S0-BNJ-346

Book of Vaadin

Vaadin 7 Draft Edition

Marko Grönroos

2012
Vaadin Ltd

Book of Vaadin: Vaadin 7 Draft Edition

Marko Grönroos
Vaadin Ltd

Vaadin 7 Draft Edition
Published: 2012-07-18
Vaadin Framework 6.7

This book can be downloaded for free at
http://vaadin.com/book

Published by
    Vaadin Ltd
    Ruukinkatu 2-4
    20540 Turku
    Finland

Abstract

Vaadin is a server-side AJAX web application development
framework that enables developers to build high-quality
user interfaces with Java. It provides a library of ready-to-
use user interface components and a clean framework for
creating your own components. The focus is on ease-of-
use, re-usability, extensibility, and meeting the requirements
of large enterprise applications.

Copyright © 2000-2012 Vaadin Ltd
All rights reserved. This work is licensed under the Creative
Commons CC-BY-ND License Version 2.0.

Printed in Turku, Finland.

ISBN 978-952-92-6753-8 (print edition)
ISBN 978-952-92-6754-5 (PDF edition)

Preface

This book provides an overview of the Vaadin Framework and covers the most important topics that you might encounter while developing applications with it. A more detailed documentation of the individual classes, interfaces, and methods is given in the Vaadin API Reference.

This is a draft of the Edition V of the book, which will cover the upcoming Vaadin 7. The release will change the basic architecture of Vaadin applications significantly, more than it did in Vaadin 6 or 5. Hence, the book must also evolve significantly.

This edition is a draft. Many new features that will be included in Vaadin 7 are not yet covered in the draft and some of the content is in fact still outdated. For the most current version, please see the on-line edition available at `http://vaadin.com/book`.

Also, many Vaadin 7 features are show-cased as mini-tutorials, which are available in the Vaadin Wiki at https://vaadin.com/wiki/-/wiki/Main/Vaadin+7.

You can also find PDF and EPUB versions of the book there. You may find the other versions more easily searchable than this printed book, but the content is the same.

Writing this manual is ongoing work and it is rarely completely up-to-date with the quick-evolving product. This edition includes an index, which is not yet complete. Many sections are under work and will be expanded in future.

Who is This Book For?

This book is intended for software developers who use, or are considering to use, Vaadin to develop web applications.

The book assumes that you have some experience with programming in Java, but if not, it is at least as easy to begin learning Java with Vaadin as with any other UI framework. No knowledge of AJAX is needed as it is well hidden from the developer.

You may have used some desktop-oriented user interface frameworks for Java, such as AWT, Swing, or SWT. Or a library such as Qt for C++. Such knowledge is useful for understanding the scope of Vaadin, the event-driven programming model, and other common concepts of UI frameworks, but not necessary.

If you do not have a web graphics designer at hand, knowing the basics of HTML and CSS can help so that you can develop presentation themes for your application. A brief introduction to CSS is provided. Knowledge of Google Web Toolkit (GWT) may be useful if you develop or integrate new client-side components.

Organization of This Book

The Book of Vaadin gives an introduction to what Vaadin is and how you use it to develop web applications.

Part I: Vaadin Core Framework

Chapter 1, *Introduction*
> The chapter gives introduction to the application architecture supported by Vaadin, the core design ideas behind the framework, and some historical background.

Chapter 2, *Getting Started with Vaadin*
> This chapter gives practical instructions for installing Vaadin and the reference toolchain, including the Vaadin Plugin for Eclipse, how to run and debug the demos, and how to create your own application project in the Eclipse IDE.

Chapter 3, *Architecture*
> This chapter gives an introduction to the architecture of Vaadin and its major technologies, including AJAX, Google Web Toolkit, and event-driven programming.

Chapter 4, *Writing a Web Application*
> This chapter gives all the practical knowledge required for creating applications with Vaadin, such as window management, application lifecycle, deployment in a servlet container, and handling events, errors, and resources.

Chapter 5, *User Interface Components*
> This chapter essentially gives the reference documentation for all the core user interface components in Vaadin and

their most significant features. The text gives examples for using each of the components.

Chapter 6, *Managing Layout*
This chapter describes the layout components, which are used for managing the layout of the user interface, just like in any desktop application frameworks.

Chapter 7, *Visual User Interface Design with Eclipse*
This chapter gives instructions for using the visual editor for Eclipse, which is included in the Vaadin Plugin for the Eclipse IDE.

Chapter 8, *Themes*
This chapter gives an introduction to Cascading Style Sheets (CSS) and explains how you can use them to build custom visual themes for your application.

Chapter 9, *Binding Components to Data*
This chapter gives an overview of the built-in data model of Vaadin, consisting of properties, items, and containers.

Chapter 10, *Vaadin SQLContainer*
This chapter gives documentation for the SQLContainer, which allows binding Vaadin components to SQL queries.

Chapter 11, *Developing New Components*
This chapter describes the process of creating new client-side widgets with Google Web Toolkit (GWT) and integrating them with server-side counterparts. The chapter also gives practical instructions for creating widget projects in Eclipse, and using the GWT Development Mode to debug widgets.

Chapter 12, *Advanced Web Application Topics*
This chapter provides many special topics that are commonly needed in applications, such as opening new browser windows, embedding applications in regular web pages, low-level management of resources, shortcut keys, debugging, etc.

Chapter 13, *Portal Integration*
This chapter is describes the development of Vaadin applications as portlets which you can deploy to any portal supporting Java Portlet API 2.0 (JSR-286). The chapter also

describes the special support for Liferay and the Control Panel, IPC, and WSRP add-ons.

Chapter 14, *Rapid Development Using Vaadin and Roo*
This chapter is a tutorial for rapid development of Vaadin applications with Spring Roo and the Vaadin Plugin for Eclipse. The tutorial includes aspects such as internationalization, testing, and database binding with the JPAContainer add-on.

Part II: Vaadin Add-ons

Chapter 15, *Using Vaadin Add-ons*
This chapter gives a instructions for downloading and installing add-on components from the Vaadin Directory.

Chapter 16, *Vaadin Calendar*
This chapter gives developer documentation for the Calendar add-on component.

Chapter 17, *Vaadin Timeline*
This chapter gives an introduction to the Timeline add-on component. The full documentation is included in the product manual.

Chapter 18, *Vaadin JPAContainer*
This chapter gives documentation for the JPAContainer add-on, which allows binding Vaadin components directly to relational and other databases using Java Persistence API (JPA).

Chapter 19, *Mobile Applications with TouchKit*
This chapter gives examples and reference documentation for using the Vaadin TouchKit add-on for developing mobile applications.

Chapter 20, *Vaadin TestBench*
This chapter gives the complete documentation for using the Vaadin TestBench tool for recording and executing user interface regression tests for Vaadin applications.

Appendix A, *Migrating from Vaadin 6*
This appendix covers migration from Vaadin 6 to Vaadin 7.

Appendix B, *Songs of Vaadin*
  Mythological background of the name Vaadin.

Supplementary Material

The Vaadin websites offer plenty of material that can help you understand what Vaadin is, what you can do with it, and how you can do it.

Demo Applications
  The most important demo application for Vaadin is the Sampler, which demonstrates the use of all basic components and features. You can run it on-line at http://demo.vaadin.com/ or download it as a WAR from the Vaadin download page.

  Most of the code examples in this book and many others can be found online at http://demo.vaadin.com/book-examples-vaadin7/book/.

Cheat Sheet
  The two-page cheat sheet illustrates the basic relationship hierarchy of the user interface and data binding classes and interfaces. You can download it at http://vaadin.com/book.

Refcard
  The six-page DZone Refcard gives an overview to application development with Vaadin. It includes a diagram of the user interface and data binding classes and interfaces. You can find more information about it at https://vaadin.com/refcard.

Address Book Tutorial
  The Address Book is a sample application accompanied with a tutorial that gives detailed step-by-step instructions for creating a real-life web application with Vaadin. You can find the tutorial from the product website.

Developer's Website
  Vaadin Developer's Site at http://dev.vaadin.com/ provides various online resources, such as the ticket system, a devel-

opment wiki, source repositories, activity timeline, development milestones, and so on.

The wiki provides instructions for developers, especially for those who wish to check-out and compile Vaadin itself from the source repository. The technical articles deal with integration of Vaadin applications with various systems, such as JSP, Maven, Spring, Hibernate, and portals. The wiki also provides answers to Frequently Asked Questions.

Online Documentation
You can read this book online at http://vaadin.com/book. Lots of additional material, including technical HOWTOs, answers to Frequently Asked Questions and other documentation is also available on Vaadin web-site.

Support

Stuck with a problem? No need to lose your hair over it, the Vaadin Framework developer community and the Vaadin company offer support for all of your needs.

Community Support Forum
You can find the user and developer community forum for Vaadin at http://vaadin.com/forum. Please use the forum to discuss any problems you might encounter, wishes for features, and so on. The answer for your problems may already lie in the forum archives, so searching the discussions is always the best way to begin.

Report Bugs
If you have found a possible bug in Vaadin, the demo applications, or the documentation, please report it by filing a ticket at the Vaadin developer's site at http://dev.vaadin.com/. You may want to check the existing tickets before filing a new one. You can make a ticket to make a request for a new feature as well, or to suggest modifications to an existing feature.

Commercial Support
Vaadin offers full commercial support and training services for the Vaadin Framework and related products. Read more

about the commercial products at http://vaadin.com/pro for details.

About the Author

Marko Grönroos is a professional writer and software developer working at Vaadin Ltd in Turku, Finland. He has been involved in web application development since 1994 and has worked on several application development frameworks in C, C++, and Java. He has been active in many open source software projects and holds an M.Sc. degree in Computer Science from the University of Turku.

Acknowledgements

Much of the book is the result of close work within the development team at Vaadin Ltd. Joonas Lehtinen, CEO of Vaadin Ltd, wrote the first outline of the book, which became the basis for the first two chapters. Since then, Marko Grönroos has become the primary author and editor. The development team has contributed several passages, answered numerous technical questions, reviewed the manual, and made many corrections.

The contributors are (in rough chronological order):

> Joonas Lehtinen
> Jani Laakso
> Marko Grönroos
> Jouni Koivuviita
> Matti Tahvonen
> Artur Signell
> Marc Englund
> Henri Sara
> Jonatan Kronqvist
> Mikael Grankvist (TestBench)
> Teppo Kurki (SQLContainer)
> Tomi Virtanen (Calendar)
> Risto Yrjänä (Calendar)
> John Ahlroos (Timeline)
> Petter Holmström (JPAContainer)

About Vaadin Ltd

Vaadin Ltd is a Finnish software company specializing in the design and development of Rich Internet Applications. The company offers planning, implementation, and support services for the software projects of its customers, as well as sub-contract software development. Vaadin Framework, previously known as IT Mill Toolkit, is the flagship open source product of the company, for which it provides commercial development and support services.

Part I

Vaadin Core Framework

Table of Contents

Chapter 1

Introduction

This chapter gives a brief introduction to software development with Vaadin. We also try to give some insight about the design philosophy behind Vaadin and its history.

1.1. Overview

The core piece of the Vaadin Framework is the Java library that is designed to make creation and maintenance of high quality web-based user interfaces easy. Vaadin supports two different programming models: server-side and client-side. The server-driven programming model is the more powerful one and essentially lets you forget the web and program user interfaces much like you would program any Java desktop application with conventional toolkits such as AWT, Swing, or SWT. But easier.

While traditional web programming is a fun way to spend your time learning new web technologies, you probably want to be productive and concentrate on the application logic. With the server-driven programming model, Vaadin takes care of managing the user interface in the browser and the *AJAX* communications between the browser and the server. With the Vaadin approach, you do not need to learn and debug browser technologies, such as HTML or JavaScript.

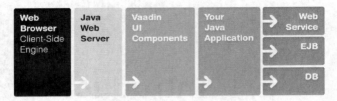

Figure 1.1. Server-Side Vaadin Application Architecture

Figure 1.1, "Server-Side Vaadin Application Architecture" illustrates the basic architecture of server-side web applications made with Vaadin. This architecture consists of the *server-side framework* and a *client-side engine* that runs in the browser, rendering the user interface and delivering user interaction to the server. The application runs as a Java Servlet session in a Java application server, and the client-side engine as JavaScript.

As the client-side engine is executed as JavaScript in the browser, no browser plugins are needed for using applications made with Vaadin. This gives it an edge over frameworks based on Flash, Java Applets, or other plugins. Vaadin relies on the support of Google Web Toolkit for a wide range of browsers, so that the developer does not need to worry about browser support.

Because HTML, JavaScript, and other browser technologies are essentially invisible to the application logic, you can think of the web browser as only a thin client platform. A thin client displays the user interface and communicates user events to the server at a low level. The control logic of the user interface runs on a Java-based web server, together with your business logic. By contrast, a normal client-server architecture with a dedicated client application would include a lot of application specific communications between the client and the server. Essentially removing the user interface tier from the application architecture makes our approach a very effective one.

Behind the server-driven development model, Vaadin makes the best use of AJAX (*Asynchronous JavaScript and XML*, see Section 3.2.1, "AJAX" for a description) techniques that make it possible to create Rich Internet Applications (RIA) that are as responsive and interactive as desktop applications.

In addition to the server-side Java application development, you can develop on the client-side by making new widgets in Java, and even pure client-side applications that run solely in the browser. The Vaadin client-side framework includes Google Web Toolkit (GWT), which provides a compiler from Java to the JavaScript that runs in the browser, as well a full-featured user interface framework. With this approach, Vaadin is pure Java on both sides.

Vaadin uses a client-side engine for rendering the user interface of a server-side application in the browser. All the client-server communications are hidden well under the hood. Vaadin is designed to be extensible, and you can indeed use any 3rd-party widgets easily, in addition to the component repertoire offered in Vaadin. If fact, you can find hundreds of add-ons from the Vaadin Directory.

Vaadin Framework defines a clear separation between the structure of the user interface and its appearance and allows you to develop them separately. Our approach to this is *themes*, which control the appearance by CSS and (optional) HTML page templates. As Vaadin provides excellent default themes, you do not usually need to make much customization, but you can if you need to. For more about themes, see Chapter 8, *Themes*.

We hope that this is enough about the basic architecture and features of Vaadin for now. You can read more about it later in Chapter 3, *Architecture*, or jump straight to more practical things in Chapter 4, *Writing a Web Application*.

1.2. Example Application Walkthrough

Let us follow the long tradition of first saying "Hello World!" when learning a new programming framework. First, using the primary server-side API.

Example 1.1. HelloWorld.java

```java
import com.vaadin.ui.*;

public class HelloWorld extends Root {
    @Override
    protected void init(WrappedRequest request) {
        // Set the window or tab title
        getPage().setTitle("Hello window");

        // Display the greeting
        addComponent(new Label("Hello World!"));
    }
}
```

Every Vaadin application has a *root* that extends the **com.vaad-in.ui.Root** class. A root is a part of the web page in which the Vaadin application runs. An application can, in fact, have multiple pages (windows) and roots in the same page, especially in portals. A Vaadin application instance is essentially a user session, and a session is created for each user who uses the application. In the context of our HelloWorld application, it is sufficient to know that the underlying session is created when the user first accesses the application by opening the page, and init() method is invoked at that time.

In the above example, the initialization of the root first accesses the web page object in which the application runs and sets the page title, which is used in the caption of the browser window or tab.

The example creates a new **Label** user interface component, which displays simple text, and sets the text to "Hello World!". Finally, the label is added to the root. So, when the application page is opened in a browser, it shows the text "Hello World!".

The result of the Hello World application is shown in Figure 1.2, "Hello World Application".

Figure 1.2. Hello World Application

Note that this example source code is complete and does not need any additional declaratively defined template files to be run. To run the program, you can just package it as a web application and deploy it to a server, as explained in Section 4.6, "Setting Up the Application Environment".

Developing a pure client-side application, you could write a Hello World just as easy, and also in Java:

```
public class HelloWorld implements EntryPoint {
    @Override
    public void onModuleLoad() {
        RootPanel.get().add(new Label("Hello, world!"));
    }
}
```

The application would be compiled into JavaScript with the GWT Compiler included in Vaadin. It is more typical, however, to write client-side widgets, which you can then use from a server-side Vaadin application. For more information regarding client-side development, see Chapter 11, *Developing New Components*.

1.3. Support for the Eclipse IDE

While Vaadin is not bound to any specific IDE, and you can in fact easily use it without any IDE altogether, we provide special support for the Eclipse IDE, which has become the most used environment for Java development. The support is provided in the Vaadin Plugin for Eclipse, which allows you to:

- Create new Vaadin projects

- Create custom themes

- Create custom widgets

- Create composite components with a visual designer

- Easily upgrade to a newer version of the Vaadin library

The Vaadin Plugin for Eclipse is our recommended way of installing Vaadin for development. Using just the JAR or loading Vaadin from a Maven repository is also possible.

Installing and updating the Eclipse plugin is covered in Section 2.2.1, "Vaadin Plugin for Eclipse" and the creation of a new Vaadin project using the plugin in Section 2.3.1, "Creating the Project". See Section 8.4, "Creating a Theme in Eclipse", Section 11.2, "Starting It Simple With Eclipse", and Chapter 7, *Visual User Interface Design with Eclipse* for instructions on using the different features of the plugin.

1.4. Goals and Philosophy

Simply put, Vaadin's ambition is to be the best possible tool when it comes to creating web user interfaces for business applications. It is easy to adopt, as it is designed to support both entry-level and advanced programmers, as well as usability experts and graphical designers.

When designing Vaadin, we have followed the philosophy inscribed in the following rules.

Right tool for the right purpose

Because our goals are high, the focus must be clear. This toolkit is designed for creating web applications. It is not designed for creating websites or advertisements demos. For such purposes, you might find (for instance) JSP/JSF or Flash more suitable.

Simplicity and maintainability

We have chosen to emphasize robustness, simplicity, and maintainability. This involves following the well-established best practices in user interface frameworks and ensuring that our implementation represents an ideal solution for its purpose without clutter or bloat.

XML is not designed for programming

The Web is inherently document-centered and very much bound to the declarative presentation of user interfaces. The Vaadin framework frees the programmer from these limitations. It is far more natural to create user interfaces by programming them than by defining them in declarative templates, which are not flexible enough for complex and dynamic user interaction.

Tools should not limit your work

There should not be any limits on what you can do with the framework: if for some reason the user interface components do not support what you need to achieve, it must be easy to add new ones to your application. When you need to create new components, the role of the framework is critical: it makes it easy to create re-usable components that are easy to maintain.

1.5. Background

The Vaadin Framework was not written overnight. After working with web user interfaces since the beginning of the Web, a group of developers got together in 2000 to form IT Mill. The team had a desire to develop a new programming paradigm that would support the creation of real user interfaces for real applications using a real programming language.

The library was originally called Millstone Library. The first version was used in a large production application that IT Mill designed and implemented for an international pharmaceutical company. IT Mill made the application already in the year 2001 and it is still in use. Since then, the company has produced dozens of large business applications with the library and it has proven its ability to solve hard problems easily.

The next generation of the library, IT Mill Toolkit Release 4, was released in 2006. It introduced an entirely new AJAX-based presentation engine. This allowed the development of AJAX applications without the need to worry about communications between the client and the server.

Release 5 Into the Open

IT Mill Toolkit 5, released initially at the end of 2007, took a significant step further into AJAX. The client-side rendering of the user interface was completely rewritten using GWT, the Google Web Toolkit.

IT Mill Toolkit 5 introduced many significant improvements both in the server-side API and in the functionality. Rewriting the Client-Side Engine with GWT allowed the use of Java both on the client and the server-side. The transition from JavaScript to GWT made the development and integration of custom components and customization of existing components much easier than before, and it also allows easy integration of existing GWT components. The adoption of GWT on the client-side did not, by itself, cause any changes in the server-side API, because GWT is a browser technology that is hidden well behind the API. Also themeing was completely revised in IT Mill Toolkit 5.

The Release 5 was published under the Apache License 2, an unrestrictive open source license, to create faster expansion of the user base and make the formation of a developer community possible.

Birth of Vaadin Release 6

IT Mill Toolkit was renamed as *Vaadin Framework*, or Vaadin in short, in spring 2009. Later IT Mill, the company, was also renamed as Vaadin Ltd. Vaadin means an adult female semi-domesticated mountain reindeer in Finnish.

Together with the Vaadin 6 was released the Vaadin Plugin for Eclipse. The initially experimental version of the visual editor, which was included with the plugin, has since then grown into to stable development tool.

With Vaadin 6, the number of developers using the framework really exploded. The introduction of Vaadin Directory in early 2010 gave it a further boost, as the number of available components multiplied almost overnight. Many of the originally experimental components have since then matured and are now used by thousands of developers. In 2012, we are seeing tremendous growth in the ecosystem around Vaadin. The size of the user community, at least if measured by forum activity, has already gone past the competing server-side frameworks and even GWT. Whether Vaadin is already past the tipping point can be seen soon.

More technical details about the history of Vaadin can be found from the Release Notes of each version.

Towards Vaadin 7

Vaadin 7 is still under development when this edition of the book is published, and will continue to evolve throughout 2012. It is a major revision that changes the Vaadin API much more than Vaadin 6 did. It will certainly be more web-oriented than Vaadin 6 was.

We are doing everything we can to help Vaadin rise high in the web universe. Some of this work is easy and almost routine - fixing bugs and implementing features. But going higher also requires standing firmer. That is one of the aims of Vaadin 7 - redesign the product so that the new architecture enables Vaadin to reach over many long-standing challenges. Many of the changes require breaking API compatibility with Vaadin 6, especially in the cliend-side, but they are made with a strong desire to avoid carrying un-necessary legacy burden far into the future. Vaadin 7 includes a compatibility layer for making adoption of Vaadin 7 in existing applications easier.

Inclusion of Google Web Toolkit in Vaadin 7 is a significant development, as it means that we now provide support for GWT as well. When Google opened the GWT development in summer 2012, Vaadin (the company) also joined the new GWT steering committee. As a member of the committee, Vaadin can work towards the success of GWT as a foundation of the Java web development community.

Vaadin 7 is targeted at the end of 2012. Alpha and beta releases allow developers to get some taste of what is coming. The most significant API changes are already there - go ahead and try them.

Chapter 2

Getting Started with Vaadin

This chapter gives practical instructions for installing the recommended toolchain and either the Vaadin Plugin for Eclipse or, if you use another IDE or no IDE at all, the Vaadin JAR.

2.1. Setting up the Development Environment

This section gives a step-by-step guide for setting up a development environment. Vaadin supports a wide variety of tools, so you can use any IDE for writing the code, most web browsers for viewing the results, any operating system or processor supported by the Java 1.5 platform, and almost any Java web server for deploying the application.

In this example, we use the following toolchain:

- Windows XP, Linux, or Mac OS X

- Sun Java 2 Standard Edition 6.0 (JDK 1.6 or newer is required)

- Eclipse IDE for Java EE Developers

- Apache Tomcat 7.0 (Core) or newer

- Mozilla Firefox browser

- Firebug debug tool (optional)

- Vaadin Framework

The above reference toolchain is a good choice of tools, but you can use almost any tools you are comfortable with.

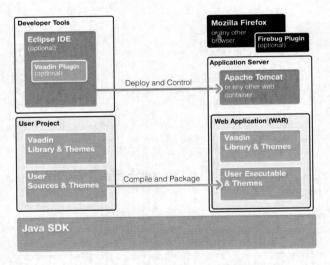

Figure 2.1. Development Toolchain and Process

Figure 2.1, "Development Toolchain and Process" illustrates the development environment and process. You develop your application as an Eclipse project. The project must include, in addition to your source code, the Vaadin Library. It can also include project-specific themes.

You must compile and deploy a project to a web container before you can use use it. You can deploy a project through the Web Tools Platform for Eclipse, which allows automatic deployment of web applications from Eclipse. You can deploy a project also manually, by creating a web application archive (WAR) and deploying it through the web container's interface.

2.1.1. Installing Java SDK

Java SDK is required by Vaadin and also by the Eclipse IDE. Vaadin is compatible with Java 1.6 and later editions.

Windows

1. Download Sun Java 2 Standard Edition 6.0 from http://java.sun.com/javase/downloads/index.jsp

2. Install the Java SDK by running the installer. The default options are fine.

Linux / UNIX

1. Download Sun Java 2 Standard Edition 6.0 from http://java.sun.com/javase/downloads/index.jsp

2. Decompress it under a suitable base directory, such as /opt. For example, for Java SDK, enter (either as root or with **sudo** in Linux):

```
# cd /opt
# sh (path-to-installation-package)/jdk-6u1-linux-
i586.bin
```

and follow the instructions in the installer.

2.1.2. Installing Eclipse IDE

Windows

Eclipse is now installed in C:\dev\eclipse and can be started from there (by double clicking eclipse.exe).

1. Download Eclipse IDE for Java EE Developers (Ganymede version) from http://www.eclipse.org/downloads/

2. Decompress the Eclipse IDE package to a suitable directory. You are free to select any directory and to use any ZIP decompressor, but in this example we decompress the ZIP file by just double-clicking it and selecting "Extract all files" task from Windows compressed folder task. In our installation example, we use `C:\dev` as the target directory.

Linux / UNIX

You have two basic options for installing Eclipse in Linux and UNIX: you can either install it using the package manager of your operating system or by downloading and installing the packages manually. The *manual installation method is recommended*, because the latest versions of the packages available in a Linux package repository may be incompatible with Eclipse plugins that are not installed using the package manager.

1. Download Download Eclipse IDE for Java EE Developers (Ganymede version) from http://www.eclipse.org/downloads/

2. Decompress the Eclipse package into a suitable base directory. It is important to make sure that there is no old Eclipse installation in the target directory. Installing a new version on top of an old one probably renders Eclipse unusable.

3. Eclipse should normally be installed as a regular user, as this makes installation of plugins easier. Eclipse also stores some user settings in the installation directory. To install the package, enter:

   ```
   $ tar zxf (path-to-installation-package)/eclipse-jee-ganymede-SR2-linux-gtk.tar.gz
   ```

   This will extract the package to a subdirectory with the name `eclipse`.

4. You may wish to add the Eclipse installation directory and the `bin` subdirectory in the installation directory of Java SDK to your system or user PATH.

An alternative to the above procedure is to use the package management system of your operating system. For example, in Ubuntu

---

Linux, which includes Sun Java SDK and Eclipse in its APT repository, you can install the programs from a package manager GUI or from command-line with a command such as:

```
$ sudo apt-get install sun-java6-jdk eclipse
```

This is, however, *not recommended*, because the Eclipse package may not include all the necessary Java EE tools, most importantly the Web Standard Tools, and it may cause incompatibilities with some components that are not installed with the package management system of your operating system.

2.1.3. Installing Apache Tomcat

Apache Tomcat is a lightweight Java web server suitable for both development and production. There are many ways to install it, but here we simply decompress the installation package.

Apache Tomcat should be installed with user permissions. During development, you will be running Eclipse or some other IDE with user permissions, but deploying web applications to a Tomcat server that is installed system-wide requires administrator or root permissions.

1. Download the installation package:

   Apache Tomcat 7.0 (Core Binary Distribution) from `http://tomcat.apache.org/`

2. Decompress Apache Tomcat package to a suitable target directory, such as `C:\dev` (Windows) or `/opt` (Linux or Mac OS X). The Apache Tomcat home directory will be `C:\dev\apache-tomcat-7.0.x` or `/opt/apache-tomcat-7.0.x`, respectively.

2.1.4. Firefox and Firebug

Vaadin supports many web browsers and you can use any of them for development. If you plan to create a custom theme, customized layouts, or create new components, we recommend that you use Firefox together with Firebug.

If you do not have Firefox installed already, go to www.getfire-fox.com and download and run the installer. In Linux, you can install it also with a package manager.

Optional. After installing Firefox, use it to open http://www.getfire-bug.com/. Follow the instructions on the site to install the latest stable version of Firebug available for the browser. You might need to tell Firefox to allow the installation by clicking the yellow warning bar at the top of the browser-window.

When Firebug is installed, it can be enabled at any time from the corner of the Firefox window. Figure 2.2, "Firebug Debugger for Firefox" shows an example of what Firebug looks like.

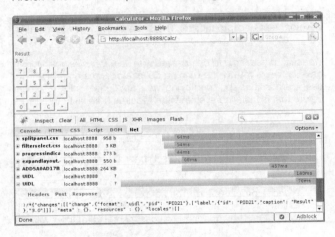

Figure 2.2. Firebug Debugger for Firefox

Now that you have installed the development environment, you can proceed to creating your first application.

2.2. Installing Vaadin

This section gives instructions for installing Vaadin in your development environment. You have two basic options for installing:

1. If you use Eclipse, we recommend that you can install the Vaadin Plugin for Eclipse, as described in Section 2.2.1, "Vaadin Plugin for Eclipse"

2. Otherwise, download and install the JAR package, as described in Section 2.2.2, "Installing the JAR Package".

These options are explained in detail in the following sections.

2.2.1. Vaadin Plugin for Eclipse

If you are using the Eclipse IDE, using the Vaadin plugin should help greatly. The plugin includes:

- An integration plugin with *wizards* for creating new Vaadin-based projects, themes, and client-side widgets and widget sets.

- A *visual editor* for editing custom composite user interface components in a WYSIWYG fashion. With full round-trip support from source code to visual model and back, the editor integrates seamlessly with your development process.

- A version of *Book of Vaadin* that you can browse in the Eclipse Help system.

You can install the plugin as follows:

1. Start Eclipse.

2. Select **Help → Software Updates…**.

3. Select the **Available Software** tab.

4. Add the Vaadin plugin update site by clicking **Add Site…**.

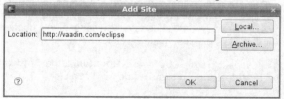

Enter the URL of the Vaadin Update Site: http://vaadin.com/eclipse and click **OK**. The Vaadin site should now appear in the **Software Updates** window.

5. Select all the Vaadin plugins in the tree.

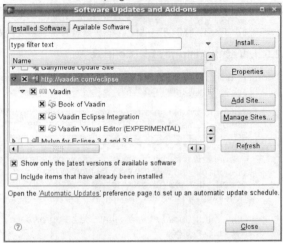

Finally, click **Install**.

Detailed and up-to-date installation instructions for the Eclipse plugin can be found at http://vaadin.com/eclipse.

Updating the Vaadin Plugin

If you have automatic updates enabled in Eclipse (see **Window → Preferences → Install/Update → Automatic Updates**), the Vaadin plugin will be updated automatically along with other plugins. Otherwise, you can update the Vaadin plugin (there are actually multiple plugins) manually as follows:

1. Select **Help → Software Updates...**, the **Software Updates and Add-ons** window will open.

2. Select the **Installed Software** tab.

3. If you want to update only the Vaadin plugins, select them in the list by clicking the plugins and holding the **Ctrl** key pressed for all but the first.

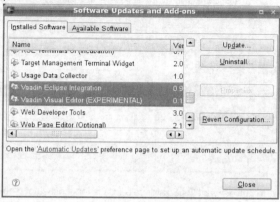

4. Click **Update**.

Notice that updating the Vaadin plugin updates only the plugin and *not* the Vaadin library, which is project specific. See below for instructions for updating the library.

Updating the Vaadin Library

Updating the Vaadin plugin does not update Vaadin library. The library is project specific, as a different version might be required for different projects, so you have to update it separately for each project. To change the library to a newer (or some other) version, do as follows:

1. Select the project in the **Project Explorer** and select **Project → Preferences** or press **Alt+Enter**.

2. In the project preferences window that opens, select **Vaadin → Vaadin Version**.

3. If the version that you want to use is not included in the **Vaadin version** drop-down list, click **Download** to open the download window.

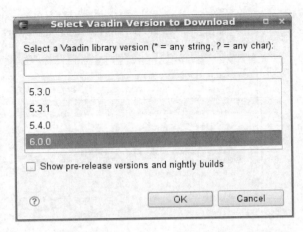

If you want to use a development version, select **Show pre-release versions and nightly builds**. Select the version that you want to download and click **OK**.

4. Select the version that you want to use from the **Vaadin version** down-down list and click **Apply**.

You can observe that the new library appears in the `WebContent/WEB-INF/lib` folder.

2.2.2. Installing the JAR Package

You can install the Vaadin JAR package in a few simple steps:

1. Download the newest Vaadin JAR package from the download page at http://vaadin.com/download/.

2. Put the JAR in the `WEB-APP/lib` web library folder in the project.

The location of the `WEB-APP/lib` folder depends on the project organization.

- In Eclipse projects: `WebContent/WEB-INF/lib`.

- In Maven projects: `src/main/webapp/WEB-INF/lib`.

2.3. Your First Project with Vaadin

This section gives instructions for creating a new Eclipse project using the Vaadin Plugin. The task will include the following steps:

1. Create a new project

2. Write the source code

3. Configure and start Tomcat (or some other web server)

4. Open a web browser to use the web application

We also show how you can debug the application in the debug mode in Eclipse.

This walkthrough assumes that you have already installed the Vaadin Plugin and set up your development environment, as instructed in Section 2.2.2, "Installing the JAR Package" and Section 2.1, "Setting up the Development Environment".

2.3.1. Creating the Project

Let us create the first application project with the tools installed in the previous section. First, launch Eclipse and follow the following steps:

1. Start creating a new project by selecting from the menu **File → New → Project...**.

2. In the **New Project** window that opens, select **Web →
   Vaadin Project** and click **Next**.

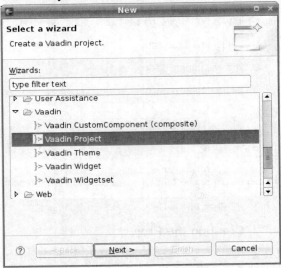

3. In the **Vaadin Project** step, you need to set the basic web project settings. You need to give at least the project name and the runtime; the default values should be good for the other settings.

Project name

Give the project a name. The name should be a valid identifier usable cross-platform as a filename and inside a URL, so using only lower-case alphanumerics, underscore, and minus sign is recommended.

Use default

Defines the directory under which the project is created. You should normally leave it as it is. You may

need to set the directory, for example, if you are creating an Eclipse project on top of a version-controlled
source tree.

Target runtime

Defines the application server to use for deploying the
application. The server that you have installed, for example Apache Tomcat, should be selected automatically. If not, click **New** to configure a new server under
Eclipse.

Configuration

Select the configuration to use; you should normally
use the default configuration for the application server.
If you need to modify the project facets, click **Modify**.

Deployment configuration

This setting defines the environment to which the application will be deployed, to generate the appropriate
project directory layout and configuration files. The
choises are:

- **Servlet** (default)

- **Google App Engine Servlet**

- **Generic Portlet (Portlet 2.0)**

- **Old Portlet (Portlet 1.0)**

The further steps in the New Project Wizard depend
on the selected deployment configuration; the steps
listed in this section are for the default servlet configuration. See Section 12.7, "Google App Engine Integration" and Chapter 13, *Portal Integration* for instructions
regarding the use of Vaadin in the alternative environments.

Vaadin version

Select the Vaadin version to use. The drop-down list
shows, by default, the latest available version of
Vaadin. If you want to use another version, click
Download. The dialog that opens lists all official releases of Vaadin.

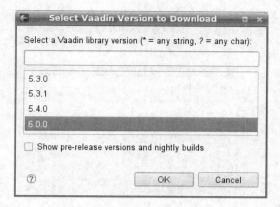

If you want to use a pre-release version or a nightly development build, select **Show pre-release versions and nightly builds**. Select a version and click **Ok** to download it. It will appear as a choise in the drop-down list.

If you want to change the project to use another version of Vaadin, for example to upgrade to a newer one, you can go to project settings and download and select the other version.

You can click **Finish** here to use the defaults for the rest of the settings, or click **Next**.

4. The settings in the **Web Module** step define the basic servlet-related settings and the structure of the web application
   project. All the settings are pre-filled, and you should normally accept them as they are.

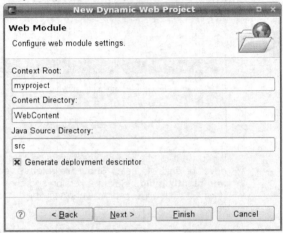

Context Root

> The context root (of the application) identifies the ap-
> plication in the URL used for accessing it. For example,
> if the server runs in the apps context and the applica-
> tion has myproject context, the URL would be ht-
> tp://example.com/app/url. The wizard will suggest
> myproject for the context name.

Content Directory

> The directory containing all the content to be included
> in the servlet and served by the web server. The direct-
> ory is relative to the root directory of the project.

Java Source Directory

> The default source directory containing the application
> sources. The src directory is suggested; another
> convention common in web applications is to use
> WebContent/WEB-INF/src, in which case the sources

are included in the servlet (but not served in HTTP requests).

Generate deployment descriptor

Should the wizard generate the `web.xml` deployment descriptor required for running the servlet in the `Web-Content/WEB-INF` directory. Strongly recommended. See Section 4.6.3, "Deployment Descriptor `web.xml`" for more details.

This will be the sub-path in the URL, for example `http://localhost:8080/myproject`. The default for the application root will be / (root).

You can just accept the defaults and click **Next**.

5. The **Vaadin project** step page has various Vaadin-specific application settings. If you are trying Vaadin out for the first time, you should not need to change anything. You can set most of the settings afterwards, except the creation of the portlet configuration.

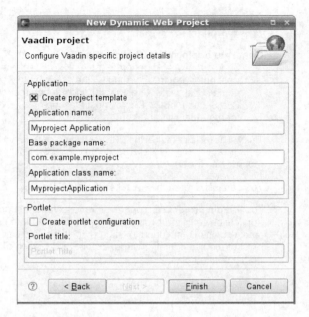

Create project template

Make the wizard create an application class stub.

Application Name

The name of the application appears in the browser window title.

Base package name

The name of the Java package under which the application class is to be placed.

Application class name

Name of the Vaadin application class.

Create portlet configuration

When this option is selected, the wizard will create the files needed for running the application in a portal. See Chapter 13, *Portal Integration* for more information on portlets.

Finally, click **Finish** to create the project.

6. Eclipse may ask to switch to J2EE perspective. A Dynamic Web Project uses an external web server and the J2EE perspective provides tools to control the server and manage application deployment. Click **Yes**.

2.3.2. Exploring the Project

After the **New Project** wizard exists, it has done all the work for us: Vaadin libraries are installed in the WebContent/WEB-INF/lib directory, an application class skeleton has been written to src directory, and WebContent/WEB-INF/web.xml already contains a deployment descriptor.

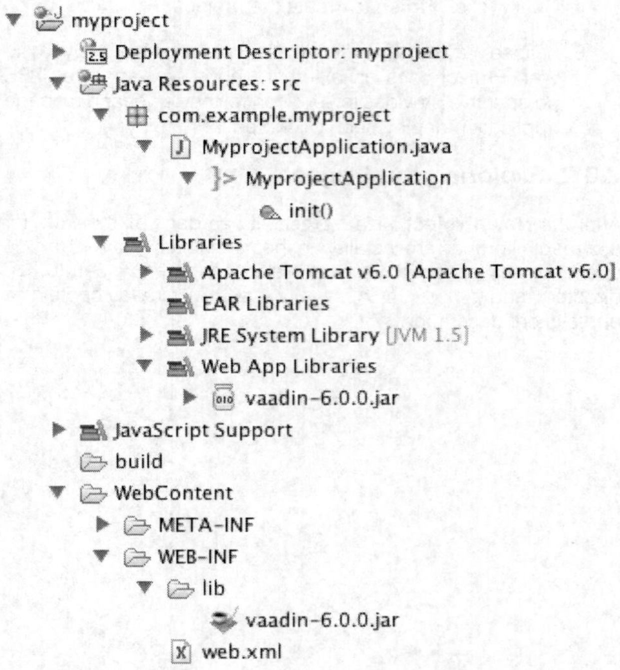

- ▼ 🏠 myproject
  - ▶ 🔧 Deployment Descriptor: myproject
  - ▼ 🗄 Java Resources: src
    - ▼ ⊞ com.example.myproject
      - ▼ 🗒 MyprojectApplication.java
        - ▼ }> MyprojectApplication
          - ⚙ init()
    - ▼ 📚 Libraries
      - ▶ 📚 Apache Tomcat v6.0 [Apache Tomcat v6.0]
      - 📚 EAR Libraries
      - ▶ 📚 JRE System Library [JVM 1.5]
      - ▼ 📚 Web App Libraries
        - ▶ 🔘 vaadin-6.0.0.jar
  - ▶ 📚 JavaScript Support
  - 📂 build
  - ▼ 📂 WebContent
    - ▶ 📂 META-INF
    - ▼ 📂 WEB-INF
      - ▼ 📂 lib
        - 🔧 vaadin-6.0.0.jar
      - X web.xml

Figure 2.3. A New Dynamic Web Project

The application class created by the plugin contains the following code:

```
package com.example.myproject;

import com.vaadin.ui.*;
import com.vaadin.terminal.WrappedRequest;

public class MyprojectRoot extends Root {
    @Override
    public void init(WrappedRequest request) {
        Label label = new Label("Hello Vaadin user");
        addComponent(label);
    }
}
```

Let us add a button to the application to make it a bit more interesting. The resulting `init()` method could look something like:

```
@Override
public void init(WrappedRequest request) {
    Label label = new Label("Hello Vaadin user");
    addComponent(label);

    addComponent(new Button("What is the time?",
                            new Button.ClickListener()
    {
        public void buttonClick(ClickEvent event) {
            Notification.show("The time is " + new
Date());
        }
    }));
}
```

The deployment descriptor `WebContent/WEB-INF/web.xml` defines Vaadin framework servlet, the application class, and servlet mapping:

Example 2.1. web.xml **Deployment Descriptor for our project**

Below is a deployment descriptor for the Hello World application.

```xml
<?xml version="1.0" encoding="UTF-8"?>
<web-app xmlns:xsi="http://www.w3.org/2001/XMLSchema-instance"
  xmlns="http://java.sun.com/xml/ns/javaee"
  xmlns:web="http://java.sun.com/xml/ns/javaee/web-app_2_5.xsd"
  id="WebApp_ID" version="2.5">

<display-name>myproject</display-name>

<context-param>
  <description>Vaadin production mode</description>
  <param-name>productionMode</param-name>
  <param-value>false</param-value>
</context-param>

<servlet>
  <servlet-name>Myproject Application</servlet-name>
  <servlet-class>
    com.vaadin.terminal.gwt.server.ApplicationServlet
  </servlet-class>
  <init-param>
    <description>Vaadin root class to use</description>
    <param-name>root</param-name>
    <param-value>
      com.example.myproject.MyprojectRoot
    </param-value>
  </init-param>
</servlet>

<servlet-mapping>
  <servlet-name>Myproject Application</servlet-name>
  <url-pattern>/*</url-pattern>
</servlet-mapping>
</web-app>
```

For a more detailed treatment of the web.xml file, see Section 4.6.3, "Deployment Descriptor web.xml".

2.3.3. Setting Up and Starting the Web Server

Eclipse IDE for Java EE Developers has the Web Standard Tools package installed, which supports control of various web servers and automatic deployment of web content to the server when changes are made to a project.

Make sure that Tomcat was installed with user permissions. Configuration of the web server in Eclipse will fail if the user does not have write permissions to the configuration and deployment directories under the Tomcat installation directory.

Follow the following steps.

1. Switch to the **Servers** tab in the lower panel in Eclipse. List of servers should be empty after Eclipse is installed. Right-click on the empty area in the panel and select **New →** **Server**.

2. Select **Apache → Tomcat v7.0 Server** and set **Server's host name** as localhost, which should be the default. If you have only one Tomcat installed, **Server runtime** has only one choice. Click **Next**.

3. Add your project to the server by selecting it on the left and clicking **Add** to add it to the configured projects on the right. Click **Finish**.

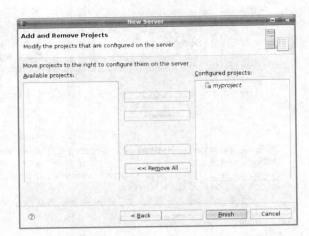

4. The server and the project are now installed in Eclipse and are shown in the **Servers** tab. To start the server, right-click on the server and select **Debug**. To start the server in non-debug mode, select **Start**.

5. The server starts and the WebContent directory of the project is published to the server on `http://local-host:8080/myproject/`.

2.3.4. Running and Debugging

Starting your application is as easy as selecting **myproject** from the **Project Explorer** and then **Run → Debug As → Debug on Server**. Eclipse then opens the application in built-in web browser.

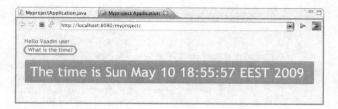

Figure 2.4. Running a Vaadin Application

You can insert break points in the Java code by double-clicking on the left margin bar of the source code window. For example, if you insert a breakpoint in the `buttonClick()` method and click the **What is the time?** button, Eclipse will ask to switch to the Debug perspective. Debug perspective will show where the execution stopped at the breakpoint. You can examine and change the state of the application. To continue execution, select **Resume** from **Run** menu.

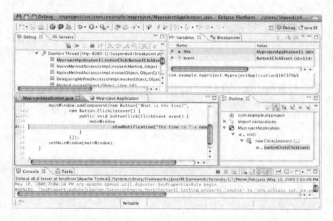

Figure 2.5. Debugging a Vaadin Application

Above, we described how to debug a server-side application. Debugging client-side widgets is described in Section 11.13, "Debugging Client-Side Code".

Restarting Application Session

When you open the URL for the application, it creates a new user session. The session is preserved even if you reload the page. Moreover, as Eclipse likes to do hot deployment to Tomcat, and Tomcat likes to persist sessions on server shutdown, you may experience a problem that the application doesn't return to its initial state after modifying code or even restarting the server.

Adding the `?restartApplication` parameter in the URL tells the Vaadin servlet to create a new application instance (user session) when reloading the page.

2.4. Creating a Project with NetBeans

Vaadin has no official plugin for NetBeans at the moment, so the tasks have to be done more manually than with Eclipse.

You have two choices to create a Vaadin project in NetBeans: as a regular web application project or as a Maven project. We cover these both ways in the following sections.

2.4.1. Regular Web Application Project

This section describes the basic way of creating a Vaadin application project in NetBeans. This approach is useful if you do not wish to use Maven, but requires more manual work.

1. Open **File → New Project**.

2. Select **Java Web → Web Application** and click **Next**.

3. Give a project name, such as `myproject`. As the project name is by default also used as the context path, it should contain only alphanumerics, underscore and minus sign. Click **Next**.

4. Select a server. The reference toolchain recommends Apache Tomcat, as many instructions in this book are given

specifically for Tomcat, but any other server should work just as fine. Click **Next**.

5. Click **Finish**.

The project is created. However, it is a simple skeleton for a JSP-based web application project. To make it a proper Vaadin project, you need to include the Vaadin library, create the application class, and define the `web.xml` deployment descriptor.

2.4.2. Maven Project from Vaadin Archetype

Creating a Maven project with the Vaadin archetype is simpler than as a normal web application project in NetBeans. It creates an application skeleton, defines the `web.xml` deployment descriptor, and also retrieves the latest Vaadin library automatically.

1. Select **File → New Project**.

2. Select **Maven → Project from Archetype** and click **Next**.

3. Select an archetype from a repository:

   - If you have used Vaadin with Maven before, you might already have the archetype in local repository - select **Archetypes from Local Repository**.

   - Add a new archetype by clicking **Add**. For **Group Id**, given `com.vaadin`. For **Artifact Id**, give `vaadin-arche-type-clean` for a normal project, `vaadin-archetype-widget` for a custom GWT widget project, or `vaadin-ar-chetype-sample` for a more advanced application skeleton. For **Version**, give `LATEST` or a specific version number. Then, click **OK**.

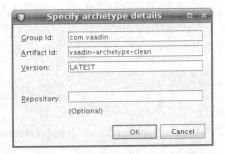

Figure 2.6. Adding a New Maven Archetype in NetBeans

Then select the **Custom archetype - vaadin-archetype-clean (LATEST)** from the selection tree.

Click **Next**.

4. In the **Name and Location** step, enter **Project Name**, which is recommended to be only lower-case alphabetics, as it is used also as a suggestion for the Java package name of the project. Modify the other parameters for your project and click **Finish**.

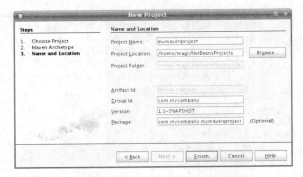

Figure 2.7. Adding a New Maven Project in NetBeans

Creating the project can take a while as Maven loads all the needed dependencies. Once created, you can run it by right-clicking on the project in the **Projects** view and selecting **Run**. In the **Select deployment server** window that opens, select **Apache Tomcat** and click **OK**. If all goes well, NetBeans starts the server and launches the default browser to display the web application.

2.5. Creating a Project with Maven

The Vaadin core library and all Vaadin add-ons are available through a Maven repository and can thereby be easily used with Apache Maven. You can use a Maven with a front-end from Eclipse or NetBeans, or by using the command-line as described in this section.

You can create a new Maven project with the following command:

```
$ mvn archetype:generate
    -DarchetypeGroupId=com.vaadin
    -DarchetypeArtifactId=vaadin-archetype-clean
    -DarchetypeVersion=LATEST
    -DgroupId=your.company
    -DartifactId=project-name
    -Dversion=1.0
    -Dpackaging=war
```

The parameters are as follows:

archetypeGroupId
> The group ID of the archetype is com.vaadin for Vaadin archetypes.

archetypeArtifactId
> The archetype ID. Vaadin currently supports the following archetypes:
>
> * vaadin-archetype-clean is a new project with a bare-bone skeleton for a regular Vaadin application. The pom.xml includes out-commented definitions for additional widgets.
>
> * vaadin-archetype-widget is a skeleton for a project with custom widgets.

- `vaadin-archetype-sample` is also for project with custom widgets, but the skeleton includes the Color Picker example used in Chapter 11, *Developing New Components*.

- `vaadin-archetype-addon` is for Vaadin add-on projects. It packages the add-on so that it can be published in Vaadin Directory. The archetype is for server-side add-ons and does not include definitions needed for building a widget set. If your add-on includes or requires other than the widgets in the Vaadin core library, you need to copy the required definitions from a POM of a `vaadin-archetype-clean` project.

- `vaadin-archetype-touchkit` is for projects using Vaadin TouchKit, described in Chapter 19, *Mobile Applications with TouchKit*. Notice that this archetype uses the AGPL-licensed version of TouchKit, which requires that your project must also be licensed under the AGPL license.

archetypeVersion
> Version of the archetype to use. This should normally be `LATEST`.

groupId
> A Maven group ID for your project. It is used for the Java package name and should normally be your domain name reversed, such as `com.example.myproject`. The group ID is used also for the Java source package name of your project, so it should be Java compatible - only alphanumerics and an underscore.

artifactId
> Identifier of the artifact, that is, your project. The identifier may contain alphanumerics, minus, and underscore.

version
> Initial version number of your application. The number must obey the Maven version numbering format.

packaging
> How will the project be packaged. It is normally `war`.

Creating a project can take a while as Maven fetches all the dependencies. The created project structure is shown in Figure 2.8, "A New Vaadin Project with `vaadin-archetype-clean`".

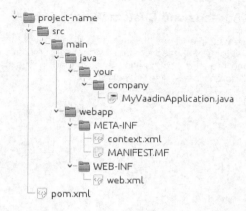

Figure 2.8. A New Vaadin Project with `vaadin-archetype-clean`

Compiling and Running the Application

Before the application can be deployed, it must be compiled and packaged as a WAR package. You can do this with the `package` goal as follows:

```
$ mvn package
```

The location of the resulting WAR package should be displayed in the command output. You can then deploy it to your favorite application server.

The easiest way to run Vaadin applications with Maven is to use the light-weight Jetty web server. After compiling the package, all you need to do is type:

```
$ mvn jetty:run
```

The special goal starts the Jetty server in port 8080 and deploys the application. You can then open it in a web browser at `http://localhost:8080/project-name`.

Using Add-ons and Custom Widget Sets

If you use Vaadin add-ons that include a widget set or make your custom widgets, you need to enable widget set compilation in the POM. The required configuration is described in Section 15.5, "Using Add-ons in a Maven Project".

Chapter 3

Architecture

This chapter provides an introduction to the architecture of Vaadin at somewhat technical level.

This edition is a draft. Many new features that will be included in Vaadin 7 are not yet covered in this chapter and some of the content may in fact be outdated. For the most current version, please see the on-line edition available at `http://vaadin.com/book`.

3.1. Overview

In Chapter 1, *Introduction*, we gave a short introduction to the general architecture of Vaadin. Let us now look deeper into it.

First of all, Vaadin provides two distinct development models: the for client-side, the browser, and for the server-side. The client-side development model allows developing widgets and applications in Java, which are executed in the browser as JavaScript. The server-driven development model, however, is the much more powerful one, allowing application development solely on the server-side, by utilizing an AJAX-based Vaadin Client-Side Engine that renders the user interface in the browser.

Figure 3.1, "Vaadin Server-Side Development Architecture" gives a basic illustration of the architecture.

Vaadin Framework consists of a *server-side API*, a *client-side API*, a horde of *user interface components* on the both sides, *themes* for controlling the appearance, and a *data model* that allows binding the server-side components directly to data. For client-side development, it includes the GWT Compiler, which allows compiling Java to JavaScript, as well as the full GWT framework.

A server-side Vaadin application runs as a servlet in a Java web server, serving HTTP requests. The Vaadin terminal adapter receives client requests through the web server's Java Servlet API, and inteprets them to user events for a particular session. Sessions are tracked using cookies. Events are associated with UI components and delivered to the application, which handles them with listeners. If the application logic makes changes to the server-side UI components, the terminal adapter renders them in the web browser by generating a response. The client-side engine running in the browser receives the responses and uses them to make any necessary changes to the page in the browser.

The entry-point of a user application consists of a *root* class that inherits **com.vaadin.ui.Root**. Its task is to create the initial user-interface and set up event listeners to handle user input. The root element can then be embedded to any HTML page. For detailed information about implementing a **Root**, see Chapter 4, *Writing a Web Application*.

The major parts of the server-driven development architecture and their function are as follows:

User Interface Components
> The user interface consists of UI components that are created and laid out by the application. Each server-side component has a client-side counterpart, with which the user interacts. The server-side components can serialize themselves over the client connection using a terminal adapter. The client-side components, in turn, can serialize user interaction back to the application, which is received in the server-side components as events. The components relay these events to the application logic. Most components are bound to a data source (see below). For a complete descrip-

---

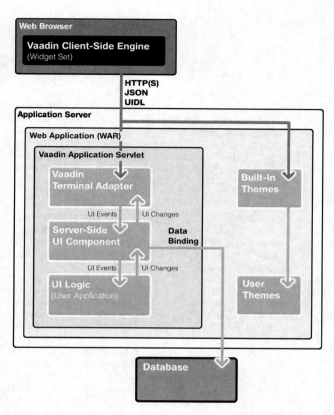

Figure 3.1. Vaadin Server-Side Development Architecture

tion of UI component architecture, see Chapter 5, *User Interface Components*.

Client-Side Engine
    The Client-Side Engine of Vaadin manages the rendering
    in the web browser. It communicates user interaction and
    UI changes with the server-side terminal adapter. The
    communications are made using asynchronous HTTP or
    HTTPS requests. See Section 3.4, "Client-Side Engine".

Terminal Adapter

The UI components do not render themselves directly as a web page, but use a *Terminal Adapter*, which handles the client-server communications at the server end. Vaadin currently has a GWT terminal adapter.

Themes

The user interface separates between presentation and logic. While the UI logic is handled as Java code, the presentation is defined in *themes* as CSS. Vaadin provides a default themes. User themes can, in addition to style sheets, include HTML templates that define custom layouts and other resources, such as images. Themes are discussed in detail in Chapter 8, *Themes*.

Events

User interaction with UI components creates events, which are first processed on the client-side with JavaScript and then passed all the way through the HTTP server, terminal adapter, and user component layers to the application. See Section 3.5, "Events and Listeners".

Data Model

In addition to the user interface model, Vaadin provides a *data model* for interfacing data presented in UI components. Using the data model, the user interface components can update the application data directly, without the need for any control code. All the UI components use this data model internally, but they can be bound to a separate data source as well. For example, you can bind a table component to an SQL query response. For a complete overview of the Vaadin Data Model, please refer to Chapter 9, *Binding Components to Data*.

3.2. Technological Background

This section provides an introduction to the various technologies and designs on which Vaadin is based: AJAX-based web applications in general and Google Web Toolkit. This knowledge is not necessary for using Vaadin, but provides some background if you need to make low-level extensions to Vaadin.

3.2.1. AJAX

AJAX (Asynchronous JavaScript and XML) is a technique for developing web applications with responsive user interaction, similar to traditional desktop applications. While conventional JavaScript-enabled HTML pages can receive new content only with page updates, AJAX-enabled pages send user interaction to the server using an asynchronous request and receive updated content in the response. This way, only small parts of the page data can be loaded. This goal is archieved by the use of a certain set of technologies: XHTML, CSS, DOM, JavaScript, XMLHttpRequest, and XML.

The web was originally not built for applications, but for hypertext pages that you can view with a browser. The purpose of web pages is to provide *content* for the user. Application software has a somewhat different purpose; usually to allow you to work on some data or content, much of which is not ever intended to be accessible through a web browser as web pages. As the web is inherently page-based, conventional web applications had to work with page requests and output HTML as response. JavaScript and AJAX have made it possible to let go of the pages.

Pages are largely an unknown concept to conventional desktop applications. At most, desktop applications can open multiple windows, but usually they work with a single main window, with an occasional dialog window here and there. Same goes usually for web applications developed with Vaadin: an application typically runs on a single page, changing the layout as needed and popping up dialog boxes.

Not having to load pages and use hyperlinks to communicate all user interaction is a relief for application development. However, they are an important feature that ordinary desktop applications lack. They allow referencing different functionalities of an application or resources managed by the application. They are also important for integration with external applications.

Certain resources can be identified through a *URL* or *Uniform Resource Locator*. A URL can easily be passed around or stored as a bookmark. We will see in Section 12.4, "Request Handlers" how you can retrieve the URL path or query parameters of a request.

Using URIs or request parameters to access functionalities or content is not as straight-forward as in conventional page-based web applications. Vaadin, just as any other AJAX framework, uses browser cookies not just for tracking users but also for tracking the application state. Cookies are unique in a browser, so any two windows share the same cookies and therefore also the state. The advantage is that you can close your browser and open it again and the application will be in the state where you left off (except for components such as text fields which did not have the immediate attribute enabled). The disadvantage is that there is no good way to distinguish between the windows, so there can usually be only a single application window. Even if there were several, you would have trouble with synchronization of application data between windows. Many conventional page-based web applications simply ignore out-of-sync situations, but such situations are risky for application platforms that are intended to be stable. Therefore it is safer to work with a single browser window. A URI can be used to fetch resources that have no particular state or to provide an entry point to the application.

With all the fuss and pomp it receives, AJAX is essentially made possible by a simple API, namely the XMLHttpRequest class in JavaScript. The API is available in all major browsers and, as of 2006, the API is under way to become a W3C standard.

Communications between the browser and the server usually require some sort of *serialization* (or *marshalling*) of data objects. The Vaadin terminal adapter handles serialization of shared state between server and client, as well as RPC calls to the other side.

3.2.2. Google Web Toolkit

Vaadin includes the Google Web Toolkit (GWT), which is a user interface framework for developing client-side web applications easily, without having to use JavaScript or other browser technologies directly. Pure client-side Vaadin applications are developed with Java and compiled into JavaScript with the GWT Compiler.

GWT is essentially a client-side technology, normally used to develop user interface logic in the web browser. Pure GWT applications still need to communicate with a server using RPC calls and by serializing any data. The server-driven development mode in Vaadin effectively hides all the client-server communications and allows handling user interaction logic in a server-side application. This makes the architecture of an AJAX-based web application much simpler.

Vaadin uses GWT to render user interfaces in the web browser and handle the low-level tasks of user interaction in the browser. Use of GWT is largely invisible in Vaadin for applications that do not need any custom GWT components.

See Section 3.4, "Client-Side Engine" for a description of how GWT is used in the Client-Side Engine of Vaadin. Chapter 11, *Developing New Components* provides information about the client-side development, as well as about the integration of client-side widgets with the server-side.

3.3. Applications as Java Servlet Sessions

Vaadin framework does basically everything it does on top of the Java Servlet API, which lies hidden deep under the hood, with the terminal adapter being the lowest level layer for handling requests from the web container.

When the web container gets the first request for a URL registered for an application, it creates an instance of the **ApplicationServlet** class in Vaadin framework that inherits the **HttpServlet** class defined in Java Servlet API. It follows sessions by using **HttpSession** interface and associates an **Application** instance with each session. During the lifetime of a session, the framework relays user actions to the proper application instance, and further to a user interface component.

3.4. Client-Side Engine

This section gives an overview of the client-side architecture of Vaadin. Knowledge of the client-side technologies is generally not needed unless you develop or use custom client-side widgets. The client-side engine is based on Google Web Toolkit (GWT) and its GWT Compiler, which allows the development of the engine and client-side components solely with Java.

Chapter 11, *Developing New Components* provides information about the integration of GWT-based user interface components with Vaadin.

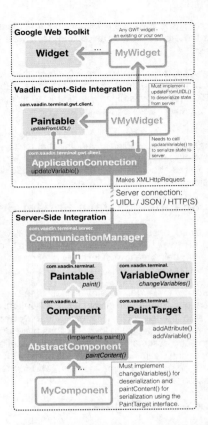

Figure 3.2. Architecture of Vaadin Client-Side Engine

Figure 3.2, "Architecture of Vaadin Client-Side Engine" illustrates the architecture of the client-side engine using a button component as an example. The user interface is managed by the **Application-Connection** class, which handles AJAX requests to the server and renders the user interface according to responses. In the server-side application, the button is used with the **Button** class of Vaadin. On the client-side, the user interface consists of various GWT components that inherit **Widget** class. In the figure above, the GWT class **Button** is used to render the button in the browser (the inheritance of **Button** is simplified in the figure). Vaadin provides an **VButton** class, which implements the **Paintable** interface needed for rendering the component with GWT.

The actual initial web page that is loaded in the browser is an empty page that loads the JavaScript code of the Vaadin Client-Side Engine. After it is loaded and started, it handles the AJAX requests to the server. All server communications are done through the **ApplicationConnection** class.

3.5. Events and Listeners

Vaadin offers an event-driven programming model for handling user interaction. When a user does something in the user interface, such as clicks a button or selects an item, the application needs to know about it. Many Java-based user interface frameworks follow the Event-Listener pattern (also known as the Observer design pattern) to communicate user input to the application logic. So does Vaadin. The design pattern involves two kinds of elements: an object that generates ("fires" or "emits") events and a number of listeners that listen for the events. When such an event occurs, the object sends a notification about it to all the listeners. In a typical case, there is only one listener.

Events can serve many kinds of purposes. In Vaadin, the usual purpose of events is handling user interaction in a user interface. Session management can require special events, such as for time-out, in which case the event would actually be the lack of user interaction. Time-out is a special case of timed or scheduled events, where an event occurs at a specific date and time or when a set time has passed. Database and other asynchronous communications can cause events as well.

To receive events of a particular type, an application must register a listener object with the event source. The listeners are registered in the components with the `addListener()` method. The method has a generic version defined at the level of **AbstractComponent**, the base class of all components.

Most components that have related events define their own event class and corresponding listener classes. For example, the **Button** has **Button.ClickEvent** events, which can be listened to through the **Button.ClickListener** interface.

In the following, we handle button clicks with a listener implemented as an anonymous class:

```
final Button button = new Button("Push it!");

button.addListener(new Button.ClickListener() {
    public void buttonClick(ClickEvent event) {
        button.setCaption("You pushed it!");
    }
});
```

Figure 3.3, "Class Diagram of a Button Click Listener" illustrates the case where an application-specific class inherits the **Button.ClickListener** interface to be able to listen for button click events. The application must instantiate the listener class and register it with addListener(). When an event occurs, an event object is instantiated, in this case a **ClickEvent**. The event object knows the related UI component, in this case the **Button**.

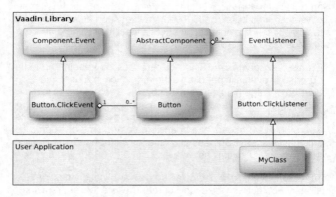

Figure 3.3. Class Diagram of a Button Click Listener

In the ancient times of C programming, *callback functions* filled largely the same need as listeners do now. In object-oriented languages, we have only classes and methods, not functions, so the application has to give a class interface instead of a callback function pointer to the framework. However, Vaadin supports defining a method as a listener as well, using the **MethodListener** wrapper.

Notice that many listener interfaces inherit the **java.util.EventListener** superinterface, but it is not generally necessary to inherit it.

Section 4.2, "Handling Events with Listeners" goes into details of handling events in practice.

Chapter 4

Writing a Web Application

This chapter provides the fundamentals of web application development with Vaadin, concentrating on the basic elements of an application from a practical point-of-view.

Vaadin provides two application development models, a server-side and client-side. In this chapter, we concentrate on the server-side model, which is usually the easiest way to create web applications. The pure client-side development model is described in Section 11.3.2, "Creating a Pure Client-Side Application".

This edition is a draft. Many new features that will be included in Vaadin 7 are not yet covered in this chapter and some of the content may in fact be outdated. For the most current version, please see the on-line edition available at http://vaadin.com/book.

4.1. Overview

A server-side application made with Vaadin runs as a Java Servlet in a Servlet container. The entry-point is the *root* class, which needs to create and manage the user interface components. User input is handled with event listeners, which can be simplified by binding user interface components directly to data. Visual appearance is defined in themes as CSS files. Icons, other images, and download-able files are handled as *resources*, which can be external or served by the application server or the application itself.

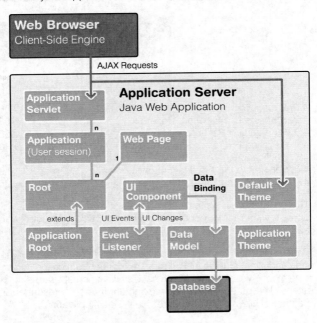

Figure 4.1. Application Architecture

Figure 4.1, "Application Architecture" above illustrates the basic architecture of an application made with the Vaadin framework, with all the major elements, which are introduced below and discussed in detail in this chapter.

First of all, a Vaadin application must have one or more root classes that extend the abstract **com.vaadin.ui.Root** class and implement the init() method. A custom theme can be defined as an annotation for the root.

```
@Theme("hellotheme")
public class HelloWorld extends Root {
    protected void init(WrappedRequest request) {
        ... initialization code goes here ...
    }
}
```

A root is a viewport to a Vaadin application running in a web page. A web page, represented by the **Page** class, can have multiple such roots embedded within it. Such situation is typical especially with portlets in a portal. An application can run in multiple browser windows, each having a **Page** and one or more roots.

The root API may seem similar to Java Servlet API, but that is only superficial. Vaadin framework associates requests with sessions so that an application instance is really a session object. Because of this, you can develop web applications much like you would develop desktop applications.

Restarting Application Session

When you first open an URL for the application, it creates a new user session. The session is preserved even if you reload the page. However, if you use Eclipse, it likes to do hot deployment to Tomcat and you may experience a problem that the application does not return to its initial state after you modify code. As Tomcat likes to persist sessions on server shutdown, the application state can remain even if you restart the server.

Adding the ?restartApplication parameter in the URL tells the Vaadin servlet to create a new **Application** instance on loading the page. If you also include a URI fragment, the parameter should be given before the fragment.

The most important task in the initialization is the creation of the initial user interface. This, and the deployment of the application as a Java Servlet in the Servlet container, as described in Section 4.6, "Setting Up the Application Environment", are the minimal requirements for an application.

Below is a short overview of the other basic elements of an application besides root:

Root

A *root* represents a HTML fragment in which a Vaadin application runs in a web page. It typically fills the entire page, but can also be just a part of a page. You normally develop a Vaadin application by extending **Root** and adding user interface components to it. A root is essentially a viewport or window connected to an application, and you can have many such views especially in a multi-window application. Normally, when the user opens a new page with the URL of the Vaadin application, a new **Root** (and the associated **Page** object) is automatically created for it.

The current root object can be globally accessed with `Root.getCurrent()`. The static method returns the thread-local root instance for the currently processed request (see Section 12.15.3, "ThreadLocal Pattern").

Page

A **Root** is associated with a **Page** object that represents the web page as well as the browser window in which the root runs.

The **Page** object for the currently processed request can be globally accessed from a Vaadin application with `Page.getCurrent()`. This is equivalent to calling `Root.getCurrent().getPage()`.

Application

A Vaadin application, as defined by the **Application** class, is essentially a user session. It can have multiple windows, each represented by a **Root**, which in turn is associated with a **Page**.

You can actually also develop a Vaadin application by extending **Application** instead of **Root**, and create the roots yourself.

User Interface Components

The user interface consists of components that are created by the application. They are laid out hierarchically using special *layout components*, with a root at the top of the hierarchy. User interaction with the components causes *events* related to the component, which the application can handle. *Field components* are intended for inputting values and can be directly bound to data using the Vaadin Data Model. You can make your own user interface components through either inheritance or composition. For a thorough reference of UI components, see Chapter 5, *User Interface Components*, for layout components, see Chapter 6, *Managing Layout*, and for composing components, see Section 5.23, "Component Composition with **CustomComponent**".

Events and Listeners

Vaadin follows an event-driven programming paradigm, in which events, and listeners that handle the events, are the basis of handling user interaction in an application. Section 3.5, "Events and Listeners" gave an introduction to events and listeners from an architectural point-of-view, while Section 4.2, "Handling Events with Listeners" later in this chapter takes a more practical view.

Resources

A user interface can display images or have links to web pages or downloadable documents. These are *resources*, which can be external or provided by the web server or the application itself. Section 4.3, "Referencing Resources" gives a practical overview of the different types of resources.

Themes

The presentation and logic of the user interface are separated. While the UI logic is handled as Java code, the presentation is defined in *themes* as CSS. Vaadin includes some built-in themes. User-defined themes can, in addition to style sheets, include HTML templates that define custom layouts and other theme resources, such as images. Themes are discussed in detail in Chapter 8, *Themes*, custom layouts in Section 6.14, "Custom Layouts", and theme resources in Section 4.3.4, "Theme Resources".

Data Binding

Field components are essentially views to data, represented in the *Vaadin Data Model*. Using the data model, the components can get their values from and update user input to the data model directly, without the need for any control code. A field component is always bound to a *property* and a group a fields to an *item* that holds the properties. Items can be collected in a *container*, which can act as a data source for some components such as tables or lists. While all the components have a default data model, they can be bound to a user-defined data source. For example, you can bind a **Table** component to an SQL query response. For a complete overview of data binding in Vaadin, please refer to Chapter 9, *Binding Components to Data*.

4.2. Handling Events with Listeners

Let us put into practice what we learned of event handling in Section 3.5, "Events and Listeners". You can handle events in three basic ways, as shown below.

The following example follows a typical pattern where you have a **Button** component and a listener that handles user interaction (clicks) communicated to the application as events. Here we define a class that listens click events.

```
public class TheButton implements Button.ClickListener {
    Button thebutton;

    /** Creates button into given container. */
    public TheButton(AbstractComponentContainer container) {
        thebutton = new Button ("Do not push this button");
        thebutton.addListener(this);
        container.addComponent(thebutton);
    }

    /** Handle button click events from the button. */
    public void buttonClick (Button.ClickEvent event) {
        thebutton.setCaption ("Do not push this button again");
    }
}
```

As an application often receives events for several components of the same class, such as multiple buttons, it has to be able to distinguish between the individual components. There are several techniques to do this, but probably the easiest is to use the property of the received event, which is set to the object sending the event. This requires keeping at hand a reference to every object that emits events.

```java
public class TheButtons implements Button.ClickListener {
    Button thebutton;
    Button secondbutton;

    /** Creates two buttons in given container. */
    public TheButtons(AbstractComponentContainer container) {
        thebutton = new Button ("Do not push this button");
        thebutton.addListener(this);
        container.addComponent(thebutton);

        secondbutton = new Button ("I am a button too");
        secondbutton.addListener(this);
        container.addComponent (secondbutton);
    }

    /** Handle button click events from the two buttons. */
    public void buttonClick (Button.ClickEvent event) {
        if (event.getButton() == thebutton)
            thebutton.setCaption("Do not push this button again");
        else if (event.getButton() == secondbutton)
            secondbutton.setCaption("I am not a number");
    }
}
```

Another solution to handling multiple events of the same class involves attaching an event source to a listener method instead of the class. An event can be attached to a method using another version of the `addListener()` method, which takes the event handler method as a parameter. The method can be passed either by the name of the method or as a **Method** object. In the example below, we use the name of the method, as a string (which is not checked at compile time).

```java
public class TheButtons2 {
    Button thebutton;
    Button secondbutton;

    /** Creates two buttons in given container. */
    public TheButtons2(AbstractComponentContainer container) {
        thebutton = new Button ("Do not push this button");
        thebutton.addListener(Button.ClickEvent.class, this,
                              "theButtonClick");
        container.addComponent(thebutton);

        secondbutton = new Button ("I am a button too");
```

```
        secondbutton.addListener(Button.ClickEvent.class, this,
                            "secondButtonClick");
        container.addComponent (secondbutton);
    }

    public void theButtonClick (Button.ClickEvent event) {
        thebutton.setCaption ("Do not push this button again");
    }

    public void secondButtonClick (Button.ClickEvent event) {
        secondbutton.setCaption ("I am not a number!");
    }
}
```

Adding a listener method with `addListener()` is really just a
wrapper that creates a **com.vaadin.event.ListenerMethod**
listener object, which is an adapter from a listener class to a
method. It implements the **java.util.EventListener** interface and
can therefore work for any event source using the interface. Notice
that not all listener classes necessarily inherit the **EventListener**
interface.

The third way, which uses anonymous local class definitions, is
often the easiest as it does not require cumbering the managing
class with new interfaces or methods. The following example
defines an anonymous class that inherits the **Button.ClickListener**
interface and implements the `buttonClick()` method.

```
public class TheButtons3 {
    Button thebutton;
    Button secondbutton;

    /** Creates two buttons in given container. */
    public TheButtons3(AbstractComponentContainer container) {
        thebutton = new Button ("Do not push this button");

        /* Define a listener in an anonymous class. */
        thebutton.addListener(new Button.ClickListener() {
            /* Handle the click. */
            public void buttonClick(ClickEvent event) {
                thebutton.setCaption (
                        "Do not push this button again");
            }
        });
        container.addComponent(thebutton);

        secondbutton = new Button ("I am a button too");
        secondbutton.addListener(new Button.ClickListener() {
            public void buttonClick(ClickEvent event) {
                secondbutton.setCaption ("I am not a number!");

            }
        });
        container.addComponent (secondbutton);
```

```
        }
    }
```

Other techniques for separating between different sources also exist. They include using object properties, names, or captions to separate between them. Using captions or any other visible text is generally discouraged, as it may create problems for internationalization. Using other symbolic strings can also be dangerous, because the syntax of such strings is checked only runtime.

Events are usually emitted by the framework, but applications may need to emit them too in some situations, such as when updating some part of the UI is required. Events can be emitted programmatically using the `fireEvent(Component.Event)` method of **AbstractComponent**. The event is then relayed to all the listeners of the particular event class for the object. Some components have a default event type, for example, a **Button** has a nested **Button.ClickEvent** class and a corresponding **Button.ClickListener** interface. These events can be triggered with `fireComponentEvent()`.

4.3. Referencing Resources

Web applications work over the web and have various resources, such as images or downloadable files, that the web browser has to get from the server. These resources are typically used in **Embedded** (images) or **Link** (downloadable files) user interface components. Various components, such as **TabSheet**, can also include icons, which are also handled as resources.

A web server can handle many of such requests for static resources without having to ask them from the application, or the **Application** object can provide them. For dynamic resources, the user application must be able to create them dynamically. Vaadin provides resource request interfaces for applications so that they can return various kinds of resources, such as files or dynamically created resources. These include the **StreamResource** class and the `RequestHandler` described in Section 12.4, "Request Handlers".

Vaadin provides also low-level facilities for retrieving the URI and other parameters of a HTTP request. We will first look into how applications can provide various kinds of resources and then look into low-level interfaces for handling URIs and parameters to provide resources and functionalities.

Notice that using request handlers to create "pages" is not meaningful in Vaadin or in AJAX applications generally. Please see Section 3.2.1, "AJAX" for a detailed explanation.

4.3.1. Resource Interfaces and Classes

Vaadin has two interfaces for resources: a generic **Resource** interface and a more specific **ApplicationResource** interface for resources provided by the application.

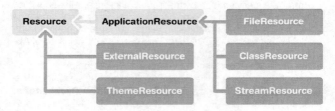

Figure 4.2. Resource Interface and Class Diagram

ApplicationResource resources are managed by the **Application** class. When you create such a resource, you give the application object to the constructor. The constructor registers the resource in the application using the **addResource** method.

Application manages requests for the resources and allows accessing resources using a URI. The URI consists of the base name of the application and a relative name of the resource. The relative name is `"APP/"+resourceid+"/"+filename`, for example `"APP/1/myimage.png"`. The `resourceid` is a generated numeric identifier to make resources unique, and `filename` is the file name of the resource given in the constructor of its class. However, the application using a resource does not usually need to consider its URI. It only needs to give the resource to an appropriate **Embedded** or **Link** or some other user interface component, which manages the rendering of the URI.

4.3.2. File Resources

File resources are files stored anywhere in the file system. The use of file resources generally falls into two main categories: downloadable files and embedded images.

A file object that can be accessed as a file resource is defined with the standard **java.io.File** class. You can create the file either with an absolute or relative path, but the base path of the relative path depends on the installation of the web server. For example, in Apache Tomcat, the default current directory is the installation path of Tomcat.

4.3.3. Class Loader Resources

The **ClassResource** allows resources to be loaded from the deployed package of the application using Java Class Loader. The one-line example below loads an image resource from the application package and displays it in an **Embedded** component.

```
mainwindow.addComponent(new Embedded ("",
        new ClassResource("smiley.jpg",
                mainwindow.getApplication())));
```

4.3.4. Theme Resources

Theme resources of **ThemeResource** class are files, typically images, included in a theme. A theme is located with path VAAD-IN/themes/themename in a web application. Name of a theme resource is given as the parameter for the constructor, with a path relative to the theme folder.

```
// A theme resource in the current theme ("book-examples")
// Located in: VAADIN/themes/book-examples/img/themeimage.png
ThemeResource resource = new ThemeResource("img/themeimage.png");

// Use the resource
Embedded image = new Embedded("My Theme Image", resource);
```

The result is shown in Figure 4.3, "Theme Resources", illustrating also the folder structure for the theme resource file in an Eclipse project.

- ✓ 🗁 WebContent
  - ➤ 🗁 META-INF
  - ✓ 🗁 VAADIN
    - ✓ 🗁 themes
      - ✓ 🗁 book-examples
        - ➤ 🗁 icons
        - ✓ 🗁 img
          - 🖼 themeimage.png
        - ➤ 🗁 layouts
          - 📄 styles.css
      - ➤ 🗁 widgetsets
  - ➤ 🗁 WEB-INF

Figure 4.3. Theme Resources

To use theme resources, you must set the theme for the application. See Chapter 8, *Themes* for more information regarding themes.

4.3.5. Stream Resources

Stream resources are application resources that allow creating dynamic resource content. Charts are typical examples of dynamic images. To define a stream resource, you need to implement the **StreamResource.StreamSource** interface and its `getStream` method. The method needs to return an **InputStream** from which the stream can be read.

The following example demonstrates the creation of a simple image in PNG image format.

```
import java.awt.image.*;

public class MyImageSource
            implements StreamResource.StreamSource {
    ByteArrayOutputStream imagebuffer = null;
    int reloads = 0;

    /* We need to implement this method that returns
     * the resource as a stream. */
    public InputStream getStream () {
        /* Create an image and draw something on it. */
        BufferedImage image = new BufferedImage (200, 200,
```

```
                            BufferedImage.TYPE_INT_RGB);
        Graphics drawable = image.getGraphics();
        drawable.setColor(Color.lightGray);
        drawable.fillRect(0,0,200,200);
        drawable.setColor(Color.yellow);
        drawable.fillOval(25,25,150,150);
        drawable.setColor(Color.blue);
        drawable.drawRect(0,0,199,199);
        drawable.setColor(Color.black);
        drawable.drawString("Reloads="+reloads, 75, 100);
        reloads++;

        try {
            /* Write the image to a buffer. */
            imagebuffer = new ByteArrayOutputStream();
            ImageIO.write(image, "png", imagebuffer);

            /* Return a stream from the buffer. */
            return new ByteArrayInputStream(
                       imagebuffer.toByteArray());
        } catch (IOException e) {
            return null;
        }
    }
}
```

The content of the generated image is dynamic, as it updates the
reloads counter with every call. The **ImageIO**.write() method
writes the image to an output stream, while we had to return an
input stream, so we stored the image contents to a temporary
buffer.

You can use resources in various ways. Some user interface
components, such as **Link** and **Embedded**, take their parameters
as a resource.

Below we display the image with the **Embedded** component. The
StreamResource constructor gets a reference to the application
and registers itself in the application's resources. Assume that
main is a reference to the main window and this is the application
object.

```
// Create an instance of our stream source.
StreamResource.StreamSource imagesource = new MyImageSource ();

// Create a resource that uses the stream source and give it a name.
// The constructor will automatically register the resource in
// the application.
StreamResource imageresource =
        new StreamResource(imagesource, "myimage.png", this);

// Create an embedded component that gets its contents
```

```
// from the resource.
main.addComponent(new Embedded("Image title", imageresource));
```

The image will look as follows:

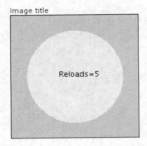

Figure 4.4. Screenshot of the stream resource example with an embedded image

We named the resource as `myimage.png`. The application adds a resource key to the file name of the resource to make it unique. The full URI will be like `http://localhost:8080/test-bench/APP/1/myimage.png`. The end `APP/1/myimage.png` is the *relative* part of the URI. You can get the relative part of a resource's URI from the application with `Application.getRelativeLocation()`.

Another way to create dynamic content is a request handler, described in Section 12.4, "Request Handlers".

4.4. Handling Errors

4.4.1. Error Indicator and message

All components have a built-in error indicator that can be set explicitly with `setComponentError()` or can be turned on implicitly if validating the component fails. As with component caption, the placement of the indicator is managed by the layout in which the component is contained. Usually, the error indicator is placed right of the caption text. Hovering the mouse pointer over the field displays the error message.

The following example shows how you can set the component error explicitly. The example essentially validates field value without using an actual validator.

```
// Create a field.
final TextField textfield = new TextField("Enter code");
main.addComponent(textfield);

// Let the component error be initially clear.
textfield.setComponentError(null); // (actually the default)

// Have a button right of the field (and align it properly).
final Button button = new Button("Ok!");
main.addComponent(button);
((VerticalLayout)main.getLayout())
        .setComponentAlignment(button, Alignment.BOTTOM_LEFT);

// Handle button clicks
button.addListener(new Button.ClickListener() {
    public void buttonClick(ClickEvent event) {
        // If the field value is bad, set its error.
        // (Allow only alphanumeric characters.)
        if (! ((String) textfield.getValue()).matches("^\\w*$")) {
            // Put the component in error state and
            // set the error message.
            textfield.setComponentError(
                new UserError("Must be letters and numbers"));
        } else {
            // Otherwise clear it.
            textfield.setComponentError(null);
        }
    }
});
```

Enter code !

Some text   Ok!
                  Must be letters and numbers

Figure 4.5. Error indicator active

4.4.2. Customizing System Messages

System messages are notifications that indicate a major invalid state in an application that usually requires restarting the application. Session timeout is perhaps the most typical such state.

System messages are strings managed in **SystemMessages** class.

sessionExpired

> Application servlet session expired. A session expires if no server requests are made during the session timeout period. The session timeout can be configured with the *session-timeout* parameter in `web.xml`, as described in Section 4.6.3, "Deployment Descriptor `web.xml`".

communicationErrorURL

> An unspecified communication problem between the Vaadin Client-Side Engine and the application server. The server may be unavailable or there is some other problem.

authenticationError

> This error occurs if 401 (Unauthorized) response to a request is received from the server.

internalError

> A serious internal problem, possibly indicating a bug in Vaadin Client-Side Engine or in some custom client-side code.

outOfSync

> The client-side state is invalid with respect to server-side state.

cookiesDisabled

> Informs the user that cookies are disabled in the browser and the application does not work without them.

Each message has four properties: a short caption, the actual message, a URL to which to redirect after displaying the message, and property indicating whether the notification is enabled.

Additional details may be written (in English) to the debug console window described in Section 12.3, "Debug and Production Mode".

You can override the default system messages by implementing the `getSystemMessages()` method in the application class. The method should return a **Application.SystemMessages** object. The easiest way to customize the messages is to use a **CustomizedSystemMessages** object as follows:

```
// Override the default implementation
public static SystemMessages getSystemMessages() {
    CustomizedSystemMessages messages =
```

```
          new CustomizedSystemMessages();
    messages.setSessionExpiredCaption("Ohno, session expired!");
    messages.setSessionExpiredMessage("Don't idle!");
    messages.setSessionExpiredNotificationEnabled(true);
    messages.setSessionExpiredURL("http://vaadin.com/");
    return messages;
}
```

Notice that the special `getSystemMessages()` method is not defined in an interface nor does it exist in the **Application** super-class.

4.4.3. Handling Uncaught Exceptions

Application development with Vaadin follows the event-driven programming model. Mouse and keyboard events in the client cause (usually higher-level) events on the server-side, which can be handled with listeners, and that is how most of the application logic works. Handling the events can result in exceptions either in the application logic or in the framework itself, but some of them may not be caught properly.

For example, in the following code excerpt, we throw an error in an event listener but do not catch it, so it falls to the framework.

```
final Button button = new Button ("Fail Me");

button.addListener(new Button.ClickListener() {
    public void buttonClick(ClickEvent event) {
        // Throw some exception.
        throw new RuntimeException("You can't catch this.");
    }
});
```

Any such exceptions that occur in the call chain, but are not caught at any other level, are eventually caught by the terminal adapter in **ApplicationServlet**, the lowest-level component that receives client requests. The terminal adapter passes all such caught exceptions as events to the error listener of the **Application** instance through the **Terminal.ErrorListener** interface. The **Application** class does not, by default, throw such exceptions forward.

The reason for this error-handling logic lies in the logic that handles component state synchronization between the client and the server. We want to handle *all* the serialized variable changes in the client request, because otherwise the client-side and server-side component states would become unsynchronized very easily, which could put the entire application in an invalid state.

The default implementation of the **Terminal.ErrorListener** interface in the **Application** class simply prints the error to console. It also tries to find out a component related to the error. If the exception occurred in a listener attached to a component, that component is considered as the component related to the exception. If a related component is found, the error handler sets the *component error* for it, the same attribute which you can set with setComponentError().

In UI, the component error is shown with a small red "!" -sign (in the default theme). If you hover the mouse pointer over it, you will see the entire backtrace of the exception in a large tooltip box, as illustrated in Figure 4.6, "Uncaught Exception in Component Error Indicator" for the above code example.

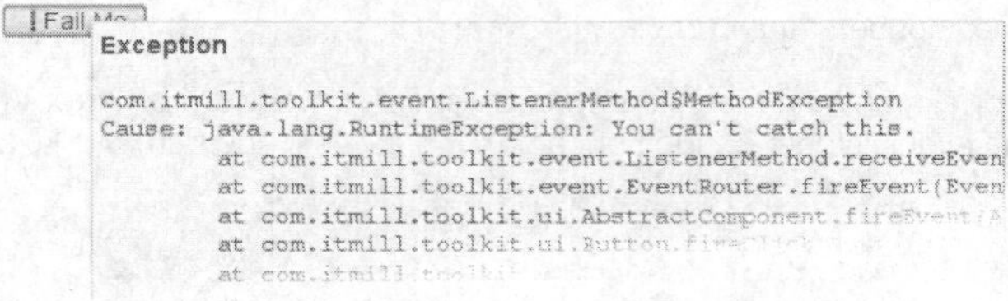

Figure 4.6. Uncaught Exception in Component Error Indicator

You can change the logic of handling the terminal errors easily by overriding the terminalError() method in your application class (the one that inherits **Application**) or by setting a custom error listener with the setErrorHandler method. You can safely discard the default handling or extend its usage with your custom error handling or logging system. In the example code below, the exceptions are also reported as notifications in the main window.

```
@Override
public void terminalError(Terminal.ErrorEvent event) {
    // Call the default implementation.
    super.terminalError(event);

    // Some custom behaviour.
    new Notification(
        "An unchecked exception occured!",
```

```
          event.getThrowable().toString(),
          Notification.TYPE_ERROR_MESSAGE)
              .show(Page.getCurrent());
}
```

Handling other exceptions works in the usual way for Java Servlets. Uncaught exceptions are finally caught and handled by the application server.

4.5. Notifications

Notifications are error or information boxes that appear briefly, typically at the center of the screen. A notification box has a caption and an optional description and icon. The box stays on the screen either for a preset time or until the user clicks it. The notification type defines the default appearance and behaviour of a notification.

There are two ways to create a notification. The easiest is to use a static shorthand `Notification.show()` method, which takes the caption of the notification as a parameter and displays it in the current page.

```
Notification.show("This is a warning");
```

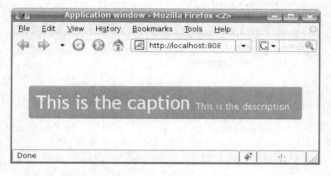

Figure 4.7. Notification

For more control, you can create a **Notification** object. Different constructors exist for taking just the caption, or also the description, notification type, and whether HTML is allowed or not. Notifications are shown in a **Page**, typically the current page.

```
new Notification("This is a warning",
    "<br/>This is the <i>last</i> warning",
    Notification.TYPE_WARNING_MESSAGE, true)
    .show(Page.getCurrent());
```

The caption and description are by default written on the same line. If you want to have a line break between them, use the XHTML line break markup "`<br/>`" if HTML is enabled, or "`\n`" if not. When HTML is enabled (it is by default), you can use any XHTML markup in the caption and description of a notification. If it is possible to get the notification content from user input, you should either disallow HTML with `setHtmlContentAllowed(false)` or sanitize the content carefully, as noted in Section 12.8.1, "Sanitizing User Input to Prevent Cross-Site Scripting".

This is a warning
This is the *last* warning

Figure 4.8. Notification with HTML Formatting

4.5.1. Notification Type

The notification type defines the overall default style and behaviour of a notification. If no notification type is given, the "humanized" type is used as the default. The notification types, listed below, are defined in the **Notification** class.

`TYPE_HUMANIZED_MESSAGE`
> A user-friendly message that does not annoy too much: it does not require confirmation by clicking and disappears quickly. It is centered and has a neutral gray color.

`TYPE_WARNING_MESSAGE`
> Warnings are messages of medium importance. They are displayed with colors that are neither neutral nor too distractive. A warning is displayed for 1.5 seconds, but the user can click the message box to dismiss it. The user can con-

tinue to interact with the application while the warning is displayed.

`TYPE_ERROR_MESSAGE`

Error messages are notifications that require the highest user attention, with alert colors and by requiring the user to click the message to dismiss it. The error message box does not itself include an instruction to click the message, although the close box in the upper right corner indicates it visually. Unlike with other notifications, the user can not interact with the application while the error message is displayed.

`TYPE_TRAY_NOTIFICATION`

Tray notifications are displayed in the "system tray" area, that is, in the lower-right corner of the browser view. As they do not usually obsure any user interface, they are displayed longer than humanized or warning messages, 3 seconds by default. The user can continue to interact with the application normally while the tray notification is displayed.

4.5.2. Customizing Notifications

All of the features of specific notification types can be controlled with the **Notification** properties. Once configured, you need to show it in the current page.

```
// Notification with default settings for a warning
Notification notif = new Notification(
    "Warning",
    "<br/>Area of reindeer husbandry",
    Notification.TYPE_WARNING_MESSAGE);

// Customize it
notif.setDelayMsec(20000);
notif.setPosition(Notification.POSITION_BOTTOM_RIGHT);
notif.setStyleName("mystyle");
notif.setIcon(new ThemeResource("img/reindeer.png"));

// Show it in the page
notif.show(Page.getCurrent());
```

The `setPosition()` method allows setting the positioning of the notification. The method takes as its parameter any of the constants:

```
Notification.POSITION_CENTERED

Notification.POSITION_CENTERED_TOP

Notification.POSITION_CENTERED_BOTTOM

Notification.POSITION_TOP_LEFT

Notification.POSITION_TOP_RIGHT

Notification.POSITION_BOTTOM_LEFT

Notification.POSITION_BOTTOM_RIGHT
```

The setDelayMSec() allows you to set the time in milliseconds for how long the notification is displayed. Parameter value -1 means that the message is displayed until the user clicks the message box. It also prevents interaction with other parts of the application window, as is default behaviour for error messages. It does not, however, add a close box that the error notification has.

4.5.3. Styling with CSS

```
.v-Notification {}
  .popupContent {}
    .gwt-HTML {}
      h1 {}
      p  {}
```

The notification box is a floating div element under the body element of the page. It has an overall v-Notification style. The content is wrapped inside an element with popupContent style. The caption is enclosed within an h1 element and the description in a p element.

To customize it, add a style for the **Notification** object with setStyleName("mystyle"), and make the settings in the theme, for example as follows:

```
.v-Notification.mystyle {
    background: #FFFF00;
    border: 10px solid #C00000;
    color: black;
}
```

The result is shown, with the icon set earlier in the customization example, in Figure 4.9, "Styled Notification".

Figure 4.9. Styled Notification

4.6. Setting Up the Application Environment

Vaadin applications are deployed as *Java web applications*. A Java "web application" can contain a number of servlets, each of which can be a Vaadin application or some other servlet, and static resources such as HTML files. Such a web application is normally packaged as WAR (Web application ARchive) file, which can be deployed to a Java application server (or a servlet container to be exact).

For a detailed tutorial on how web applications are packaged, please refer to any Java book that discusses Java Servlets. Sun has an excellent reference online at http://java.sun.com/j2ee/tutorial/1_3-fcs/doc/WCC3.html .

Remember that, in the Java Servlet parlance, "web application" means a collection of Java servlets or portlets, JSP and static HTML pages, and various other resources that form an application. Such a Java web application is typically packaged as a WAR package for deployment. Vaadin applications, on the other hand, run as servlets within such a Java web application. There exists also other kinds of web applications. To avoid confusion with the general meaning of "web application", we often refer to Java web application as "WAR" in this book.

4.6.1. Creating Deployable WAR in Eclipse

To deploy an application to a web server, you need to create a WAR package. Here we give the instructions for Eclipse.

1. Select **File → Export** and then **Web → WAR File**. Or, right-click the project in the Project Explorer and select **Web → WAR File**.

2. Select the **Web project** to export. Enter **Destination** file name (`.war`).

3. Make any other settings in the dialog, and click **Finish**.

4.6.2. Web Application Contents

The following files are required in a web application in order to run it.

Web application organization

`WEB-INF/web.xml`

> This is the standard web application descriptor that defines how the application is organized. You can refer to any Java book about the contents of this file. Also see an example in Example 4.1, "web.xml".

`WEB-INF/lib/vaadin-7.x.x.jar`

> This is the Vaadin library. It is included in the product package in `lib` directory.

Your application classes

> You must include your application classes either in a JAR file in `WEB-INF/lib` or as classes in `WEB-INF/classes`

Your own theme files (OPTIONAL)

> If your application uses a special theme (look and feel), you must include it in `VAADIN/themes/themename` directory.

Widget sets (OPTIONAL)

> If your application uses a project-specific widget set, it must be compiled in the `VAADIN/widgetset/` directory.

4.6.3. Deployment Descriptor `web.xml`

The deployment descriptor is an XML file with the name `web.xml` in the `WEB-INF` directory of a web application. It is a standard component in Java EE describing how a web application should be deployed. The structure of the deployment descriptor is illus-

---

trated by the following example. You simply deploy applications as servlets implemented by the special `com.vaadin.terminal.gwt.server.ApplicationServlet` wrapper class.

If your application has a single root, you simply specify the root class by giving the `root` parameter with the name of the specific root class for the servlet. The servlet is then connected to a URL in a standard way for Java Servlets.

Example 4.1. web.xml

```xml
<?xml version="1.0" encoding="UTF-8"?>
<web-app
  id="WebApp_ID" version="2.4"
  xmlns="http://java.sun.com/xml/ns/j2ee"
  xmlns:xsi="http://www.w3.org/2001/XMLSchema-instance"
  xsi:schemaLocation="http://java.sun.com/xml/ns/j2ee
    http://java.sun.com/xml/ns/j2ee/web-app_2_4.xsd">

  <servlet>
    <servlet-name>myservlet</servlet-name>
    <servlet-class>
        com.vaadin.terminal.gwt.server.ApplicationServlet
    </servlet-class>
    <init-param>
      <param-name>root</param-name>
      <param-value>MyRoot</param-value>
    </init-param>
  </servlet>

  <servlet-mapping>
    <servlet-name>myservlet</servlet-name>
    <url-pattern>/*</url-pattern>
  </servlet-mapping>
</web-app>
```

The descriptor defines a servlet with name `myservlet`. The servlet class, **com.vaadin.terminal.gwt.server.ApplicationServlet**, is provided by Vaadin framework and is normally the same for all Vaadin projects. For some purposes, you may need to use a custom servlet class.

Root or Application Class

The servlet can take either an application class or the root class of an application as a parameter. A root class is normally given in

---

applications with a single root inside a page, while using an application class as the entry-point allows multiple roots.

If the `root` parameter is given, its value must be the class name of the root class, such as **com.example.MyRoot**, including the full package path to the class. If the class is in the default package, the package path is obviously not used.

If your application has multiple roots in one page, or for other purposes, you can extend the **Application** class instead of **Root** and define your application class with the `application` parameter for the servlet. For roots created during the execution of an application, such as for displaying popup windows, you can add new roots dynamically to the application instance.

Servlet Mapping with URL Patterns

The `url-pattern` is defined above as `/*`. This matches to any URL under the project context. We defined above the project context as `myproject` so the URL for the page of the root will be `http://localhost:8080/myproject/`. If the project were to have multiple roots or servlets, they would have to be given different names to distinguish them. For example, `url-pattern /myroot/*` would match a URL such as `http://localhost:8080/myproject/myroot/`. Notice that the slash and the asterisk *must* be included at the end of the pattern.

Notice also that if the URL pattern is other than `/*` (such as `/myroot/*`), you will also need to make a servlet mapping to `/VAADIN/*` (unless you are serving it statically as noted below). For example:

```
...
<servlet-mapping>
    <servlet-name>myservlet</servlet-name>
    <url-pattern>/myurl/*</url-pattern>
</servlet-mapping>

<servlet-mapping>
    <servlet-name>myservlet</servlet-name>
    <url-pattern>/VAADIN/*</url-pattern>
</servlet-mapping>
```

If you have multiple servlets, you should specify only one /VAAD-IN/* mapping. It does not matter which servlet you map the pattern to, as long as it is a Vaadin servlet.

You do not have to provide the above /VAADIN/* mapping if you serve both the widget sets and (custom and default) themes statically in the WebContent/VAADIN/ directory. The mapping simply allows serving them dynamically from the Vaadin JAR. Serving them statically is recommended for production environments as it is faster. If you serve the content from within the same web application, you may not have the root pattern /* for the Vaadin servlet, as then all the requests would be mapped to the servlet.

Other Deployment Parameters

Deployment descriptor can have many parameters and options that control the execution of a servlet. You can find a complete documentation of the deployment descriptor in Java Servlet Specification at http://java.sun.com/products/servlet/.

By default, Vaadin applications run in *debug mode*, which should be used during development. This enables various debugging features. For production use, you should have put in your web.xml the following parameter:

```
<context-param>
  <param-name>productionMode</param-name>
  <param-value>true</param-value>
  <description>Vaadin production mode</description>
</context-param>
```

The parameter and the debug and production modes are described in detail in Section 12.3, "Debug and Production Mode".

One often needed option is the session timeout. Different servlet containers use varying defaults for timeouts, such as 30 minutes for Apache Tomcat. You can set the timeout with:

```
<session-config>
    <session-timeout>30</session-timeout>
</session-config>
```

4.7. Basic Application Architecture

Once your application grows beyond a dozen or so lines, which is actually quite soon, you need to start considering the application architecture. You are free to use any object-oriented techniques available in Java to organize your code in methods, classes, packages, and libraries. An architecture defines how these modules communicate together and what sort of dependencies they have between them. It also defines the scope of the application. The scope of this book, however, only gives a possibility to mention some of the most common architectural patterns in Vaadin applications.

The following sections describe some basic application patterns. You may also want to consider the advanced architectures presented in Section 12.14, "Advanced Application Architectures". The Section 12.15, "Accessing Session-Global Data" discusses the problem of passing essentially global references around, a common problem which is also visited in later in this section, in Section 4.7.3, "Accessing Root, Page, and Application".

4.7.1. Compositing Components

User interfaces typically contain many user interface components in a layout hierarchy. Vaadin provides many layout components for laying contained components vertically, horizontally, in a grid, and in many other ways. You can extend layout components to create composite components.

```
class MyView extends VerticalLayout {
    TextField entry   = new TextField("Enter this");
    Label     display = new Label("See this");
    Button    click   = new Button("Click This");

    public MyView() {
        addComponent(entry);
        addComponent(display);
        addComponent(click);

        // Configure it a bit
        setSizeFull();
        addStyleName("myview");
    }
}
```

```
// Use it
Layout myview = new MyView();
```

This composition pattern is especially supported for creating forms, as described in Section 9.4.3, "Binding Member Fields".

While extending layouts is an easy way to make component composition, it is a good practice to encapsulate implementation details, such as the exact layout component used. Otherwise, the users of such a composite could begin to rely on such implementation details, which would make changes harder. For this purpose, Vaadin has a special **CustomComponent** wrapper, which hides the content representation.

```
class MyView extends CustomComponent {
    TextField entry   = new TextField("Enter this");
    Label     display = new Label("See this");
    Button    click   = new Button("Click This");

    public MyView() {
        Layout layout = new VerticalLayout();

        layout.addComponent(entry);
        layout.addComponent(display);
        layout.addComponent(click);

        setCompositionRoot(layout);

        setSizeFull();
    }
}

// Use it
MyView myview = new MyView();
```

For a more detailed description of the **CustomComponent**, see Section 5.23, "Component Composition with **CustomComponent**". The Vaadin Plugin for Eclipse also includes a visual editor for composite components, as described in Chapter 7, *Visual User Interface Design with Eclipse*.

4.7.2. View Navigation

While the most simple applications have just a single *view* (or *screen*), perhaps most have many. Even in a single view, you often want to have sub-views, for example to display different content. Figure 4.10, "Navigation Between Views" illustrates a typical navigation between different top-level views of an application, and a main view with sub-views.

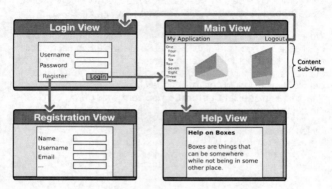

Figure 4.10. Navigation Between Views

The **Navigator** described in Section 12.10, "Navigating in an Application" is a view manager that provides a flexible way to navigate between views and sub-views, while managing the URI fragment in the page URL to allow bookmarking, linking, and going back in browser history.

Often Vaadin application views are part of something bigger. In such cases, you may need to integrate the Vaadin applications with the other website. You can use the embedding techniques described in Section 12.2, "Embedding Applications in Web Pages".

4.7.3. Accessing Root, Page, and Application

You can access the current root, page, and application objects from anywhere in the application using the static `getCurrent()` method in the respective **Root**, **Page**, and **Application** classes.

```
// Opens a sub-window
Root.getCurrent().addWindow(new Window("My Window"));

// Set the page title (window or tab caption)
```

```
Page.getCurrent().setTitle("My Page");

// Set the logout URL
Application.getCurrent().setLogoutURL(
        "http://en.wikipedia.org/wiki/Reindeer");
```

These methods use the built-in ThreadLocal support for application and root objects. The pattern is described in detail in Section 12.15.3, "ThreadLocal Pattern".

Chapter 5

User Interface Components

This chapter provides an overview and a detailed description of all non-layout components in Vaadin.

This chapter is a draft. Many new features that will be included in the final version of Vaadin 7 are not yet covered in the draft and some of the content may be outdated. For the most current version, please see the on-line edition available at `http://vaad-in.com/book`.

5.1. Overview

Vaadin provides a comprehensive set of user interface components and allows you to define custom components. Figure 5.1, "UI Component Inheritance Diagram" illustrates the inheritance hierarchy of the UI component classes and interfaces. Interfaces are displayed in gray, abstract classes in orange, and regular classes in blue. An annotated version of the diagram is featured in the *Vaadin Cheat Sheet*.

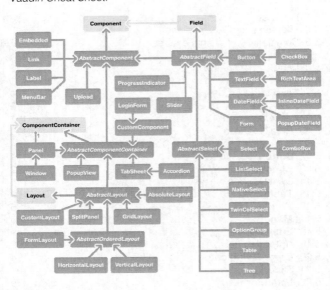

Figure 5.1. UI Component Inheritance Diagram

At the top of the interface hierarchy, we have the **Component** interface. At the top of the class hierarchy, we have the **Abstract-Component** class. It is inherited by two other abstract classes: **AbstractField**, inherited further by field components, and **Abstract-ComponentContainer**, inherited by various container and layout components. Components that are not bound to a content data model, such as labels and links, inherit **AbstractComponent** directly.

The layout of the various components in a window is controlled, logically, by layout components, just like in conventional Java UI toolkits for desktop applications. In addition, with the **CustomLayout** component, you can write a custom layout as an XHTML template that includes the locations of any contained components. Looking at the inheritance diagram, we can see that layout components inherit the **AbstractComponentContainer** and the **Layout** interface. Layout components are described in detail in Chapter 6, *Managing Layout*.

Looking at it from the perspective of an object hierarchy, we would have a **Window** object, which contains a hierachy of layout components, which again contain other layout components, field components, and other visible components.

You can browse the built-in UI components of Vaadin library in the Sampler application of the Vaadin Demo. The Sampler shows a description, JavaDoc documentation, and a code samples for each of the components.

In addition to the built-in components, many components are available as add-ons, either from the Vaadin Directory or from independent sources. Both commercial and free components exist. The installation of add-ons is described in Chapter 15, *Using Vaadin Add-ons*.

Vaadin Cheat Sheet and Refcard

Figure 5.1, "UI Component Inheritance Diagram" is included in the Vaadin Cheat Sheet that illustrates the basic relationship hierarchy of the user interface components and data binding classes and interfaces. You can download it at http://dev.vaadin.com/browser/doc/trunk/cheatsheet/vaadin-cheatsheet-duplex.pdf.

The diagram is also included in the six-page DZone Refcard, which you can find at https://vaadin.com/refcard.

5.2. Interfaces and Abstractions

Vaadin user interface components are built on a skeleton of interfaces and abstract classes that define and implement the features common to all components and the basic logic how the component states are serialized between the server and the client.

This section gives details on the basic component interfaces and abstractions. The layout and other component container abstractions are described in Chapter 6, *Managing Layout*. The interfaces that define the Vaadin data model are described in Chapter 9, *Binding Components to Data*.

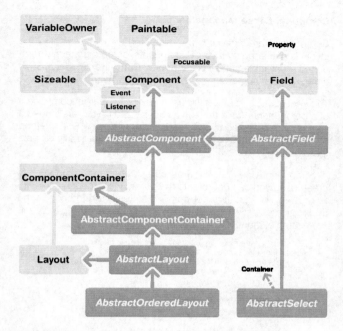

Figure 5.2. Component Interfaces and Abstractions

All components also implement the **Paintable** interface, which is used for serializing ("painting") the components to the client, and the reverse **VariableOwner** interface, which is needed for deserializing component state or user interaction from the client.

In addition to the interfaces defined within the Vaadin framework, all components implement the **java.io.Serializable** interface to allow serialization. Serialization is needed in many clustering and cloud computing solutions.

5.2.1. Component Interface

The **Component** interface is paired with the **AbstractComponent** class, which implements all the methods defined in the interface.

Component Tree Management

Components are laid out in the user interface hierarchically. The layout is managed by layout components, or more generally components that implement the **ComponentContainer** interface. Such a container is the parent of the contained components.

The getParent() method allows retrieving the parent component of a component. While there is a setParent(), you rarely need it as you usually add components with the addComponent() method of the **ComponentContainer** interface, which automatically sets the parent.

A component does not know its parent when the component is created, so you can not refer to the parent in the constructor with getParent(). Also, it is not possible to fetch a reference to the application object with getApplication() before having a parent. For example, the following is invalid:

```
public class AttachExample extends CustomComponent {
    public AttachExample() {
        // ERROR: We can't access the application object yet.
        ClassResource r = new ClassResource("smiley.jpg",
                                            getApplication());
        Embedded image = new Embedded("Image:", r);
        setCompositionRoot(image);
    }
}
```

Adding a component to an application triggers calling the attach() method for the component. Correspondingly, removing a component from a container triggers calling the detach() method. If the parent of an added component is already connected to the application, the attach() is called immediately from setParent().

```
public class AttachExample extends CustomComponent {
    public AttachExample() {
    }

    @Override
    public void attach() {
        super.attach(); // Must call.

        // Now we know who ultimately owns us.
        ClassResource r = new ClassResource("smiley.jpg",
                                            getApplication());
        Embedded image = new Embedded("Image:", r);
        setCompositionRoot(image);
    }
}
```

The attachment logic is implemented in **AbstractComponent**, as described in Section 5.2.2, "**AbstractComponent**".

5.2.2. AbstractComponent

AbstractComponent is the base class for all user interface components. It is the (only) implementation of the **Component** interface, implementing all the methods defined in the interface.

AbstractComponent has a single abstract method, `getTag()`, which returns the serialization identifier of a particular component class. It needs to be implemented when (and only when) creating entirely new components. **AbstractComponent** manages much of the serialization of component states between the client and the server. Creation of new components and serialization is described in Chapter 11, *Developing New Components*.

5.2.3. Field Components (Field and AbstractField)

Fields are components that have a value that the user can change through the user interface. Figure 5.3, "Field Components" illustrates the inheritance relationships and the important interfaces and base classes.

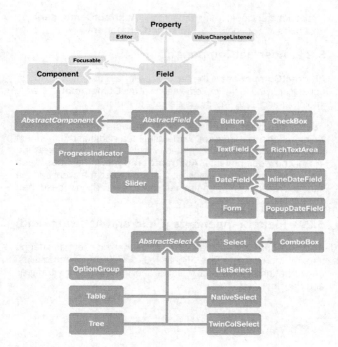

Figure 5.3. Field Components

Field components are built upon the framework defined in the **Field** interface and the **AbstractField** base class.

The description of the field interfaces and base classes is broken down in the following sections.

Field Interface

The **Field** interface inherits the **Component** superinterface and also the **Property** interface to have a value for the field. **Abstract-Field** is the only class implementing the **Field** interface directly. The relationships are illustrated in Figure 5.4, "**Field** Interface Inheritance Diagram".

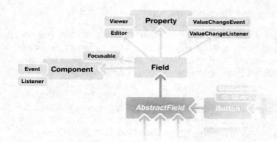

Figure 5.4. Field Interface Inheritance Diagram

You can set the field value with the `setValue()` and read with the `getValue()` method defined in the **Property** interface. The actual value type depends on the component.

The **Field** interface defines a number of attributes, which you can retrieve or manipulate with the corresponding setters and getters.

`description`
> All fields have a description. Notice that while this attribute is defined in the **Field** component, it is implemented in **AbstractField**, which does not directly implement **Field**, but only through the **AbstractField** class.

`required`
> When enabled, a required indicator (usually the asterisk * character) is displayed on the left, above, or right the field, depending on the containing layout and whether the field has a caption. If such fields are validated but are empty and the `requiredError` property (see below) is set, an error indicator is shown and the component error is set to the text defined with the error property. Without validation, the required indicator is merely a visual guide.

`requiredError`
> Defines the error message to show when a value is required, but none is entered. The error message is set as the component error for the field and is usually displayed in a tooltip when the mouse pointer hovers over the error indicator.

Data Binding and Conversions

Fields are strongly coupled with the Vaadin data model. The field value is handled as a **Property** of the field component, as documented in Section 9.2, "Properties". Selection fields allow management of the selectable items through the **Container** interface.

Fields edit some particular type. For example, **TextField** allows editing **String** values. When bound to a data source, the property type of the data model can be something different, say an **Integer**. *Converters* are used for converting the values between the representation and the model. They are described in Section 9.2.3, "Converting Between Property Type and Representation".

Handling Field Value Changes

Field inherits **Property.ValueChangeListener** to allow listening for field value changes and **Property.Editor** to allow editing values.

When the value of a field changes, a **Property.ValueChangeEvent** is triggered for the field. You should not implement the `valueChange()` method in a class inheriting **AbstractField**, as it is already implemented in **AbstractField**. You should instead implement the method explicitly by adding the implementing object as a listener.

AbstractField Base Class

AbstractField is the base class for all field components. In addition to the component features inherited from **AbstractComponent**, it implements a number of features defined in **Property**, **Buffered**, **Validatable**, and **Component.Focusable** interfaces.

5.3. Common Component Features

The component base classes and interfaces provide a large number of features. Let us look at some of the most commonly needed features. Features not documented here can be found from the Java API Reference.

The interface defines a number of properties, which you can retrieve or manipulate with the corresponding setters and getters.

5.3.1. Caption

A caption is an explanatory textual label accompanying a user interface component, usually shown above, left of, or inside the component. The contents of a caption are automatically quoted, so no raw XHTML can be rendered in a caption.

The caption text can usually be given as the first parameter of a constructor of a component or with `setCaption()`.

```
// New text field with caption "Name"
TextField name = new TextField("Name");
layout.addComponent(name);
```

The caption of a component is, by default, managed and displayed by the layout component or component container inside which the component is placed. For example, the **VerticalLayout** component shows the captions left-aligned above the contained components, while the **FormLayout** component shows the captions on the left side of the vertically laid components, with the captions and their associated components left-aligned in their own columns. The **CustomComponent** does not manage the caption of its composition root, so if the root component has a caption, it will not be rendered.

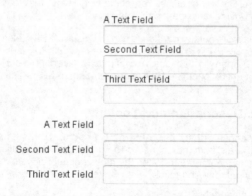

Figure 5.5. Caption Management by VerticalLayout and FormLayout components.

Some components, such as **Button** and **Panel**, manage the caption themselves and display it inside the component.

Icon (see Section 5.3.4, "Icon") is closely related to caption and is usually displayed horizontally before or after it, depending on the component and the containing layout. Also the required indicator in field components is usually shown before or after the caption.

An alternative way to implement a caption is to use another component as the caption, typically a **Label**, a **TextField**, or a **Panel**. A **Label**, for example, allows highlighting a shortcut key with XHTML markup or to bind the caption to a data source. The **Panel** provides an easy way to add both a caption and a border around a component.

CSS Style Rules

```
.v-caption {}
  .v-captiontext {}
  .v-caption-clearelem {}
  .v-required-field-indicator {}
```

A caption is be rendered inside an HTML element that has the `v-caption` CSS style class. The containing layout may enclose a caption inside other caption-related elements.

Some layouts put the caption text in a `v-captiontext` element. A `v-caption-clearelem` is used in some layouts to clear a CSS `float` property in captions. An optional required indicator in field components is contained in a separate element with `v-required-field-indicator` style.

5.3.2. Description and Tooltips

All components (that inherit **AbstractComponent**) have a description separate from their caption. The description is usually shown as a tooltip that appears when the mouse pointer hovers over the component for a short time.

You can set the description with `setDescription()` and retrieve with `getDescription()`.

```
Button button = new Button("A Button");
button.setDescription("This is the tooltip");
```

The tooltip is shown in Figure 5.6, "Component Description as a Tooltip".

Figure 5.6. Component Description as a Tooltip

A description is rendered as a tooltip in most components.

When a component error has been set with `setComponentError()`, the error is usually also displayed in the tooltip, below the description. Components that are in error state will also display the error indicator. See Section 4.4.1, "Error Indicator and message".

The description is actually not plain text, but you can use XHTML tags to format it. Such a rich text description can contain any HTML elements, including images.

```
button.setDescription(
    "<h2><img src=\"../VAADIN/themes/sampler/icons/comment_yellow.gif\"/>"+

    "A richtext tooltip</h2>"+
    "<ul>"+
    "  <li>Use rich formatting with XHTML</li>"+
    "  <li>Include images from themes</li>"+
    "  <li>etc.</li>"+
    "</ul>");
```

The result is shown in Figure 5.7, "A Rich Text Tooltip".

Figure 5.7. A Rich Text Tooltip

Notice that the setter and getter are defined for all fields in the **Field** interface, not for all components in the **Component** interface.

5.3.3. Enabled

The *enabled* property controls whether the user can actually use the component. A disabled component is visible, but grayed to indicate the disabled state.

Components are always enabled by default. You can disable a component with `setEnabled(false)`.

```
Button enabled = new Button("Enabled");
enabled.setEnabled(true); // The default
layout.addComponent(enabled);

Button disabled = new Button("Disabled");
disabled.setEnabled(false);
layout.addComponent(disabled);
```

Figure 5.8, "An Enabled and Disabled **Button**" shows the enabled and disabled buttons.

Figure 5.8. An Enabled and Disabled Button

A disabled component is automatically put in read-only state. No client interaction with such a component is sent to the server and, as an important security feature, the server-side components do not receive state updates from the client in the read-only state. This feature exists in all built-in components in Vaadin and is automatically handled for all **Field** components for the field property value. For custom widgets, you need to make sure that the read-only state is checked on the server-side for all safety-critical variables.

CSS Style Rules

Disabled components have the `v-disabled` CSS style in addition to the component-specific style. To match a component with both the styles, you have to join the style class names with a dot as done in the example below.

```
.v-textfield.v-disabled {
    border: dotted;
}
```

This would make the border of all disabled text fields dotted.

```
TextField disabled = new TextField("Disabled");
disabled.setValue("Read-only value");
disabled.setEnabled(false);
layout.addComponent(disabled);
```

The result is illustrated in Figure 5.9, "Styling Disabled Components".

Figure 5.9. Styling Disabled Components

5.3.4. Icon

An icon is an explanatory graphical label accompanying a user interface component, usually shown above, left of, or inside the component. Icon is closely related to caption (see Section 5.3.1, "Caption") and is usually displayed horizontally before or after it, depending on the component and the containing layout.

The icon of a component can be set with the `setIcon()` method. The image is provided as a resource, perhaps most typically a **ThemeResource**.

```
// Component with an icon from a custom theme
TextField name = new TextField("Name");
name.setIcon(new ThemeResource("icons/user.png"));
layout.addComponent(name);

// Component with an icon from another theme ('runo')
Button ok = new Button("OK");
ok.setIcon(new ThemeResource("../runo/icons/16/ok.png"));
layout.addComponent(ok);
```

The icon of a component is, by default, managed and displayed by the layout component or component container in which the component is placed. For example, the **VerticalLayout** component shows the icons left-aligned above the contained components, while the **FormLayout** component shows the icons on the left side of the vertically laid components, with the icons and their associated components left-aligned in their own columns. The **Custom-**

Component does not manage the icon of its composition root, so if the root component has an icon, it will not be rendered.

Figure 5.10. Displaying an Icon from a Theme Resource.

Some components, such as **Button** and **Panel**, manage the icon themselves and display it inside the component.

CSS Style Rules

An icon will be rendered inside an HTML element that has the v-icon CSS style class. The containing layout may enclose an icon and a caption inside elements related to the caption, such as v-caption.

5.3.5. Locale

The locale property defines the country and language used in a component. You can use the locale information in conjunction with an internationalization scheme to acquire localized resources. Some components, such as **DateField**, use the locale for component localization.

You can set the locale of a component (or the application) with setLocale().

```
// Component for which the locale is meaningful
InlineDateField date = new InlineDateField("Datum");

// German language specified with ISO 639-1 language
// code and ISO 3166-1 alpha-2 country code.
date.setLocale(new Locale("de", "DE"));

date.setResolution(DateField.RESOLUTION_DAY);
layout.addComponent(date);
```

The resulting date field is shown in Figure 5.11, "Set Locale for **InlineDateField**".

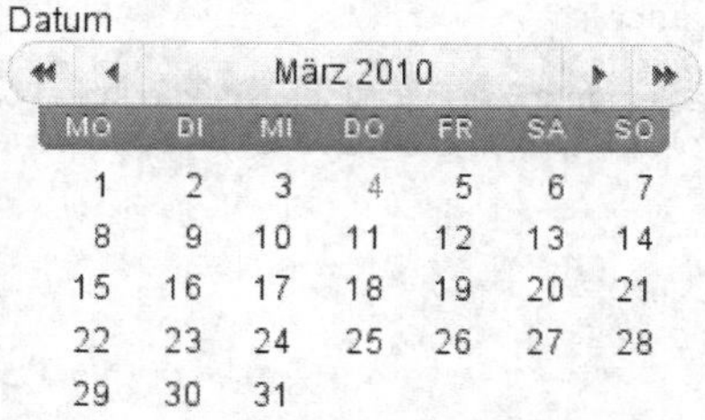

Datum

⏪	◀		März 2010			▶	⏩
MO	**DI**	**MI**	**DO**	**FR**	**SA**	**SO**
	1	2	3	4	5	6	7
	8	9	10	11	12	13	14
	15	16	17	18	19	20	21
	22	23	24	25	26	27	28
	29	30	31				

Figure 5.11. Set Locale for InlineDateField

You can get the locale of a component with `getLocale()`. If the locale is undefined for a component, that is, not explicitly set, the locale of the parent component is used. If none of the parent components have a locale set, the locale of the application is used, and if that is not set, the default system locale is set, as given by `Locale.getDefault()`.

Because of the requirement that the component must be attached to the application, it is awkward to use `getLocale()` for internationalization. You can not use it in the constructor, so you would have to get the locale in `attach()` as shown in the following example:

```
Button cancel = new Button() {
    @Override
    public void attach() {
        ResourceBundle bundle = ResourceBundle.getBundle(
                MyAppCaptions.class.getName(), getLocale());
        setCaption(bundle.getString("CancelKey"));
    }
};
layout.addComponent(cancel);
```

It is normally a better practice to get the locale from an application-global parameter and use it to get the localized resource right when the component is created.

```
// Captions are stored in MyAppCaptions resource bundle
// and the application object is known in this context.
ResourceBundle bundle =
    ResourceBundle.getBundle(MyAppCaptions.class.getName(),
                             getApplication().getLocale());

// Get a localized resource from the bundle
Button cancel = new Button(bundle.getString("CancelKey"));
layout.addComponent(cancel);
```

Selecting a Locale

A common task in many applications is selecting a locale. This is done in the following example with a **Select** component.

```
// The locale in which we want to have the language
// selection list
Locale displayLocale = Locale.ENGLISH;

// All known locales
final Locale[] locales = Locale.getAvailableLocales();

// Allow selecting a language. We are in a constructor of a
// CustomComponent, so preselecting the current
// language of the application can not be done before
// this (and the selection) component are attached to
// the application.
final Select select = new Select("Select a language") {
    @Override
    public void attach() {
        setValue(getLocale());
    }
};
for (int i=0; i<locales.length; i++) {
    select.addItem(locales[i]);
    select.setItemCaption(locales[i],
                    locales[i].getDisplayName(displayLocale));

    // Automatically select the current locale
    if (locales[i].equals(getLocale()))
        select.setValue(locales[i]);
}
layout.addComponent(select);

// Locale code of the selected locale
final Label localeCode = new Label("");
layout.addComponent(localeCode);

// A date field which language the selection will change
final InlineDateField date =
    new InlineDateField("Calendar in the selected language");
date.setResolution(DateField.RESOLUTION_DAY);
layout.addComponent(date);

// Handle language selection
select.addListener(new Property.ValueChangeListener() {
    public void valueChange(ValueChangeEvent event) {
        Locale locale = (Locale) select.getValue();
        date.setLocale(locale);
        localeCode.setValue("Locale code: " +
                        locale.getLanguage() + "_" +
                        locale.getCountry());
    }
});
select.setImmediate(true);
```

The user interface is shown in Figure 5.12, "Selecting a Locale".

Figure 5.12. Selecting a Locale

5.3.6. Read-Only

The property defines whether the value of a component can be changed. The property is mainly applicable to **Field** components, as they have a value that can be edited by the user.

```
TextField readwrite = new TextField("Read-Write");
readwrite.setValue("You can change this");
readwrite.setReadOnly(false); // The default
layout.addComponent(readwrite);

TextField readonly = new TextField("Read-Only");
readonly.setValue("You can't touch this!");
readonly.setReadOnly(true);
layout.addComponent(readonly);
```

The resulting read-only text field is shown in Figure 5.13, "A Read-Only Component.".

Read-Write | Read-Only
You can change this | You can't touch this!

Figure 5.13. A Read-Only Component.

Setting a layout or some other component container as read-only does not usually make the contained components read-only recursively. This is different from, for example, the disabled state, which is usually applied recursively.

Notice that the value of a selection component is the selection, not its items. A read-only selection component doesn't therefore allow its selection to be changed, but other changes are possible. For example, if you have a read-only **Table** in editable mode, its contained fields and the underlying data model can still be edited, and the user could sort it or reorder the columns.

Client-side state modifications will not be communicated to the server-side and, more importantly, server-side field components will not accept changes to the value of a read-only **Field** component. The latter is an important security feature, because a malicious user can not fabricate state changes in a read-only field. This is handled at the level of **AbstractField** in setValue(), so you can not change the value programmatically either. Calling setValue() on a read-only field results in **Property.ReadOnlyException**.

Also notice that while the read-only status applies automatically to the property value of a field, it does not apply to other component variables. A read-only component can accept some other variable changes from the client-side and some of such changes could be acceptable, such as change in the scroll bar position of a **Table**. Custom widgets should check the read-only state for variables bound to business data.

CSS Style Rules

Setting a normally editable component to read-only state can change its appearance to disallow editing the value. In addition to CSS styling, also the HTML structure can change. For example, **TextField** loses the edit box and appears much like a **Label**.

A read-only component will have the v-readonly style. The following CSS rule would make the text in all read-only **TextField** components appear in italic.

```
.v-textfield.v-readonly {
    font-style: italic;
}
```

5.3.7. Style Name

The *style name* property defines one or more custom CSS style class names for the component. The `getStyleName()` returns the current style names as a space-separated list. The `setStyleName()` replaces all the styles with the given style name or a space-separated list of style names. You can also add and remove individual style names with `addStylename()` and `removeStyleName()`. A style name must be a valid CSS style name.

```
Label label = new Label("This text has a lot of style");
label.addStyleName("mystyle");
layout.addComponent(label);
```

The style name will appear in the component's HTML element in two forms: literally as given and prefixed with the component class specific style name. For example, if you add a style name `mystyle` to a **Button**, the component would get both `mystyle` and `v-button-mystyle` styles. Neither form may conflict with built-in style names of Vaadin. For example, `focus` style would conflict with a built-in style of the same name, and an `option` style for a **Select** component would conflict with the built-in `v-select-option` style.

The following CSS rule would apply the style to any component that has the `mystyle` style.

```
.mystyle {
    font-family: fantasy;
    font-style:  italic;
    font-size:   25px;
    font-weight: bolder;
    line-height: 30px;
}
```

The resulting styled component is shown in Figure 5.14, "Component with a Custom Style"

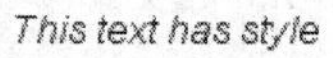

This text has style

Figure 5.14. Component with a Custom Style

5.3.8. Visible

Components can be hidden by setting the *visible* property to *false*. Also the caption, icon and any other component features are made hidden. Hidden components are not just invisible, but their content is not communicated to the browser at all. That is, they are not made invisible cosmetically with only CSS rules. This feature is important for security if you have components that contain security-critical information that must only be shown in specific application states.

```
TextField readonly = new TextField("Read-Only");
readonly.setValue("You can't see this!");
readonly.setVisible(false);
layout.addComponent(readonly);
```

The resulting invisible component is shown in Figure 5.15, "An Invisible Component.".

Figure 5.15. An Invisible Component.

Beware that invisible beings can leave footprints. The containing layout cell that holds the invisible component will not go away, but will show in the layout as extra empty space. Also expand ratios work just like if the component was visible - it is the layout cell that expands, not the component.

If you need to make a component only cosmetically invisible, you should use a custom theme to set it `display: none` style. This is mainly useful for certain special components such as **ProgressIndicator**, which have effects even when made invisible in CSS. If the hidden component has undefined size and is enclosed in a layout that also has undefined size, the containing layout will collapse when the component disappears. If you want to have the component keep its size, you have to make it invisible by setting all its font and other attributes to be transparent. In such cases, the invisible content of the component can be made visible easily in the browser.

A component made invisible with the *visible* property has no particular CSS style class to indicate that it is hidden. The element does exist though, but has `display: none` style, which overrides any CSS styling.

5.3.9. Sizing Components

Vaadin components are sizeable; not in the sense that they were fairly large or that the number of the components and their features are sizeable, but in the sense that you can make them fairly large on the screen if you like, or small or whatever size.

The **Sizeable** interface, shared by all components, provides a number of manipulation methods and constants for setting the height and width of a component in absolute or relative units, or for leaving the size undefined.

The size of a component can be set with setWidth() and setHeight() methods. The methods take the size as a floating-point value. You need to give the unit of the measure as the second parameter for the above methods. The available units are listed in Table 5.1, "Size Units" below.

```
mycomponent.setWidth(100, Sizeable.UNITS_PERCENTAGE);
mycomponent.setWidth(400, Sizeable.UNITS_PIXELS);
```

Alternatively, you can speficy the size as a string. The format of such a string must follow the HTML/CSS standards for specifying measures.

```
mycomponent.setWidth("100%");
mycomponent.setHeight("400px");
```

The "100%" percentage value makes the component take all avail-able size in the particular direction (see the description of *Sizeable.UNITS_PERCENTAGE* in the table below). You can also use the shorthand method setSizeFull() to set the size to 100% in both directions.

The size can be *undefined* in either or both dimensions, which means that the component will take the minimum necessary space. Most components have undefined size by default, but some layouts have full size in horizontal direction. You can set the height or width as undefined with *Sizeable.SIZE_UNDEFINED* parameter for setWidth() and setHeight().

You always need to keep in mind that *a layout with undefined size may not contain components with defined relative size*, such as "full size". See Section 6.13.1, "Layout Size" for details.

The Table 5.1, "Size Units" lists the available units and their codes defined in the **Sizeable** interface.

Table 5.1. Size Units

UNITS_PIXELS	px	The *pixel* is the basic hardware-specific measure of one physical display pixel.
UNITS_POINTS	pt	The *point* is a typographical unit, which is usually defined as 1/72 inches or about 0.35 mm. However, on displays the size can vary significantly depending on display metrics.
UNITS_PICAS	pc	The *pica* is a typographical unit, defined as 12 points, or 1/7 inches or about 4.233 mm. On displays, the size can vary depending on display metrics.
UNITS_EM	em	A unit relative to the used font, the width of the upper-case "M" letter.
UNITS_EX	ex	A unit relative to the used font, the height of the lower-case "x" letter.
UNITS_MM	mm	A physical length unit, millimeters on the surface of a display device. However, the actual size

		depends on the display, its metrics in the operating system, and the browser.
UNITS_CM	cm	A physical length unit, *centimeters* on the surface of a display device. However, the actual size depends on the display, its metrics in the operating system, and the browser.
UNITS_INCH	in	A physical length unit, *inches* on the surface of a display device. However, the actual size depends on the display, its metrics in the operating system, and the browser.
UNITS_PERCENTAGE	%	A relative percentage of the available size. For example, for the top-level layout *100%* would be the full width or height of the browser window. The percentage value must be between 0 and 100.

If a component inside **HorizontalLayout** or **VerticalLayout** has full size in the namesake direction of the layout, the component will expand to take all available space not needed by the other components. See Section 6.13.1, "Layout Size" for details.

5.3.10. Managing Input Focus

When the user clicks on a component, the component gets the *input focus*, which is indicated by highlighting according to style definitions. If the component allows inputting text, the focus and insertion point are indicated by a cursor. Pressing the **Tab** key moves the focus to the component next in the *focus order*.

Focusing is supported by all **Field** components and also by **Upload**.

The focus order or *tab index* of a component is defined as a positive integer value, which you can set with `setTabIndex()` and get with `getTabIndex()`. The tab index is managed in the context of the application-level **Window** in which the components are contained. The focus order can therefore jump between two any lower-level component containers, such as sub-windows or panels.

The default focus order is determined by the natural hierarchical order of components in the order in which they were added under their parents. The default tab index is 0 (zero).

Giving a negative integer as the tab index removes the component from the focus order entirely.

CSS Style Rules

The component having the focus will have an additional style class with the `-focus` suffix. For example, a **TextField**, which normally has the `v-textfield` style, would additionally have the `v-textfield-focus` style.

For example, the following would make a text field blue when it has focus.

```
.v-textfield-focus {
    background: lightblue;
}
```

5.4. Component Extensions

Components can have extensions which are attached to a component dynamically. Especially many add-on features are extensions.

To add an extension to a component, call the `extend()` method in the extension.

```
TextField tf = new TextField("Hello");
layout.addComponent(tf);

// Add a simple extension
new CapsLockWarning().extend(tf);

// Add an extension that requires some parameters
CSValidator validator = new CSValidator();
validator.setRegExp("[0-9]*");
validator.setErrorMessage("Must be a number");
validator.extend(tf);
```

5.5. Label

Label is a text component that displays non-editable text. In addition to regular text, you can also display preformatted text and HTML, depending on the *content mode* of the label.

```
// A container that is 100% wide by default
VerticalLayout layout = new VerticalLayout();

Label label = new Label("Labeling can be dangerous");
layout.addComponent(label);
```

The text will wrap around and continue on the next line if it exceeds the width of the **Label**. The default width is 100%, so the containing layout must also have a defined width. Some layout components have undefined width by default, such as **HorizontalLayout**, so you need to pay special care with them.

```
// A container with a defined width. The default content layout
// of Panel is VerticalLayout, which has 100% default width.
Panel panel = new Panel("Panel Containing a Label");
panel.setWidth("300px");

panel.addComponent(
    new Label("This is a Label inside a Panel. There is " +
              "enough text in the label to make the text " +
              "wrap when it exceeds the width of the panel."));
```

As the size of the **Panel** in the above example is fixed and the width of **Label** is the default 100%, the text in the **Label** will wrap to fit the panel, as shown in Figure 5.16, "The Label Component".

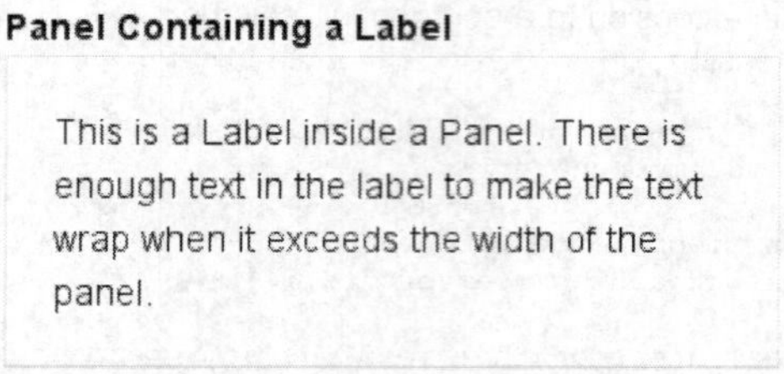

Panel Containing a Label

> This is a Label inside a Panel. There is
> enough text in the label to make the text
> wrap when it exceeds the width of the
> panel.

Figure 5.16. The Label Component

Setting **Label** to undefined width will cause it to not wrap at the end of the line, as the width of the content defines the width. If placed inside a layout with defined width, the **Label** will overflow the layout horizontally and, normally, be truncated.

Even though **Label** is text and often used as a caption, it also has a caption, just like any other component. As with other components, the caption is managed by the containing layout.

5.5.1. Content Mode

The contents of a label are formatted depending on the content mode. By default, the text is assumed to be plain text and any contained XML-specific characters will be quoted appropriately to allow rendering the contents of a label in XHTML in a web browser. The content mode can be set in the constructor or with `setContentMode()`, and can have the values defined in the **Label.ContentMode** enumeration type:

DEFAULT
> The default content mode is TEXT (see below).

TEXT
> Content mode where the label contains only plain text. All characters are allowed, including the special <, >, and & characters in XML or HTML, which are quoted properly in XHTML while rendering the component. This is the default mode.

PREFORMATTED

Content mode where the label contains preformatted text. It will be, by default, rendered with a fixed-width typewriter font. Preformatted text can contain line breaks, written in Java with the \n escape sequence for a newline character (ASCII 0x0a), or tabulator characters written with \t (ASCII 0x08).

RAW

Content mode where the label contains raw text. Output is not required to be valid XML. It can be, for example, HTML, which can be unbalanced or otherwise invalid XML. The example below uses the <br> tag in HTML. While XHTML should be preferred in most cases, this can be useful for some specific purposes where you may need to display loosely formatted HTML content. The raw mode also preserves character entities, some of which might otherwise be interpreted incorrectly.

Please note the security and validity warnings regarding the content mode later in this section.

XHTML

Content mode where the label contains XHTML. The content will be enclosed in a DIV element having the namespace "http://www.w3.org/TR/xhtml1/DTD/xhtml1-strict.dtd".

Please note the security and validity warnings regarding the content mode later in this section.

XML

Content mode, where the label contains well-formed and well-balanced XML. Each of the root elements must have their default namespace specified.

Please note the security and validity warnings regarding the content mode later in this section.

UIDL

Formatted content mode, where the contents are XML that is restricted to UIDL 1.0, the internal language of Vaadin for AJAX communications between the server and the browser. Obsolete since IT Mill Toolkit 5.0.

Cross-Site Scripting Warning

Having **Label** in RAW, XHTML, or XML content modes allows pure HTML content. If the content comes from user input, you should always carefully sanitize it to prevent cross-site scripting (XSS) attacks. Please see Section 12.8.1, "Sanitizing User Input to Prevent Cross-Site Scripting".

Also, the validity of the XML content is not checked when rendering the component and any errors can result in an error in the browser. If the content comes from an uncertain source, you should always validate it before displaying it in the component.

The following example demonstrates the use of **Label** in different modes.

```
GridLayout labelgrid = new GridLayout (2,1);

labelgrid.addComponent (new Label ("DEFAULT"));
labelgrid.addComponent (
    new Label ("This is a label in default mode: <plain text>",
               Label.ContentMode.DEFAULT));

labelgrid.addComponent (new Label ("PREFORMATTED"));
labelgrid.addComponent (
    new Label ("This is a preformatted label.\n"+
               "The newline character \\n breaks the line.",
               Label.ContentMode.PREFORMATTED));

labelgrid.addComponent (new Label ("RAW"));
labelgrid.addComponent (
    new Label ("This is a label in raw mode.<br>It can contain, "+
               "for example, unbalanced markup.",
               Label.ContentMode.RAW));

labelgrid.addComponent (new Label ("TEXT"));
labelgrid.addComponent (
    new Label ("This is a label in (plain) text mode",
               Label.ContentMode.TEXT));

labelgrid.addComponent (new Label ("XHTML"));
labelgrid.addComponent (
    new Label ("<i>This</i> is an <b>XHTML</b> formatted label",
               Label.ContentMode.XHTML));

labelgrid.addComponent (new Label ("XML"));
labelgrid.addComponent (
    new Label ("This is an <myelement>XML</myelement> "+
               "formatted label",
               Label.ContentMode.XML));
```

```
main.addComponent(labelgrid);
```

The rendering will look as follows:

CONTENT_DEFAULT	This is a label in default mode: <plain text>
CONTENT_PREFORMATTED	This is a preformatted label. The newline character \n breaks the line.
CONTENT_RAW	This is a label in raw mode. It can contain, for example, unbalanced markup.
CONTENT_TEXT	This is a label in (plain) text mode
CONTENT_XHTML	*This* is an **XHTML** formatted label
CONTENT_XML	This is an XML formatted label

Figure 5.17. Label Modes Rendered on Screen

5.5.2. Making Use of the XHTML Mode

Using the XHTML, XML, or raw modes allow inclusion of, for example, images within the text flow, which is not possible with any regular layout components. The following example includes an image within the text flow, with the image coming from a class loader resource.

```
ClassResource labelimage = new ClassResource ("labelimage.jpg",
                                               this);
main.addComponent(new Label("Here we have an image <img src=\"" +
                            this.getRelativeLocation(labelimage) +
                            "\"/> within text.",
                            Label.ContentMode.XHTML));
```

When you use a class loader resource, the image has to be included in the JAR of the web application. In this case, the `labelimage.jpg` needs to be in the default package. When rendered in a web browser, the output will look as follows:

Here we have an image 😊 within some text.

Figure 5.18. Referencing An Image Resource in Label

Another solution would be to use the **CustomLayout** component, where you can write the component content as an XHTML fragment in a theme, but such a solution may be too heavy for most cases.

Notice that the rendering of XHTML depends on the assumption that the client software and the terminal adapter are XHTML based. It is possible to write a terminal adapter for a custom thin client application, which may not be able to render XHTML at all. There are also differences between web browsers in their support of XHTML.

5.5.3. Spacing with a Label

You can use a **Label** to create vertical or horizontal space in a layout. If you need a empty "line" in a vertical layout, having just a label with empty text is not enough, as it will collapse to zero height. The same goes for a label with only whitespace as the label text. You need to use a non-breaking space character, either ` ` or ` `:

```
layout.addComponent(new Label(" ", Label.ContentMode.XHTML));
```

Using the *Label.ContentMode.PREFORMATTED* mode has the same effect; preformatted spaces do not collapse in a vertical layout. In a **HorizontalLayout**, the width of a space character may be unpredictable if the label font is proportional, so you can use the preformatted mode to add em-width wide spaces.

If you want a gap that has adjustable width or height, you can use an empty label if you specify a height or width for it. For example, to create vertical space in a **VerticalLayout**:

```
Label gap = new Label();
gap.setHeight("1em");
verticalLayout.addComponent(gap);
```

You can make a flexible expanding spacer by having a relatively sized empty label with `100%` height or width and setting the label as expanding in the layout.

```
// A wide component bar
HorizontalLayout horizontal = new HorizontalLayout();
horizontal.setWidth("100%");

// Have a component before the gap (a collapsing cell)
Button button1 = new Button("I'm on the left");
horizontal.addComponent(button1);

// An expanding gap spacer
Label expandingGap = new Label();
```

```
expandingGap.setWidth("100%");
horizontal.addComponent(expandingGap);
horizontal.setExpandRatio(expandingGap, 1.0f);

// A component after the gap (a collapsing cell)
Button button2 = new Button("I'm on the right");
horizontal.addComponent(button2);
```

5.5.4. CSS Style Rules

The **Label** component has a `v-label` overall style.

The Reindeer theme includes a number of predefined styles for typical formatting cases. These include `"h1"` (`Reindeer.LABEL_H1`) and `"h2"` (`Reindeer.LABEL_H2`) heading styles and `"light"` (`Reindeer.LABEL_SMALL`) style.

5.6. Link

The **Link** component allows making hyperlinks. References to locations are represented as resource objects, explained in Section 4.3, "Referencing Resources". The **Link** is a regular HTML hyperlink, that is, an `<a href>` anchor element that is handled natively by the browser. Unlike when clicking a **Button**, clicking a **Link** does not cause an event on the server-side.

Links to an arbitrary URL can be made by using an **ExternalResource** as follows:

```
// Textual link
Link link = new Link("Click Me!",
        new ExternalResource("http://vaadin.com/"));
```

You can use `setIcon()` to make image links as follows:

```
// Image link
Link iconic = new Link(null,
        new ExternalResource("http://vaadin.com/"));
iconic.setIcon(new ThemeResource("img/nicubunu_Chain.png"));

// Image + caption
Link combo = new Link("To appease both literal and visual",
        new ExternalResource("http://vaadin.com/"));
combo.setIcon(new ThemeResource("img/nicubunu_Chain.png"));
```

The resulting links are shown in Figure 5.19, "**Link** Example". You could add a "`display: block`" style for the icon element to place the caption below it.

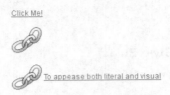

Click Me!

To appease both literal and visual

Figure 5.19. Link Example

With the simple constructor used in the above example, the resource is opened in the current window. Using the constructor that takes the target window as a parameter, or by setting the target window with `setTargetName()`, you can open the resource in another window, such as a native popup window. As the target name is an HTML `target` string managed by the browser, the target can be any window, including windows not managed by the application itself. You can use the special underscored target names, such as `_blank` to open the link to a new browser window or tab.

```
// Hyperlink to a given URL
Link link = new Link("Take me a away to a faraway land",
        new ExternalResource("http://vaadin.com/"));

// Open the URL in a new window/tab
link.setTargetName("_blank");

// Indicate visually that it opens in a new window/tab
link.setIcon(new ThemeResource("icons/external-link.png"));
link.addStyleName("icon-after-caption");
```

Normally, the link icon is before the caption. You can have it right of the caption by reversing the text direction in the containing element.

```
/* Position icon right of the link caption. */
.icon-after-caption {
    direction: rtl;
}
/* Add some padding around the icon. */
.icon-after-caption .v-icon {
    padding: 0 3px;
}
```

The resulting link is shown in Figure 5.20, "Link That Opens a New Window".

Take me a away to a faraway land 🖉

Figure 5.20. Link That Opens a New Window

With the `_blank` target, a normal new browser window is opened. If you wish to open it in a popup window, you need to give a size for the window with `setTargetWidth()` and `setTargetHeight()`. You can control the window border style with `setTargetBorder()`, which takes any of the defined border styles *TARGET_BORDER_DEFAULT*, *TARGET_BORDER_MINIMAL*, and *TARGET_BORDER_NONE*. The exact result depends on the browser.

```
// Open the URL in a popup
link.setTargetName("_blank");
link.setTargetBorder(Link.TARGET_BORDER_NONE);
link.setTargetHeight(300);
link.setTargetWidth(400);
```

In addition to the **Link** component, Vaadin allows alternative ways to make hyperlinks. The **Button** component has a *Reindeer.BUTTON_LINK* style name that makes it look like a hyperlink, while handling clicks in a server-side click listener instead of in the browser. Also, you can make hyperlinks (or any other HTML) in a **Label** in XHTML content mode.

CSS Style Rules

```
.v-link { }
  a { }
    .v-icon {}
    span {}
```

The overall style for the **Link** component is `v-link`. The root element contains the `<a href>` hyperlink anchor. Inside the anchor are the icon, with `v-icon` style, and the caption in a text span.

Hyperlink anchors have a number of *pseudo-classes* that are active at different times. An unvisited link has `a:link` class and a visited link `a:visited`. When the mouse pointer hovers over the link, it will have `a:hover`, and when the mouse button is being pressed over the link, the `a:active` class. When combining the pseudo-classes in a selector, please notice that `a:hover` must come after an `a:link` and `a:visited`, and `a:active` after the `a:hover`.

5.7. TextField

TextField is one of the most commonly used user interface components. It is a **Field** component that allows entering textual values using keyboard.

The following example creates a simple text field:

```
// Create a text field
TextField tf = new TextField("A Field");

// Put some initial content in it
tf.setValue("Stuff in the field");
```

See the result in Figure 5.21, "**TextField** Example".

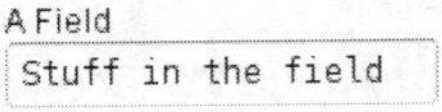

A Field
```
Stuff in the field
```

Figure 5.21. TextField Example

Value changes are handled with a **Property.ValueChangeListener**, as in most other fields. The value can be acquired with `getValue()` directly from the text field, as is done in the example below, or from the property reference of the event.

```
// Handle changes in the value
tf.addListener(new Property.ValueChangeListener() {
    public void valueChange(ValueChangeEvent event) {
        // Assuming that the value type is a String
        String value = (String) tf.getValue();

        // Do something with the value
        Notification.show("Value is:", value);
    }
});

// Fire value changes immediately when the field loses focus
tf.setImmediate(true);
```

Much of the API of **TextField** is defined in **AbstractTextField**, which allows different kinds of text input fields, such as rich text editors, which do not share all the features of the single-line text fields.

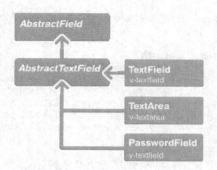

Figure 5.22. Text Field Class Relationships

5.7.1. Data Binding

TextField edits **String** values, but you can bind it to any property type that has a proper converter, as described in Section 9.2.3, "Converting Between Property Type and Representation".

```
// Have an initial data model. As Double is unmodificable and
// doesn't support assignment from String, the object is
// reconstructed in the wrapper when the value is changed.
Double trouble = 42.0;

// Wrap it in a property data source
final ObjectProperty<Double> property =
    new ObjectProperty<Double>(trouble);

// Create a text field bound to it
// (StringToDoubleConverter is used automatically)
TextField tf = new TextField("The Answer", property);
tf.setImmediate(true);

// Show that the value is really written back to the
// data source when edited by user.
Label feedback = new Label(property);
feedback.setCaption("The Value");
```

When you put a **Table** in editable mode or create fields with a **FieldGroup**, the **DefaultFieldFactory** creates a **TextField** for almost every property type by default. You often need to make a custom factory to customize the creation and to set the field tooltip, validation, formatting, and so on.

See Chapter 9, *Binding Components to Data* for more details on data binding, field factories for **Table** in Section 5.15.3, "Editing the Values in a Table", and Section 9.4, "Binding Fields to Items" regarding forms.

5.7.2. String Length

The `setMaxLength()` method sets the maximum length of the input string so that the browser prevents the user from entering a longer one. As a security feature, the input value is automatically truncated on the server-side, as the maximum length setting could be bypassed on the client-side. The maximum length property is defined at **AbstractTextField** level.

Notice that the maximum length setting does not affect the width of the field. You can set the width with `setWidth()`, as with other components. Using *em* widths is recommended to better approximate the proper width in relation to the size of the used font. There is no standard way in HTML for setting the width exactly to a number of letters (in a monospaced font). You can trick your way around this restriction by putting the text field in an undefined-width **VerticalLayout** together with an undefined-width **Label** that contains a sample text, and setting the width of the text field as 100%. The layout will get its width from the label, and the text field will use that.

5.7.3. Handling Null Values

As with any field, the value of a **TextField** can be set as *null*. This occurs most commonly when you create a new field without setting a value for it or bind the field value to a data source that allows null values. In such case, you might want to show a special value that stands for the null value. You can set the null representation with the `setNullRepresentation()` method. Most typically, you use an empty string for the null representation, unless you want to differentiate from a string that is explicitly empty. The default null representation is "null", which essentially warns that you may have forgotten to initialize your data objects properly.

The `setNullSettingAllowed()` controls whether the user can actually input a null value by using the null value representation. If the setting is `false`, which is the default, inputting the null value representation string sets the value as the literal value of the string, not null. This default assumption is a safeguard for data sources that may not allow null values.

```
// Create a text field without setting its value
TextField tf = new TextField("Field Energy (J)");
tf.setNullRepresentation("-- null-point energy --");

// The null value is actually the default
tf.setValue(null);

// Allow user to input the null value by
// its representation
tf.setNullSettingAllowed(true);

// Feedback to see the value
Label value = new Label(tf);
value.setCaption("Current Value:");
```

The **Label**, which is bound to the value of the **TextField**, displays a null value as empty. The resulting user interface is shown in Figure 5.23, "Null Value Representation".

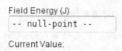

Figure 5.23. Null Value Representation

5.7.4. Text Change Events

Often you want to receive a change event immediately when the text field value changes. The *immediate* mode is not literally immediate, as the changes are transmitted only after the field loses focus. In the other extreme, using keyboard events for every keypress would make typing unbearably slow and also processing the keypresses is too complicated for most purposes. *Text change events* is transmitted asynchronously soon after typing and do not block typing while an event is being processed.

Text change events are received with a **TextChangeListener**, as is done in the following example that demonstrates how to create a text length counter:

```
// Text field with maximum length
final TextField tf = new TextField("My Eventful Field");
tf.setValue("Initial content");
tf.setMaxLength(20);

// Counter for input length
```

```
final Label counter = new Label();
counter.setValue(tf.toString().length() +
                 " of " + tf.getMaxLength());

// Display the current length interactively in the counter
tf.addListener(new TextChangeListener() {
    public void textChange(TextChangeEvent event) {
        int len = event.getText().length();
        counter.setValue(len + " of " + tf.getMaxLength());
    }
});

// This is actually the default
tf.setTextChangeEventMode(TextChangeEventMode.LAZY);
```

The result is shown in Figure 5.24, "Text Change Events".

Figure 5.24. Text Change Events

The *text change event mode* defines how quickly the changes are transmitted to the server and cause a server-side event. Lazier change events allow sending larger changes in one event if the user is typing fast, thereby reducing server requests.

You can set the text change event mode of a **TextField** with set-TextChangeEventMode(). The allowed modes are defined in **TextChangeEventMode** class and are the following:

TextChangeEventMode.LAZY (default)
>An event is triggered when there is a pause in editing the text. The length of the pause can be modified with setInputEventTimeout(). As with the *TIMEOUT* mode, a text change event is forced before a possible **ValueChangeEvent**, even if the user did not keep a pause while entering the text.

>This is the default mode.

TextChangeEventMode.TIMEOUT
>A text change in the user interface causes the event to be communicated to the application after a timeout period. If more changes are made during this period, the event sent to the server-side includes the changes made up to the last

change. The length of the timeout can be set with `setInputEventTimeout()`.

If a **ValueChangeEvent** would occur before the timeout period, a **TextChangeEvent** is triggered before it, on the condition that the text content has changed since the previous **TextChangeEvent**.

`TextChangeEventMode.EAGER`
An event is triggered immediately for every change in the text content, typically caused by a key press. The requests are separate and are processed sequentially one after another. Change events are nevertheless communicated asynchronously to the server, so further input can be typed while event requests are being processed.

5.7.5. CSS Style Rules

```
.v-textfield { }
```

The HTML structure of **TextField** is extremely simple, consisting only of an element with `v-textfield` style.

For example, the following custom style uses dashed border:

```
.v-textfield-dashing {
    border:     thin dashed;
    background: white; /* Has shading image by default */
}
```

The result is shown in Figure 5.25, "Styling TextField with CSS".

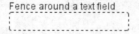

Figure 5.25. Styling TextField with CSS

The style name for **TextField** is also used in several components that contain a text input field, even if the text input is not an actual **TextField**. This ensures that the style of different text input boxes is similar.

5.8. TextArea

TextArea is a multi-line version of the **TextField** component described in Section 5.7, "**TextField**".

The following example creates a simple text area:

```
// Create the area
TextArea area = new TextArea("Big Area");

// Put some content in it
area.setValue("A row\n"+
              "Another row\n"+
              "Yet another row");
```

The result is shown in Figure 5.26, "**TextArea** Example".

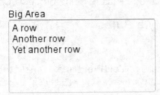

Figure 5.26. TextArea Example

You can set the number of visible rows with setRows() or use the regular setHeight() to define the height in other units. If the actual number of rows exceeds the number, a vertical scrollbar will appear. Setting the height with setRows() leaves space for a horizontal scrollbar, so the actual number of visible rows may be one higher if the scrollbar is not visible.

You can set the width with the regular setWidth() method. Setting the size with the *em* unit, which is relative to the used font size, is recommended.

Word Wrap

The setWordwrap() sets whether long lines are wrapped (true - default) when the line length reaches the width of the writing area. If the word wrap is disabled (false), a vertical scrollbar will appear instead. The word wrap is only a visual feature and wrapping a long line does not insert line break characters in the field value; shortening a wrapped line will undo the wrapping.

```
TextArea areal = new TextArea("Wrapping");
areal.setWordwrap(true); // The default
areal.setValue("A quick brown fox jumps over the lazy dog");

TextArea area2 = new TextArea("Nonwrapping");
area2.setWordwrap(false);
area2.setValue("Victor jagt zw&ouml;lf Boxk&auml;mpfer quer "+
               "&uuml;ber den Sylter Deich");
```

The result is shown in Figure 5.27, "Word Wrap in **TextArea**".

Figure 5.27. Word Wrap in TextArea

CSS Style Rules

```
.v-textarea { }
```

The HTML structure of **TextArea** is extremely simple, consisting only of an element with v-textarea style.

5.9. PasswordField

The **PasswordField** is a variant of **TextField** that hides the typed input from visual inspection.

```
PasswordField tf = new PasswordField("Keep it secret");
```

The result is shown in Figure 5.28, "**PasswordField**".

Figure 5.28. PasswordField

You should note that the **PasswordField** hides the input only from "over the shoulder" visual observation. Unless the server connection is encrypted with a secure connection, such as HTTPS, the input is transmitted in clear text and may be intercepted by anyone with low-level access to the network. Also phishing attacks that intercept the input in the browser may be possible by exploiting JavaScript execution security holes in the browser.

CSS Style Rules

```
.v-textfield { }
```

The **PasswordField** does not have its own CSS style name but uses the same `v-textfield` style as the regular **TextField**. See Section 5.7.5, "CSS Style Rules" for information on styling it.

5.10. RichTextArea

The **RichTextArea** field allows entering or editing formatted text. The toolbar provides all basic editing functionalities. The text content of **RichTextArea** is represented in HTML format. **RichTextArea** inherits **TextField** and does not add any API functionality over it. You can add new functionality by extending the client-side components **VRichTextArea** and **VRichTextToolbar**.

As with **TextField**, the textual content of the rich text area is the **Property** of the field and can be set with `setValue()` and read with `getValue()`.

```
// Create a rich text area
final RichTextArea rtarea = new RichTextArea();
rtarea.setCaption("My Rich Text Area");

// Set initial content as HTML
rtarea.setValue("<h1>Hello</h1>\n" +
    "<p>This rich text area contains some text.</p>");
```

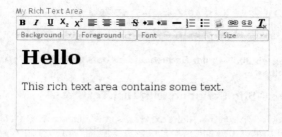

Figure 5.29. Rich Text Area Component

Above, we used context-specific tags such as `<h1>` in the initial HTML content. The rich text area component does not allow creating such tags, only formatting tags, but it does preserve them unless the user edits them away. Any non-visible whitespace such as the new line character (`\n`) are removed from the content. For example, the value set above will be as follows when read from the field with `getValue()`:

```
<h1>Hello</h1> <p>This rich text area contains some
text.</p>
```

The rich text area is one of the few components in Vaadin that contain textual labels. The selection boxes in the toolbar are in English and currently can not be localized in any other way than by inheriting or reimplementing the client-side **VRichTextToolbar** widget. The buttons can be localized simply with CSS by downloading a copy of the toolbar background image, editing it, and replacing the default toolbar. The toolbar is a single image file from which the individual button icons are picked, so the order of the icons is different from the rendered. The image file depends on the client-side implementation of the toolbar.

```
.v-richtextarea-richtextexample .gwt-ToggleButton
.gwt-Image {
  background-image: url(img/richtextarea-toolbar-fi.png)
                    !important;
}
```

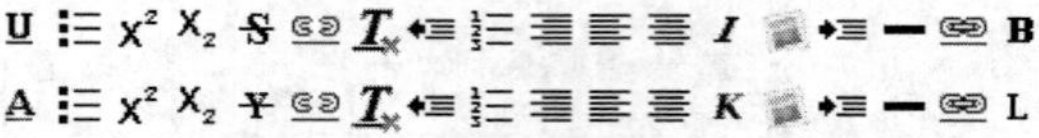

$$\underline{U} \; \vdots\equiv \; x^2 \; x_2 \; \cdot\!S \; \text{\textcircled{s}\textcircled{\tiny 9}} \; \underline{T_\times} \; \cdot\!\equiv \; \vdots\equiv \; \equiv \; \equiv \; \equiv \; I \; \text{\scriptsize\faImage} \; \cdot\!\equiv \; - \; \text{\textcircled{s}\textcircled{\tiny 9}} \; \mathbf{B}$$

$$\underline{A} \; \vdots\equiv \; x^2 \; x_2 \; \cdot\!\mathbf{Y} \; \text{\textcircled{s}\textcircled{\tiny 9}} \; \underline{T_\times} \; \cdot\!\equiv \; \vdots\equiv \; \equiv \; \equiv \; \equiv \; K \; \text{\scriptsize\faImage} \; \cdot\!\equiv \; - \; \text{\textcircled{s}\textcircled{\tiny 9}} \; \mathbf{L}$$

Figure 5.30. Regular English and a Localized Rich Text Area Toolbar

Cross-Site Scripting with RichTextArea

The user input from a **RichTextArea** is transmitted as XHTML from the browser to server-side and is not sanitized. As the entire purpose of the **RichTextArea** component is to allow input of formatted text, you can not sanitize it just by removing all HTML tags. Also many attributes, such as *style*, should pass through the sanitization.

See Section 12.8.1, "Sanitizing User Input to Prevent Cross-Site Scripting" for more details on Cross-Site scripting vulnerabilities and sanitization of user input.

CSS Style Rules

```
.v-richtextarea { }
.v-richtextarea .gwt-RichTextToolbar { }
.v-richtextarea .gwt-RichTextArea { }
```

The rich text area consists of two main parts: the toolbar with overall style `.gwt-RichTextToolbar` and the editor area with style `.gwt-RichTextArea`. The editor area obviously contains all the elements and their styles that the HTML content contains. The toolbar contains buttons and drop-down list boxes with the following respective style names:

```
.gwt-ToggleButton { }
.gwt-ListBox { }
```

5.11. Date and Time Input with DateField

The **DateField** component provides the means to display and input date and time. The field comes in two variations: **PopupDateField**, with a numeric input box and a popup calendar view, and **InlineDateField**, with the calendar view always visible. The **DateField** base class defaults to the popup variation.

The example below illustrates the use of the **DateField** baseclass, which is equivalent to the **PopupDateField**. We set the initial time of the date field to current time by using the default constructor of the **java.util.Date** class.

```
// Create a DateField with the default style
DateField date = new DateField();

// Set the date and time to present
date.setValue(new Date());
```

The result is shown in Figure 5.31, "**DateField** (**PopupDateField**) for Selecting Date and Time".

Figure 5.31. DateField (PopupDateField) for Selecting Date and Time

5.11.1. PopupDateField

The **PopupDateField** provides date input using a text box for the date and time. As the **DateField** defaults to this component, the use is exactly the same as described earlier. Clicking the handle right of the date opens a popup view for selecting the year, month, and day, as well as time. Also the **Down** key opens the popup. Once opened, the user can navigate the calendar using the cursor keys.

The date and time selected from the popup are displayed in the text box according to the default date and time format of the current locale, or as specified with `setDateFormat()`. The same format definitions are used for parsing user input.

Date and Time Format

The date and time are normally displayed according to the default format for the current locale (see Section 5.3.5, "Locale"). You can specify a custom format with `setDateFormat()`. It takes a format string that follows the format of the **SimpleDateFormat** in Java.

```
// Display only year, month, and day in ISO format
date.setDateFormat("yyyy-MM-dd");
```

The result is shown in Figure 5.32, "Custom Date Format for **PopupDateField**".

Figure 5.32. Custom Date Format for PopupDateField

The same format specification is also used for parsing user-input date and time, as described later.

Handling Malformed User Input

A user can easily input a malformed or otherwise invalid date or time. **DateField** has two validation layers: first on the client-side and then on the server-side.

The validity of the entered date is first validated on the client-side, immediately when the input box loses focus. If the date format is invalid, the `v-datefield-parseerror` style is set. Whether this causes a visible indication of a problem depends on the theme. The built-in `reindeer` theme does not shown any indication by default, making server-side handling of the problem more convenient.

```
.mydate.v-datefield-parseerror .v-textfield {
    background: pink;
}
```

The `setLenient(true)` setting enables relaxed interpretation of dates, so that invalid dates, such as February 30th or March 0th, are wrapped to the next or previous month, for example.

The server-side validation phase occurs when the date value is sent to the server. If the date field is set in immediate state, it occurs immediately after the field loses focus. Once this is done and if the status is still invalid, an error indicator is displayed beside the component. Hovering the mouse pointer over the indicator shows the error message.

You can handle the errors by overriding the `handleUnparsableDateString()` method. The method gets the user input as a string parameter and can provide a custom parsing mechanism, as shown in the following example.

```
// Create a date field with a custom parsing and a
// custom error message for invalid format
PopupDateField date = new PopupDateField("My Date") {
    @Override
    protected Date handleUnparsableDateString(String dateString)
    throws Property.ConversionException {
        // Try custom parsing
        String fields[] = dateString.split("/");
        if (fields.length >= 3) {
            try {
                int year  = Integer.parseInt(fields[0]);
                int month = Integer.parseInt(fields[1])-1;
                int day   = Integer.parseInt(fields[2]);
                GregorianCalendar c =
                    new GregorianCalendar(year, month, day);
                return c.getTime();
            } catch (NumberFormatException e) {
                throw new Property.
                    ConversionException("Not a number");
            }
        }

        // Bad date
        throw new Property.
            ConversionException("Your date needs two slashes");
    }
};

// Display only year, month, and day in slash-delimited format
date.setDateFormat("yyyy/MM/dd");

// Don't be too tight about the validity of dates
// on the client-side
date.setLenient(true);
```

The handler method must either return a parsed **Date** object or throw a **ConversionException**. Returning *null* will set the field value to *null* and clear the input box.

Customizing the Error Message

In addition to customized parsing, overriding the handler method for unparseable input is useful for internationalization and other customization of the error message. You can also use it for another way for reporting the errors, as is done in the example below:

```
// Create a date field with a custom error message for invalid format
PopupDateField date = new PopupDateField("My Date") {
    @Override
    protected Date handleUnparsableDateString(String dateString)
    throws Property.ConversionException {
        // Have a notification for the error
        Notification.show(
                "Your date needs two slashes",
                Notification.TYPE_WARNING_MESSAGE);

        // A failure must always also throw an exception
        throw new Property.ConversionException("Bad date");
    }
};
```

If the input is invalid, you should always throw the exception; returning a *null* value would make the input field empty, which is probably undesired.

Input Prompt

Like other fields that have a text box, **PopupDateField** allows an input prompt that is visible until the user has input a value. You can set the prompt with setInputPrompt.

```
PopupDateField date = new PopupDateField();

// Set the prompt
date.setInputPrompt("Select a date");

// Set width explicitly to accommodate the prompt
date.setWidth("10em");
```

The date field doesn't automatically scale to accommodate the prompt, so you need to set it explicitly with setWidth().

The input prompt is not available in the **DateField** superclass.

CSS Style Rules

```
.v-datefield, v-datefield-popupcalendar {}
  .v-textfield, v-datefield-textfield {}
  .v-datefield-button {}
```

The top-level element of **DateField** and all its variants have `v-datefield` style. The base class and the **PopupDateField** also have the `v-datefield-popupcalendar` style.

In addition, the top-level element has a style that indicates the resolution, with `v-datefield-` basename and an extension, which is one of `full`, `day`, `month`, or `year`. The `-full` style is enabled when the resolution is smaller than a day. These styles are used mainly for controlling the appearance of the popup calendar.

The text box has `v-textfield` and `v-datefield-textfield` styles, and the calendar button `v-datefield-button`.

Once opened, the calendar popup has the following styles at the top level:

```
.v-datefield-popup {}
  .v-popupcontent {}
    .v-datefield-calendarpanel {}
```

The top-level element of the floating popup calendar has `.v-datefield-popup` style. Observe that the popup frame is outside the HTML structure of the component, hence it is not enclosed in the `v-datefield` element and does not include any custom styles. The content in the `v-datefield-calendarpanel` is the same as in **InlineDateField**, as described in Section 5.11.2, "**InlineDate-Field**".

5.11.2. InlineDateField

The **InlineDateField** provides a date picker component with a month view. The user can navigate months and years by clicking the appropriate arrows. Unlike with the popup variant, the month view is always visible in the inline field.

```
// Create a DateField with the default style
InlineDateField date = new InlineDateField();

// Set the date and time to present
date.setValue(new java.util.Date());
```

The result is shown in Figure 5.33, "Example of the **InlineDate-Field**".

Figure 5.33. Example of the InlineDateField

The user can also navigate the calendar using the cursor keys.

CSS Style Rules

```
.v-datefield {}
  .v-datefield-calendarpanel {}
    .v-datefield-calendarpanel-header {}
      .v-datefield-calendarpanel-prevyear {}
      .v-datefield-calendarpanel-prevmonth {}
      .v-datefield-calendarpanel-month {}
      .v-datefield-calendarpanel-nextmonth {}
      .v-datefield-calendarpanel-nextyear {}
    .v-datefield-calendarpanel-body {}
      .v-datefield-calendarpanel-weekdays,
      .v-datefield-calendarpanel-weeknumbers {}
        .v-first {}
        .v-last {}
      .v-datefield-calendarpanel-weeknumber {}
      .v-datefield-calendarpanel-day {}
    .v-datefield-calendarpanel-time {}
      .v-datefield-time {}
        .v-select {}
        .v-label {}
```

The top-level element has the v-datefield style. In addition, the top-level element has a style name that indicates the resolution of the calendar, with v-datefield- basename and an extension, which is one of full, day, month, or year. The -full style is enabled when the resolution is smaller than a day.

The v-datefield-calendarpanel-weeknumbers and v-date-field-calendarpanel-weeknumber styles are enabled when the week numbers are enabled. The former controls the appearance of the weekday header and the latter the actual week numbers.

The other style names should be self-explanatory. For weekdays, the v-first and v-last styles allow making rounded endings for the weekday bar.

5.11.3. Time Resolution

The **DateField** displays dates by default. It can also display the time in hours and minutes, or just the month or year. The visibility of the input components is controlled by *time resolution*, which can be set with setResolution() method. The method takes as its parameters the lowest visible component, typically *RESOLUTION_DAY* for just dates and *RESOLUTION_MIN* for dates with time in hours and minutes. Please see the API Reference for the complete list of resolution parameters.

5.11.4. DateField Locale

The date and time are displayed according to the locale of the user, as reported by the browser. You can set a custom locale with the setLocale() method of **AbstractComponent**, as described in Section 5.3.5, "Locale". Only Gregorian calendar is supported.

5.12. Button

The **Button** is a user interface component that is normally used for finalizing input and initiating some action. When the user clicks a button, a **Button.ClickEvent** is emitted. A listener that inherits the **Button.ClickListener** interface can handle clicks with the buttonClick() method.

```
public class TheButton extends CustomComponent
                       implements Button.ClickListener {
    Button thebutton;

    public TheButton() {
        // Create a Button with the given caption.
        thebutton = new Button ("Do not push this button");

        // Listen for ClickEvents.
        thebutton.addListener(this);

        setCompositionRoot(thebutton);
    }
```

```
/** Handle click events for the button. */
public void buttonClick (Button.ClickEvent event) {
    thebutton.setCaption ("Do not push this button again");
}
}
```

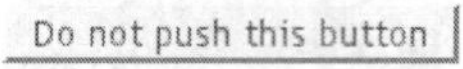

| Do not push this button |

Figure 5.34. An Example of a Button

As a user interface often has several buttons, you can differentiate between them either by comparing the **Button** object reference returned by the `getButton()` method of **Button.ClickEvent** to a kept reference or by using a separate listener method for each button. The listening object and method can be given to the constructor. For a detailed description of these patterns together with some examples, please see Section 3.5, "Events and Listeners".

CSS Style Rules

`.v-button { }`

The exact CSS style name can be different if a **Button** has the *switchMode* attribute enabled. See the alternative CSS styles below.

Adding the `"small"` style name enables a smaller style for the **Button**. You can also use the *BUTTON_SMALL* constant in **Runo** and **Reindeer** theme classes as well. The **BaseTheme** class also has a *BUTTON_LINK* style, with `"link"` style name, which makes the button look like a hyperlink.

5.13. CheckBox

CheckBox is a two-state selection component that can be either checked or unchecked. The caption of the check box will be placed right of the actual check box. Vaadin provides two ways to create check boxes: individual check boxes with the **CheckBox** component described in this section and check box groups with the **OptionGroup** component in multiple selection mode, as described in Section 5.14.5, "Radio Button and Check Box Groups with **OptionGroup**".

Clicking on a check box will change its state. The state is a **Boolean** property that you can set with the `setValue()` method and obtain with the `getValue()` method of the **Property** interface. Changing the value of a check box will cause a **ValueChangeEvent**, which can be handled by a **ValueChangeListener**.

```
// A check box with default state (not checked, false).
final CheckBox checkbox1 = new CheckBox("My CheckBox");
main.addComponent(checkbox1);

// Another check box with explicitly set checked state.
final CheckBox checkbox2 = new CheckBox("Checked CheckBox");
checkbox2.setValue(true);
main.addComponent(checkbox2);

// Make some application logic. We use anonymous listener
// classes here. The above references were defined as final
// to allow accessing them from inside anonymous classes.
checkbox1.addListener(new ValueChangeListener() {
    public void valueChange(ValueChangeEvent event) {
        // Copy the value to the other checkbox.
        checkbox2.setValue(checkbox1.getValue());
    }
});
checkbox2.addListener(new ValueChangeListener() {
    public void valueChange(ValueChangeEvent event) {
        // Copy the value to the other checkbox.
        checkbox1.setValue(checkbox2.getValue());
    }
});
```

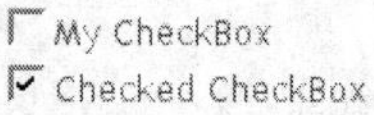

Figure 5.35. An Example of a Check Box

For an example on the use of check boxes in a table, see Section 5.15, "**Table**".

CSS Style Rules

```
.v-checkbox { }
  .v-checkbox > input { }
  .v-checkbox > label { }
```

The top-level element of a **CheckBox** has the `v-checkbox` style. It contains two sub-elements: the actual check box `input` element and the `label` element. If you want to have the label on the left, you can change the positions with `"direction: rtl"` for the top element.

5.14. Selecting Items

Vaadin gives many alternatives for selecting one or more items from a list, using drop-down and regular lists, radio button and check box groups, tables, trees, and so on.

The core library includes the following selection components, all based on the **AbstractSelect** class:

Select

> In single selection mode, a drop-down list with a text input area, which the user can use to filter the displayed items. In multiselect mode, a list box equivalent to **ListSelect**.

ComboBox

> A drop-down list for single selection. Otherwise as **Select**, but the user can also enter new items. The component also provides an input prompt.

ListSelect

> A vertical list box for selecting items in either single or multiple selection mode.

NativeSelect

> Provides selection using the native selection component of the browser, typically a drop-down list for single selection and a multi-line list in multiselect mode. This uses the `<select>` element in HTML.

OptionGroup

> Shows the items as a vertically arranged group of radio buttons in the single selection mode and of check boxes in multiple selection mode.

TwinColSelect

> Shows two list boxes side by side where the user can select items from a list of available items and move them to a list of selected items using control buttons.

In addition, the **Tree** and **Table** components allow special forms of selection. They also inherit the **AbstractSelect**.

5.14.1. Binding Selection Components to Data

The selection components are strongly coupled with the Vaadin Data Model. The selectable items in all selection components are objects that implement the **Item** interface and are contained in a **Container**. The current selection is bound to the **Property** interface.

Even though the data model is used, the selection components allow simple use in the most common cases. Each selection component is bound to a default container type, which supports management of items without need to implement a container.

See Chapter 9, *Binding Components to Data* for a detailed description of the data model, its interfaces, and built-in implementations.

Adding New Items

New items are added with the `addItem()` method defined in the **Container** interface.

```
// Create a selection component
Select select = new Select ("Select something here");

// Add some items and give each an item ID
select.addItem("Mercury");
select.addItem("Venus");
select.addItem("Earth");
```

The `addItem()` method creates an empty **Item**, which is identified by its *item identifier* (IID) object, given as the parameter. This item ID is by default used also as the caption of the item, as explained in the next section. The identifier is typically a **String**. The item is of a type specific to the container and has itself little relevance for most selection components, as the properties of an item may not be used in any way (except in **Table**), only the item ID.

The item identifier can be of any object type. We could as well have given integers for the item identifiers and set the captions explicitly with setItemCaption(). You could also add an item with the parameterless addItem(), which returns an automatically generated item ID.

```
// Create a selection component
Select select = new Select("My Select");

// Add an item with a generated ID
Object itemId = select.addItem();
select.setItemCaption(itemId, "The Sun");

// Select the item
select.setValue(itemId);
```

Some container types may support passing the actual data object to the add method. For example, you can add items to a **BeanItemContainer** with addBean(). Such implementations can use a separate item ID object, or the data object itself as the item ID, as is done in addBean(). In the latter case you can not depend on the default way of acquiring the item caption; see the description of the different caption modes later.

The following section describes the different options for determining the item captions.

Item Captions

The displayed captions of items in a selection component can be set explicitly with setItemCaption() or determined from the item IDs or item properties. This behaviour is defined with the *caption mode*, which you can set with setItemCaptionMode(). The default mode is ITEM_CAPTION_MODE_EXPLICIT_DEFAULTS_ID, which uses the item identifiers for the captions, unless given explicitly.

In addition to a caption, an item can have an icon. The icon is set with setItemIcon().

Caption Modes for Selection Components

ITEM_CAPTION_MODE_EXPLICIT_DEFAULTS_ID
    This is the default caption mode and its flexibility allows using it in most cases. By default, the item identifier will be used as the caption. The identifier object does not necessarily have to be a string; the caption is retrieved with to-

`String()` method. If the caption is specified explicitly with `setItemCaption()`, it overrides the item identifier.

```
Select select = new Select("Moons of Mars");

// Use the item ID also as the caption of this item
select.addItem(new Integer(1));

// Set item caption for this item explicitly
select.addItem(2); // same as "new Integer(2)"
select.setItemCaption(2, "Deimos");
```

ITEM_CAPTION_MODE_EXPLICIT

Captions must be explicitly specified with `setItemCaption()`. If they are not, the caption will be empty. Such items with empty captions will nevertheless be displayed in the **Select** component as empty items. If they have an icon, they will be visible.

ITEM_CAPTION_MODE_ICON_ONLY

Only icons are shown, captions are hidden.

ITEM_CAPTION_MODE_ID

String representation of the item identifier object is used as caption. This is useful when the identifier is a string, and also when the identifier is an complex object that has a string representation. For example:

```
Select select = new Select("Inner Planets");
select.setItemCaptionMode(Select.ITEM_CAPTION_MODE_ID);

// A class that implements toString()
class PlanetId extends Object implements Serializable {
    String planetName;
    PlanetId (String name) {
        planetName = name;
    }
    public String toString () {
        return "The Planet " + planetName;
    }
}

// Use such objects as item identifiers
String planets[] = {"Mercury", "Venus", "Earth", "Mars"};
for (int i=0; i<planets.length; i++)
    select.addItem(new PlanetId(planets[i]));
```

ITEM_CAPTION_MODE_INDEX

Index number of item is used as caption. This caption mode is applicable only to data sources that implement the **Con-**

tainer.Indexed interface. If the interface is not available, the component will throw a **ClassCastException**. The **Select** component itself does not implement this interface, so the mode is not usable without a separate data source. An **IndexedContainer**, for example, would work.

ITEM_CAPTION_MODE_ITEM

String representation of item, acquired with `toString()`, is used as the caption. This is applicable mainly when using a custom **Item** class, which also requires using a custom **Container** that is used as a data source for the **Select** component.

ITEM_CAPTION_MODE_PROPERTY

Item captions are read from the **String** representation of the property with the identifier specified with `setItemCaptionPropertyId()`. This is useful, for example, when you have a container that you use as the data source for a **Select**, and you want to use a specific property for caption.

In the example below, we bind a selection component to a bean container and use a property of the bean as the caption.

```
/* A bean with a "name" property. */
public class Planet implements Serializable {
    String name;

    public Planet(String name) {
        this.name = name;
    }

    public void setName(String name) {
        this.name = name;
    }

    public String getName() {
        return name;
    }
}

void propertyModeExample() {
    VerticalLayout layout = new VerticalLayout();

    // Have a bean container to put the beans in
    BeanItemContainer<Planet> container =
        new BeanItemContainer<Planet>(Planet.class);

    // Put some example data in it
    container.addItem(new Planet("Mercury"));
    container.addItem(new Planet("Venus"));
```

```
container.addItem(new Planet("Earth"));
container.addItem(new Planet("Mars"));

// Create a selection component bound to the container
Select select = new Select("Planets", container);

// Set the caption mode to read the caption directly
// from the 'name' property of the bean
select.setItemCaptionMode(
        Select.ITEM_CAPTION_MODE_PROPERTY);
select.setItemCaptionPropertyId("name");

layout.addComponent(select);
```

Getting and Setting Selection

A selection component provides the current selection as the property of the component (with the **Property** interface). The property value is an item identifier object that identifies the selected item. You can get the identifier with `getValue()` of the **Property** interface.

You can select an item with the corresponding `setValue()` method. In multiselect mode, the property will be an unmodifiable set of item identifiers. If no item is selected, the property will be *null* in single selection mode or an empty collection in multiselect mode.

The **Select** and **NativeSelect** components will show "-" selection when no actual item is selected. This is the *null selection item identifier*. You can set an alternative ID with `setNullSelection-ItemId()`. Setting the alternative null ID is merely a visual text; the `getValue()` will still return *null* value if no item is selected, or an empty set in multiselect mode.

The item identifier of the currently selected item will be set as the property of the **Select** object. You can access it with the `getValue()` method of the **Property** interface of the component. Also, when handling changes in a **Select** component with the **Property.ValueChangeListener** interface, the **Property.ValueChangeEvent** will have the selected item as the property of the event, accessible with the `getProperty()` method.

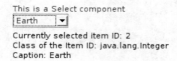

Currently selected item ID: 2
Class of the Item ID: java.lang.Integer
Caption: Earth

Figure 5.36. Selected Item

5.14.2. Basic Select Component

The **Select** component allows, in single selection mode, selecting an item from a drop-down list. The component also has a text field area, which allows entering search text by which the items shown in the drop-down list are filtered.

In multiple selection mode, the component shows the items in a vertical list box, identical to **ListSelect**.

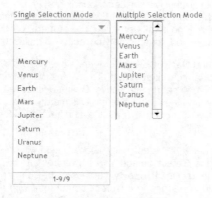

Figure 5.37. The Select Component

Filtered Selection

The **Select** component allows filtering the items available for selection. The component shows as an input box for entering text. The text entered in the input box is used for filtering the available items shown in a drop-down list. Pressing **Enter** will complete the item in the input box. Pressing **Up**- and **Down**-arrows can be used for selecting an item from the drop-down list. The drop-down list is paged and clicking on the scroll buttons will change to the next or previous page. The list selection can also be done with the arrow keys on the keyboard. The shown items are loaded from the server as needed, so the number of items held in the component can be quite large.

Vaadin provides two filtering modes: `FILTERINGMODE_CONTAINS` matches any item that contains the string given in the text field part of the component and `FILTERINGMODE_STARTSWITH` matches only items that begin with the given string. The filtering mode is set with `setFilteringMode()`. Setting the filtering mode to the default value `FILTERINGMODE_OFF` disables filtering.

```
Select select = new Select("Enter containing substring");

select.setFilteringMode(AbstractSelect.Filtering.FILTERINGMODE_CON-
TAINS);

/* Fill the component with some items. */
final String[] planets = new String[] {
        "Mercury", "Venus", "Earth", "Mars",
        "Jupiter", "Saturn", "Uranus", "Neptune" };

for (int i = 0; i < planets.length; i++)
    for (int j = 0; j < planets.length; j++) {
        select.addItem(planets[j] + " to " + planets[i]);
```

The above example uses the containment filter that matches to all items containing the input string. As shown in Figure 5.38, "Filtered Selection" below, when we type some text in the input area, the drop-down list will show all the matching items.

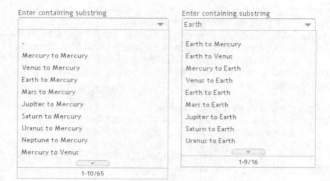

Figure 5.38. Filtered Selection

CSS Style Rules

```
.v-filterselect { }
.v-filterselect-input { }
.v-filterselect-button { }
.v-filterselect-suggestpopup { }
.v-filterselect-prefpage-off { }
.v-filterselect-suggestmenu { }
.v-filterselect-status { }
.v-select { }
.v-select-select { }
```

In its default state, only the input field of the **Select** component is visible. The entire component is enclosed in v-filterselect style, the input field has v-filterselect-input style and the button in the right end that opens and closes the drop-down result list has v-filterselect-button style.

The drop-down result list has an overall v-filterselect-suggest-popup style. It contains the list of suggestions with v-filterse-lect-suggestmenu style and a status bar in the bottom with v-filterselect-status style. The list of suggestions is padded with an area with v-filterselect-prefpage-off style above and below the list.

In multiselect-mode, the styles of the component aere identical to **ListSelect** component, with `v-select` overall style and `v-select-select` for the native selection element.

5.14.3. ListSelect

The **ListSelect** component is list box that shows the selectable items in a vertical list. If the number of items exceeds the height of the component, a scrollbar is shown. The component allows both single and multiple selection modes, which you can set with `setMultiSelect()`. It is visually identical in both modes.

```
// Create the selection component
ListSelect select = new ListSelect("My Selection");

// Add some items
select.addItem("Mercury");
select.addItem("Venus");
select.addItem("Earth");
...

select.setNullSelectionAllowed(false);

// Show 5 items and a scrollbar if there are more
select.setRows(5);
```

The number of visible items is set with `setRows()`.

Figure 5.39. The ListSelect Component

CSS Style Rules

```
.v-select {}
.v-select-select {}
```

The component has a `v-select` overall style. The native `select` element has `v-select-select` style.

5.14.4. Native Selection Component NativeSelect

NativeSelect offers the native selection component of web browsers, using the HTML `<select>` element. The component is shown as a drop-down list.

```
// Create the selection component
final NativeSelect select = new NativeSelect("Native Selection");

// Add some items
select.addItem("Mercury");
select.addItem("Venus");
...

// Set the width in "columns" as in TextField
select.setColumns(10);

select.setNullSelectionAllowed(false);
```

The `setColumns()` allows setting the width of the list as "columns", which is a measure that depends on the browser.

Figure 5.40. The NativeSelect Component

Multiple selection mode is not allowed; you should use the **ListSelect** component instead. Also adding new items, which would be enabled with `setNewItemsAllowed()`, is not allowed.

CSS Style Rules

```
.v-select {}
.v-select-select {}
```

The component has a `v-select` overall style. The native `select` element has `v-select-select` style.

5.14.5. Radio Button and Check Box Groups with OptionGroup

The **OptionGroup** class provides selection from alternatives using a group of radio buttons in single selection mode. In multiple selection mode, the items show up as check boxes.

```
OptionGroup optiongroup = new OptionGroup("My Option Group");

// Use the multiple selection mode.
myselect.setMultiSelect(true);
```

Figure 5.41, "Option Button Group in Single and Multiple Selection Mode" shows the **OptionGroup** in both single and multiple selection mode.

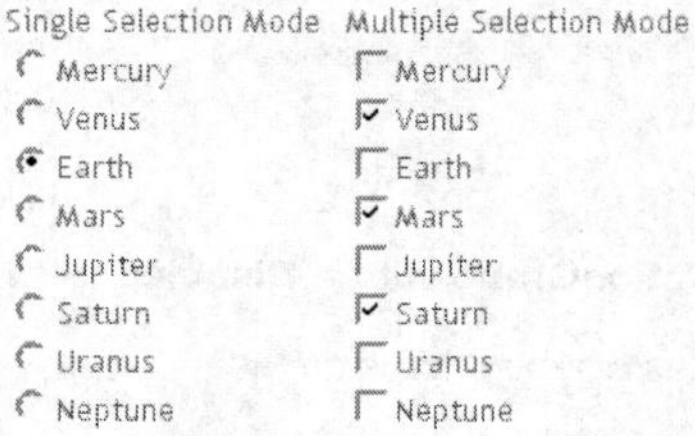

Figure 5.41. Option Button Group in Single and Multiple Selection Mode

You can create check boxes individually using the **CheckBox** class, as described in Section 5.13, "**CheckBox**". The advantages of the **OptionGroup** component are that as it maintains the individual check box objects, you can get an array of the currently selected items easily, and that you can easily change the appearance of a single component.

Disabling Items

You can disable individual items in an **OptionGroup** with `setItemEnabled()`. The user can not select or deselect disabled items in multi-select mode, but in single-select mode the use can change the selection from a disabled to an enabled item. The selections can be changed programmatically regardless of whether an item is enabled or disabled. You can find out whether an item is enabled with `isItemEnabled()`.

The `setItemEnabled()` identifies the item to be disabled by its item ID.

```
// Have an option group
OptionGroup group = new OptionGroup("My Disabled Group");
group.addItem("One");
group.addItem("Two");
group.addItem("Three");

// Disable one item
group.setItemEnabled("Two", false);
```

The item IDs are also used for the captions in this example. The result is shown in Figure 5.42, "**OptionGroup** with a Disabled Item".

Figure 5.42. OptionGroup with a Disabled Item

Setting an item as disabled turns on the `v-disabled` style for it.

CSS Style Rules

```
.v-select-optiongroup {}
.v-select-option.v-checkbox {}
.v-select-option.v-radiobutton {}
```

The `v-select-optiongroup` is the overall style for the component. Each check box will have the `v-checkbox` style, borrowed from the **CheckBox** component, and each radio button the `v-radiobutton` style. Both the radio buttons and check boxes will also have the `v-select-option` style that allows styling regardless of the option type. Disabled items have additionally the `v-disabled` style.

The options are normally laid out vertically. You can use horizontal layout by setting `display: inline-block` for the options. The `nowrap` setting for the overall element prevents wrapping if there

is not enough horizontal space in the layout, or if the horizontal
width is undefined.

```
/* Lay the options horizontally */
.v-select-optiongroup-horizontal .v-select-option {
    display: inline-block;
}

/* Avoid wrapping if the layout is too tight */
.v-select-optiongroup-horizontal {
    white-space: nowrap;
}

/* Some extra spacing is needed */
.v-select-optiongroup-horizontal
  .v-select-option.v-radiobutton {
    padding-right: 10px;
}
```

Use of the above rules requires setting a custom `horizontal` style
name for the component. The result is shown in Figure 5.43, "Horizontal **OptionGroup**".

Figure 5.43. Horizontal OptionGroup

5.14.6. Twin Column Selection with TwinColSelect

The **TwinColSelect** field provides a multiple selection component
that shows two lists side by side, with the left column containing
unselected items and the right column the selected items. The
user can select items from the list on the left and click on the ">>"
button to move them to the list on the right. Items can be deselected
by selecting them in the right list and clicking on the "<<" button.

TwinColSelect is always in multi-select mode, so its property
value is always a collection of the item IDs of the selected items,
that is, the items in the right column.

The selection columns can have their own captions, separate from
the overall component caption, which is managed by the containing
layout. You can set the column captions with `setLeftColumnCap-
tion()` and `setRightColumnCaption()`.

```
final TwinColSelect select =
    new TwinColSelect("Select Targets to Destroy");
```

```
// Set the column captions (optional)
select.setLeftColumnCaption("These are left");
select.setRightColumnCaption("These are done for");

// Put some data in the select
String planets[] = {"Mercury", "Venus", "Earth", "Mars",
        "Jupiter", "Saturn", "Uranus", "Neptune"};
for (int pl=0; pl<planets.length; pl++)
    select.addItem(planets[pl]);

// Set the number of visible items
select.setRows(planets.length);
```

The resulting component is shown in Figure 5.44, "Twin Column Selection".

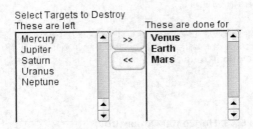

Figure 5.44. Twin Column Selection

The setRows() method sets the height of the component by the number of visible items in the selection boxes. Setting the height with setHeight() to a defined value overrides the rows setting.

CSS Style Rules

```
.v-select-twincol {}
  .v-select-twincol-options-caption {}
  .v-select-twincol-selections-caption {}
  .v-select-twincol-options {}
  .v-select-twincol-buttons {}
    .v-button {}
      .v-button-wrap {}
        .v-button-caption {}
    .v-select-twincol-deco {}
  .v-select-twincol-selections {}
```

The **TwinColSelect** component has an overall v-select-twincol style. If set, the left and right column captions have v-select-

`twincol-options-caption` and `v-select-twincol-options-caption` style names, respectively. The left box, which displays the unselected items, has `v-select-twincol-options-caption` style and the right box, which displays the selected items, has `v-select-twincol-options-selections` style. Between them is the button area, which has overall `v-select-twincol-buttons` style; the actual buttons reuse the styles for the **Button** component. Between the buttons is a divider element with `v-select-twincol-deco` style.

5.14.7. Allowing Adding New Items

The selection components allow the user to add new items, with a user interface similar to combo boxes in desktop user interfaces. You need to enable the *newItemsAllowed* mode with the `setNewItemsAllowed()` method.

```
myselect.setNewItemsAllowed(true);
```

The user interface for adding new items depends on the selection component and the selection mode. The regular **Select** component in single selection mode, which appears as a combo box, allows you to simply type the new item in the combo box and hit **Enter** to add it. In most other selection components, as well as in the multiple selection mode of the regular **Select** component, a text field that allows entering new items is shown below the selection list, and clicking the **+** button will add the item in the list, as illustrated in Figure 5.45, "Select Component with Adding New Items Allowed".

Figure 5.45. Select Component with Adding New Items Allowed

The identifier of an item added by the user will be a **String** object identical to the caption of the item. You should consider this if the item identifier of automatically filled items is some other type or otherwise not identical to the caption.

Adding new items is possible in both single and multiple selection modes and in all styles. Adding new items may not be possible if the **Select** is bound to an external **Container** that does not allow adding new items.

5.14.8. Multiple Selection Mode

Setting the **Select**, **NativeSelect**, or **OptionGroup** components to multiple selection mode with the `setMultiSelect()` method changes their appearance to allow selecting multiple items.

Select and **NativeSelect**
> These components appear as a native HTML selection list, as shown in Figure 5.45, "Select Component with Adding New Items Allowed". By holding the **Ctrl** or **Shift** key pressed, the user can select multiple items.

OptionGroup
> The option group, which is a radio button group in single selection mode, will show as a check box group in multiple selection mode. See Section 5.14.5, "Radio Button and Check Box Groups with **OptionGroup**".

The **TwinColSelect**, described in Section 5.14.6, "Twin Column Selection with **TwinColSelect**", is a special multiple selection mode that is not meaningful for single selection.

```
myselect.setMultiSelect(true);
```

As in single selection mode, the selected items are set as the property of the **Select** object. In multiple selection mode, the property is a **Collection** of currently selected items. You can get and set the property with the `getValue()` and `setValue()` methods as usual.

A change in the selection will trigger a **ValueChangeEvent**, which you can handle with a **Propery.ValueChangeListener**. As usual, you should use `setImmediate(true)` to trigger the event immediately when the user changes the selection. The following example shows how to handle selection changes with a listener.

```
public class SelectExample
        extends CustomComponent
        implements Property.ValueChangeListener {
    // Create a Select object with a caption.
    Select select = new Select("This is a Select component");

    VerticalLayout layout = new VerticalLayout();
    Label status = new Label("-");

    SelectExample () {
        setCompositionRoot (layout);
        layout.addComponent(select);

        // Fill the component with some items.
        final String[] planets = new String[] {
            "Mercury", "Venus", "Earth", "Mars",
            "Jupiter", "Saturn", "Uranus", "Neptune"};
        for (int i=0; i<planets.length; i++)
            select.addItem(planets[i]);

        // By default, the change event is not triggered
        // immediately when the selection changes.
        // This enables the immediate events.
        select.setImmediate(true);

        // Listen for changes in the selection.
        select.addListener(this);

        layout.addComponent(status);
    }

    /* Respond to change in the selection. */
    public void valueChange(Property.ValueChangeEvent event) {
        // The event.getProperty() returns the Item ID (IID)
        // of the currently selected item in the component.
        status.setValue("Currently selected item ID: " +
                        event.getProperty());
    }
}
```

5.14.9. Other Common Features

Item Icons

You can set an icon for each item with `setItemIcon()`, or define an item property that provides the icon resource with `setItemIcon-PropertyId()`, in a fashion similar to captions. Notice, however, that icons are not supported in **NativeSelect**, **TwinColSelect**, and some other selection components and modes. This is because HTML does not support images inside the native `select` elements. Icons are also not really visually applicable.

5.15. Table

The **Table** component is intended for presenting tabular data organized in rows and columns. The **Table** is one of the most versatile components in Vaadin. Table cells can include text or arbitrary UI components. You can easily implement editing of the table data, for example clicking on a cell could change it to a text field for editing.

The data contained in a **Table** is managed using the Data Model of Vaadin (see Chapter 9, *Binding Components to Data*), through the **Container** interface of the **Table**. This makes it possible to bind a table directly to a data source, such as a database query. Only the visible part of the table is loaded into the browser and moving the visible window with the scrollbar loads content from the server. While the data is being loaded, a tooltip will be displayed that shows the current range and total number of items in the table. The rows of the table are *items* in the container and the columns are *properties*. Each table row (item) is identified with an *item identifier* (IID), and each column (property) with a *property identifier* (PID).

When creating a table, you first need to define columns with `addContainerProperty()`. This method comes in two flavors. The simpler one takes the property ID of the column and uses it also as the caption of the column. The more complex one allows differing PID and header for the column. This may make, for example, internationalization of table headers easier, because if a PID is internationalized, the internationalization has to be used everywhere where the PID is used. The complex form of the method also allows defining an icon for the column from a resource. The "default value" parameter is used when new properties (columns) are added to the table, to fill in the missing values. (This default has no meaning in the usual case, such as below, where we add items after defining the properties.)

```
/* Create the table with a caption. */
Table table = new Table("This is my Table");

/* Define the names and data types of columns.
 * The "default value" parameter is meaningless here. */
table.addContainerProperty("First Name", String.class,  null);
table.addContainerProperty("Last Name",  String.class,  null);
table.addContainerProperty("Year",       Integer.class, null);

/* Add a few items in the table. */
```

```
table.addItem(new Object[] {
    "Nicolaus","Copernicus",new Integer(1473)}, new Integer(1));
table.addItem(new Object[] {
    "Tycho",   "Brahe",    new Integer(1546)}, new Integer(2));
table.addItem(new Object[] {
    "Giordano","Bruno",    new Integer(1548)}, new Integer(3));
table.addItem(new Object[] {
    "Galileo", "Galilei",  new Integer(1564)}, new Integer(4));
table.addItem(new Object[] {
    "Johannes","Kepler",   new Integer(1571)}, new Integer(5));
table.addItem(new Object[] {
    "Isaac",   "Newton",   new Integer(1643)}, new Integer(6));
```

In this example, we used an increasing **Integer** object as the Item
Identifier, given as the second parameter to `addItem()`. The actual
rows are given simply as object arrays, in the same order in which
the properties were added. The objects must be of the correct
class, as defined in the `addContainerProperty()` calls.

This is my Table

First Name	Last Name	Year
Nicolaus	Copernicus	1473
Tycho	Brahe	1546
Giordano	Bruno	1548
Galileo	Galilei	1564
Johannes	Kepler	1571

Figure 5.46. Basic Table Example

Scalability of the **Table** is largely dictated by the container. The
default **IndexedContainer** is relatively heavy and can cause
scalability problems, for example, when updating the values. Use
of an optimized application-specific container is recommended.
Table does not have a limit for the number of items and is just as
fast with hundreds of thousands of items as with just a few. With
the current implementation of scrolling, there is a limit of around
500 000 rows, depending on the browser and the pixel height of
rows.

5.15.1. Selecting Items in a Table

The **Table** allows selecting one or more items by clicking them
with the mouse. When the user selects an item, the IID of the item
will be set as the property of the table and a **ValueChangeEvent**
is triggered. To enable selection, you need to set the table *select-*

able. You will also need to set it as *immediate* in most cases, as we do below, because without it, the change in the property will not be communicated immediately to the server.

The following example shows how to enable the selection of items in a **Table** and how to handle **ValueChangeEvent** events that are caused by changes in selection. You need to handle the event with the `valueChange()` method of the **Property.ValueChangeListener** interface.

```
// Allow selecting items from the table.
table.setSelectable(true);

// Send changes in selection immediately to server.
table.setImmediate(true);

// Shows feedback from selection.
final Label current = new Label("Selected: -");

// Handle selection change.
table.addListener(new Property.ValueChangeListener() {
    public void valueChange(ValueChangeEvent event) {
        current.setValue("Selected: " + table.getValue());
    }
});
```

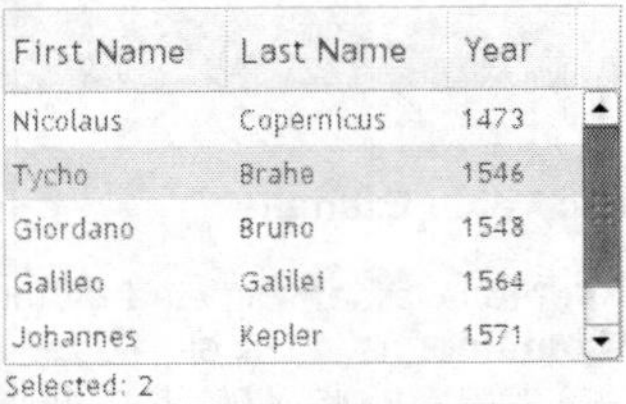

First Name	Last Name	Year
Nicolaus	Copernicus	1473
Tycho	Brahe	1546
Giordano	Bruno	1548
Galileo	Galilei	1564
Johannes	Kepler	1571

Selected: 2

Figure 5.47. Table Selection Example

If the user clicks on an already selected item, the selection will deselected and the table property will have *null* value. You can disable this behaviour by setting `setNullSelectionAllowed(false)` for the table.

The selection is the value of the table's property, so you can get it with `getValue()`. You can get it also from a reference to the table itself. In single selection mode, the value is the item identifier of the selected item or *null* if no item is selected. In multiple selection mode (see below), the value is a **Set** of item identifiers. Notice that the set is unmodifiable, so you can not simply change it to change the selection.

Multiple Selection Mode

A table can also be in *multiselect* mode, where a user can select multiple items by clicking them with left mouse button while holding the **Ctrl** key (or **Meta** key) pressed. If **Ctrl** is not held, clicking an item will select it and other selected items are deselected. The user can select a range by selecting an item, holding the **Shift** key pressed, and clicking another item, in which case all the items between the two are also selected. Multiple ranges can be selected by first selecting a range, then selecting an item while holding **Ctrl**, and then selecting another item with both **Ctrl** and **Shift** pressed.

The multiselect mode is enabled with the `setMultiSelect()` method of the **Select** interface of **Table**. Setting table in multiselect mode does not implicitly set it as *selectable*, so it must be set separately.

The `setMultiSelectMode()` property affects the control of multiple selection: `MultiSelectMode.DEFAULT` is the default behaviour, which requires holding the **Ctrl** (or **Meta**) key pressed while selecting items, while in `MultiSelectMode.SIMPLE` holding the **Ctrl** key is not needed. In the simple mode, items can only be deselected by clicking them.

5.15.2. Table Features

Page Length and Scrollbar

The default style for **Table** provides a table with a scrollbar. The scrollbar is located at the right side of the table and becomes visible when the number of items in the table exceeds the page length, that is, the number of visible items. You can set the page length with `setPageLength()`.

Setting the page length to zero makes all the rows in a table visible, no matter how many rows there are. Notice that this also effectively disables buffering, as all the entire table is loaded to the browser at once. Using such tables to generate reports does not scale up very well, as there is some inevitable overhead in rendering a table with Ajax. For very large reports, generating HTML directly is a more scalable solution.

Resizing Columns

You can set the width of a column programmatically from the server-side with `setColumnWidth()`. The column is identified by the property ID and the width is given in pixels.

The user can resize table columns by dragging the resize handle between two columns. Resizing a table column causes a **ColumnResizeEvent**, which you can handle with a **Table.ColumnResizeListener**. The table must be set in immediate mode if you want to receive the resize events immediately, which is typical.

```
table.addListener(new Table.ColumnResizeListener() {
    public void columnResize(ColumnResizeEvent event) {
        // Get the new width of the resized column
        int width = event.getCurrentWidth();

        // Get the property ID of the resized column
        String column = (String) event.getPropertyId();

        // Do something with the information
        table.setColumnFooter(column, String.valueOf(width) + "px");
    }
});

// Must be immediate to send the resize events immediately
table.setImmediate(true);
```

See Figure 5.48, "Resizing Columns" for a result after the columns of a table has been resized.

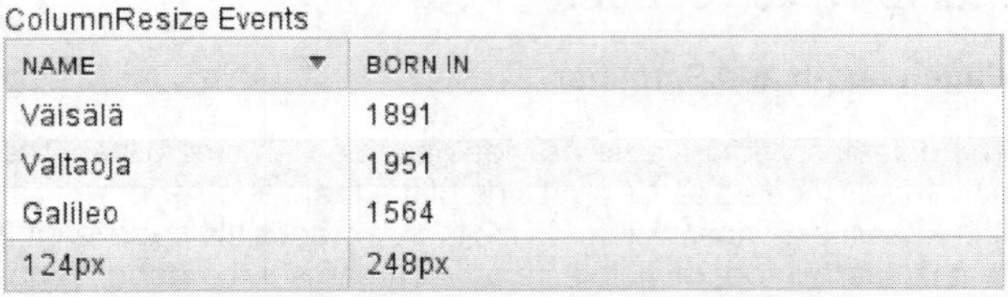

ColumnResize Events

NAME ▼	BORN IN
Väisälä	1891
Valtaoja	1951
Galileo	1564
124px	248px

Figure 5.48. Resizing Columns

Reordering Columns

If `setColumnReorderingAllowed(true)` is set, the user can reorder table columns by dragging them with the mouse from the column header,

Collapsing Columns

When `setColumnCollapsingAllowed(true)` is set, the right side of the table header shows a drop-down list that allows selecting which columns are shown. Collapsing columns is different than hiding columns with `setVisibleColumns()`, which hides the columns completely so that they can not be made visible (uncollapsed) from the user interface.

You can collapse columns programmatically with `setColumnCollapsed()`. Collapsing must be enabled before collapsing columns with the method or it will throw an **IllegalAccessException**.

```
// Allow the user to collapse and uncollapse columns
table.setColumnCollapsingAllowed(true);

// Collapse this column programmatically
try {
    table.setColumnCollapsed("born", true);
} catch (IllegalAccessException e) {
    // Can't occur - collapsing was allowed above
    System.err.println("Something horrible occurred");
}

// Give enough width for the table to accommodate the
// initially collapsed column later
table.setWidth("250px");
```

See Figure 5.49, "Collapsing Columns".

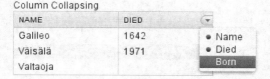

Figure 5.49. Collapsing Columns

If the table has undefined width, it minimizes its width to fit the width of the visible columns. If some columns are initially collapsed, the width of the table may not be enough to accomodate them later, which will result in an ugly horizontal scrollbar. You should consider giving the table enough width to accomodate columns uncollapsed by the user.

Components Inside a Table

The cells of a **Table** can contain any user interface components, not just strings. If the rows are higher than the row height defined in the default theme, you have to define the proper row height in a custom theme.

When handling events for components inside a **Table**, such as for the **Button** in the example below, you usually need to know the item the component belongs to. Components do not themselves know about the table or the specific item in which a component is contained. Therefore, the handling method must use some other means for finding out the Item ID of the item. There are a few possibilities. Usually the easiest way is to use the setData() method to attach an arbitrary object to a component. You can subclass the component and include the identity information there. You can also simply search the entire table for the item with the component, although that solution may not be so scalable.

The example below includes table rows with a **Label** in XHTML formatting mode, a multiline **TextField**, a **CheckBox**, and a **Button** that shows as a link.

```
// Create a table and add a style to allow setting the row height
in theme.
final Table table = new Table();
table.addStyleName("components-inside");

/* Define the names and data types of columns.
 * The "default value" parameter is meaningless here. */
table.addContainerProperty("Sum",            Label.class,    null);
table.addContainerProperty("Is Transferred", CheckBox.class, null);
table.addContainerProperty("Comments",       TextField.class, null);
table.addContainerProperty("Details",        Button.class,   null);

/* Add a few items in the table. */
for (int i=0; i<100; i++) {
    // Create the fields for the current table row
    Label sumField = new Label(String.format(
                "Sum is <b>$%04.2f</b><br/><i>(VAT incl.)</i>",
                new Object[] {new Double(Math.random()*1000)}),
                      Label.CONTENT_XHTML);
    CheckBox transferredField = new CheckBox("is transferred");

    // Multiline text field. This required modifying the
    // height of the table row.
    TextField commentsField = new TextField();
    commentsField.setRows(3);

    // The Table item identifier for the row.
    Integer itemId = new Integer(i);
```

```
    // Create a button and handle its click. A Button does not
    // know the item it is contained in, so we have to store the
    // item ID as user-defined data.
    Button detailsField = new Button("show details");
    detailsField.setData(itemId);
    detailsField.addListener(new Button.ClickListener() {
        public void buttonClick(ClickEvent event) {
            // Get the item identifier from the user-defined data.
            Integer iid = (Integer)event.getButton().getData();
            Notification.show("Link " +
                                iid.intValue() + " clicked.");
        }
    });
    detailsField.addStyleName("link");

    // Create the table row.
    table.addItem(new Object[] {sumField, transferredField,
                                commentsField, detailsField},
                  itemId);
}

// Show just three rows because they are so high.
table.setPageLength(3);
```

The row height has to be set higher than the default with a style
rule such as the following:

```
/* Table rows contain three-row TextField components. */
.v-table-components-inside .v-table-cell-content {
 height: 54px;
}
```

The table will look as shown in Figure 5.50, "Components in a
Table".

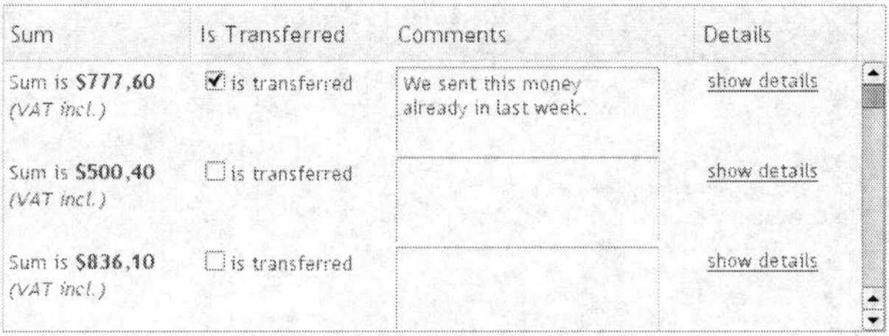

Figure 5.50. Components in a Table

Iterating Over a Table

As the items in a **Table** are not indexed, iterating over the items has to be done using an iterator. The `getItemIds()` method of the **Container** interface of **Table** returns a **Collection** of item identifiers over which you can iterate using an **Iterator**. For an example about iterating over a **Table**, please see Section 9.5, "Collecting Items in Containers". Notice that you may not modify the **Table** during iteration, that is, add or remove items. Changing the data is allowed.

Filtering Table Contents

A table can be filtered if its container data source implements the **Filterable** interface, as the default **IndexedContainer** does. See Section 9.5.4, "**Filterable** Containers".

5.15.3. Editing the Values in a Table

Normally, a **Table** simply displays the items and their fields as text. If you want to allow the user to edit the values, you can either put them inside components as we did above, or you can simply call `setEditable(true)` and the cells are automatically turned into editable fields.

Let us begin with a regular table with a some columns with usual Java types, namely a **Date**, **Boolean**, and a **String**.

```
// Create a table. It is by default not editable.
final Table table = new Table();

// Define the names and data types of columns.
table.addContainerProperty("Date",     Date.class,  null);
table.addContainerProperty("Work",     Boolean.class, null);
table.addContainerProperty("Comments", String.class,  null);

// Add a few items in the table.
for (int i=0; i<100; i++) {
    Calendar calendar = new GregorianCalendar(2008,0,1);
    calendar.add(Calendar.DAY_OF_YEAR, i);

    // Create the table row.
    table.addItem(new Object[] {calendar.getTime(),
                                new Boolean(false),
                                ""},
                  new Integer(i)); // Item identifier
}

table.setPageLength(8);
layout.addComponent(table);
```

You could put the table in editable mode right away if you need to. We'll continue the example by adding a mechanism to switch the **Table** from and to the editable mode.

```
final CheckBox switchEditable = new CheckBox("Editable");
switchEditable.addListener(new Property.ValueChangeListener() {
    public void valueChange(ValueChangeEvent event) {
        table.setEditable(((Boolean)event.getProperty()
                            .getValue()).booleanValue());
    }
});
switchEditable.setImmediate(true);
layout.addComponent(switchEditable);
```

Now, when you check to checkbox, the components in the table turn into editable fields, as shown in Figure 5.51, "A Table in Normal and Editable Mode".

Figure 5.51. A Table in Normal and Editable Mode

Field Factories

The field components that allow editing the values of particular types in a table are defined in a field factory that implements the **TableFieldFactory** interface. The default implementation is **DefaultFieldFactory**, which offers the following crude mappings:

Table 5.2. Type to Field Mappings in DefaultFieldFactory

Property Type	Mapped to Field Class
Date	A **DateField**.
Boolean	A **CheckBox**.
Item	A **Form** (deprecated in Vaadin 7). The fields of the form are automatically created from the item's properties using a **Form-**

Property Type	Mapped to Field Class
	FieldFactory. The normal use for this property type is inside a **Form** and is less useful inside a **Table**.
other	A **TextField**. The text field manages conversions from the basic types, if possible.

Field factories are covered with more detail in Section 9.4, "Binding Fields to Items". You could just implement the **TableFieldFactory** interface, but we recommend that you extend the **DefaultField-Factory** according to your needs. In the default implementation, the mappings are defined in the `createFieldByPropertyType()` method (you might want to look at the source code) both for tables and forms.

Navigation in Editable Mode

In the editable mode, the editor fields can have focus. Pressing **Tab** moves the focus to next column or, at the last column, to the first column of the next item. Respectively, pressing **Shift+Tab** moves the focus backward. If the focus is in the last column of the last visible item, the pressing **Tab** moves the focus outside the table. Moving backward from the first column of the first item moves the focus to the table itself. Some updates to the table, such as changing the headers or footers or regenerating a column, can move the focus from an editor component to the table itself.

The default behaviour may be undesirable in many cases. For example, the focus also goes through any read-only editor fields and can move out of the table inappropriately. You can provide better navigation is to use event handler for shortcut keys such as **Tab**, **Arrow Up**, **Arrow Down**, and **Enter**.

```
// Keyboard navigation
class KbdHandler implements Handler {
    Action tab_next = new ShortcutAction("Tab",
            ShortcutAction.KeyCode.TAB, null);
    Action tab_prev = new ShortcutAction("Shift+Tab",
            ShortcutAction.KeyCode.TAB,
            new int[] {ShortcutAction.ModifierKey.SHIFT});
    Action cur_down = new ShortcutAction("Down",
            ShortcutAction.KeyCode.ARROW_DOWN, null);
    Action cur_up   = new ShortcutAction("Up",
```

```
            ShortcutAction.KeyCode.ARROW_UP,  null);
    Action enter  = new ShortcutAction("Enter",
            ShortcutAction.KeyCode.ENTER,     null);
    public Action[] getActions(Object target, Object sender) {
        return new Action[] {tab_next, tab_prev, cur_down,
                             cur_up, enter};
    }

    public void handleAction(Action action, Object sender,
                             Object target) {
        if (target instanceof TextField) {
            // Move according to keypress
            int itemid = (Integer) ((TextField) target).getData();
            if (action == tab_next || action == cur_down)
                itemid++;
            else if (action == tab_prev || action == cur_up)
                itemid--;
            // On enter, just stay where you were. If we did
            // not catch the enter action, the focus would be
            // moved to wrong place.

            if (itemid >= 0 && itemid < table.size()) {
                TextField newTF = valueFields.get(itemid);
                if (newTF != null)
                    newTF.focus();
            }
        }
    }
}

// Panel that handles keyboard navigation
Panel navigator = new Panel();
navigator.addStyleName(Reindeer.PANEL_LIGHT);
navigator.addComponent(table);
navigator.addActionHandler(new KbdHandler());
```

The main issue in implementing keyboard navigation in an editable table is that the editor fields do not know the table they are in. To find the parent table, you can either look up in the component container hierarchy or simply store a reference to the table with setData() in the field component. The other issue is that you can not acquire a reference to an editor field from the **Table** component. One solution is to use some external collection, such as a **HashMap**, to map item IDs to the editor fields.

```
// Can't access the editable components from the table so
// must store the information
final HashMap<Integer,TextField> valueFields =
    new HashMap<Integer,TextField>();
```

The map has to be filled in a **TableFieldFactory**, such as in the following. You also need to set the reference to the table there and you can also set the initial focus there.

```
table.setTableFieldFactory(new TableFieldFactory () {
    public Field createField(Container container, Object itemId,
            Object propertyId, Component uiContext) {
        TextField field = new TextField((String) propertyId);

        // User can only edit the numeric column
        if ("Source of Fear".equals(propertyId))
            field.setReadOnly(true);
        else { // The numeric column
            // The field needs to know the item it is in
            field.setData(itemId);

            // Remember the field
            valueFields.put((Integer) itemId, field);

            // Focus the first editable value
            if (((Integer)itemId) == 0)
                field.focus();
        }
        return field;
    }
});
```

The issues are complicated by the fact that the editor fields are
not generated for the entire table, but only for a cache window that
includes the visible items and some items above and below it. For
example, if the beginning of a big scrollable table is visible, the
editor component for the last item does not exist. This issue is relevant mostly if you want to have wrap-around navigation that jumps
from the last to first item and vice versa.

5.15.4. Column Headers and Footers

Table supports both column headers and footers; the headers are
enabled by default.

Headers

The table header displays the column headers at the top of the
table. You can use the column headers to reorder or resize the
columns, as described earlier. By default, the header of a column
is the property ID of the column, unless given explicitly with set-
ColumnHeader().

```
// Define the properties
table.addContainerProperty("lastname", String.class, null);
table.addContainerProperty("born", Integer.class, null);
table.addContainerProperty("died", Integer.class, null);

// Set nicer header names
table.setColumnHeader("lastname", "Name");
```

```
table.setColumnHeader("born", "Born");
table.setColumnHeader("died", "Died");
```

The text of the column headers and the visibility of the header depends on the *column header mode*. The header is visible by default, but you can disable it with `setColumnHeader-Mode(Table.COLUMN_HEADER_MODE_HIDDEN)`.

Footers

The table footer can be useful for displaying sums or averages of values in a column, and so on. The footer is not visible by default; you can enable it with `setFooterVisible(true)`. Unlike in the header, the column headers are empty by default. You can set their value with `setColumnFooter()`. The columns are identified by their property ID.

The following example shows how to calculate average of the values in a column:

```
// Have a table with a numeric column
Table table = new Table("Custom Table Footer");
table.addContainerProperty("Name", String.class, null);
table.addContainerProperty("Died At Age", Integer.class, null);

// Insert some data
Object people[][] = {{"Galileo",  77},
                     {"Monnier",  83},
                     {"Vaisala",  79},
                     {"Oterma",   86}};
for (int i=0; i<people.length; i++)
    table.addItem(people[i], new Integer(i));

// Calculate the average of the numeric column
double avgAge = 0;
for (int i=0; i<people.length; i++)
    avgAge += (Integer) people[i][1];
avgAge /= people.length;

// Set the footers
table.setFooterVisible(true);
table.setColumnFooter("Name", "Average");
table.setColumnFooter("Died At Age", String.valueOf(avgAge));

// Adjust the table height a bit
table.setPageLength(table.size());
```

The resulting table is shown in Figure 5.52, "A Table with a Footer".

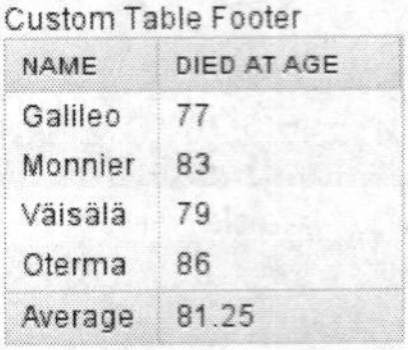

Custom Table Footer

NAME	DIED AT AGE
Galileo	77
Monnier	83
Väisälä	79
Oterma	86
Average	81.25

Figure 5.52. A Table with a Footer

Handling Mouse Clicks on Headers and Footers

Normally, when the user clicks a column header, the table will be sorted by the column, assuming that the data source is **Sortable** and sorting is not disabled. In some cases, you might want some other functionality when the user clicks the column header, such as selecting the column in some way.

Clicks in the header cause a **HeaderClickEvent**, which you can handle with a **Table.HeaderClickListener**. Click events on the table header (and footer) are, like button clicks, sent immediately to server, so there is no need to set setImmediate().

```
// Handle the header clicks
table.addListener(new Table.HeaderClickListener() {
    public void headerClick(HeaderClickEvent event) {
        String column = (String) event.getPropertyId();
        Notification.show("Clicked " + column +
                "with " + event.getButtonName());
    }
});

// Disable the default sorting behavior
table.setSortDisabled(true);
```

Setting a click handler does not automatically disable the sorting behavior of the header; you need to disable it explicitly with set-SortDisabled(true). Header click events are not sent when the user clicks the column resize handlers to drag them.

The **HeaderClickEvent** object provides the identity of the clicked column with getPropertyId(). The getButton() reports the mouse button with which the click was made: *BUTTON_LEFT*, *BUTTON_RIGHT*, or *BUTTON_MIDDLE*. The getButtonName() a human-readable button name in English: "*left*", "*right*", or "*middle*". The `isShiftKey()`, `isCtrlKey()`, etc., methods indicate if the **Shift**, **Ctrl**, **Alt** or other modifier keys were pressed during the click.

Clicks in the footer cause a **FooterClickEvent**, which you can handle with a **Table.FooterClickListener**. Footers do not have any default click behavior, like the sorting in the header. Otherwise, handling clicks in the footer is equivalent to handling clicks in the header.

5.15.5. Generated Table Columns

You might want to have a column that has values calculated from other columns. Or you might want to format table columns in some way, for example if you have columns that display currencies. The **ColumnGenerator** interface allows defining custom generators for such columns.

You add new generated columns to a **Table** with `addGenerated-Column()`. It takes the column identifier as its parameters. Usually you want to have a more user-friendly and possibly internationalized column header. You can set the header and a possible icon by calling `addContainerProperty()` *before* adding the generated column.

```
// Define table columns.
table.addContainerProperty(
    "date",     Date.class,   null, "Date",        null, null);
table.addContainerProperty(
    "quantity", Double.class, null, "Quantity (l)", null, null);
table.addContainerProperty(
    "price",    Double.class, null, "Price (e/l)", null, null);
table.addContainerProperty(
    "total",    Double.class, null, "Total (e)",    null, null);

// Define the generated columns and their generators.
table.addGeneratedColumn("date",
                    new DateColumnGenerator());
table.addGeneratedColumn("quantity",
                    new ValueColumnGenerator("%.2f l"));
table.addGeneratedColumn("price",
                    new PriceColumnGenerator());
table.addGeneratedColumn("total",
                    new ValueColumnGenerator("%.2f e"));
```

Notice that the `addGeneratedColumn()` always places the generated columns as the last column, even if you defined some other order previously. You will have to set the proper order with `setVisibleColumns()`.

```
table.setVisibleColumns(new Object[] {"date", "quantity", "price",
  "total"});
```

The generators are objects that implement the **Table.ColumnGenerator** interface and its `generateCell()` method. The method gets the identity of the item and column as its parameters, in addition to the table object. It has to return a component object.

The following example defines a generator for formatting **Double** valued fields according to a format string (as in **java.util.Formatter**).

```
/** Formats the value in a column containing Double objects. */
class ValueColumnGenerator implements Table.ColumnGenerator {
    String format; /* Format string for the Double values. */

    /**
     * Creates double value column formatter with the given
     * format string.
     */
    public ValueColumnGenerator(String format) {
        this.format = format;
    }

    /**
     * Generates the cell containing the Double value.
     * The column is irrelevant in this use case.
     */
    public Component generateCell(Table source, Object itemId,
                                  Object columnId) {
        // Get the object stored in the cell as a property
        Property prop =
            source.getItem(itemId).getItemProperty(columnId);
        if (prop.getType().equals(Double.class)) {
            Label label = new Label(String.format(format,
                new Object[] { (Double) prop.getValue() }));

            // Set styles for the column: one indicating that it's
            // a value and a more specific one with the column
            // name in it. This assumes that the column name
            // is proper for CSS.
            label.addStyleName("column-type-value");
            label.addStyleName("column-" + (String) columnId);
            return label;
        }
        return null;
    }
}
```

The generator is called for all the visible (or more accurately cached) items in a table. If the user scrolls the table to another position in the table, the columns of the new visible rows are generated dynamically. The columns in the visible (cached) rows are also generated always when an item has a value change. It is therefore usually safe to calculate the value of generated cells from the values of different rows (items).

When you set a table as *editable*, regular fields will change to editing fields. When the user changes the values in the fields, the generated columns will be updated automatically. Putting a table with generated columns in editable mode has a few quirks. The editable mode of **Table** does not affect generated columns. You have two alternatives: either you generate the editing fields in the generator or, in case of formatter generators, remove the generator in the editable mode. The example below uses the latter approach.

```
// Have a check box that allows the user
// to make the quantity and total columns editable.
final CheckBox editable = new CheckBox(
    "Edit the input values - calculated columns are regenerated");

editable.setImmediate(true);
editable.addListener(new ClickListener() {
    public void buttonClick(ClickEvent event) {
        table.setEditable(editable.booleanValue());

        // The columns may not be generated when we want to
        // have them editable.
        if (editable.booleanValue()) {
            table.removeGeneratedColumn("quantity");
            table.removeGeneratedColumn("total");
        } else { // Not editable
            // Show the formatted values.
            table.addGeneratedColumn("quantity",
                new ValueColumnGenerator("%.2f l"));
            table.addGeneratedColumn("total",
                new ValueColumnGenerator("%.2f e"));
        }
        // The visible columns are affected by removal
        // and addition of generated columns so we have
        // to redefine them.
        table.setVisibleColumns(new Object[] {"date", "quantity",
            "price", "total", "consumption", "dailycost"});
    }
});
```

You will also have to set the editing fields in *immediate* mode to have the update occur immediately when an edit field loses the focus. You can set the fields in *immediate* mode with the a custom **TableFieldFactory**, such as the one given below, that just extends the default implementation to set the mode:

```
public class ImmediateFieldFactory extends DefaultFieldFactory {
    public Field createField(Container container,
                            Object itemId,
                            Object propertyId,
                            Component uiContext) {
```

```
            // Let the DefaultFieldFactory create the fields...
            Field field = super.createField(container, itemId,
                                            propertyId, uiContext);

            // ...and just set them as immediate.
            ((AbstractField)field).setImmediate(true);

            return field;
        }
    }
    ...
    table.setTableFieldFactory(new ImmediateFieldFactory());
```

If you generate the editing fields with the column generator, you avoid having to use such a field factory, but of course have to generate the fields for both normal and editable modes.

Figure 5.53, "Table with Generated Columns in Normal and Editable Mode" shows a table with columns calculated (blue) and simply formatted (black) with column generators.

Date	Quantity (l)	Price (€/l)	Total (€)	Consumption (l/day)	Daily Cost (€/day)
2005-02-19	44,96 l	1,14 €	51,21 €	N/A	N/A
2005-03-30	44,91 l	1,20 €	53,67 €	1,15 l	1,38 €
2005-04-20	42,96 l	1,14 €	49,06 €	2,05 l	2,34 €
2005-05-23	47,37 l	1,17 €	55,28 €	1,44 l	1,68 €
2005-06-06	35,34 l	1,17 €	41,52 €	2,52 l	2,97 €
2005-06-30	16,07 l	1,24 €	20,00 €	0,67 l	0,83 €
2005-07-02	36,40 l	0,99 €	36,19 €	18,20 l	18,10 €

Date	Quantity (l)	Price (€/l)	Total (€)	Consumption (l/day)	Daily Cost (€/day)
2005-02-19	44.96	1,14 €	51.21	N/A	N/A
2005-03-30	44.91	1,20 €	53.67	1,15 l	1,38 €
2005-04-20	42.96	1,14 €	49.06	2,05 l	2,34 €
2005-05-23	47.37	1,17 €	55.28	1,44 l	1,68 €
2005-06-06	35.34	1,17 €	41.52	2,52 l	2,97 €
2005-06-30	16.07	1,24 €	20.0	0,67 l	0,83 €
2005-07-02	36.4	0,99 €	36.19	18,20 l	18,10 €

Figure 5.53. Table with Generated Columns in Normal and Editable Mode

5.15.6. Formatting Table Columns

The displayed values of properties shown in a table are normally formatted using the toString() method of each property. Customizing the format of a column can be done in several ways:

- Using **ColumnGenerator** to generate a second column that is formatted. The original column needs to be set invisible. See Section 5.15.5, "Generated Table Columns".

- Using a **PropertyFormatter** as a proxy between the table and the data property. This also normally requires using an mediate container in the table.

- Overriding the default `formatPropertyValue()` in **Table**.

As using a **PropertyFormatter** is generally much more awkward than overriding the `formatPropertyValue()`, its use is not described here.

You can override `formatPropertyValue()` as is done in the following example:

```
// Create a table that overrides the default
// property (column) format
final Table table = new Table("Formatted Table") {
    @Override
    protected String formatPropertyValue(Object rowId,
            Object colId, Property property) {
        // Format by property type
        if (property.getType() == Date.class) {
            SimpleDateFormat df =
                new SimpleDateFormat("yyyy-MM-dd hh:mm:ss");
            return df.format((Date)property.getValue());
        }

        return super.formatPropertyValue(rowId, colId, property);
    }
};

// The table has some columns
table.addContainerProperty("Time", Date.class, null);

... Fill the table with data ...
```

You can also distinguish between columns by the `colId` parameter, which is the property ID of the column. **DecimalFormat** is useful for formatting decimal values.

```
... in formatPropertyValue() ...
} else if ("Value".equals(pid)) {
    // Format a decimal value for a specific locale
    DecimalFormat df = new DecimalFormat("#.00",
        new DecimalFormatSymbols(locale));
    return df.format((Double) property.getValue());
}
...
table.addContainerProperty("Value", Double.class, null);
```

A table with the formatted date and decimal value columns is shown in Figure 5.54, "Formatted Table Columns".

Formatted Table

TIME	VALUE	MESSAGE
1970-01-01 02:00:00	708,42	Msg #55
1970-03-29 05:16:33	44,31	Msg #33
1970-07-22 04:40:13	741,61	Msg #1
1970-09-01 12:11:49	757,91	Msg #36
1970-12-21 02:32:50	793,82	Msg #92
1971-01-13 05:25:15	700,79	Msg #65

Figure 5.54. Formatted Table Columns

You can use CSS for further styling of table rows, columns, and individual cells by using a **CellStyleGenerator**. It is described in Section 5.15.7, "CSS Style Rules".

5.15.7. CSS Style Rules

Styling the overall style of a **Table** can be done with the following CSS rules.

```
.v-table {}
  .v-table-header-wrap {}
    .v-table-header {}
      .v-table-header-cell {}
        .v-table-resizer {} /* Column resizer handle. */
        .v-table-caption-container {}
  .v-table-body {}
    .v-table-row-spacer {}
    .v-table-table {}
      .v-table-row {}
        .v-table-cell-content {}
```

Notice that some of the widths and heights in a table are calculated dynamically and can not be set in CSS.

Setting Individual Cell Styles

The **Table.CellStyleGenerator** interface allows you to set the CSS style for each individual cell in a table. You need to implement the getStyle(), which gets the row (item) and column (property) identifiers as parameters and can return a style name for the cell. The returned style name will be concatenated to prefix "`v-table-cell-content-`".

The `getStyle()` is called also for each row, so that the *propertyId* parameter is `null`. This allows setting a row style.

Alternatively, you can use a **Table.ColumnGenerator** (see Section 5.15.5, "Generated Table Columns") to generate the actual UI components of the cells and add style names to them.

```
Table table = new Table("Table with Cell Styles");
table.addStyleName("checkerboard");

// Add some columns in the table. In this example, the property
// IDs of the container are integers so we can determine the
// column number easily.
table.addContainerProperty("0", String.class, null, "", null, null);
for (int i=0; i<8; i++)
    table.addContainerProperty(""+(i+1), String.class, null,
                       String.valueOf((char) (65+i)), null, null);

// Add some items in the table.
table.addItem(new Object[]{
    "1", "R", "N", "B", "Q", "K", "B", "N", "R"}, new Integer(0));
table.addItem(new Object[]{
    "2", "P", "P", "P", "P", "P", "P", "P", "P"}, new Integer(1));
for (int i=2; i<6; i++)
    table.addItem(new Object[]{String.valueOf(i+1),
                "", "", "", "", "", "", "", ""}, new Integer(i));
table.addItem(new Object[]{
    "7", "P", "P", "P", "P", "P", "P", "P", "P"}, new Integer(6));
table.addItem(new Object[]{
    "8", "R", "N", "B", "Q", "K", "B", "N", "R"}, new Integer(7));
table.setPageLength(8);

// Set cell style generator
table.setCellStyleGenerator(new Table.CellStyleGenerator() {
    public String getStyle(Object itemId, Object propertyId) {
        // Row style setting, not relevant in this example.
        if (propertyId == null)
            return "green"; // Will not actually be visible

        int row = ((Integer)itemId).intValue();
        int col = Integer.parseInt((String)propertyId);

        // The first column.
        if (col == 0)
            return "rowheader";

        // Other cells.
        if ((row+col)%2 == 0)
            return "black";
        else
            return "white";
```

```
        }
});
```

You can then style the cells, for example, as follows:

```css
/* Center the text in header. */
.v-table-header-cell {
    text-align: center;
}

/* Basic style for all cells. */
.v-table-checkerboard .v-table-cell-content {
    text-align: center;
    vertical-align: middle;
    padding-top: 12px;
    width: 20px;
    height: 28px;
}

/* Style specifically for the row header cells. */
.v-table-cell-content-rowheader {
 background: #E7EDF3
     url(../default/table/img/header-bg.png) repeat-x scroll 0 0;
}

/* Style specifically for the "white" cells. */
.v-table-cell-content-white {
    background: white;
    color: black;
}

/* Style specifically for the "black" cells. */
.v-table-cell-content-black {
    background: black;
    color: white;
}
```

The table will look as shown in Figure 5.55, "Cell Style Generator
for a Table".

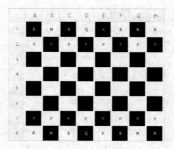

Figure 5.55. Cell Style Generator for a Table

5.16. Tree

The **Tree** component allows a natural way to represent data that has hierarchical relationships, such as filesystems or message threads. The **Tree** component in Vaadin works much like the tree components of most modern desktop user interface toolkits, for example in directory browsing.

The typical use of the **Tree** component is for displaying a hierachical menu, like a menu on the left side of the screen, as in Figure 5.56, "A **Tree** Component as a Menu", or for displaying filesystems or other hierarchical datasets. The *menu* style makes the appearance of the tree more suitable for this purpose.

```
final Object[][] planets = new Object[][]{
        new Object[]{"Mercury"},
        new Object[]{"Venus"},
        new Object[]{"Earth", "The Moon"},
        new Object[]{"Mars", "Phobos", "Deimos"},
        new Object[]{"Jupiter", "Io", "Europa", "Ganymedes",
                                "Callisto"},
        new Object[]{"Saturn",  "Titan", "Tethys", "Dione",
                                "Rhea", "Iapetus"},
        new Object[]{"Uranus",  "Miranda", "Ariel", "Umbriel",
                                "Titania", "Oberon"},
        new Object[]{"Neptune", "Triton", "Proteus", "Nereid",
                                "Larissa"}};

Tree tree = new Tree("The Planets and Major Moons");

/* Add planets as root items in the tree. */
for (int i=0; i<planets.length; i++) {
    String planet = (String) (planets[i][0]);
    tree.addItem(planet);
```

```
        if (planets[i].length == 1) {
            // The planet has no moons so make it a leaf.
            tree.setChildrenAllowed(planet, false);
        } else {
            // Add children (moons) under the planets.
            for (int j=1; j<planets[i].length; j++) {
                String moon = (String) planets[i][j];

                // Add the item as a regular item.
                tree.addItem(moon);

                // Set it to be a child.
                tree.setParent(moon, planet);

                // Make the moons look like leaves.
                tree.setChildrenAllowed(moon, false);
            }

            // Expand the subtree.
            tree.expandItemsRecursively(planet);
        }
    }

main.addComponent(tree);
```

Figure 5.56, "A **Tree** Component as a Menu" below shows the tree from the code example in a practical situation.

You can read or set the currently selected item by the value property of the **Tree** component, that is, with getValue() and setValue(). When the user clicks an item on a tree, the tree will receive an **ValueChangeEvent**, which you can catch with a **ValueChangeListener**. To receive the event immediately after the click, you need to set the tree as **setImmediate(true)**.

The **Tree** component uses **Container** data sources much like the **Table** component, with the addition that it also utilizes hierarchy information maintained by a **HierarchicalContainer**. The contained items can be of any item type supported by the container. The default container and its addItem() assume that the items are strings and the string value is used as the item ID.

5.17. MenuBar

The **MenuBar** component allows creating horizontal dropdown menus, much like the main menu in desktop applications.

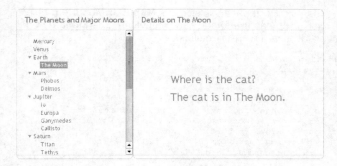

Figure 5.56. A Tree Component as a Menu

```
// Create a menu bar
final MenuBar menubar = new MenuBar();
main.addComponent(menubar);
```

You insert the top-level menu items to a **MenuBar** object with the addItem() method. It takes a string label, an icon resource, and a command as its parameters. The icon and command are not required and can be *null*.

```
MenuBar.MenuItem beverages =
        menubar.addItem("Beverages", null, null);
```

The command is called when the user clicks the item. A menu command is a class that implements the **MenuBar.Command** interface.

```
// A feedback component
final Label selection = new Label("-");
main.addComponent(selection);

// Define a common menu command for all the menu items.
MenuBar.Command mycommand = new MenuBar.Command() {
    public void menuSelected(MenuItem selectedItem) {
        selection.setValue("Ordered a " +
                           selectedItem.getText() +
                           " from menu.");
    }
};
```

The `addItem()` method returns a **MenuBar.MenuItem** object, which you can use to add sub-menu items. The **MenuItem** has an identical `addItem()` method.

```
// Put some items in the menu hierarchically
MenuBar.MenuItem beverages =
    menubar.addItem("Beverages", null, null);
MenuBar.MenuItem hot_beverages =
    beverages.addItem("Hot", null, null);
hot_beverages.addItem("Tea", null, mycommand);
hot_beverages.addItem("Coffee", null, mycommand);
MenuBar.MenuItem cold_beverages =
    beverages.addItem("Cold", null, null);
cold_beverages.addItem("Milk", null, mycommand);

// Another top-level item
MenuBar.MenuItem snacks =
    menubar.addItem("Snacks", null, null);
snacks.addItem("Weisswurst", null, mycommand);
snacks.addItem("Salami", null, mycommand);

// Yet another top-level item
MenuBar.MenuItem services =
    menubar.addItem("Services", null, null);
services.addItem("Car Service", null, mycommand);
```

The menu will look as follows:

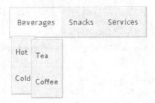

Figure 5.57. Menu Bar

CSS Style Rules

```
.v-menubar { }
.gwt-MenuItem {}
.gwt-MenuItem-selected {}
```

The menu bar has the overall style name `.v-menubar`. Each menu item has `.gwt-MenuItem` style normally and `.gwt-MenuItem-selected` when the item is selected.

5.18. Embedded

The **Embedded** component allows displaying embedded media objects, such as images, animations, or any embeddable media type supported by the browser. The contents of an **Embedded** component are managed as *resources*. For documentation on resources, see Section 4.3, "Referencing Resources".

The following example displays an image from the same Java package as the class itself using the class loader.

```
Embedded image = new Embedded("Yes, logo:",
    new ClassResource("vaadin-logo.png", this));
main.addComponent(image);
```

Yes, logo:

Figure 5.58. Embedded Image

The **Embedded** component supports several different content types, which are rendered differently in HTML. You can set the content type with `setType()`, although for images, as in the above example, the type is determined automatically.

Embedded.TYPE_OBJECT
> The default embedded type, allows embedding certain file types inside HTML `<object>` and `<embed>` elements.

Embedded.TYPE_IMAGE
> Embeds an image inside a HTML `<img>` element.

Embedded.TYPE_BROWSER
> Embeds a browser frame inside a HTML `<iframe>` element.

5.18.1. Embedded Objects

The *Embedded.TYPE_OBJECT* is the default and most generic embedded type, which allows embedding media objects inside HTML `<object>` and `<embed>` elements. You need define the MIME type for the object type.

Currently, only Shockwave Flash animations are supported (MIME type `application/x-shockwave-flash`).

```
// Create a Shockware Flash resource
final ClassResource flashResource =
    new ClassResource("itmill_spin.swf", getApplication());

// Display the resource in a Embedded compoant
final Embedded embedded =
    new Embedded("Embedded Caption", flashResource);

// This is the default type, but we set it anyway.
embedded.setType(Embedded.TYPE_OBJECT);

// This is recorgnized automatically, but set it anyway.
embedded.setMimeType("application/x-shockwave-flash");
```

You can set object parameters with `setParameter()`, which takes a parameter's name and value as strings. The object parameters are included in the HTML as `<param>` elements.

5.18.2. Embedded Images

Images are embedded with the type *Embedded.TYPE_IMAGE*, although you do not normally need to set the type explicitly, as it is recognized automatically from the MIME type of the resource, as in the example above.

Embedded component has by default undefined size in both directions, so it will automatically fit the size of the embedded image. If you want scrolling with scroll bars, you can put the **Embedded** inside a **Panel** that has a defined size to enable scrolling, as described in Section 6.6.1, "Scrolling the Panel Content". You can also give it a defined size and set the `overflow: auto` CSS property for it in a theme.

You can find another example of displaying an image from **FileResource** in Section 5.19, "**Upload**". Another example, in Section 4.3.5, "Stream Resources", shows how you can generate the content of an **Embedded** component dynamically using a **StreamResource**.

If you have a dynamically generated image, for example with a **StreamResource**, and the data changes, you need to reload the image in the browser. Because of how caching is handled in some browsers, you are best off by renaming the filename of the resource with a unique name, such as one including a timestamp. You should set cache time to zero with `setCacheTime()` for the resource object when you create it.

```
// Create the stream resource with some initial filename.
StreamResource imageResource =
    new StreamResource(imageSource, "initial-filename.png",
                       getApplication());

// Instruct browser not to cache the image.
imageResource.setCacheTime(0);

// Display the image in an Embedded component.
Embedded embedded = new Embedded("", imageResource);
```

When refreshing, you also need to call `requestRepaint()` for the **Embedded** object.

```
// This needs to be done, but is not sufficient.
embedded.requestRepaint();

// Generate a filename with a timestamp.
SimpleDateFormat df = new SimpleDateFormat("yyyyMMddHHmmssSSS");
String filename = "myfilename-" + df.format(new Date()) + ".png";

// Replace the filename in the resource.
imageResource.setFilename(makeImageFilename());
```

You can find more detailed information about the **StreamResource** in Section 4.3.5, "Stream Resources".

5.18.3. Browser Frames

The browser frame type allows you to embed external content inside an HTML `<iframe>` element. You can refer to a URL with an **ExternalResource** object. URLs are given with the standard Java **URL** class.

```
URL url = new URL("http://dev.vaadin.com/");
Embedded browser = new Embedded("", new ExternalResource(url));
browser.setType(Embedded.TYPE_BROWSER);
main.addComponent(browser);
```

5.19. Upload

The **Upload** component allows a user to upload files to the server. It displays a file name entry box, a file selection button, and an upload submit button. The user can either write the filename in the text area or click the **Browse** button to select a file. After the file is selected, the user sends the file by pressing the upload submit button.

```
// Create the Upload component.
Upload upload = new Upload("Upload the file here", this);
```

Figure 5.59. Upload Component

You can set the text of the upload button with `setButtonCaption()`, as in the example above, but it is difficult to change the look of the **Browse** button. This is a security feature of web browsers. The language of the **Browse** button is determined by the browser, so if you wish to have the language of the **Upload** component consistent, you will have to use the same language in your application.

```
upload.setButtonCaption("Upload Now");
```

The uploaded files are typically stored as files in a file system, in a database, or as temporary objects in memory. The upload component writes the received data to an **java.io.OutputStream** so you have plenty of freedom in how you can process the upload content.

To use the **Upload** component, you need to define a class that implements the **Upload.Receiver** interface. The `receiveUpload()` method is called when the user clicks the submit button. The method must return an **OutputStream**. To do this, it typically creates a **File** or a memory buffer where the stream is written. The method gets the file name and MIME type of the file, as reported by the browser.

When an upload is finished, successfully or unsuccessfully, the **Upload** component will emit the **Upload.FinishedEvent** event. To receive it, you need to implement the **Upload.FinishedListener** interface, and register the listening object in the **Upload** component. The event object will also include the file name, MIME type,

---

and length of the file. Notice that the more specific **Upload.Faile-dEvent** and **Upload.SucceededEvent** events will be called in the cases where the upload failed or succeeded, respectively.

The following example allows uploading images to /tmp/uploads directory in (UNIX) filesystem (the directory must exist or the upload fails). The component displays the last uploaded image in an **Embedded** component.

```
// Create the upload with a caption and set receiver later
Upload upload = new Upload("Upload Image Here", null);
upload.setButtonCaption("Start Upload");

// Put the upload component in a panel
Panel panel = new Panel("Cool Image Storage");
panel.addComponent(upload);

// Show uploaded file in this placeholder
final Embedded image = new Embedded("Uploaded Image");
image.setVisible(false);
panel.addComponent(image);

// Implement both receiver that saves upload in a file and
// listener for successful upload
class ImageUploader implements Receiver, SucceededListener {
    public File file;

    public OutputStream receiveUpload(String filename,
                                      String mimeType) {
        // Create upload stream
        FileOutputStream fos = null; // Stream to write to
        try {
            // Open the file for writing.
            file = new File("/tmp/uploads/" + filename);
            fos = new FileOutputStream(file);
        } catch (final java.io.FileNotFoundException e) {
            Notification.show(
                    "Could not open file<br/>", e.getMessage(),
                    Notification.TYPE_ERROR_MESSAGE);
            return null;
        }
        return fos; // Return the output stream to write to
    }

    public void uploadSucceeded(SucceededEvent event) {
        // Show the uploaded file in the image viewer
        image.setVisible(true);
        image.setSource(new FileResource(file,
                                         getApplication())));
    }
};
final ImageUploader uploader = new ImageUploader();
upload.setReceiver(uploader);
upload.addListener(uploader);
```

The example does not check the type of the uploaded files in any way, which will cause an error if the content is anything else but an image. The program also assumes that the MIME type of the file is resolved correctly based on the file name extension. After uploading an image, the component will look as show in Figure 5.60, "Image Upload Example" below.

Cool Image Storage

Figure 5.60. Image Upload Example

5.20. ProgressIndicator

The **ProgressIndicator** component allows displaying the progress of a task graphically. The progress is given as a floating-point value between 0.0 and 1.0.

Figure 5.61. The Progress Indicator Component

The progress indicator polls the server for updates for its value. If the value has changed, the progress is updated. Notice that the user application does not have to handle any polling event, but updating the component is done automatically.

Creating a progress indicator is just like with any other component. You can give the initial progress value as a parameter for the constructor. The default polling frequency is 1000 milliseconds (one second), but you can set some other interval with the `set-PollingInterval()` method.

```
// Create the indicator
final ProgressIndicator indicator =
        new ProgressIndicator(new Float(0.0));
main.addComponent(indicator);

// Set polling frequency to 0.5 seconds.
indicator.setPollingInterval(500);
```

CSS Style Rules

```
/* Base element. */
.v-progressindicator {}

/* Progress indication element on top of the base. */
.v-progressindicator div {}
```

The default style for the progress indicator uses an animated GIF image (`img/base.gif`) as the base background for the component. The progress is a `<div>` element inside the base. When the progress element grows, it covers more and more of the base background. By default, the graphic of the progress element is defined in `img/progress.png` under the default style directory. See `com.vaadin.terminal.gwt/public/default/progressindicator/progressindicator.css`.

5.20.1. Doing Heavy Computation

The progress indicator is often used to display the progress of a heavy server-side computation task. In the following example, we create a thread in the server to do some "heavy work". All the thread needs to do is to set the value of the progress indicator with `set-Value()` and the current progress is displayed automatically when the browser polls the server.

```java
// Create an indicator that makes you look busy
final ProgressIndicator indicator =
        new ProgressIndicator(new Float(0.0));
main.addComponent(indicator);

// Set polling frequency to 0.5 seconds.
indicator.setPollingInterval(500);

// Add a button to start working
final Button button = new Button("Click to start");
main.addComponent(button);

// Another thread to do some work
class WorkThread extends Thread {
    public void run () {
        double current = 0.0;
        while (true) {
            // Do some "heavy work"
            try {
                sleep(50); // Sleep for 50 milliseconds
            } catch (InterruptedException) {}

            // Show that you have made some progress:
            // grow the progress value until it reaches 1.0.
            current += 0.01;
            if (current>1.0)
                indicator.setValue(new Float(1.0));
            else
                indicator.setValue(new Float(current));

            // After all the "work" has been done for a while,
            // take a break.
            if (current > 1.2) {
                // Restore the state to initial.
                indicator.setValue(new Float(0.0));
                button.setVisible(true);
                break;
            }
        }
    }
}

// Clicking the button creates and runs a work thread
button.addListener(new Button.ClickListener() {
    public void buttonClick(ClickEvent event) {
        final WorkThread thread = new WorkThread();
        thread.start();

        // The button hides until the work is done.
        button.setVisible(false);
    }
});
```

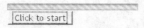

Figure 5.62. Starting Heavy Work

5.21. Slider

The **Slider** is a vertical or horizontal bar that allows setting a numeric value within a defined range by dragging a bar handle with the mouse. The value is shown when dragging the handle.

Slider has a number of different constructors that take a combination of the caption, *minimum* and *maximum* value, *resolution*, and the *orientation* of the slider.

```
// Create a vertical slider
final Slider vertslider = new Slider(1, 100);
vertslider.setOrientation(Slider.ORIENTATION_VERTICAL);
```

Slider Properties

min
> Minimum value of the slider range. The default is 0.0.

max
> Maximum value of the slider range. The default is 100.0.

resolution
> The number of digits after the decimal point. The default is 0.

orientation
> The orientation can be either horizontal (`Slider.ORIENTA-TION_HORIZONTAL`) or vertical (`Slider.ORIENTATION_VER-TICAL`). The default is horizontal.

As the **Slider** is a field component, you can handle value changes with a **ValueChangeListener**. The value of the **Slider** field is a **Double** object.

```
// Shows the value of the vertical slider
final Label vertvalue = new Label();
vertvalue.setSizeUndefined();

// Handle changes in slider value.
vertslider.addListener(new Property.ValueChangeListener() {
```

```
    public void valueChange(ValueChangeEvent event) {
        double value = (Double) vertslider.getValue();

        // Use the value
        box.setHeight((float) value, Sizeable.UNITS_PERCENTAGE);
        vertvalue.setValue(String.valueOf(value));
    }
});

// The slider has to be immediate to send the changes
// immediately after the user drags the handle.
vertslider.setImmediate(true);
```

You can set the value with the `setValue()` method defined in **Slider** that takes the value as a native double value. The setter can throw a **ValueOutOfBoundsException**, which you must handle.

```
// Set the initial value. This has to be set after the
// listener is added if we want the listener to handle
// also this value change.
try {
 vertslider.setValue(50.0);
} catch (ValueOutOfBoundsException e) {
}
```

Alternatively, you can use the regular `setValue(Object)`, which does not do bounds checking.

Figure 5.63, "The **Slider** Component" shows both vertical (from the code examples) and horizontal sliders that control the size of a box. The slider values are displayed also in separate labels.

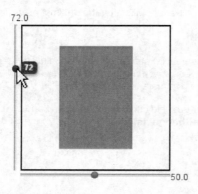

Figure 5.63. The Slider Component

CSS Style Rules

```
.v-slider {}
.v-slider-base {}
.v-slider-handle {}
```

The enclosing style for the **Slider** is v-slider. The slider bar has style v-slider-base. Even though the handle is higher (for horizontal slider) or wider (for vertical slider) than the bar, the handle element is nevertheless contained within the slider bar element. The appearance of the handle comes from a background image defined in the *background* CSS property.

5.22. LoginForm

The **LoginForm** component is a login form that allows a password manager in the web browser to remember and later automatically fill in the username and password. This commonly used functionality does not work with regular Vaadin components and is a common problem with Ajax applications.

```
// A wrapper with a caption for the login form
Panel loginPanel = new Panel("Login");
loginPanel.setWidth("250px");

LoginForm login = new LoginForm();
loginPanel.addComponent(login);
```

The resulting form is shown in Figure 5.64, "The **LoginForm** Component".

Figure 5.64. The LoginForm Component

The **LoginForm** uses static HTML inside an `iframe` element to enable the functionality. The component provides a default implementation of the static HTML; if you want to change the layout, you need to reimplement the `getLoginHtml()` method.

The login form has by default 100%x100% relative size, taking all the space given by the containing layout. You may set the size to fixed values, but not undefined in either direction, because the contained `iframe` element takes all of this size (it also has 100%x100% size). How the actual form uses this space depends on the static HTML. Giving too little space for the form results in scroll bars.

5.22.1. Customizing LoginForm

Customization of the login form is necessary, for example, if you need to change the layout or internationalize the form. Customization is done by overriding the `getLoginHtml()` method, which returns the static HTML of the form. The customization layer is very "unvaadin"-like, and at best hack-ish, but dictated by the form management in browsers.

Let us look at a custom login form that lets the user of the form to give the field captions:

```
class MyLoginForm extends LoginForm {
    String usernameCaption;
    String passwordCaption;
    String submitCaption;

    public MyLoginForm(String usernameCaption,
            String passwordCaption, String submitCaption) {
        this.usernameCaption = usernameCaption;
        this.passwordCaption = passwordCaption;
        this.submitCaption  = submitCaption;
    }
```

Then we override the method that generates the static HTML for the form:

```
@Override
protected byte[] getLoginHTML() {
    // Application URI needed for submitting form
    String appUri = getApplication().getURL().toString()
            + getWindow().getName() + "/";

    String x, h, b; // XML header, HTML head and body
```

The XML header is needed for the validity of the XHTML page:

```
x = "<!DOCTYPE html PUBLIC \"-//W3C//DTD "
  + "XHTML 1.0 Transitional//EN\" "
  + "\"http://www.w3.org/TR/xhtml1/"
  + "DTD/xhtml1-transitional.dtd\">\n";
```

Notice that it is important to have a newline (\n) at the end of the XML header line.

The HTML header part contains JavaScript definitions that handle submitting the form data. It also copies the style sheet references from the parent window.

```
h = "<head><script type='text/javascript'>"
  + "var setTarget = function() {"
  + "  var uri = '" + appUri + "loginHandler';"
  + "  var f = document.getElementById('loginf');"
  + "  document.forms[0].action = uri;"
  + "  document.forms[0].username.focus();"
  + "};"
  + ""
  + "var styles = window.parent.document.styleSheets;"
  + "for(var j = 0; j < styles.length; j++) {\n"
  + "  if(styles[j].href) {"
  + "    var stylesheet = document.createElement('link');\n"
  + "    stylesheet.setAttribute('rel', 'stylesheet');\n"
  + "    stylesheet.setAttribute('type', 'text/css');\n"
  + "    stylesheet.setAttribute('href', styles[j].href);\n"
  + "    document.getElementsByTagName('head')[0]"
  + "             .appendChild(stylesheet);\n"
  + "  }"
  + "}\n"
  + "function submitOnEnter(e) {"
  + "  var keycode = e.keyCode || e.which;"
  + "  if (keycode == 13) {document.forms[0].submit();}"
  + "}\n"
  + "</script>"
  + "</head>";
```

The HTML body element contains the actual form. Notice that it is contained within an inner `iframe`. The form and the button must have JavaScript calls to submit the form content.

```
b = "<body onload='setTarget();'"
  + "  style='margin:0;padding:0; background:transparent;'"
  + "  class='"
  + ApplicationConnection.GENERATED_BODY_CLASSNAME + "'>"
  + "<div class='v-app v-app-loginpage'"
  + "     style='background:transparent;'>"
  + "<iframe name='logintarget' style='width:0;height:0;"
  + "border:0;margin:0;padding:0;'></iframe>"
  + "<form id='loginf' target='logintarget'"
  + "      onkeypress='submitOnEnter(event)'"
  + "      method='post'>"
  + "<table>"
  + "<tr><td>" + usernameCaption + "</td>"
```

```
+   "<td><input class='v-textfield' style='display:block;'"
+   "          type='text' name='username'></td></tr>"
+ "<tr><td>" + passwordCaption + "</td>"
+   "    <td><input class='v-textfield'"
+   "          style='display:block;' type='password'"
+   "          name='password'></td></tr>"
+ "</table>"
+ "<div>"
+ "<div onclick='document.forms[0].submit();'"
+ "     tabindex='0' class='v-button' role='button'>"
+ "<span class='v-button-wrap'>"
+ "<span class='v-button-caption'>"
+ submitCaption + "</span>"
+ "</span></div></div></form></div></body>";
```

Then combine and return the page as a byte array.

```
    return (x + "<html>" + h + b + "</html>").getBytes();
}
```

We can use the custom login form as follows:

```
MyLoginForm loginForm = new MyLoginForm("Name of the User",
    "A passing word", "Login Me Now");
```

The customized **LoginForm** is shown in Figure 5.65, "Customizing the **LoginForm**".

Figure 5.65. Customizing the LoginForm

Styling with CSS

```
.v-customcomponent {}
.v-customcomponent .v-embedded {}
.v-app-loginpage {}
.v-app-loginpage .v-textfield {}
.v-app-loginpage .v-button  {}
```

The **LoginForm** component is a purely server-side component that extends **CustomComponent** and therefore has a v-custom-component base style. If you wish to do any styling for the component, you should give it a custom style name to distinguish it from the regular **CustomComponent**.

The component contains an `iframe` in an element with `v-embedded` style. The other styles are defined in the static HTML code returned by the `getLoginHTML()` method. The default implementation reuses the styles of the **TextField** and **Button** components for the input fields and the button, that is, `v-textfield` and `v-button`. The root element has the same `v-app` style as a regular Vaadin application would have, and an additional `v-app-loginpage` style.

```
...
+ "<div class='v-app v-app-loginpage'
        style=\"background:transparent;\">"
...
+ "<input class='v-textfield' ...
...
+ "<div><input class='v-textfield' ...
...
<div ... class='v-button' role='button'>
```

5.23. Component Composition with Custom-Component

The ease of making new user interface components is one of the core features of Vaadin. Typically, you simply combine existing built-in components to produce composite components. In many applications, such composite components make up the majority of the user interface.

To create a composite component, you need to inherit the **Custom-Component** and call the `setCompositionRoot()` in the constructor to set the *composition root* component. The root component is typically a layout component that contains multiple components.

For example:

```
class MyComposite extends CustomComponent {
    public MyComposite(String message) {
        // A layout structure used for composition
        Panel panel = new Panel("My Custom Component");
        panel.setContent(new VerticalLayout());

        // Compose from multiple components
        Label label = new Label(message);
        label.setSizeUndefined(); // Shrink
        panel.addComponent(label);
        panel.addComponent(new Button("Ok"));

        // Set the size as undefined at all levels
        panel.getContent().setSizeUndefined();
        panel.setSizeUndefined();
        setSizeUndefined();
```

```
            // The composition root MUST be set
            setCompositionRoot(panel);
    }
}
```

Take note of the sizing when trying to make a customcomponent that shrinks to fit the contained components. You have to set the size as undefined at all levels; the sizing of the composite component and the composition root are separate.

You can use the component as follows:

```
MyComposite mycomposite = new MyComposite("Hello");
```

The rendered component is shown in Figure 5.66, "A Custom Composite Component".

Figure 5.66. A Custom Composite Component

You can also inherit any other components, such as layouts, to attain similar composition. Even further, you can create entirely new low-level components, by integrating pure client-side components or by extending the client-side functionality of built-in components. Development of new components is covered in Chapter 11, *Developing New Components*.

Chapter 6

Managing Layout

This edition is a draft. Many new features that will be included in the final version of Vaadin 7 are not yet covered in the draft and some of the content may be outdated. For the most current version, please see the on-line edition available at `http://vaad-in.com/book`.

Ever since the ancient xeroxians invented graphical user interfaces, programmers have wanted to make GUI programming ever easier for themselves. Solutions started simple. When GUIs appeared on PC desktops, practically all screens were of the VGA type and fixed into 640x480 size. Mac or X Window System on UNIX were not much different. Everyone was so happy with such awesome graphics resolutions that they never thought that an application would have to work on a radically different screen size. At worst, screens could only grow, they thought, giving more space for more windows. In the 80s, the idea of having a computer screen in your pocket was simply not realistic. Hence, the GUI APIs allowed placing UI components using screen coordinates. Visual Basic and some other systems provided an easy way for the designer to drag and drop components on a fixed-sized window. One would have thought that at least translators would have complained about the awkwardness of such a solution, but apparently they were not, as non-engineers, heard or at least cared about. At best, engineers could throw at them a resource editor that would allow them to resize the UI components by hand. Such was the spirit back then.

After the web was born, layout design was doomed to change for ever. At first, layout didn't matter much, as everyone was happy with plain headings, paragraphs, and a few hyperlinks here and there. Designers of HTML wanted the pages to run on any screen size. The screen size was actually not pixels but rows and columns of characters, as the baby web was really just hyper*text*, not graphics. That was soon to be changed. The first GUI-based browser, NCSA Mosaic, launched a revolution that culminated in Netscape Navigator. Suddenly, people who had previously been doing advertisement brochures started writing HTML. This meant that layout design had to be easy not just for programmers, but also allow the graphics designer to do his or her job without having to know a thing about programming. The W3C committee designing web standards came up with the CSS (Cascading Style Sheet) specification, which allowed trivial separation of appearance from content. Later versions of HTML followed, XHTML appeared, as did countless other standards.

Page description and markup languages are a wonderful solution for static presentations, such as books and most web pages. Real applications, however, need to have more control. They need to be able to change the state of user interface components and even their layout on the run. This creates a need to separate the presentation from content on exactly the right level.

Thanks to the attack of graphics designers, desktop applications were, when it comes to appearance, far behind web design. Sun Microsystems had come in 1995 with a new programming language, Java, for writing cross-platform desktop applications. Java's original graphical user interface toolkit, AWT (Abstract Windowing Toolkit), was designed to work on multiple operating systems as well as embedded in web browsers. One of the special aspects of AWT was the layout manager, which allowed user interface components to be flexible, growing and shrinking as needed. This made it possible for the user to resize the windows of an application flexibly and also served the needs of localization, as text strings were not limited to some fixed size in pixels. It became even possible to resize the pixel size of fonts, and the rest of the layout adapted to the new size.

Layout management of Vaadin is a direct successor of the web-based concept for separation of content and appearance and of the Java AWT solution for binding the layout and user interface components into objects in programs. Vaadin layout components allow you to position your UI components on the screen in a hierarchical fashion, much like in conventional Java UI toolkits such as AWT, Swing, or SWT. In addition, you can approach the layout from the direction of the web with the **CustomLayout** component, which you can use to write your layout as a template in XHTML that provides locations of any contained components.

The moral of the story is that, because Vaadin is intended for web applications, appearance is of high importance. The solutions have to be the best of both worlds and satisfy artists of both kind: code and graphics. On the API side, the layout is controlled by UI components, particularly the layout components. On the visual side, it is controlled by themes. Themes can contain any HTML, CSS, and JavaScript that you or your web artists create to make people feel good about your software.

6.1. Overview

The user interface components in Vaadin can roughly be divided in two groups: components that the user can interact with and layout components for placing the other components to specific places in the user interface. The layout components are identical in their purpose to layout managers in regular desktop frameworks for Java and you can use plain Java to accomplish sophisticated component layouting.

You start by creating a root layout for the main window, unless you use the default, and then add the other layout components hierarchically, and finally the interaction components as the leaves of the component tree.

```
// Set the root layout (VerticalLayout is actually the default).
VerticalLayout root = new VerticalLayout();
setContent(root);

// Add the topmost component.
root.addComponent(new Label("The Ultimate Cat Finder"));

// Add a horizontal layout for the bottom part.
HorizontalLayout bottom = new HorizontalLayout();
root.addComponent(bottom);

bottom.addComponent(new Tree("Major Planets and Their Moons"));
bottom.addComponent(new Panel());
...
```

You will usually need to tune the layout components a bit by setting sizes, expansion ratios, alignments, spacings, and so on. The general settings are described in Section 6.13, "Layout Formatting", while the layout component specific settings are described in connection with the component.

Layouts are coupled with themes that specify various layout features, such as backgrounds, borders, text alignment, and so on. Definition and use of themes is described in Chapter 8, *Themes*

You can see the finished version of the above example in Figure 6.1, "Layout Example".

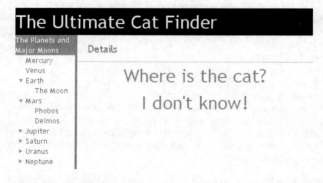

Figure 6.1. Layout Example

The alternative for using layout components is to use the special **CustomLayout** that allows using HTML templates. This way, you can let the web page designers take responsibility of component layouting using their own set of tools. What you lose is the ability to manage the layout dynamically.

The Visual Editor

While you can always program the layout by hand, the Vaadin plugin for the Eclipse IDE includes a visual (WYSIWYG) editor that you can use to create user interfaces visually. The editor generates the code that creates the user interface and is useful for rapid application development and prototyping. It is especially helpful when you are still learning the framework, as the generated code, which is designed to be as reusable as possible, also works as an example of how you create user interfaces with Vaadin. You can find more about the editor in Chapter 7, *Visual User Interface Design with Eclipse*.

6.2. Window and Panel Root Layout

The **Window** and its superclass **Panel** have a single root layout component. The component is usually a **Layout**, but any **ComponentContainer** is allowed. When you create the components, they create a default root layout, usually **VerticalLayout**, but you can change it with the **setContent()** method.

```
Window main = new Window("My Application");
setMainWindow(main);

// Set another root layout for the main window.
TabSheet tabsheet = new TabSheet();
main.setContent(tabsheet);
```

The size of the root layout is the default size of the particular layout component, for example, a **VerticalLayout** has 100% width and undefined height by default. In many applications, you want to use the full area of the browser view. Setting the components contained inside the root layout to full size is not enough, and would actually lead to an invalid state if the height of the root layout is undefined.

```
// This is actually the default.
main.setContent(new VerticalLayout());

// Set the size of the root layout to full width and height.
main.getContent().setSizeFull();

// Add a title area on top of the screen. This takes just the
// vertical space it needs.
main.addComponent(new Label("My Application"));

// Add a menu-view area that takes rest of the vertical space.
HorizontalLayout menuview = new HorizontalLayout();
menuview.setSizeFull();
main.addComponent(menuview);
```

See Section 6.13.1, "Layout Size" for more information about setting layout sizes.

6.3. VerticalLayout and HorizontalLayout

VerticalLayout and **HorizontalLayout** are containers for laying components out either vertically or horizontally, respectively. These are the two most important layout components in Vaadin and some components, such as **Window** and **Panel**, have a **VerticalLayout** as the root layout, which you can set with setContent().

Typical use of the layouts goes as follows:

```
VerticalLayout vertical = new VerticalLayout ();
vertical.addComponent(new TextField("Name"));
vertical.addComponent(new TextField("Street address"));
vertical.addComponent(new TextField("Postal code"));
main.addComponent(vertical);
```

In these layouts, component captions are placed above the component. The layout will look on screen as follows:

Name

Street address

Postal code

Using **HorizontalLayout** gives the following layout:

Name   Street address   Postal code

The layouts can have spacing between the horizontal or vertical cells, defined with `setSpacing()`, as described in Section 6.13.3, "Layout Cell Spacing". The contained components can be aligned within their cells with `setComponentAlignment()`, as described in Section 6.13.2, "Layout Cell Alignment".

6.3.1. Sizing Contained Components

The components contained within an ordered layout can be laid out in a number of different ways depending on how you specify their height or width in the primary direction of the layout component.

Figure 6.2. Component Widths in HorizontalLayout

Figure 6.2, "Component Widths in **HorizontalLayout**" above gives a summary of the sizing options for a **HorizontalLayout**. The figure is broken down in the following subsections.

Layout with Undefined Size

If a **VerticalLayout** has undefined height or **HorizontalLayout** undefined width, the layout will shrink to fit the contained components so that there is no extra space between them.

```
HorizontalLayout fittingLayout = new HorizontalLayout();
fittingLayout.setWidth(Sizeable.SIZE_UNDEFINED, 0); // Default
fittingLayout.addComponent(new Button("Small"));
fittingLayout.addComponent(new Button("Medium-sized"));
fittingLayout.addComponent(new Button("Quite a big component"));
parentLayout.addComponent(fittingLayout);
```

The both layouts actually have undefined height by default and **HorizontalLayout** has also undefined width, while **VerticalLayout** has 100% relative width.

If such a vertical layout with undefined height continues below the bottom of a window (a **Window** object), the window will pop up a vertical scroll bar on the right side of the window area. This way, you get a "web page". The same applies to **Panel**.

A layout that contains components with percentual size must have a defined size!

If a layout has undefined size and a contained component has, say, 100% size, the component would fill the space given by the layout, while the layout would shrink to fit the space taken by the component, which would be a paradox. This requirement holds for height and width separately. The debug mode allows detecting such invalid cases; see Section 12.3.1, "Debug Mode".

An exception to the above rule is a case where you have a layout with undefined size that contains a component with a fixed or undefined size together with one or more components with relative size. In this case, the contained component with fixed (or undefined) size in a sense defines the size of the containing layout, removing the paradox. That size is then used for the relatively sized components.

The technique can be used to define the width of a **VerticalLayout** or the height of a **HorizontalLayout**.

```
// Vertical layout would normally have 100% width
VerticalLayout vertical = new VerticalLayout();

// Shrink to fit the width of contained components
vertical.setWidth(Sizeable.SIZE_UNDEFINED, 0);

// Label has normally 100% width, but we set it as
// undefined so that it will take only the needed space
Label label =
    new Label("\u2190 The VerticalLayout shrinks to fit "+
              "the width of this Label \u2192");
label.setWidth(Sizeable.SIZE_UNDEFINED, 0);
vertical.addComponent(label);
```

```
// Button has undefined width by default
Button butt = new Button("\u2190 This Button takes 100% "+
                         "of the width \u2192");
butt.setWidth("100%");
vertical.addComponent(butt);
```

This is a VerticalLayout with two components

← The VerticalLayout shrinks to fit the width of this Label →

← **This Button takes 100% of the width** →

Figure 6.3. Defining the Size with a Component

Layout with Defined Size

If you set a **HorizontalLayout** to a defined size horizontally or a
VerticalLayout vertically, and there is space left over from the
contained components, the extra space is distributed equally
between the component cells. The components are aligned within
these cells according to their alignment setting, top left by default,
as in the example below.

```
fixedLayout.setWidth("400px");
```

Small   Medium-sized   Quite a big component

Using percentual sizes for components contained in a layout requires answering the question, "Percentage of what?" There is no
sensible default answer for this question in the current implementation of the layouts, so in practice, you may not define "100%" size
alone.

Expanding Components

Often, you want to have one component that takes all the available
space left over from other components. You need to set its size as
100% and set it as *expanding* with setExpandRatio(). The second
parameter for the method is an expansion ratio, which is relevant
if there are more than one expanding component, but its value is
irrelevant for a single expanding component.

```
HorizontalLayout layout = new HorizontalLayout();
layout.setWidth("400px");
```

```
// These buttons take the minimum size.
layout.addComponent(new Button("Small"));
layout.addComponent(new Button("Medium-sized"));

// This button will expand.
Button expandButton = new Button("Expanding component");

// Use 100% of the expansion cell's width.
expandButton.setWidth("100%");

// The component must be added to layout before setting
 the ratio.
layout.addComponent(expandButton);

// Set the component's cell to expand.
layout.setExpandRatio(expandButton, 1.0f);

parentLayout.addComponent(layout);
```

| Small | Medium-sized | Expanding component |

Notice that you must call setExpandRatio() *after* addComponent(), because the layout can not operate on an component that it doesn't (yet) include.

Expand Ratios

If you specify an expand ratio for multiple components, they will all try to use the available space according to the ratio.

```
HorizontalLayout layout = new HorizontalLayout();
layout.setWidth("400px");

// Create three equally expanding components.
String[] captions = { "Small", "Medium-sized",
                      "Quite a big component" };
for (int i = 1; i <= 3; i++) {
    Button button = new Button(captions[i-1]);
    button.setWidth("100%");
    layout.addComponent(button);

    // Have uniform 1:1:1 expand ratio.
    layout.setExpandRatio(button, 1.0f);
}
```

| Small | Medium-sized | Quite a big compone|

As the example used the same ratio for all components, the ones with more content may have the content cut. Below, we use differing ratios:

```
// Expand ratios for the components are 1:2:3.
layout.setExpandRatio(button, i * 1.0f);
```

| Small | Medium-sized | Quite a big component |

If the size of the expanding components is defined as a percentage (typically "100%"), the ratio is calculated from the *overall* space available for the relatively sized components. For example, if you have a 100 pixels wide layout with two cells with 1.0 and 4.0 respective expansion ratios, and both the components in the layout are set as `setWidth("100%")`, the cells will have respective widths of 20 and 80 pixels, regardless of the minimum size of the components.

However, if the size of the contained components is undefined or fixed, the expansion ratio is of the *excess* available space. In this case, it is the excess space that expands, not the components.

```
for (int i = 1; i <= 3; i++) {
    // Button with undefined size.
    Button button = new Button(captions[i - 1]);

    layout4.addComponent(button);

    // Expand ratios are 1:2:3.
    layout4.setExpandRatio(button, i * 1.0f);
}
```

| Small | Medium-sized | Quite a big component |

It is not meaningful to combine expanding components with percentually defined size and components with fixed or undefined size. Such combination can lead to a very unexpected size for the percentually sized components.

Percentage of Cells

A percentual size of a component defines the size of the component *within its cell*. Usually, you use "100%", but a smaller percentage or a fixed size (smaller than the cell size) will leave an empty space in the cell and align the component within the cell according to its alignment setting, top left by default.

```
HorizontalLayout layout50 = new HorizontalLayout();
layout50.setWidth("400px");

String[] captions1 = { "Small 50%", "Medium 50%",
                       "Quite a big 50%" };
for (int i = 1; i <= 3; i++) {
    Button button = new Button(captions1[i-1]);
    button.setWidth("50%");
    layout50.addComponent(button);

    // Expand ratios for the components are 1:2:3.
    layout50.setExpandRatio(button, i * 1.0f);
}
parentLayout.addComponent(layout50);
```

6.4. GridLayout

GridLayout container lays components out on a grid, defined by the number of columns and rows. The columns and rows of the grid serve as coordinates that are used for laying out components on the grid. Each component can use multiple cells from the grid, defined as an area (x1,y1,x2,y2), although they typically take up only a single grid cell.

The grid layout maintains a cursor for adding components in left-to-right, top-to-bottom order. If the cursor goes past the bottom-right corner, it will automatically extend the grid downwards by adding a new row.

The following example demonstrates the use of **GridLayout**. The addComponent takes a component and optional coordinates. The coordinates can be given for a single cell or for an area in x,y (column,row) order. The coordinate values have a base value of 0. If coordinates are not given, the cursor will be used.

```
// Create a 4 by 4 grid layout.
GridLayout grid = new GridLayout(4, 4);
grid.addStyleName("example-gridlayout");

// Fill out the first row using the cursor.
grid.addComponent(new Button("R/C 1"));
for (int i = 0; i < 3; i++) {
    grid.addComponent(new Button("Col " + (grid.getCursorX() + 1)));
}

// Fill out the first column using coordinates.
for (int i = 1; i < 4; i++) {
    grid.addComponent(new Button("Row " + i), 0, i);
}

// Add some components of various shapes.
grid.addComponent(new Button("3x1 button"), 1, 1, 3, 1);
grid.addComponent(new Label("1x2 cell"), 1, 2, 1, 3);
InlineDateField date = new InlineDateField("A 2x2 date field");
date.setResolution(DateField.RESOLUTION_DAY);
grid.addComponent(date, 2, 2, 3, 3);
```

The resulting layout will look as follows. The borders have been made visible to illustrate the layout cells.

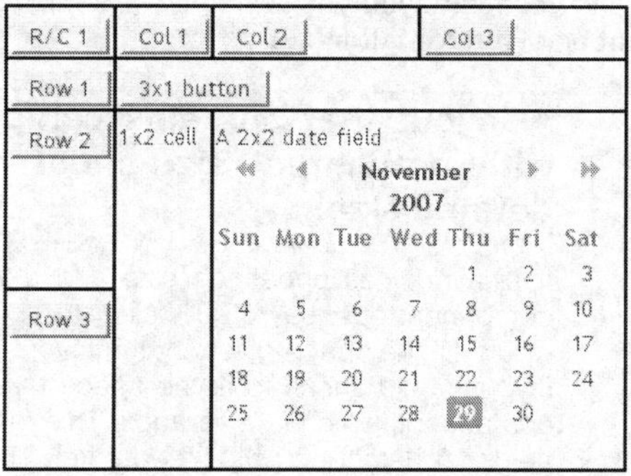

Figure 6.4. The Grid Layout Component

A component to be placed on the grid must not overlap with existing components. A conflict causes throwing a **GridLayout.OverlapsException**.

6.4.1. Sizing Grid Cells

You can define the size of both a grid layout and its components in either fixed or percentual units, or leave the size undefined altogether, as described in Section 5.3.9, "Sizing Components". Section 6.13.1, "Layout Size" gives an introduction to sizing of layouts.

The size of the **GridLayout** component is undefined by default, so it will shrink to fit the size of the components placed inside it. In most cases, especially if you set a defined size for the layout but do not set the contained components to full size, there will be some unused space. The position of the non-full components within the grid cells will be determined by their *alignment*. See Section 6.13.2, "Layout Cell Alignment" for details on how to align the components inside the cells.

The components contained within a **GridLayout** layout can be laid out in a number of different ways depending on how you specify their height or width. The layout options are similar to **HorizontalLayout** and **VerticalLayout**, as described in Section 6.3, "**VerticalLayout** and **HorizontalLayout**".

A layout that contains components with percentual size must have a defined size!

If a layout has undefined size and a contained component has, say, 100% size, the component would fill the space given by the layout, while the layout would shrink to fit the space taken by the component, which is a paradox. This requirement holds for height and width separately. The debug mode allows detecting such invalid cases; see Section 12.3.1, "Debug Mode".

Often, you want to have one or more rows or columns that take all the available space left over from non-expanding rows or columns. You need to set the rows or columns as *expanding* with `setRowExpandRatio()` and `setColumnExpandRatio()`. The first parameter for these methods is the index of the row or column to set as expanding. The second parameter for the methods is an expansion ratio, which is relevant if there are more than one expanding row or column, but its value is irrelevant if there is only one. With multiple expanding rows or columns, the ratio parameter sets the relative portion how much a specific row/column will take in relation with the other expanding rows/columns.

```
GridLayout grid = new GridLayout(3,2);

// Layout containing relatively sized components must have
// a defined size, here is fixed size.
grid.setWidth("600px");
grid.setHeight("200px");

// Add some content
String labels [] = {
        "Shrinking column<br/>Shrinking row",
        "Expanding column (1:)<br/>Shrinking row",
        "Expanding column (5:)<br/>Shrinking row",
        "Shrinking column<br/>Expanding row",
        "Expanding column (1:)<br/>Expanding row",
        "Expanding column (5:)<br/>Expanding row"
};
for (int i=0; i<labels.length; i++) {
    Label label = new Label(labels[i], Label.CONTENT_XHTML);
    label.setWidth(null); // Set width as undefined
    grid.addComponent(label);
}

// Set different expansion ratios for the two columns
grid.setColumnExpandRatio(1, 1);
grid.setColumnExpandRatio(2, 5);

// Set the bottom row to expand
grid.setRowExpandRatio(1, 1);

// Align and size the labels.
for (int col=0; col<grid.getColumns(); col++) {
    for (int row=0; row<grid.getRows(); row++) {
        Component c = grid.getComponent(col, row);
        grid.setComponentAlignment(c, Alignment.TOP_CENTER);

        // Make the labels high to illustrate the empty
        // horizontal space.
        if (col != 0 || row != 0)
            c.setHeight("100%");
    }
}
```

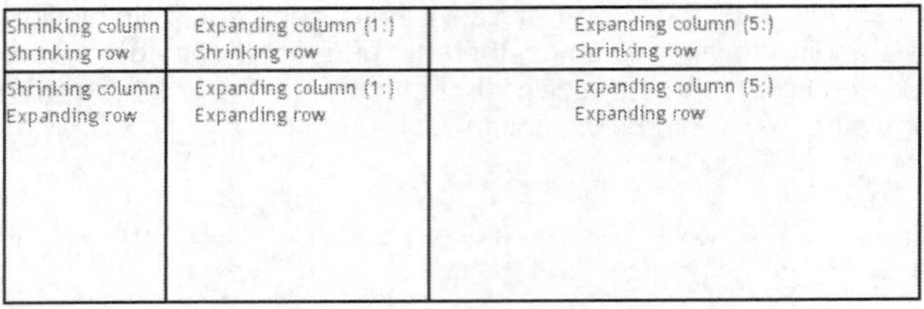

Shrinking column Shrinking row	Expanding column {1:} Shrinking row	Expanding column {5:} Shrinking row
Shrinking column Expanding row	Expanding column {1:} Expanding row	Expanding column {5:} Expanding row

Figure 6.5. Expanding Rows and Columns in GridLayout

If the size of the contained components is undefined or fixed, the expansion ratio is of the *excess* space, as in Figure 6.5, "Expanding Rows and Columns in **GridLayout**" (excess horizontal space is shown in white). However, if the size of the all the contained components in the expanding rows or columns is defined as a percentage, the ratio is calculated from the *overall* space available for the percentually sized components. For example, if we had a 100 pixels wide grid layout with two columns with 1.0 and 4.0 respective expansion ratios, and all the components in the grid were set as setWidth("100%"), the columns would have respective widths of 20 and 80 pixels, regardless of the minimum size of their contained components.

CSS Style Rules

```
.v-gridlayout {}
.v-gridlayout-margin {}
```

The v-gridlayout is the root element of the **GridLayout** component. The v-gridlayout-margin is a simple element inside it that allows setting a padding between the outer element and the cells.

For styling the individual grid cells, you should style the components inserted in the cells. The implementation structure of the grid can change, so depending on it, as is done in the example below, is not generally recommended. Normally, if you want to have, for example, a different color for a certain cell, just make set the component inside it setSizeFull(), and add a style name for it. Sometimes you may need to use a layout component between a cell and its actual component just for styling.

The following example shows how to make the grid borders visible, as in Figure 6.5, "Expanding Rows and Columns in **GridLayout**".

```
.v-gridlayout-gridexpandratio {
    background: blue; /* Creates a "border" around the grid. */
    margin:     10px; /* Empty space around the layout. */
}

/* Add padding through which the background color shows. */
.v-gridlayout-gridexpandratio .v-gridlayout-margin {
    padding: 2px;
}

/* Add cell borders and make the cell backgrounds white.
 * Warning: This depends heavily on the HTML structure. */
.v-gridlayout-gridexpandratio > div > div > div {
    padding:    2px;   /* Layout background will show through. */
    background: white; /* The cells will be colored white. */
}

/* Components inside the layout are a safe way to style cells. */
.v-gridlayout-gridexpandratio .v-label {
    text-align: left;
    background: #ffffc0; /* Pale yellow */
}
```

You should beware of `margin`, `padding`, and `border` settings in CSS as they can mess up the layout. The dimensions of layouts are calculated in the Client-Side Engine of Vaadin and some settings can interfere with these calculations. For more information, on margins and spacing, see Section 6.13.3, "Layout Cell Spacing" and Section 6.13.4, "Layout Margins"

6.5. FormLayout

FormLayout lays the components and their captions out in two columns, with optional indicators for required fields and errors that can be shown for each field. The field captions can have an icon in addition to the text.

```
// A FormLayout used outside the context of a Form
FormLayout fl = new FormLayout();

// Make the FormLayout shrink to its contents
fl.setSizeUndefined();

TextField tf = new TextField("A Field");
fl.addComponent(tf);

// Mark the first field as required
tf.setRequired(true);
tf.setRequiredError("The Field may not be empty.");
```

```
TextField tf2 = new TextField("Another Field");
fl.addComponent(tf2);

// Set the second field straing to error state with a message.
tf2.setComponentError(
    new UserError("This is the error indicator of a Field."));
```

The resulting layout will look as follows. The error message shows in a tooltip when you hover the mouse pointer over the error indicator.

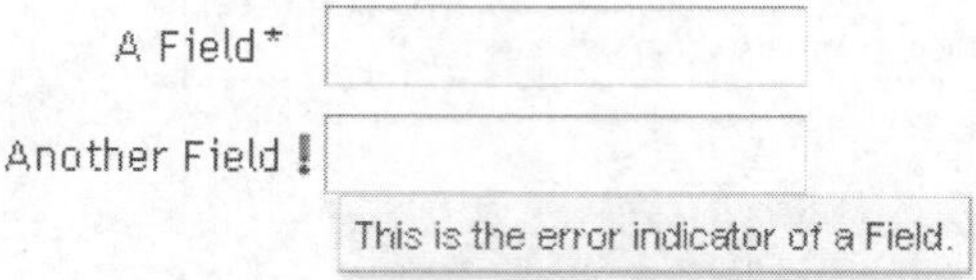

Figure 6.6. A FormLayout Layout for Forms

CSS Style Rules

```
.v-formlayout {}
.v-formlayout .v-caption {}

/* Columns in a field row. */
.v-formlayout-contentcell {} /* Field content. */
.v-formlayout-captioncell {} /* Field caption. */
.v-formlayout-errorcell {}   /* Field error indicator. */

/* Overall style of field rows. */
.v-formlayout-row {}
.v-formlayout-firstrow {}
.v-formlayout-lastrow {}

/* Required field indicator. */
.v-formlayout .v-required-field-indicator {}
.v-formlayout-captioncell .v-caption
        .v-required-field-indicator {}

/* Error indicator. */
.v-formlayout-cell .v-errorindicator {}
.v-formlayout-error-indicator .v-errorindicator {}
```

The top-level element of **FormLayout** has the v-formlayout style. The layout is tabular with three columns: the caption column, the error indicator column, and the field column. These can be styled with `v-formlayout-captioncell`, `v-formlayout-errorcell`, and `v-formlayout-contentcell`, respectively. While the error indicator is shown as a dedicated column, the indicator for required fields is currently shown as a part of the caption column.

For information on setting margins and spacing, see also Section 6.13.3, "Layout Cell Spacing" and Section 6.13.4, "Layout Margins".

6.6. Panel

Panel is a simple container with a frame and an optional caption. The content area is bound to a an inner layout component for laying out the contained components. The default content layout is a **VerticalLayout**, but you can change it with the `setContent()` method to be any class implementing the **ComponentContainer** interface.

The caption can have an icon in addition to the text.

```
// Create a panel with a caption.
final Panel panel = new Panel("Contact Information");
panel.addStyleName("panelexample");

// The width of a Panel is 100% by default, make it
// shrink to fit the contents.
panel.setWidth(Sizeable.SIZE_UNDEFINED, 0);

// Create a layout inside the panel
final FormLayout form = new FormLayout();

// Have some margin around it.
form.setMargin(true);

// Add some components
form.addComponent(new TextField("Name"));
form.addComponent(new TextField("Email"));

// Set the layout as the root layout of the panel
panel.setContent(form);
```

The resulting layout is shown in Figure 6.7, "A **Panel** Layout in Runo Theme" with the Runo theme.

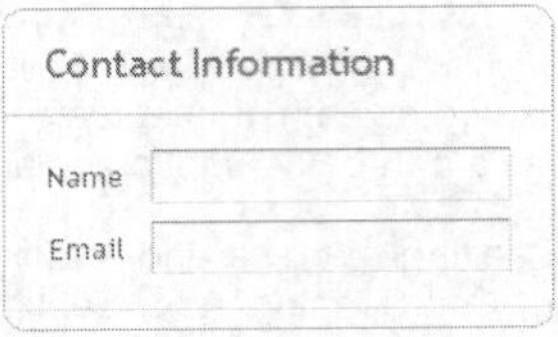

Figure 6.7. A Panel Layout in Runo Theme

See Section 6.2, "Window and Panel Root Layout" for more information about setting the content layout.

Panel has 100% width and undefined width by default. This corresponds with the default sizing of **VerticalLayout**, the default root layout of **Panel**. If you set undefined width for a panel, also the root layout must have undefined width to avoid a paradox.

CSS Style Rules

```
.v-panel {}
.v-panel-caption {}
.v-panel-nocaption {}
.v-panel-content {}
.v-panel-deco {}
```

The entire panel has v-panel style. A panel consists of three parts: the caption, content, and bottom decorations (shadow). These can be styled with v-panel-caption, v-panel-content, and v-panel-deco, respectively. If the panel has no caption, the caption element will have the style v-panel-nocaption.

The built-in *light* style has no borders or border decorations for the **Panel**. You enable it simply by adding the light style name for the panel, as is done in the example below. You can also use the *PANEL_LIGHT* constant defined in **BaseTheme** class; it is usable in all subthemes.

```
// Have a window with a SplitPanel.
final Window window = new Window("Window with a Light Panel");
window.setWidth("400px");
window.setHeight("200px");
final HorizontalSplitPanel splitter =
        new HorizontalSplitPanel();
window.setContent(splitter);

// Create a panel with a caption.
```

```
final Panel light = new Panel("Light Panel");
light.setSizeFull();

// The "light" style is a predefined style without borders
light.addStyleName(Runo.PANEL_LIGHT);

light.addComponent(new Label("The light Panel has no borders."));
light.getLayout().setMargin(true);

// The Panel will act as a "caption" of the left panel
// in the SplitPanel.
splitter.addComponent(light);
splitter.setSplitPosition(250, Sizeable.UNITS_PIXELS);

main.addWindow(window);
```

Figure 6.8, "A **Panel** with Light Style" shows the rendered **Panel** in the Runo theme.

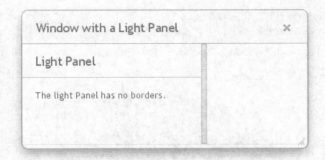

Figure 6.8. A Panel with Light Style

The *light* style is typical when using a **Panel** as the root layout of a window or some similar layout, as in the example above.

6.6.1. Scrolling the Panel Content

Normally, if a panel has undefined size in a direction, as it has by default vertically, it will fit the size of the content and grow as the content grows. However, if it has a fixed or percentual size and its content becomes too big to fit in the content area, a scroll bar will appear for the particular direction. Scroll bars in a **Panel** are handled natively by the browser with the `overflow: auto` property in CSS.

In the following example, the **Embedded** component has undefined size in both dimensions by default, but we also have to set undefined size for the root layout of the panel as the default **Vertical-Layout** only has undefined height by default.

```
// Serve the image from the theme
Resource rsrc = new ThemeResource("img/embedded-journalist.jpg");

// Display the image without caption
Embedded image = new Embedded(null, rsrc);
image.setSizeUndefined(); // Actually the default

// The panel will give it scrollbars. The root layout
// (VerticalLayout) must have undefined width to make the
// horizontal scroll bar appear.
Panel panel = new Panel("Embedding");
panel.setWidth("400px");
panel.setHeight("300px");
panel.getContent().setSizeUndefined();
panel.addComponent(image);

layout.addComponent(panel);
```

The result is shown in Figure 6.9, "Panel with Scroll Bars".

Embedding

Figure 6.9. Panel with Scroll Bars

Programmatic Scrolling with Scrollable

Panel implements the Scrollable interface to allow *programmatic scrolling*. You first need to enable programmatic scrolling with setScrollable(true), after which you can set the scroll position in pixels with setScrollTop() and setScrollLeft().

Consider the following example:

```
final Panel panel = new Panel("Scrolling Panel");
panel.setHeight("300px");
panel.setWidth("400px");
panel.getContent().setHeight("1000px");
panel.setScrollable(true);

layout.addComponent(panel);

HorizontalLayout scrollButtons = new HorizontalLayout();
layout.addComponent(scrollButtons);

Button scrollUp = new Button("Scroll Up");
scrollUp.addListener(new Button.ClickListener() {
    public void buttonClick(ClickEvent event) {
        int scrollPos = panel.getScrollTop() - 250;
        if (scrollPos < 0)
            scrollPos = 0;
        panel.setScrollTop(scrollPos);
    }
});
scrollButtons.addComponent(scrollUp);

Button scrollDown = new Button("Scroll Down");
scrollDown.addListener(new Button.ClickListener() {
    public void buttonClick(ClickEvent event) {
        int scrollPos = panel.getScrollTop();
        if (scrollPos > 1000)
            scrollPos = 1000;
        panel.setScrollTop(scrollPos + 250);
    }
});
scrollButtons.addComponent(scrollDown);
```

6.7. Sub-Windows

Sub-windows are floating panels within a native browser window.
Unlike native windows, they are managed by the client-side runtime
of Vaadin using HTML features. Vaadin allows opening and closing
sub-windows, refreshing one window from another, resizing windows, and scrolling the window content. Sub-windows are typically
used for *Dialog Windows* and *Multiple Document Interface* applications. Sub-windows are by default not modal; you can set them
modal as described in Section 6.7.4, "Modal Windows".

As with all user interface components, the appearance of a window
and its contents is defined with themes.

User control of a sub-window is limited to moving, resizing, and
closing the window. Maximizing or minimizing are not yet supported.

6.7.1. Opening and Closing a Sub-Window

You can open a new window by creating a new **Window** object and adding it to the main window with `addWindow()` method of the **Application** class.

```
mywindow = new Window("My Window");
mainwindow.addWindow(mywindow);
```

You close the window in a similar fashion, by calling the `removeWindow()` of the **Application** class:

```
myapplication.removeWindow (mywindow);
```

The user can, by default, close a sub-window by clicking the close button in the upper-right corner of the window. You can disable the button by setting the window as *read-only* with `setReadOnly(true)`. Notice that you could disable the button also by making it invisible in CSS with a "*display: none*" formatting. The problem with such a cosmetic disabling is that a malicious user might re-enable the button and close the window, which might cause problems and possibly be a security hole. Setting the window as read-only not only disables the close button on the client side, but also prevents processing the close event on the server side.

The following example demonstrates the use of a sub-window in an application. The example manages the window using a custom component that contains a button for opening and closing the window.

```
/** Component contains a button that allows opening a window. */
public class WindowOpener extends CustomComponent
                      implements Window.CloseListener {
    Window mainwindow; // Reference to main window
    Window mywindow;   // The window to be opened
    Button openbutton; // Button for opening the window
    Button closebutton; // A button in the window
    Label  explanation; // A descriptive text

    public WindowOpener(String label, Window main) {
        mainwindow = main;

        // The component contains a button that opens the window.
        final VerticalLayout layout = new VerticalLayout();

        openbutton = new Button("Open Window", this,
                            "openButtonClick");
        explanation = new Label("Explanation");
        layout.addComponent(openbutton);
```

```
            layout.addComponent(explanation);

            setCompositionRoot(layout);
        }

        /** Handle the clicks for the two buttons. */
        public void openButtonClick(Button.ClickEvent event) {
            /* Create a new window. */
            mywindow = new Window("My Dialog");
            mywindow.setPositionX(200);
            mywindow.setPositionY(100);

            /* Add the window inside the main window. */
            mainwindow.addWindow(mywindow);

            /* Listen for close events for the window. */
            mywindow.addListener(this);

            /* Add components in the window. */
            mywindow.addComponent(
                    new Label("A text label in the window."));
            closebutton = new Button("Close", this, "closeButtonClick");

            mywindow.addComponent(closebutton);

            /* Allow opening only one window at a time. */
            openbutton.setEnabled(false);

            explanation.setValue("Window opened");
        }

        /** Handle Close button click and close the window. */
        public void closeButtonClick(Button.ClickEvent event) {
            /* Windows are managed by the application object. */
            mainwindow.removeWindow(mywindow);

            /* Return to initial state. */
            openbutton.setEnabled(true);

            explanation.setValue("Closed with button");
        }

        /** In case the window is closed otherwise. */
        public void windowClose(CloseEvent e) {
            /* Return to initial state. */
            openbutton.setEnabled(true);

            explanation.setValue("Closed with window controls");
        }
    }
```

The example implements a custom component that inherits the
CustomComponent class. It consists of a **Button** that it uses to
open a window and a **Label** to describe the state of the window.
When the window is open, the button is disabled. When the window
is closed, the button is enabled again.

You can use the above custom component in the application class with:

```
public void init() {
    Window main = new Window("The Main Window");
    setMainWindow(main);

    main.addComponent(new WindowOpener("Window Opener",
main));
}
```

When added to an application, the screen will look as illustrated in the following screenshot:

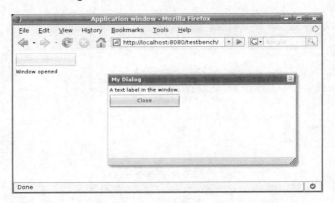

Figure 6.10. Opening a Sub-Window

6.7.2. Window Positioning

When created, a window will have a default size and position. You can specify the size of a window with setHeight() and setWidth() methods. You can set the position of the window with setPositionX() and setPositionY() methods.

```
/* Create a new window. */
mywindow = new Window("My Dialog");

/* Set window size. */
mywindow.setHeight("200px");
mywindow.setWidth("400px");
```

```
/* Set window position. */
mywindow.setPositionX(200);
mywindow.setPositionY(50);
```

Notice that the size of the main window is unknown and the getHeight and getWidth methods will return -1.

6.7.3. Scrolling Sub-Window Content

If a sub-window has a fixed or percentual size and its content becomes too big to fit in the content area, a scroll bar will appear for the particular direction. On the other hand, if the sub-window has undefined size in the direction, it will fit the size of the content and never get a scroll bar. Scroll bars in sub-windows are handled with regular HTML features, namely overflow: auto property in CSS.

As **Window** extends **Panel**, windows are also Scrollable. Note that the interface defines *programmatic scrolling*, not scrolling by the user. Please see Section 6.6, "**Panel**".

6.7.4. Modal Windows

A modal window is a child window that has to be closed by the user before the use of the parent window can continue. Dialog windows are typically modal. The advantage of modal windows is the simplification of user interaction, which may contribute to the clarity of the user interface. Modal windows are also easy to use from a development perspective, because as user interaction is isolated to them, changes in application state are more limited while the modal window is open. The disadvantage of modal windows is that they can restrict workflow too much.

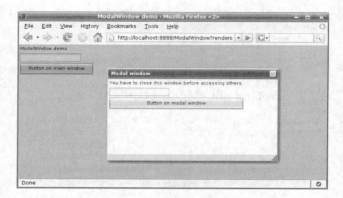

Figure 6.11. Screenshot of the Modal Window Demo Application

Depending on theme settings, the parent window may be grayed while the modal window is open.

The demo application of Vaadin includes an example of using modal windows. Figure 6.11, "Screenshot of the Modal Window Demo Application" above is from the demo application. The example includes the source code.

 Security Warning

> Modality of child windows is purely a client-side feature and can be circumvented with client-side attack code. You should not trust in the modality of child windows in security-critical situations such as login windows.

6.8. HorizontalSplitPanel and VerticalSplit-Panel

HorizontalSplitPanel and **VerticalSplitPanel** are a two-component containers that divide the available space into two areas to accomodate the two components. **HorizontalSplitPanel** makes the split horizontally with a vertical splitter bar, and **VerticalSplit-**

Panel vertically with a horizontal splitter bar. The user can drag the bar to adjust its position.

You can set the two components with the `setFirstComponent()` and `setSecondComponent()` methods, or with the regular `addComponent()` method.

```
// Have a panel to put stuff in
Panel panel = new Panel("Split Panels Inside This Panel");

// Have a horizontal split panel as its root layout
HorizontalSplitPanel hsplit = new HorizontalSplitPanel();
panel.setContent(hsplit);

// Put a component in the left panel
Tree tree = new Tree("Menu", TreeExample.createTreeContent());
hsplit.setFirstComponent(tree);

// Put a vertical split panel in the right panel
VerticalSplitPanel vsplit = new VerticalSplitPanel();
hsplit.setSecondComponent(vsplit);

// Put other components in the right panel
vsplit.addComponent(new Label("Here's the upper panel"));
vsplit.addComponent(new Label("Here's the lower panel"));
```

The result is shown in Figure 6.12, "**HorizontalSplitPanel** and **VerticalSplitPanel**". Observe that the tree is cut horizontally as it can not fit in the layout. If its height exceeds the height of the panel, a vertical scroll bar will appear automatically. If horizontal scroll bar is necessary, you could put the content in a **Panel**, which can have scroll bars in both directions.

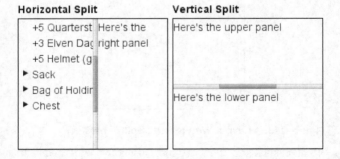

Figure 6.12. HorizontalSplitPanel and VerticalSplitPanel

You can set the split position with `setSplitPosition()`. It accepts any units defined in the **Sizeable** interface, with percentual size relative to the size of the component.

```
// Have a horizontal split panel
HorizontalSplitPanel hsplit = new HorizontalSplitPanel();
hsplit.setFirstComponent(new Label("75% wide panel"));
hsplit.setSecondComponent(new Label("25% wide panel"));

// Set the position of the splitter as percentage
hsplit.setSplitPosition(75, Sizeable.UNITS_PERCENTAGE);
```

Another version of the `setSplitPosition()` method allows leaving out the unit, using the same unit as previously. The method also has versions take take a boolean parameter, *reverse*, which allows defining the size of the right or bottom panel instead of the left or top panel.

The split bar allows the user to adjust the split position by dragging the bar with mouse. To lock the split bar, use `setLocked(true)`. When locked, the move handle in the middle of the bar is disabled.

```
// Lock the splitter
hsplit.setLocked(true);
```

Setting the split position programmatically and locking the split bar is illustrated in Figure 6.13, "A Layout With Nested SplitPanels".

Locked Split Position

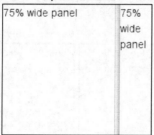

Figure 6.13. A Layout With Nested SplitPanels

Notice that the size of a split panel must not be undefined in the split direction.

CSS Style Rules

```
/* For a horizontal SplitPanel. */
.v-splitpanel-horizontal {}
.v-splitpanel-hsplitter {}
.v-splitpanel-hsplitter-locked {}

/* For a vertical SplitPanel. */
.v-splitpanel-vertical {}
.v-splitpanel-vsplitter {}
.v-splitpanel-vsplitter-locked {}

/* The two container panels. */
.v-splitpanel-first-container {}   /* Top or left panel. */
.v-splitpanel-second-container {} /* Bottom or right panel. */
```

The entire split panel has the style v-splitpanel-horizontal or
v-splitpanel-vertical, depending on the panel direction. The
split bar or *splitter* between the two content panels has either the
...-splitter or ...-splitter-locked style, depending on
whether its position is locked or not.

6.9. TabSheet

The **TabSheet** is a multicomponent container that allows switching
between the components with "tabs". The tabs are organized as a
tab bar at the top of the tab sheet. Clicking on a tab opens its
contained component in the main display area of the layout.

You add new tabs to a tab sheet with the addTab() method. The
simple version of the method takes as its parameter the root component of the tab. You can use the root component to retrieve its
corresponding **Tab** object. Typically, you put a layout component
as the root component.

```
// Create an empty tab sheet.
TabSheet tabsheet = new TabSheet();

// Create a component to put in a tab and put
// some content in it.
VerticalLayout myTabRoot = new VerticalLayout();
myTabRoot.addComponent(new Label("Hello, I am a Tab!"));

// Add the component to the tab sheet as a new tab.
tabsheet.addTab(myTabRoot);

// Get the Tab holding the component and set its caption.
tabsheet.getTab(myTabRoot).setCaption("My Tab");
```

Each tab in a tab sheet is represented as a **Tab** object, which manages the tab caption, icon, and attributes such as hidden and visible. You can set the caption with `setCaption()` and the icon with `setIcon()`. If the component added with `addTab()` has a caption or icon, it is used as the default for the **Tab** object. However, changing the attributes of the root component later does not affect the tab, but you must make the setting through the **Tab** object. The `addTab()` returns the new **Tab** object, so you can easily set an attribute using the reference.

```
// Set an attribute using the returned reference
tabsheet.addTab(myTab).setCaption("My Tab");
```

You can also give the caption and the icon as parameters for the `addTab()` method. The following example demonstrates the creation of a simple tab sheet, where each tab shows a different **Label** component. The tabs have an icon, which are (in this example) loaded as Java class loader resources from the application.

```
TabSheet tabsheet = new TabSheet();

// Make the tabsheet shrink to fit the contents.
tabsheet.setSizeUndefined();

tabsheet.addTab(new Label("Contents of the first tab"),
        "First Tab",
        new ClassResource("images/Mercury_small.png", this));
tabsheet.addTab(new Label("Contents of the second tab"),
        "Second Tab",
        new ClassResource("images/Venus_small.png", this));
tabsheet.addTab(new Label("Contents of the third tab"),
        "Third tab",
        new ClassResource("images/Earth_small.png", this));
```

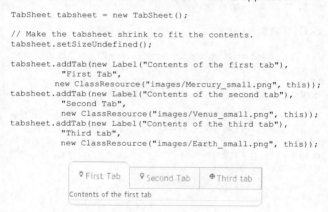

Figure 6.14. A Simple TabSheet Layout

The `hideTabs()` method allows hiding the tab bar entirely. This can be useful in tabbed document interfaces (TDI) when there is only one tab. An individual tab can be made invisible by setting `setVisible(false)` for the **Tab** object. A tab can be disabled by setting `setEnabled(false)`.

Clicking on a tab selects it. This fires a **TabSheet.SelectedTabChangeEvent**, which you can handle by implementing the **TabSheet.SelectedTabChangeListener** interface. The source component of the event, which you can retrieve with `getSource()` method of the event, will be the **TabSheet** component. You can find the currently selected tab with `getSelectedTab()` and select (open) a particular tab programmatically with `setSelectedTab()`. Notice that also adding the first tab fires the **SelectedTabChangeEvent**, which may cause problems in your handler if you assume that everything is initialized before the first change event.

The example below demonstrates handling **TabSheet** related events and enabling and disabling tabs. The sort of logic used in the example is useful in sequential user interfaces, often called *wizards*, where the user goes through the tabs one by one, but can return back if needed.

```
import com.vaadin.ui.*;
import com.vaadin.ui.Button.ClickEvent;
import com.vaadin.ui.TabSheet.SelectedTabChangeEvent;

public class TabSheetExample extends CustomComponent implements
        Button.ClickListener, TabSheet.SelectedTabChangeListener {
    TabSheet tabsheet = new TabSheet();
    Button tab1 = new Button("Push this button");
    Label tab2 = new Label("Contents of Second Tab");
    Label tab3 = new Label("Contents of Third Tab");

    TabSheetExample() {
        setCompositionRoot(tabsheet);

        // Listen for changes in tab selection.
        tabsheet.addListener(this);

        // First tab contains a button, for which we
        // listen button click events.
        tab1.addListener(this);

        // This will cause a selectedTabChange() call.
        tabsheet.addTab(tab1, "First Tab", null);

        // A tab that is initially invisible.
        tabsheet.addTab(tab2, "Second Tab", null);
        tabsheet.getTab(tab2).setVisible(false);

        // A tab that is initially disabled.
        tabsheet.addTab(tab3, "Third tab", null);
        tabsheet.getTab(tab3).setEnabled(false);
    }

    public void buttonClick(ClickEvent event) {
```

```
        // Enable the invisible and disabled tabs.
    tabsheet.getTab(tab2).setVisible(true);
    tabsheet.getTab(tab3).setEnabled(true);

        // Change selection automatically to second tab.
        tabsheet.setSelectedTab(tab2);
    }

    public void selectedTabChange(SelectedTabChangeEvent event) {
        // Cast to a TabSheet. This isn't really necessary in
    // this example, as we have only one TabSheet component,
    // but would be useful if there were multiple TabSheets.
        final TabSheet source = (TabSheet) event.getSource();

        if (source == tabsheet) {
            // If the first tab was selected.
            if (source.getSelectedTab() == tab1) {
                // The 2. and 3. tabs may not have been set yet.
                if (tabsheet.getTab(tab2) != null
                    && tabsheet.getTab(tab3) != null) {
                  tabsheet.getTab(tab2).setVisible(false);
                    tabsheet.getTab(tab3).setEnabled(false);
                }
            }
        }
    }
}
```

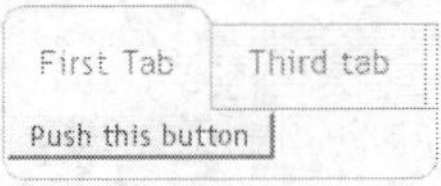

Figure 6.15. A TabSheet with Hidden and Disabled Tabs

CSS Style Rules

```
.v-tabsheet {}
.v-tabsheet-tabs {}
.v-tabsheet-content {}
.v-tabsheet-deco {}
.v-tabsheet-tabcontainer {}
.v-tabsheet-tabsheetpanel {}
.v-tabsheet-hidetabs {}

.v-tabsheet-scroller {}
.v-tabsheet-scrollerPrev {}
.v-tabsheet-scrollerNext {}
.v-tabsheet-scrollerPrev-disabled{}
.v-tabsheet-scrollerNext-disabled{}

.v-tabsheet-tabitem {}
```

```
.v-tabsheet-tabitem-selected {}
.v-tabsheet-tabitemcell {}
.v-tabsheet-tabitemcell-first {}

.v-tabsheet-tabs td {}
.v-tabsheet-spacertd {}
```

The entire tabsheet has the `v-tabsheet` style. A tabsheet consists of three main parts: the tabs on the top, the main content pane, and decorations around the tabsheet.

The tabs area at the top can be styled with `v-tabsheet-tabs`, `v-tabsheet-tabcontainer` and `v-tabsheet-tabitem*`.

The style `v-tabsheet-spacertd` is used for any empty space after the tabs. If the tabsheet has too little space to show all tabs, scroller buttons enable browsing the full tab list. These use the styles `v-tabsheet-scroller*`.

The content area where the tab contents are shown can be styled with `v-tabsheet-content`, and the surrounding decoration with `v-tabsheet-deco`.

6.10. Accordion

Accordion is a multicomponent container similar to **TabSheet**, except that the "tabs" are arranged vertically. Clicking on a tab opens its contained component in the space between the tab and the next one. You can use an **Accordion** identically to a **TabSheet**, which it actually inherits. See Section 6.9, "**TabSheet**" for more information.

The following example shows how you can create a simple accordion. As the **Accordion** is rather naked alone, we put it inside a Panel that acts as its caption and provides it a border.

```
// Create the Accordion.
Accordion accordion = new Accordion();

// Have it take all space available in the layout.
accordion.setSizeFull();

// Some components to put in the Accordion.
Label l1 = new Label("There are no previously saved actions.");
Label l2 = new Label("There are no saved notes.");
Label l3 = new Label("There are currently no issues.");
```

```
// Add the components as tabs in the Accordion.
accordion.addTab(l1, "Saved actions", null);
accordion.addTab(l2, "Notes", null);
accordion.addTab(l3, "Issues", null);

// A container for the Accordion.
Panel panel = new Panel("Tasks");
panel.setWidth("300px");
panel.setHeight("300px");
panel.addComponent(accordion);

// Trim its layout to allow the Accordion take all space.
panel.getLayout().setSizeFull();
panel.getLayout().setMargin(false);
```

Figure 6.16, "An Accordion" shows what the example would look like with the default theme.

Figure 6.16. An Accordion

CSS Style Rules

```
.v-accordion {}
.v-accordion-item {}
.v-accordion-item-open {}
.v-accordion-item-first {}
.v-accordion-item-caption {}
.v-accordion-item-caption .v-caption {}
.v-accordion-item-content {}
```

The top-level element of **Accordion** has the `v-accordion` style.
An **Accordion** consists of a sequence of item elements, each of
which has a caption element (the tab) and a content area element.

The selected item (tab) has also the `v-accordion-open` style. The
content area is not shown for the closed items.

6.11. AbsoluteLayout

AbsoluteLayout allows placing components in arbitrary positions
in the layout area. The positions are specified in the `addCompon-
ent()` method with horizontal and vertical coordinates relative to
an edge of the layout area. The positions can include a third depth
dimension, the *z-index*, which specifies which components are
displayed in front and which behind other components.

The positions are specified by a CSS absolute position string, using
the `left`, `right`, `top`, `bottom`, and `z-index` properties known from
CSS. In the following example, we have a 300 by 150 pixels large
layout and position a text field 50 pixels from both the left and the
top edge:

```
// A 400x250 pixels size layout
AbsoluteLayout layout = new AbsoluteLayout();
layout.setWidth("400px");
layout.setHeight("250px");

// A component with coordinates for its top-left corner
TextField text = new TextField("Somewhere someplace");
layout.addComponent(text, "left: 50px; top: 50px;");
```

The `left` and `top` specify the distance from the left and top edge,
respectively. The `right` and `bottom` specify the distances from
the right and top edge.

```
// At the top-left corner
Button button = new Button( "left: 0px; top: 0px;");
layout.addComponent(button, "left: 0px; top: 0px;");

// At the bottom-right corner
Button buttCorner = new Button( "right: 0px; bottom: 0px;");
layout.addComponent(buttCorner, "right: 0px; bottom: 0px;");

// Relative to the bottom-right corner
Button buttBrRelative = new Button( "right: 50px; bottom: 50px;");
layout.addComponent(buttBrRelative, "right: 50px; bottom: 50px;");

// On the bottom, relative to the left side
Button buttBottom = new Button( "left: 50px; bottom: 0px;");
layout.addComponent(buttBottom, "left: 50px; bottom: 0px;");
```

```
// On the right side, up from the bottom
Button buttRight = new Button( "right: 0px; bottom: 100px;");
layout.addComponent(buttRight, "right: 0px; bottom: 100px;");
```

The result of the above code examples is shown in Figure 6.17, "Components Positioned Relative to Various Edges".

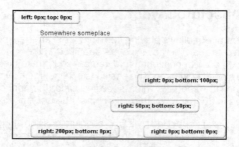

Figure 6.17. Components Positioned Relative to Various Edges

In the above examples, we had components of undefined size and specified the positions of components by a single pair of coordinates. The other possibility is to specify an area and let the component fill the area by specifying a proportional size for the component, such as "100%". Normally, you use setSizeFull() to take the entire area given by the layout.

```
// Specify an area that a component should fill
Panel panel = new Panel("A Panel filling an area");
panel.setSizeFull(); // Fill the entire given area
layout.addComponent(panel, "left: 25px; right: 50px; "+
                           "top: 100px; bottom: 50px;");
```

The result is shown in Figure 6.18, "Component Filling an Area Specified by Coordinates"

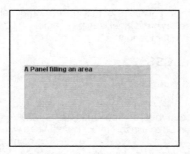

Figure 6.18. Component Filling an Area Specified by Coordinates

You can also use proportional coordinates to specify the coordinates:

```
// A panel that takes 30% to 90% horizontally and
// 20% to 80% vertically
Panel panel = new Panel("A Panel");
panel.setSizeFull(); // Fill the specified area
layout.addComponent(panel, "left: 30%; right: 10%;" +
                           "top: 20%; bottom: 20%;");
```

The result is shown in Figure 6.19, "Specifying an Area by Proportional Coordinates"

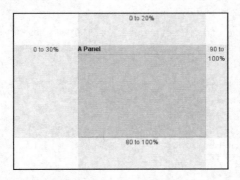

Figure 6.19. Specifying an Area by Proportional Coordinates

Drag and drop is very useful for moving the components contained in an **AbsoluteLayout**. Check out the example in Section 12.11.6, "Dropping on a Component".

Styling with CSS

```
.v-absolutelayout {}
.v-absolutelayout-wrapper {}
```

The **AbsoluteLayout** component has `v-absolutelayout` root style. Each component in the layout is contained within an element that has the `v-absolutelayout-wrapper`. The component captions are outside the wrapper elements, in a separate element with the usual `v-caption` style.

6.12. CssLayout

CssLayout allows strong control over styling of the components contained inside the layout. The components are contained in a simple DOM structure consisting of `<div>` elements. By default, the contained components are laid out horizontally and wrap naturally when they reach the width of the layout, but you can control this and most other behaviour with CSS. You can also inject custom CSS for each contained component. As **CssLayout** has a very simple DOM structure and no dynamic rendering logic, relying purely on the built-in rendering logic of the browsers, it is the fastest of the layout components.

The basic use of **CssLayout** is just like with any other layout component:

```
CssLayout layout = new CssLayout();

// Component with a layout-managed caption and icon
TextField tf = new TextField("A TextField");
tf.setIcon(new ThemeResource("icons/user.png"));
layout.addComponent(tf);

// Labels are 100% wide by default so must unset width
Label label = new Label("A Label");
label.setWidth(Sizeable.SIZE_UNDEFINED, 0);
layout.addComponent(label);

layout.addComponent(new Button("A Button"));
```

The result is shown in Figure 6.20, "Basic Use of **CssLayout**". Notice that the default spacing and alignment of the layout is quite crude and CSS styling is nearly always needed.

Figure 6.20. Basic Use of CssLayout

The `display` attribute of **CssLayout** is `inline-block` by default, so the components are laid out horizontally following another. **CssLayout** has 100% width by default. If the components reach the width of the layout, they are wrapped to the next "line" just as text would be. If you add a component with 100% width, it will take an entire line by wrapping before and after the component.

Overriding the `getCss()` method allows injecting custom CSS for each component. The CSS returned by the method is inserted in the `style` attribute of the `<div>` element of the component, so it will override any style definitions made in CSS files.

```
CssLayout layout = new CssLayout() {
    @Override
    protected String getCss(Component c) {
        if (c instanceof Label) {
            // Color the boxes with random colors
            int rgb = (int) (Math.random()*(1<<24));
            return "background: #" + Integer.toHexString(rgb);
        }
        return null;
    }
};
layout.setWidth("400px"); // Causes to wrap the contents

// Add boxes of various sizes
for (int i=0; i<40; i++) {
    Label box = new Label(" ", Label.CONTENT_XHTML);
    box.addStyleName("flowbox");
    box.setWidth((float) Math.random()*50,
                Sizeable.UNITS_PIXELS);
    box.setHeight((float) Math.random()*50,
                Sizeable.UNITS_PIXELS);
    layout.addComponent(box);
}
```

The style name added to the components allows making common styling in a CSS file:

```
.v-label-flowbox {
  border: thin black solid;
}
```

Figure 6.21, "Use of `getCss()` and line wrap" shows the rendered result.

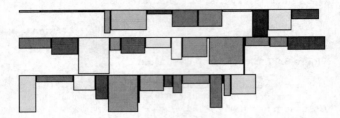

Figure 6.21. Use of `getCss()` and line wrap

The stregth of the **CssLayout** is also its weakness. Much of the logic behind the other layout components is there to give nice default behaviour and to handle the differences in different browsers. Some browsers, no need to say which, are notoriously incompatible with the CSS standards, so they require a lot of custom CSS. You may need to make use of the browser-specific style classes in the root element of the application. Some features in the other layouts are not even solvable in pure CSS, at least in all browsers.

Styling with CSS

```
.v-csslayout {}
.v-csslayout-margin {}
.v-csslayout-container {}
```

The **CssLayout** component has `v-csslayout` root style. The margin element with `v-csslayout-margin` style is always enabled. The components are contained in an element with `v-csslayout-container` style.

For example, we could style the basic **CssLayout** example shown earlier as follows:

```
/* Have the caption right of the text box, bottom-aligned */
.csslayoutexample .mylayout .v-csslayout-container {
    direction: rtl;
    line-height: 24px;
    vertical-align: bottom;
}

/* Have some space before and after the caption */
.csslayoutexample .mylayout .v-csslayout-container .v-caption {
```

```
    padding-left:  3px;
    padding-right: 10px;
}
```

The example would now be rendered as shown in Figure 6.22,
"Styling **CssLayout**".

```
┌─────────────────────────────────┐
│                                 │  Here's a field
└─────────────────────────────────┘
```

Figure 6.22. Styling CssLayout

Captions and icons that are managed by the layout are contained
in an element with `v-caption` style. These caption elements are
contained flat at the same level as the actual component elements.
This may cause problems with wrapping in `inline-block` mode,
as wrapping can occur between the caption and its corresponding
component element just as well as between components. Such
use case is therefore not feasible.

6.13. Layout Formatting

While the formatting of layouts is mainly done with style sheets,
just as with other components, style sheets are not ideal or even
possible to use in some situations. For example, CSS does not allow
defining the spacing of table cells, which is done with the `cellspa-
cing` attribute in HTML.

Moreover, as many layout sizes are calculated dynamically in the
Client-Side Engine of Vaadin, some CSS settings can fail altogether.

6.13.1. Layout Size

The size of a layout component can be specified with the
`setWidth()` and `setHeight()` methods defined in the **Sizeable**
interface, just like for any component. It can also be undefined, in
which case the layout shrinks to fit the component(s) inside it.
Section 5.3.9, "Sizing Components" gives details on the interface.

| Undefined width layout: | Small | Medium-sized | Quite a big component |
| Defined width layout: | Small | Medium-sized | Quite a big component |

Figure 6.23. HorizontalLayout with Undefined vs Defined size

Many layout components take 100% width by default, while they have the height undefined.

The sizes of components inside a layout can also be defined as a percentage of the space available in the layout, for example with `setWidth("100%")`; or with the (most commonly used method) `setFullSize()` that sets 100% size in both directions. If you use a percentage in a **HorizontalLayout**, **VerticalLayout**, or **GridLayout**, you will also have to set the component as *expanding*, as noted below.

> **Warning**
>
> *A layout that contains components with percentual size must have a defined size!*
>
> If a layout has undefined size and a contained component has, say, 100% size, the component will try to fill the space given by the layout, while the layout will shrink to fit the space taken by the component, which is a paradox. This requirement holds for height and width separately. The debug mode allows detecting such invalid cases; see Section 12.3.1, "Debug Mode".

For example:

```
// This takes 100% width but has undefined height.
VerticalLayout layout = new VerticalLayout();

// A button that takes all the space available in the layout.
Button button = new Button("100%x100% button");
button.setSizeFull();
layout.addComponent(button);

// We must set the layout to a defined height vertically, in
// this case 100% of its parent layout, which also must
// not have undefined size.
layout.setHeight("100%");
```

The default layout of **Window** and **Panel** is **VerticalLayout** with undefined height. If you insert enough components in such a layout, it will grow outside the bottom of the view area and scrollbars will appear in the browser. If you want your application to use all the browser view, nothing more or less, you should use `setFullSize()` for the root layout.

```
// Create the main window.
Window main = new Window("Main Window");
setMainWindow(main);

// Use full size.
main.getLayout().setSizeFull();
```

Expanding Components

If you set a **HorizontalLayout** to a defined size horizontally or a **VerticalLayout** vertically, and there is space left over from the contained components, the extra space is distributed equally between the component cells. The components are aligned within these cells, according to their alignment setting, top left by default, as in the example below.

Often, you don't want such empty space, but want one or more components to take all the leftover space. You need to set such a component to 100% size and use `setExpandRatio()`. If there is just one such expanding component in the layout, the ratio parameter is irrelevant.

If you set multiple components as expanding, the expand ratio dictates how large proportion of the available space (overall or excess depending on whether the components are sized as a percentage or not) each component takes. In the example below, the buttons have 1:2:3 ratio for the expansion.

GridLayout has corresponding method for both of its directions, `setRowExpandRatio()` and `setColumnExpandRatio()`.

Expansion is dealt in detail in the documentation of the layout components that support it. See Section 6.3, "**VerticalLayout** and **HorizontalLayout**" and Section 6.4, "**GridLayout**" for details on components with relative sizes.

6.13.2. Layout Cell Alignment

You can set the alignment of the component inside a specific layout cell with the setComponentAlignment() method. The method takes as its parameters the component contained in the cell to be formatted, and the horizontal and vertical alignment.

Figure 6.24, "Cell Alignments" illustrates the alignment of components within a **GridLayout**.

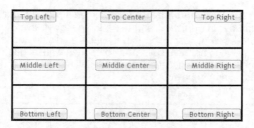

Figure 6.24. Cell Alignments

The easiest way to set alignments is to use the constants defined in the **Alignment** class. Let us look how the buttons in the top row of the above **GridLayout** are aligned with constants:

```
// Create a grid layout
final GridLayout grid = new GridLayout(3, 3);

grid.setWidth(400, Sizeable.UNITS_PIXELS);
grid.setHeight(200, Sizeable.UNITS_PIXELS);

Button topleft = new Button("Top Left");
grid.addComponent(topleft, 0, 0);
grid.setComponentAlignment(topleft, Alignment.TOP_LEFT);

Button topcenter = new Button("Top Center");
grid.addComponent(topcenter, 1, 0);
grid.setComponentAlignment(topcenter, Alignment.TOP_CENTER);
```

```
Button topright = new Button("Top Right");
grid.addComponent(topright, 2, 0);
grid.setComponentAlignment(topright, Alignment.TOP_RIGHT);
...
```

The following table lists all the **Alignment** constants by their respective locations:

Table 6.1. Alignment Constants

TOP_LEFT	*TOP_CENTER*	*TOP_RIGHT*
MIDDLE_LEFT	*MIDDLE_CENTER*	*MIDDLE_RIGHT*
BOTTOM_LEFT	*BOTTOM_CENTER*	*BOTTOM_RIGHT*

Another way to specify the alignments is to create an **Alignment** object and specify the horizontal and vertical alignment with separate constants. You can specify either of the directions, in which case the other alignment direction is not modified, or both with a bitmask operation between the two directions.

```
Button middleleft = new Button("Middle Left");
grid.addComponent(middleleft, 0, 1);
grid.setComponentAlignment(middleleft,
        new Alignment(Bits.ALIGNMENT_VERTICAL_CENTER |
                    Bits.ALIGNMENT_LEFT));

Button middlecenter = new Button("Middle Center");
grid.addComponent(middlecenter, 1, 1);
grid.setComponentAlignment(middlecenter,
        new Alignment(Bits.ALIGNMENT_VERTICAL_CENTER |
                    Bits.ALIGNMENT_HORIZONTAL_CENTER));

Button middleright = new Button("Middle Right");
grid.addComponent(middleright, 2, 1);
grid.setComponentAlignment(middleright,
        new Alignment(Bits.ALIGNMENT_VERTICAL_CENTER |
                    Bits.ALIGNMENT_RIGHT));
```

Obviously, you may combine only one vertical bitmask with one horizontal bitmask, though you may leave either one out. The following table lists the available alignment bitmask constants:

Table 6.2. Alignment Bitmasks

Horizontal	*Bits.ALIGNMENT_LEFT*

	Bits.ALIGNMENT_HORIZONT-AL_CENTER
	Bits.ALIGNMENT_RIGHT
Vertical	Bits.ALIGNMENT_TOP
	Bits.ALIGNMENT_VERTICAL_CEN-TER
	Bits.ALIGNMENT_BOTTOM

You can determine the current alignment of a component with getComponentAlignment(), which returns an **Alignment** object. The class provides a number of getter methods for decoding the alignment, which you can also get as a bitmask value.

Size of Aligned Components

You can only align a component that is smaller than its containing cell in the direction of alignment. If a component has 100% width, as many components have by default, horizontal alignment does not have any effect. For example, **Label** is 100% wide by default and can not therefore be horizontally aligned as such. The problem can be hard to notice, as the text inside a **Label** is left-aligned.

You usually need to set either a fixed size, undefined size, or less than a 100% relative size for the component to be aligned - a size that is smaller than the containing layout has.

For example, assuming that a **Label** has short content that is less wide than the containing **VerticalLayout**, you could center it as follows:

```
VerticalLayout layout = new VerticalLayout(); // 100% default width
Label label = new Label("Hello"); // 100% default width
label.setSizeUndefined();
layout.addComponent(label);
layout.setComponentAlignment(label, Alignment.MIDDLE_CENTER);
```

If you set the size as undefined and the component itself contains components, make sure that the contained components also have either undefined or fixed size. For example, if you set the size of a **Form** as undefined, its containing layout **FormLayout** has 100% default width, which you also need to set as undefined. But then, any components inside the **FormLayout** must have either un-defined or fixed size.

6.13.3. Layout Cell Spacing

The **VerticalLayout**, **HorizontalLayout**, and **GridLayout** layouts offer a setSpacing() method for enabling space between the cells in the layout. Enabling the spacing adds a spacing style for all cells except the first so that, by setting the left or top padding, you can specify the amount of spacing.

To enable spacing, simply call setSpacing(true) for the layout as follows:

```
HorizontalLayout layout2 = new HorizontalLayout();
layout2.addStyleName("spacingexample");
layout2.setSpacing(true);
layout2.addComponent(new Button("Component 1"));
layout2.addComponent(new Button("Component 2"));
layout2.addComponent(new Button("Component 3"));

VerticalLayout layout4 = new VerticalLayout();
layout4.addStyleName("spacingexample");
layout4.setSpacing(true);
layout4.addComponent(new Button("Component 1"));
layout4.addComponent(new Button("Component 2"));
layout4.addComponent(new Button("Component 3"));
```

In practise, the setSpacing() method toggles between the "v-COMPONENTCLASSNAME-spacing-on" and "-off" CSS class names in the cell elements. Elements having those class names can be used to define the spacing metrics in a theme.

The layouts have a spacing style name to define spacing also when spacing is off. This allows you to define a small default spacing between components by default and a larger one when the spacing is actually enabled.

Spacing can be horizontal (for **HorizontalLayout**), vertical (for **VerticalLayout**), or both (for **GridLayout**). The name of the spacing style for horizontal and vertical spacing is the base name of the component style name plus the "-spacing-on" suffix, as shown in the following table:

Table 6.3. Spacing Style Names

VerticalLayout	v-verticallayout-spacing-on

HorizontalLayout	`v-horizontallayout-spacing-on`
GridLayout	`v-gridlayout-spacing-on`

In the CSS example below, we specify the exact amount of spacing for the code example given above, for the layouts with the custom `"spacingexample"` style:

```
/* Set the amount of horizontal cell spacing in a
 * specific element with the "-spacingexample" style. */
.v-horizontallayout-spacingexample .v-horizontallayout-spacing-on
{
    padding-left: 30px;
}

/* Set the amount of vertical cell spacing in a
 * specific element with the "-spacingexample" style. */
.v-verticallayout-spacingexample .v-verticallayout-spacing-on {
    padding-top: 30px;
}

/* Set the amount of both vertical and horizontal cell spacing
 * in a specific element with the "-spacingexample" style. */
.v-gridlayout-spacingexample .v-gridlayout-spacing-on {
    padding-top: 30px;
    padding-left: 50px;
}
```

The resulting layouts will look as shown in Figure 6.25, "Layout Spacings", which also shows the layouts with no spacing.

				No spacing	Vertical spacing
No spacing:	Component 1	Component 2	Component 3	Component 1	Component 1
				Component 2	
				Component 3	Component 2
Horizontal spacing:	Component 1	Component 2	Component 3		
					Component 3

Figure 6.25. Layout Spacings

Note

Spacing is unrelated to "cell spacing" in HTML tables. While many layout components are implemented with HTML tables in the browser, this implementation is not guaranteed to stay the same and at least **Vertical**-/**HorizontalLayout** could be implemented with `<div>` elements as well. In fact, as GWT compiles widgets separately for different browsers, the implementation could even vary between browsers.

Also note that HTML elements with spacing class-names don't necessarily exist in a component after rendering, because the Client-Side Engine of Vaadin processes them.

6.13.4. Layout Margins

By default, layout components do not have any margin around them. You can add margin with CSS directly to the layout component. Below we set margins for a specific layout component (here a `horizontallayout`):

```
layout1.addStyleName("marginexample1");
```

```
.v-horizontallayout-marginexample1
        .v-horizontallayout-margin {
 padding-left:    200px;
 padding-right:   100px;
 padding-top:     50px;
 padding-bottom:  25px;
}
```

Similar settings exist for other layouts such as `verticallayout`.

The layout size calculations require the margins to be defined as CSS `padding` rather than as CSS `margin`.

As an alternative to the pure CSS method, you can set up a margin around the layout that can be enabled with `setMargin(true)`. The margin element has some default margin widths, but you can adjust the widths in CSS if you need to.

Let us consider the following example, where we enable the margin on all sides of the layout:

```
// Create a layout
HorizontalLayout layout2 = new HorizontalLayout();
containinglayout.addComponent(
    new Label("Layout with margin on all sides:"));
containinglayout.addComponent(layout2);
```

```
// Set style name for the layout to allow styling it
layout2.addStyleName("marginexample");

// Have margin on all sides around the layout
layout2.setMargin(true);

// Put something inside the layout
layout2.addComponent(new Label("Cell 1"));
layout2.addComponent(new Label("Cell 2"));
layout2.addComponent(new Label("Cell 3"));
```

You can enable the margins only for specific sides. The margins are specified for the `setMargin()` method in clockwise order for top, right, bottom, and left margin. The following would enable the top and left margins:

```
layout2.setMargin(true, false, false, true);
```

You can specify the actual margin widths in the CSS if you are not satisfied with the default widths (in this example for a **HorizontalLayout**):

```
.v-horizontallayout-marginexample .v-horizontallay-
out-margin-left    {padding-left:   200px;}
.v-horizontallayout-marginexample .v-horizontallay-
out-margin-right   {padding-right:  100px;}
.v-horizontallayout-marginexample .v-horizontallay-
out-margin-top     {padding-top:    50px; }
.v-horizontallayout-marginexample .v-horizontallay-
out-margin-bottom  {padding-bottom: 25px; }
```

The resulting margins are shown in Figure 6.26, "Layout Margins" below. The two ways produce identical margins.

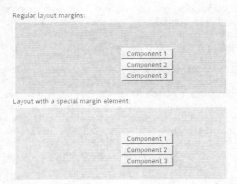

Figure 6.26. Layout Margins

CSS Style Rules

The CSS style names for the margin widths for `setMargin()` consist of the specific layout name plus `-margin-left` and so on. The CSS style names for CSS-only margins consist of the specific layout name plus `-margin`. Below, the style rules are given for **Vertical-Layout**:

```
/* Alternative 1: CSS only style */
.v-verticallayout-margin {
    padding-left:    ___px;
    padding-right:   ___px;
    padding-top:     ___px;
    padding-bottom: ___px;
}
/* Alternative 2: CSS rules to be enabled in code */
.v-verticallayout-margin-left   {padding-left:    ___px;}
.v-verticallayout-margin-right  {padding-right:   ___px;}
.v-verticallayout-margin-top    {padding-top:     ___px;}
.v-verticallayout-margin-bottom {padding-bottom: ___px;}
```

6.14. Custom Layouts

While it is possible to create almost any typical layout with the standard layout components, it is sometimes best to separate the layout completely from code. With the **CustomLayout** component, you can write your layout as a template in XHTML that provides locations of any contained components. The layout template is in-cluded in a theme. This separation allows the layout to be designed separately from code, for example using WYSIWYG web designer tools such as Adobe Dreamweaver.

A template is a HTML file located under `layouts` folder under a theme folder under the `WebContent/VAADIN/themes/` folder, for example, `WebContent/VAADIN/themes/themename/layouts/mylay-out.html`. (Notice that the root path `WebContent/VAADIN/themes/` for themes is fixed.) A template can also be provided dynamically from an **InputStream**, as explained below. A template includes `<div>` elements with a `location` attribute that defines the location identifier. All custom layout HTML-files must be saved using UTF-8 character encoding.

```html
<table width="100%" height="100%">
  <tr height="100%">
    <td>
      <table align="center">
        <tr>
          <td align="right">User name:</td>
          <td><div location="username"></div></td>
        </tr>
        <tr>
          <td align="right">Password:</td>
          <td><div location="password"></div></td>
        </tr>
      </table>
    </td>
  </tr>
  <tr>
    <td align="right" colspan="2">
      <div location="okbutton"></div>
    </td>
  </tr>
</table>
```

The client-side engine of Vaadin will replace contents of the location elements with the components. The components are bound to the location elements by the location identifier given to `addCompon-ent()`, as shown in the example below.

```java
// Have a Panel where to put the custom layout.
Panel panel = new Panel("Login");
panel.setSizeUndefined();
main.addComponent(panel);

// Create custom layout from "layoutname.html" template.
```

```
CustomLayout custom = new CustomLayout("layoutname");
custom.addStyleName("customlayoutexample");

// Use it as the layout of the Panel.
panel.setContent(custom);

// Create a few components and bind them to the location tags
// in the custom layout.
TextField username = new TextField();
custom.addComponent(username, "username");

TextField password = new TextField();
custom.addComponent(password, "password");

Button ok = new Button("Login");
custom.addComponent(ok, "okbutton");
```

The resulting layout is shown below in Figure 6.27, "Example of a Custom Layout Component".

Figure 6.27. Example of a Custom Layout Component

You can use `addComponent()` also to replace an existing component in the location given in the second parameter.

In addition to a static template file, you can provide a template dynamically with the **CustomLayout** constructor that accepts an **InputStream** as the template source. For example:

```
new CustomLayout(new ByteArrayInputStream("<b>Tem-
plate</b>".getBytes()));
```

or

```
new CustomLayout(new FileInputStream(file));
```

Chapter 7

Visual User Interface Design with Eclipse

This chapter provides instructions for developing the graphical user interface of Vaadin components with the Vaadin Plugin for the Eclipse IDE.

7.1. Overview

The visual designer feature in the Vaadin Plugin for Eclipse allows you to design the user interface of an entire application or of specific composite components. The plugin generates the actual Java code, which is designed to be reusable, so you can design the basic layout of the user interface with the visual designer and build the user interaction logic on top of the generated code. You can use inheritance and composition to modify the components further.

The designer works with classes that extend the **CustomComponent** class, which is the basic technique in Vaadin for creating

composite components. Component composition is described in
Section 5.23, "Component Composition with **CustomComponent**".
Any **CustomComponent** will not do for the visual designer; you
need to create a new one as instructed below.

For instructions on installing the Eclipse plugin, see Section 2.2.1,
"Vaadin Plugin for Eclipse".

Using a Composite Component

You can use a composite component as you would use any
Vaadin component. Just remember that the component as well as
its root layout, which is an **AbsoluteLayout**, are 100% wide and
high by default. A component with full size (expand-to-fit container)
may not be inside a layout with undefined size (shrink-to-fit content).
The default root layout for **Window** is a **VerticalLayout**, which by
default has undefined height, so you have to set it explicitly to a
defined size, usually to full (100%) height.

```
public class MyApplication extends Application {
    public void init() {
        Window mainWindow = new Window("My Application");
        setMainWindow(mainWindow);

        // Needed because composites are full size
        mainWindow.getContent().setSizeFull();

        MyComposite myComposite = new MyComposite();
        mainWindow.addComponent(myComposite);
    }
}
```

You could also set the size of the root layout of the composite to
a fixed height (in component properties in the visual editor). An
AbsoluteLayout may not have undefined size.

7.2. Creating a New Composite

If the Vaadin Plugin is installed in Eclipse, you can create a new composite component as follows.

1. Select **File → New → Other...** in the main menu or right-click the **Project Explorer** and select **New → Other...** to open the **New** window.

2. In the first, **Select a wizard** step, select **Vaadin → Vaadin Composite** and click **Next**.

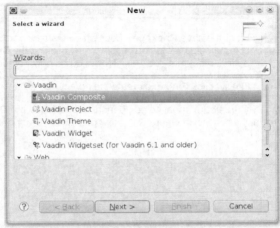

3. The **Source folder** is the root source directory where the new component will be created. This is by default the default source directory of your project.

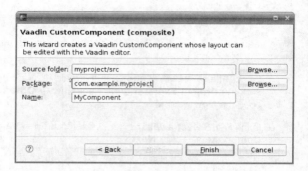

Enter the Java **Package** under which the new component class should be created or select it by clicking the **Browse** button. Also enter the class **Name** of the new component.

Finally, click **Finish** to create the component.

A newly created composite component is opened in the **Design** window, as shown in Figure 7.1, "New Composite Component".

```
MyComponent.java ⊠                                              ─ □
    package com.vaadin.book.examples.editor;

 ⊕ import com.vaadin.annotations.AutoGenerated;□

    public class MyComponent extends CustomComponent {

        @AutoGenerated
        private AbsoluteLayout mainLayout;

        /**
         * The constructor should first build the main layout, set the
         * composition root and then do any custom initialization.
         *
         * The constructor will not be automatically regenerated by the
         * visual editor.
         */
        public MyComponent() {
            buildMainLayout();
            setCompositionRoot(mainLayout);

            // TODO add user code here
        }

        @AutoGenerated
        private void buildMainLayout() {
            // the main layout and components will be created here
            mainLayout = new AbsoluteLayout();
        }

    }

Source Design
```

Figure 7.1. New Composite Component

You can observe that a component that you can edit with the
visual designer has two tabs at the bottom of the view: **Source**
and **Design**. These tabs allow switching between the source view
and the visual design view.

If you later open the source file for editing, the **Source** and **Design**
tabs should appear below the source editor. If they do not, right-
click the file in the Project Explorer and select **Open With**.

7.3. Using The Visual Designer

The visual editor view consists of, on the left side, an *editing area*
that displays the current layout and, on the right side, a *control
panel* that contains a *component list* for selecting new components
to add, the current *component tree*, and a *component property
panel*.

7.3.1. Adding New Components

Adding new components to the user interface is done as follows by dragging them from the component list to either the editing area or to the component tree. If you drag the components to the tree,

1. Select which components are shown in the component list by entering a search string or by expanding the filters and selecting only the desired component categories.

2. Drag a component from the component list to either:

   a. Editing area, where you can easily move and resize the component. Dragging a component onto a layout component will add it in it and you can also position components within a layout by dragging them.

   b. Component tree. Remember that you can only add components under a layout component or other component container.

3. Edit the component properties

   a. In the editing area, you can move and resize the components, and set their alignment in the containing layout.

   b. In the property panel, you can set the component name, size, position and other properties.

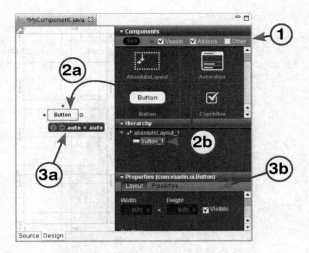

Figure 7.2. Adding a New Component Node

You can delete a component by right-clicking it in the component tree and selecting **Remove**. The context menu also allows copying and pasting components.

A composite component created by the plugin must have a **AbsoluteLayout** as its root layout. While it is suitable for the visual designer, absolute layouts are rarely used otherwise in Vaadin applications. If you want to use another root layout, you can add another layout inside the `mainLayout` and set that as the root with `setCompositionRoot()` in the source view. It will be used as the root when the component is actually used in an application.

7.3.2. Setting Component Properties

The property setting sub-panel of the control panel allows setting component properties. The panel has two tabs: **Layout** and **Properties**, where the latter defines the various basic properties.

Basic Properties

The top section of the property panel, shown in Figure 7.3, "Basic Component Properties", allows setting basic component properties. The panel also includes properties such as field properties for field components.

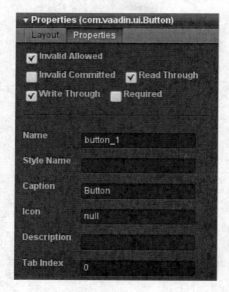

Figure 7.3. Basic Component Properties

The properties are as follows:

Name
> The name of the component, which is used for the reference to the component, so it must obey Java notation for variable names.

Style Name
> A space-separated list of CSS style class names for the component. See Chapter 8, *Themes* for information on component styles in themes.

Caption
> The caption of a component is usually displayed above the component. Some components, such as **Button**, display the caption inside the component. For **Label** text, you should set the value of the label instead of the caption, which should be left empty.

Description (tooltip)
> The description is usually displayed as a tooltip when the mouse pointer hovers over the component for a while. Some components, such as **Form** have their own way of displaying the description.

Icon
> The icon of a component is usually displayed above the component, left of the caption. Some components, such as **Button**, display the icon inside the component.

Formatting type
> Some components allow different formatting types, such as **Label**, which allow formatting either as **Text**, **XHTML**, **Preformatted**, and **Raw**.

Value
> The component value. The value type and how it is displayed by the component varies between different component types and each value type has its own editor. The editor opens by clicking on the **...** button.

Most of the basic component properties are defined in the **Component** interface; see Section 5.2.1, "**Component** Interface" for further details.

Layout Properties

The size of a component is determined by its width and height, which you can give in the two edit boxes in the control panel. You can use any unit specifiers for components, as described in Section 5.3.9, "Sizing Components". Emptying a size box will make the size "automatic", which means setting the size as *undefined*. In the generated code, the undefined value will be expressed as "`-1px`".

Setting width of "100px" and *auto* (undefined or empty) height would result in the following generated settings for a button:

```
// myButton
myButton = new Button();
...
myButton.setHeight("-1px");
myButton.setWidth("100px");
...
```

Figure 7.4, "Layout Properties" shows the control panel area for the size and position.

Figure 7.4. Layout Properties

The generated code for the example would be:

```
// myButton
myButton = new Button();
myButton.setWidth("-1px");
myButton.setHeight("-1px");
myButton.setImmediate(true);
myButton.setCaption("My Button");
mainLayout.addComponent(myButton,
                        "top:243.0px;left:152.0px;");
```

The position is given as a CSS position in the second parameter for addComponent(). The values "-1px" for width and height will make the button to be sized automatically to the minimum size required by the caption.

When editing the position of a component inside an **AbsoluteLayout**, the editor will display vertical and horizontal guides, which you can use to set the position of the component. See Section 7.3.3, "Editing an **AbsoluteLayout**" for more information about editing absolute layouts.

The **ZIndex** setting controls the "Z coordinate" of the components, that is, which component will overlay which when they overlap. Value -1 means automatic, in which case the components added to the layout later will be on top.

7.3.3. Editing an AbsoluteLayout

The visual editor has interactive support for the **AbsoluteLayout** component that allows positioning components exactly at specified coordinates. You can position the components using guides that control the position attributes, shown in the control panel on the right. The position values are measured in pixels from the corresponding edge; the vertical and horizontal rulers show the distances from the top and left edge.

Figure 7.5, "Positioning with **AbsoluteLayout**" shows three components, a **Label**, a **Table**, and a **Button**, inside an **AbsoluteLayout**.

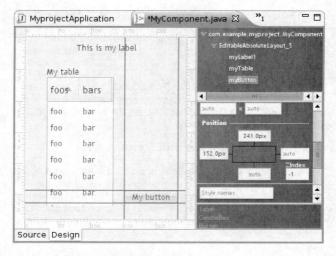

Figure 7.5. Positioning with AbsoluteLayout

Position attributes that are empty are *automatic* and can be either zero (at the edge) or dynamic to make it shrink to fit the size of the component, depending on the component. Guides are shown also for the automatic position attributes and move automatically; in Figure 7.5, "Positioning with **AbsoluteLayout**" the right and bottom edges of the **Button** are automatic.

Moving an automatic guide manually makes the guide and the corresponding the position attribute non-automatic. To make a manually set attribute automatic, empty it in the control panel. Figure 7.6, "Manually positioned **Label**" shows a **Label** component with all the four edges set manually. Notice that if an automatic position is 0, the guide is at the edge of the ruler.

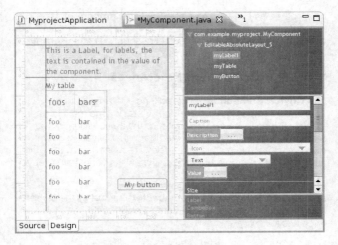

Figure 7.6. Manually positioned Label

7.4. Structure of a Visually Editable Component

A component created by the wizard and later managed by the visual editor has a very specific structure that allows you to insert your user interface logic in the component while keeping a minimal amount of code off-limits. You need to know what you can edit yourself and what exactly is managed by the editor. The managed member variables and methods are marked with the **AutoGenerated** annotation, as you can see later.

A visually editable component consists of:

- Member variables containing sub-component references
- Sub-component builder methods
- The constructor

The structure of a composite component is hierarchical, a nested hierarchy of layout components containing other layout components as well as regular components. The root layout of the component tree, or the *composition root* of the **CustomComponent**, is named `mainLayout`. See Section 5.23, "Component Composition with **CustomComponent**" for a detailed description of the structure of custom (composite) components.

7.4.1. Sub-Component References

The **CustomComponent** class will include a reference to each contained component as a member variable. The most important of these is the `mainLayout` reference to the composition root layout. Such automatically generated member variables are marked with the `@AutoGenerated` annotation. They are managed by the editor, so you should not edit them manually, unless you know what you are doing.

A composite component with an **AbsoluteLayout** as the composition root, containing a **Button** and a **Table** would have the references as follows:

```
public class MyComponent extends CustomComponent {

    @AutoGenerated
    private AbsoluteLayout mainLayout;
    @AutoGenerated
    private Button myButton;
    @AutoGenerated
    private Table myTable;
    ...
```

The names of the member variables are defined in the component properties panel of the visual editor, in the **Component name** field, as described in the section called "Basic Properties". While you can change the name of any other components, the name of the root layout is always `mainLayout`. It is fixed because the editor does not make changes to the constructor, as noted in Section 7.4.3, "The Constructor". You can, however, change the type of the root layout, which is an **AbsoluteLayout** by default.

Certain typically static components, such as the **Label** label component, will not have a reference as a member variable. See the description of the builder methods below for details.

7.4.2. Sub-Component Builders

Every managed layout component will have a builder method that creates the layout and all its contained components. The builder

---

puts references to the created components in their corresponding member variables, and it also returns a reference to the created layout component.

Below is an example of an initial main layout:

```
@AutoGenerated
private AbsoluteLayout buildMainLayout() {
    // common part: create layout
    mainLayout = new AbsoluteLayout();

    // top-level component properties
    setHeight("100.0%");
    setWidth("100.0%");

    return mainLayout;
}
```

Notice that while the builder methods return a reference to the created component, they also write the reference directly to the member variable. The returned reference might not be used by the generated code at all (in the constructor or in the builder methods), but you can use it for your purposes.

The builder of the main layout is called in the constructor, as explained in Section 7.4.3, "The Constructor". When you have a layout with nested layout components, the builders of each layout will call the appropriate builder methods of their contained layouts to create their contents.

7.4.3. The Constructor

When you create a new composite component using the wizard, it will create a constructor for the component and fill its basic content.

```
public MyComponent() {
    buildMainLayout();
    setCompositionRoot(mainLayout);

    // TODO add user code here
}
```

The most important thing to do in the constructor is to set the composition root of the **CustomComponent** with the setCompositionRoot() (see Section 5.23, "Component Composition with **CustomComponent**" for more details on the composition root).

The generated constructor first builds the root layout of the composite component with `buildMainLayout()` and then uses the `mainLayout` reference.

The editor will not change the constructor afterwards, so you can safely change it as you want. The editor does not allow changing the member variable holding a reference to the root layout, so it is always named `mainLayout`.

Chapter 8

Themes

This chapter provides details about using and creating *themes* that control the visual look of web applications. Themes consist of Cascading Style Sheets (CSS) and other theme resources such as images. We provide an introduction to CSS, especially concerning the styling of HTML by element classes.

This chapter is a draft. Many new features that will be included in the final version of Vaadin 7 are not yet covered in the draft and some of the content may be outdated. For the most current version, please see the on-line edition available at `http://vaad-in.com/book`.

8.1. Overview

Vaadin separates the appearance of the user interface from its logic using *themes*. Themes can include CSS style sheets, custom HTML layouts, and any necessary graphics. Theme resources can also be accessed from an application as **ThemeResource** objects.

Custom themes are placed under the `WebContent/VAADIN/themes/` folder of the web application. This location is fixed -- the `VAADIN` folder specifies that these are static resources specific to Vaadin.

The folder should normally contain also the built-in themes, although you can let them be loaded dynamically from the Vaadin JAR (even though that is somewhat inefficient). Figure 8.1, "Contents of a Theme" illustrates the contents of a theme.

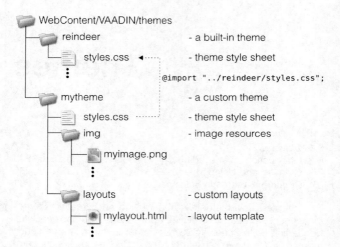

Figure 8.1. Contents of a Theme

The name of a theme folder defines the name of the theme. The name is used in the `@Theme` annotation that sets the theme. A theme must contain the `styles.css` stylesheet, but other contents have free naming. We suggest a convention for naming the folders as `img` for images, `layouts` for custom layouts, and `css` for additional stylesheets.

Custom themes that use an existing complete theme need to inherit the theme. See Section 8.3.2, "Built-in Themes" and Section 8.3.4, "Theme Inheritance" for details on inheriting a theme. Copying and modifying a complete theme is also possible, but it may need more work to maintain if the modifications are small.

You use a theme with by specifying it with the `@Theme` annotation for the root class of the application as follows:

```
@Theme("mytheme")
public class MyRoot extends Root {
    @Override
    protected void init(WrappedRequest request) {
        ...
    }
}
```

A theme can contain alternate styles for user interface components, which can be changed as needed.

In addition to style sheets, a theme can contain HTML templates for custom layouts used with **CustomLayout**. See Section 6.14, "Custom Layouts" for details.

Resources provided in a theme can also be accessed using the **ThemeResource** class, as described in Section 4.3.4, "Theme Resources". This allows using theme resources, such as images, for example in **Embedded** objects and other objects that allow inclusion of images using resources.

8.2. Introduction to Cascading Style Sheets

Cascading Style Sheets or CSS is a technique to separate the appearance of a web page from the content represented in HTML or XHTML. Let us give a short introduction to Cascading Style Sheets and look how they are relevant to software development with Vaadin.

8.2.1. Basic CSS Rules

A style sheet is a file that contains a set of *rules*. Each rule consists of one or more *selectors*, separated with commas, and a *declaration block* enclosed in curly braces. A declaration block contains a list of *property* statements. Each property has a label and a value, separated with a colon. A property statement ends with a semi-colon.

Let us look at an example:

```
p, td {
  color: blue;
}

td {
```

```
  background: yellow;
  font-weight: bold;
}
```

In the example above, `p` and `td` are element type selectors that match with `<p>` and `<td>` elements in HTML, respectively. The first rule matches with both elements, while the second matches only with `<td>` elements. Let us assume that you have saved the above style sheet with the name `mystylesheet.css` and consider the following HTML file located in the same folder.

```
<html>
    <head>
        <link rel="stylesheet" type="text/css"
            href="mystylesheet.css"/>
    </head>
    <body>
        <p>This is a paragraph</p>
        <p>This is another paragraph</p>
        <table>
            <tr>
                <td>This is a table cell</td>
                <td>This is another table cell</td>
            </tr>
        </table>
    </body>
</html>
```

The `<link>` element defines the style sheet to use. The HTML elements that match the above rules are emphasized. When the page is displayed in the browser, it will look as shown in the figure below.

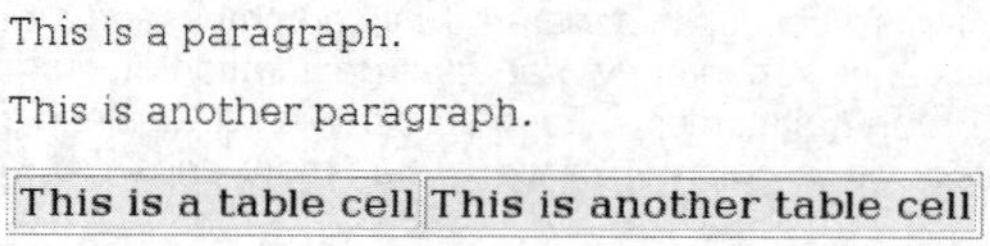

This is a paragraph.

This is another paragraph.

| This is a table cell | This is another table cell |

Figure 8.2. Simple Styling by Element Type

CSS has an *inheritance* mechanism where contained elements inherit the properties of their parent elements. For example, let us change the above example and define it instead as follows:

```
table {
    color: blue;
    background: yellow;
}
```

All elements contained in the `<table>` element would have the same properties. For example, the text in the contained `<td>` elements would be in blue color.

Each HTML element type accepts a certain set of properties. The `<div>` elements are generic elements that can be used to create almost any layout and formatting that can be created with a specific HTML element type. Vaadin uses `<div>` elements extensively, especially for layouts.

Matching elements by their type is, however, rarely if ever used in style sheets for Vaadin components or Google Web Toolkit widgets.

8.2.2. Matching by Element Class

Matching HTML elements by the *class* attribute of the elements is the most relevant form of matching with Vaadin. It is also possible to match with the *identifier* of a HTML element.

The class of an HTML element is defined with the `class` attribute as follows:

```html
<html>
  <body>
    <p class="normal">This is the first paragraph</p>

    <p class="another">This is the second paragraph</p>

    <table>
      <tr>
        <td class="normal">This is a table cell</td>
        <td class="another">This is another table cell</td>
      </tr>
    </table>
  </body>
</html>
```

The class attributes of HTML elements can be matched in CSS rules with a selector notation where the class name is written after a period following the element name. This gives us full control of matching elements by their type and class.

```
p.normal     {color: red;}
p.another    {color: blue;}
td.normal    {background: pink;}
td.another   {background: yellow;}
```

The page would look as shown below:

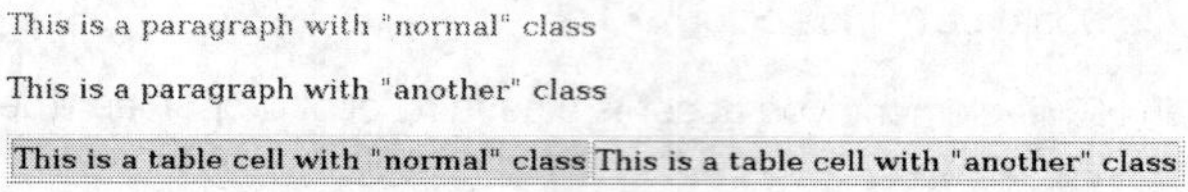

This is a paragraph with "normal" class

This is a paragraph with "another" class

| This is a table cell with "normal" class | This is a table cell with "another" class |

Figure 8.3. Matching HTML Element Type and Class

We can also match solely by the class by using the universal selector * for the element name, for example *.normal. The universal selector can also be left out altogether so that we use just the class name following the period, for example .normal.

```
.normal {
    color: red;
}

.another {
    blackground: yellow;
}
```

In this case, the rule will match with all elements of the same class regardless of the element type. The result is shown in Figure 8.4, "Matching Only HTML Element Class". This example illustrates a technique to make style sheets compatible regardless of the exact HTML element used in drawing a component.

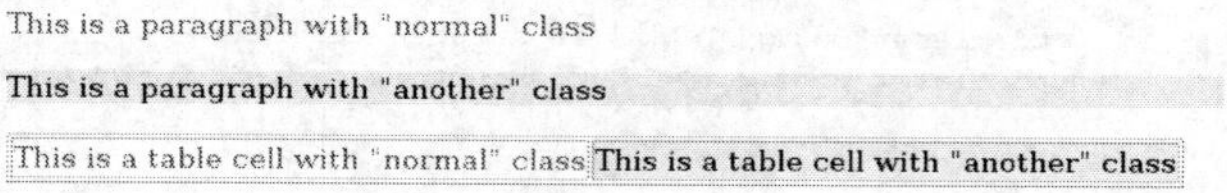

This is a paragraph with "normal" class

This is a paragraph with "another" class

| This is a table cell with "normal" class | This is a table cell with "another" class |

Figure 8.4. Matching Only HTML Element Class

To assure compatibility, we recommend that you use only matching based on the element classes and *do not* match for specific HTML element types in CSS rules, because either Vaadin or GWT may use different HTML elements to render some components in the future. For example, IT Mill Toolkit Release 4 used `<div>` elements extensively for layout components. However, IT Mill Toolkit Release 5 and Vaadin use GWT to render the components, and GWT uses the `<table>` element to implement most layouts. Similarly, IT Mill Toolkit Release 4 used `<div>` element also for buttons, but in Release 5, GWT uses the `<button>` element. Vaadin has little control over how GWT renders its components, so we can not guarantee compatibility in different versions of GWT. However, both `<div>` and `<table>` as well as `<tr>` and `<td>` elements accept most of the same properties, so matching only the class hierarchy of the elements should be compatible in most cases.

8.2.3. Matching by Descendant Relationship

CSS allows matching HTML by their containment relationship. For example, consider the following HTML fragment:

```
<body>
  <p class="mytext">Here is some text inside a
                    paragraph element</p>
  <table class="mytable">
    <tr>
      <td class="mytext">Here is text inside
                    a table and inside a td element.</td>
    </tr>
  </table>
</body>
```

Matching by the class name `.mytext` alone would match both the `<p>` and `<td>` elements. If we want to match only the table cell, we could use the following selector:

```
.mytable .mytext {color: blue;}
```

To match, a class listed in a rule does not have to be an immediate descendant of the previous class, but just a descendant. For example, the selector "`.v-panel .v-button`" would match all elements with class `.v-button` somewhere inside an element with class `.v-panel`.

Let us give an example with a real case. Consider the following Vaadin component.

```
public class LoginBox extends CustomComponent {
    Panel          panel  = new Panel("Log In");

    public LoginBox () {
```

```
            setCompositionRoot(panel);

        panel.addComponent(new TextField("Username:"));
        panel.addComponent(new TextField("Password:"));
        panel.addComponent(new Button("Login"));
    }
}
```

The component will look by default as shown in the following figure.

Figure 8.5. Themeing Login Box Example with 'runo' theme.

Now, let us look at the HTML structure of the component. The following listing assumes that the application contains only the above
component in the main window of the application.

```
<body>
   <div id="v-app">
     <div>
       <div class="v-orderedlayout">
         <div>
           <div class="v-panel">
             <div class="v-panel-caption">Log In</div>
             <div class="v-panel-content">
               <div class="v-orderedlayout">
                 <div>
                   <div>
                     <div class="v-caption">
                       <span>Username:</span>
                     </div>
                   </div>
                   <input type="text" class="v-textfield"/>
                 </div>
                 <div>
                   <div>
                     <div class="v-caption">
                       <span>Password:</span>
                     </div>
                   </div>
                   <input type="password"
```

```
                                class="v-textfield"/>
                </div>
                <div>
                  <button type="button"
                          class="v-button">Login</button>
                </div>
              </div>
            </div>
            <div class="v-panel-deco"/>
          </div>
        </div>
      </div>
    </div>
  </div>
</body>
```

Now, consider the following theme where we set the backgrounds
of various elements.

```
.v-panel .v-panel-caption {
 background: #80ff80; /* pale green */
}

.v-panel .v-panel-content {
 background: yellow;
}

.v-panel .v-textfield {
 background: #e0e0ff; /* pale blue */
}

.v-panel .v-button {
 background: pink;
}
```

The coloring has changed as shown in the following figure.

Figure 8.6. Themeing Login Box Example with Custom Theme

An element can have multiple classes separated with a space. With multiple classes, a CSS rule matches an element if any of the classes match. This feature is used in many Vaadin components to allow matching based on the state of the component. For example, when the mouse is over a **Link** component, `over` class is added to the component. Most of such styling is a feature of Google Web Toolkit.

8.2.4. Notes on Compatibility

CSS was first proposed in 1994. The specification of CSS is maintained by the CSS Working Group of World Wide Web Consortium (W3C). Its versions are specified as *levels* that build upon the earlier version. CSS Level 1 was published in 1996, Level 2 in 1998. Development of CSS Level 3 was started in 1998 and is still under way.

While the support for CSS has been universal in all graphical web browsers since at least 1995, the support has been very incomplete at times and there still exists an unfortunate number of incompatibilities between browsers. While we have tried to take these incompatibilities into account in the built-in themes in Vaadin, you need to consider them while developing custom themes.

Compatibility issues are detailed in various CSS handbooks.

8.3. Creating and Using Themes

Custom themes are placed in `VAADIN/themes` folder of the web application (in the `WebContent` directory) as illustrated in Figure 8.1, "Contents of a Theme". This location is fixed. You need to have a theme folder for each theme you use in your application, although applications rarely need more than a single theme. For example, if you want to define a theme with the name `mytheme`, you will place it in folder `VAADIN/themes/mytheme`.

A custom theme must also inherit a built-in theme, as shown in the example below:

```
@import "../reindeer/styles.css";

.v-app {
    background: yellow;
}
```

Vaadin 6.0 includes two built-in themes: `reindeer` and `runo`. The latter is a compatibility theme for IT Mill Toolkit 5; there is no longer a "default" theme. See Section 8.3.2, "Built-in Themes" and Section 8.3.4, "Theme Inheritance" below for details on inheriting themes.

8.3.1. Styling Standard Components

Each user interface component in Vaadin has a CSS style class that you can use to control the appearance of the component. Some components have additional sub-elements that also allow styling.

Table 8.1, "Default CSS Style Names of Vaadin Components" lists the style classes of all Vaadin components, together with their client-side widgets. Notice that a single server-side component can have multiple client-side implementations. For example, a **Button** can be rendered on the client side either as a regular button or a check box, depending on the `switchMode` attribute of the button. For details regarding the mapping to client-side components, see Section 11.11, "Defining a Client-Side Module Descriptor". Each client-side component type has its own style class and a number of additional classes that depend on the client-side state of the component. For example, a text field will have `v-textfield-focus` class when mouse pointer hovers over the component. This state is purely on the client-side and is not passed to the server.

Table 8.1. Default CSS Style Names of Vaadin Components

Server-Side Component	Client-Side Widget	CSS Class Name
AbsoluteLayout	VAbsoluteLayout	v-absolutelayout
Accordion	VAccordion	v-accordion
Button	VButton	v-button
CheckBox	VCheckBox	v-checkbox
CssLayout	VCssLayout	v-csslayout
CustomComponent	VCustomComponent	v-customcomponent
CustomLayout	VCustomLayout	v-customlayout
DateField	VDateField	v-datefield

Server-Side Component	Client-Side Widget	CSS Class Name
	VCalendar	v-datefield-entrycalendar
	VDateFieldCalendar	v-datefield-calendar
	VPopupCalendar	v-datefield-calendar
	VTextualDate	
Embedded	VEmbedded	-
Form	VForm	v-form
FormLayout	VFormLayout	-
GridLayout	VGridLayout	-
Label	VLabel	v-label
Link	VLink	v-link
OptionGroup	VOptionGroup	v-select-optiongroup
HorizontalLayout	VHorizontalLayout	v-horizontallayout
VerticalLayout	VVerticalLayout	v-verticallayout
Panel	VPanel	v-panel
Select		
	VListSelect	v-listselect
	VFilterSelect	v-filterselect
Slider	VSlider	v-slider
SplitPanel	VSplitPanel	-
	VSplitPanelHorizontal	-
	VSplitPanelVertical	-
Table	VScrollTable	v-table
	VTablePaging	v-table
TabSheet	VTabSheet	v-tabsheet
TextField	VTextField	v-textfield
	VTextArea	
	VPasswordField	

Server-Side Component	Client-Side Widget	CSS Class Name
Tree	VTree	v-tree
TwinColSelect	VTwinColSelect	v-select-twincol
Upload	VUpload	-
Window	VWindow	v-window
-	CalendarEntry	-
-	CalendarPanel	v-datefield-calendarpanel
-	ContextMenu	v-contextmenu
-	VUnknownComponent	vaadin-unknown
-	VView	-
-	Menubar	gwt-MenuBar
-	MenuItem	gwt-MenuItem
-	Time	v-datefield-time

Please see the documentation of the particular components for a listing of possible sub-component styles.

Some client-side components can be shared by different server-side components. There is also the **VUnknownComponent**, which is a component that indicates an internal error in a situation where the server asked to render a component which is not available on the client-side.

8.3.2. Built-in Themes

Vaadin currently includes two built-in themes: reindeer and runo. The default theme in Vaadin 6 and 7 is reindeer. The runo was the default theme for IT Mill Toolkit 5 (where its name was "default").

The built-in themes are provided in the respective VAADIN/themes/reindeer/styles.css and VAADIN/themes/runo/styles.css stylesheets in the Vaadin library JAR. These stylesheets are compilations of the separate stylesheets for each component in the corresponding subdirectory. The stylesheets are compiled to a single file for efficiency: the browser needs to load just a single file.

Various constants related to the built-in themes are defined in the theme classes in com.vaadin.ui.themes package. These are mostly special style names for specific components.

```
@Theme("runo")
public class MyRoot extends Root {
    @Override
    protected void init(WrappedRequest request) {
        ...
        Panel panel = new Panel("Regular Panel in the Runo Theme");

        panel.addComponent(new Button("Regular Runo Button"));

        // A button with the "small" style
        Button smallButton = new Button("Small Runo Button");
        smallButton.addStyleName(Runo.BUTTON_SMALL);

        Panel lightPanel = new Panel("Light Panel");
        lightPanel.addStyleName(Runo.PANEL_LIGHT);
        lightPanel.addComponent(new Label("With addStyle-
Name(\"light\")"));
        ...
```

The example with the Runo theme is shown in Figure 8.7, "Runo Theme".

Figure 8.7. Runo Theme

Serving Built-In Themes Statically

The built-in themes included in the Vaadin library JAR are served dynamically from the JAR by the servlet. Serving themes and widget sets statically by the web server is more efficient. You only need to extract the VAADIN/ directory from the JAR under

> your `WebContent` directory. Just make sure to up-
> date it if you upgrade to a newer version of Vaadin.

Creation of a default theme for custom GWT widgets is described in Section 11.9, "Styling a Widget".

8.3.3. Using Themes

Using a theme is simple, you just set it for a **Root** class with the `@Theme` annotation.

8.3.4. Theme Inheritance

When you define your own theme, you will need to inherit a built-in theme (unless you just copy the built-in theme, which is not recommended).

Inheritance in CSS is done with the `@import` statement. In the typical case, when you define your own theme, you inherit a built-in theme as follows:

```
@import "../reindeer/styles.css";

.v-app {
    background: yellow;
}
```

You can even create a deep hierarchy of themes by inheritance.

8.4. Creating a Theme in Eclipse

The Eclipse plugin provides a wizard for creating custom themes. Do the following steps to create a new theme.

1. Select **File → New → Other...** in the main menu or right-click the **Project Explorer** and select **New → Other...**. A window will open.

2. In the **Select a wizard** step, select the **Vaadin → Vaadin Theme** wizard.

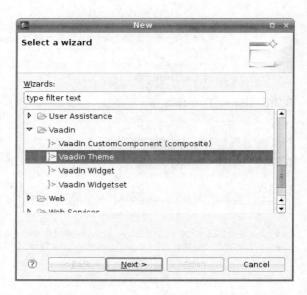

Click **Next** to proceed to the next step.

3. In the **Create a new Vaadin theme** step, you have the following settings:

   Project (mandatory)
   > The project in which the theme should be created.

   Theme name (mandatory)
   > The theme name is used as the name of the theme folder and in a CSS tag (prefixed with "v-theme-"), so it must be a proper identifier. Only latin alphanumerics, underscore, and minus sign are allowed.

   Modify application classes to use theme (optional)
   > The setting allows the wizard to write a code statement that enables the theme in the constructor of the selected application class(es). If you need to control the theme with dynamic logic, you can leave the setting unchecked or change the generated line later.

Click **Finish** to create the theme.

The wizard creates the theme folder under the `WebContent/VAAD-IN/themes` folder and the actual style sheet as `styles.css`, as illustrated in Figure 8.8, "Newly Created Theme".

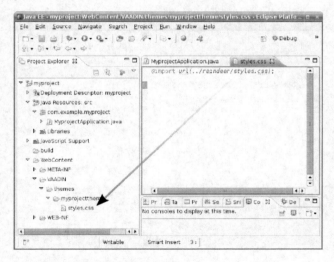

Figure 8.8. Newly Created Theme

The created theme inherits a built-in base theme with an `@import` statement. See the explanation of theme inheritance in Section 8.3,

"Creating and Using Themes". Notice that the `reindeer` theme is not located in the `widgetsets` folder, but in the Vaadin JAR. See Section 8.3.2, "Built-in Themes" for information for serving the built-in themes.

If you selected an application class or classes in the **Modify application classes to use theme** in the theme wizard, the wizard will add the `@Theme` annotation to the application root class.

If you later rename the theme in Eclipse, notice that changing the name of the folder will not automatically change the `@Theme` annotation. You need to change such references to theme names in the calls manually.

Chapter 9

Binding Components to Data

This chapter describes the Vaadin Data Model and shows how you can use it to bind components directly to data sources, such as database queries.

This edition is a draft. Many new features that will be included in the final version of Vaadin 7 are not yet covered in the draft and some of the content may be outdated. For the most current version, please see the on-line edition available at `http://vaad-in.com/book`.

9.1. Overview

The Vaadin Data Model is one of the core concepts of the library. To allow the view (user interface components) to access the data model of an application directly, we have introduced a standard data interface.

The model allows binding user interface components directly to the data that they display and possibly allow to edit. There are three nested levels of hierarchy in the data model: *property*, *item*, and *container*. Using a spreadsheet application as an analogy, these would correspond to a cell, a row, and a table, respectively.

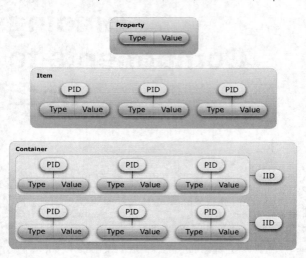

Figure 9.1. Vaadin Data Model

The Data Model is realized as a set of interfaces in the **com.vaadin.data** package. The package contains the **Property**, **Item**, and **Container** interfaces, along with a number of more specialized interfaces and classes.

Notice that the Data Model does not define data representation, but only interfaces. This leaves the representation fully to the implementation of the containers. The representation can be almost anything, such as a plain old Java object (POJO) structure, a filesystem, or a database query.

The Data Model is used heavily in the core user interface components of Vaadin, especially the field components, that is, components that implement the **Field** interface or more typically extend **AbstractField**, which defines many common features. A key feature of all the built-in field components is that they can either maintain their data by themselves or be bound to an external data source. The value of a field is always available through the **Property** interface. As more than one component can be bound to the same data source, it is easy to implement various viewer-editor patterns.

The relationships of the various interfaces are shown in Figure 9.2, "Interface Relationships in Vaadin Data Model"; the value change event and listener interfaces are shown only for the **Property** interface, while the notifier interfaces are omitted altogether.

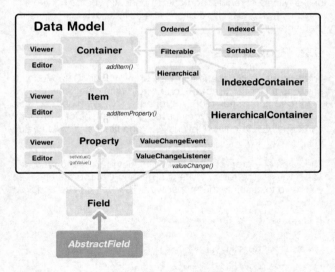

Figure 9.2. Interface Relationships in Vaadin Data Model

The Data Model has many important and useful features, such as support for change notification. Especially containers have many helper interfaces, including ones that allow indexing, ordering, sorting, and filtering the data. Also **Field** components provide a

---

number of features involving the data model, such as buffering, validation, and lazy loading.

Vaadin provides a number of built-in implementations of the data model interfaces. The built-in implementations are used as the default data models in many field components.

In addition to the built-in implementations, many data model implementations, such as containers, are available as add-ons, either from the Vaadin Directory or from independent sources. Both commercial and free implementations exist. The JPAContainer, described in Chapter 18, *Vaadin JPAContainer*, is the most often used conmmercial container add-on. The installation of add-ons is described in Chapter 15, *Using Vaadin Add-ons*. Notice that unlike with most regular add-on components, you do not need to compile a widget set for add-ons that include just data model implementations.

9.2. Properties

The **Property** interface is the base of the Vaadin Data Model. It provides a standardized API for a single data object that can be read (get) and written (set). A property is always typed, but can optionally support data type conversions. The type of a property can be any Java class. Optionally, properties can provide value change events for following their changes.

The value of a property is written with `setValue()` and read with `getValue()`. The return value is a generic **Object** reference, so you need to cast it to the proper type. The type can be acquired with `getType()`.

```
final TextField tf = new TextField("Name");

// Set the value
tf.setValue("The text field value");

// When the field value is edited by the user
tf.addListener(new Property.ValueChangeListener() {
    public void valueChange(ValueChangeEvent event) {
        // Get the value and cast it to proper type
        String value = (String) tf.getValue();

        // Do something with it
        layout.addComponent(new Label(value));
    }
});
```

Changes in the property value usually emit a **ValueChangeEvent**, which can be handled with a **ValueChangeListener**. The event object provides reference to the property with `getProperty()`.

Properties are in themselves unnamed. They are collected in *items*, which associate the properties with names: the *Property Identifiers* or *PID*s. Items can be further contained in containers and are identified with *Item Identifiers* or *IID*s. In the spreadsheet analogy, *Property Identifiers* would correspond to column names and *Item Identifiers* to row names. The identifiers can be arbitrary objects, but must implement the `equals(Object)` and `hashCode()` methods so that they can be used in any standard Java **Collection**.

The **Property** interface can be utilized either by implementing the interface or by using some of the built-in property implementations. Vaadin includes a **Property** interface implementation for arbitrary function pairs and bean properties, with the **MethodProperty** class, and for simple object properties, with the **ObjectProperty** class, as described later.

In addition to the simple components, many selection components such as **Select**, **Table**, and **Tree** provide their current selection through the **Property** property. In single selection mode, the property is a single item identifier, while in multiple selection mode it is a set of item identifiers. Please see the documentation of the selection components for further details.

Components that can be bound to a property have an internal default data source object, typically a **ObjectProperty**, which is described later. As all such components are viewers or editors, also described later, so you can rebind a component to any data source with `setPropertyDataSource()`.

9.2.1. Property Viewers and Editors

The most important function of the **Property** as well as of the other data model interfaces is to connect classes implementing the interface directly to editor and viewer classes. This means connecting a data source (model) to a user interface component (views) to allow editing or viewing the data model.

A property can be bound to a component implementing the **Viewer** interface with `setPropertyDataSource()`.

```
// Have a data model
ObjectProperty property =
    new ObjectProperty("Hello", String.class);

// Have a component that implements Viewer
Label viewer = new Label();

// Bind it to the data
viewer.setPropertyDataSource(property);
```

You can use the same method in the **Editor** interface to bind a component that allows editing a particular property type to a property.

```
// Have a data model
ObjectProperty property =
    new ObjectProperty("Hello", String.class);

// Have a component that implements Viewer
TextField editor = new TextField("Edit Greeting");

// Bind it to the data
editor.setPropertyDataSource(property);
```

As all field components implement the **Property** interface, you can bind any component implementing the **Viewer** interface to any field, assuming that the viewer is able the view the object type of the field. Continuing from the above example, we can bind a **Label** to the **TextField** value:

```
Label viewer = new Label();
viewer.setPropertyDataSource(editor);

// The value shown in the viewer is updated immediately
// after editing the value in the editor (once it
// loses the focus)
editor.setImmediate(true);
```

9.2.2. ObjectProperty Implementation

The **ObjectProperty** class is a simple implementation of the **Property** interface that allows storing an arbitrary Java object.

```
// Have a component that implements Viewer interface
final TextField tf = new TextField("Name");

// Have a data model with some data
String myObject = "Hello";

// Wrap it in an ObjectProperty
ObjectProperty property =
    new ObjectProperty(myObject, String.class);
```

```
// Bind the property to the component
tf.setPropertyDataSource(property);
```

9.2.3. Converting Between Property Type and Representation

Fields allow editing a certain type, such as a **String** or **Date**. The bound property, on the other hand, could have some entirely different type. Conversion between a representation edited by the field and the model defined in the property is handler with a converter that implements the `Converter` interface.

Most common type conversions, such as between string and integer, are handled by the default converters. They are created in a converter factory global in the application.

Basic Use of Converters

The `setConverter(Converter)` method sets the converter for a field. The method is defined in **AbstractField**.

```
// Have an integer property
final ObjectProperty<Integer> property =
        new ObjectProperty<Integer>(42);

// Create a TextField, which edits Strings
final TextField tf = new TextField("Name");

// Use a converter between String and Integer
tf.setConverter(new StringToIntegerConverter());

// And bind the field
tf.setPropertyDataSource(property);
```

The built-in converters are the following:

Table 9.1. Built-in Converters

StringToInteger-Converter	String	Integer
StringToDouble-Converter	String	Double
StringToNumber-Converter	String	Number

StringTo- BooleanConverter	String	Boolean
StringToDateCon- verter	String	Date
DateToLongCon- verter	Date	Long

In addition, there is a **ReverseConverter** that takes a converter
as a parameter and reverses the conversion direction.

If a converter already exists for a type, the `setConverter(Class)`
retrieves the converter for the given type from the converter factory,
and then sets it for the field. This method is used implicitly when
binding field to a property data source.

Implementing a Converter

A conversion always occurs between a *representation type*, edited
by the field component, and a *model type*, that is, the type of the
property data source. Converters implement the `Converter` interface defined in the com.vaadin.data.util.converter package.

For example, let us assume that we have a simple **Complex** type
for storing complex values.

```
public class ComplexConverter
    implements Converter<String, Complex> {
    @Override
    public Complex convertToModel(String value, Locale locale)
        throws ConversionException {
        String parts[] =
            value.replaceAll("[\\(\\)]", "").split(",");
        if (parts.length != 2)
            throw new ConversionException(
                "Unable to parse String to Complex");
        return new Complex(Double.parseDouble(parts[0]),
                           Double.parseDouble(parts[1]));
    }

    @Override
    public String convertToPresentation(Complex value,
                                        Locale locale)
        throws ConversionException {
        return "("+value.getReal()+","+value.getImag()+")";
    }

    @Override
    public Class<Complex> getModelType() {
        return Complex.class;
```

```
    }

    @Override
    public Class<String> getPresentationType() {
        return String.class;
    }
}
```

The conversion methods get the locale for the conversion as a parameter.

Converter Factory

If a field does not directly allow editing a property type, a default converter is attempted to create using an application-global converter factory. If you define your own converters that you wish to include in the converter factory, you need to implement one yourself. While you could implement the ConverterFactory interface, it is usually easier to just extend **DefaultConverterFactory**.

```
class MyConverterFactory extends DefaultConverterFactory {
    @Override
    public <PRESENTATION, MODEL> Converter<PRESENTATION, MODEL>
            createConverter(Class<PRESENTATION> presentationType,
                            Class<MODEL> modelType) {
        // Handle one particular type conversion
        if (String.class == presentationType &&
            Complex.class == modelType)
            return (Converter<PRESENTATION, MODEL>)
                new ComplexConverter();

        // Default to the supertype
        return super.createConverter(presentationType,
                                     modelType);
    }
}

// Use the factory globally in the application
Application.getCurrentApplication().setConverterFactory(
        new MyConverterFactory());
```

9.2.4. Implementing the Property Interface

Implementation of the **Property** interface requires defining setters and getters for the value and the *read-only* mode. Only a getter is needed for the property type, as the type is often fixed in property implementations.

The following example shows a simple implementation of the **Property** interface:

```
class MyProperty implements Property {
    Integer data     = 0;
    boolean readOnly = false;

    // Return the data type of the model
    public Class<?> getType() {
        return Integer.class;
    }

    public Object getValue() {
        return data;
    }

    // Override the default implementation in Object
    @Override
    public String toString() {
        return Integer.toHexString(data);
    }

    public boolean isReadOnly() {
        return readOnly;
    }

    public void setReadOnly(boolean newStatus) {
        readOnly = newStatus;
    }

    public void setValue(Object newValue)
            throws ReadOnlyException, ConversionException {
        if (readOnly)
            throw new ReadOnlyException();

        // Already the same type as the internal representation
        if (newValue instanceof Integer)
            data = (Integer) newValue;

        // Conversion from a string is required
        else if (newValue instanceof String)
            try {
                data = Integer.parseInt((String) newValue, 16);
            } catch (NumberFormatException e) {
                throw new ConversionException();
            }
        else
            // Don't know how to convert any other types
            throw new ConversionException();

        // Reverse decode the hexadecimal value
    }
}

// Instantiate the property and set its data
MyProperty property = new MyProperty();
property.setValue(42);

// Bind it to a component
final TextField tf = new TextField("Name", property);
```

The components get the displayed value by the `toString()` method, so it is necessary to override it. To allow editing the value, value returned in the `toString()` must be in a format that is accepted by the `setValue()` method, unless the property is read-only. The `toString()` can perform any type conversion necessary to make the internal type a string, and the `setValue()` must be able to make a reverse conversion.

The implementation example does not notify about changes in the property value or in the read-only mode. You should normally also implement at least the **Property.ValueChangeNotifier** and **Property.ReadOnlyStatusChangeNotifier**. See the **ObjectProperty** class for an example of the implementation.

9.3. Holding properties in Items

The **Item** interface provides access to a set of named properties. Each property is identified by a *property identifier* (PID) and a reference to such a property can be queried from an **Item** with `getItemProperty()` using the identifier.

Examples on the use of items include rows in a **Table**, with the properties corresponding to table columns, nodes in a **Tree**, and the the data bound to a **Form**, with item's properties bound to individual form fields.

Items are generally equivalent to objects in the object-oriented model, but with the exception that they are configurable and provide an event handling mechanism. The simplest way to utilize **Item** interface is to use existing implementations. Provided utility classes include a configurable property set (**PropertysetItem**) and a bean-to-item adapter (**BeanItem**). Also, a **Form** implements the interface and can therefore be used directly as an item.

In addition to being used indirectly by many user interface components, items provide the basic data model underlying the **Form** component. In simple cases, forms can even be generated automatically from items. The properties of the item correspond to the fields of the form.

The **Item** interface defines inner interfaces for maintaining the item property set and listening changes made to it. **PropertySetChangeEvent** events can be emitted by a class implementing the

PropertySetChangeNotifier interface. They can be received through the **PropertySetChangeListener** interface.

9.3.1. The PropertysetItem Implementation

The **PropertysetItem** is a generic implementation of the **Item** interface that allows storing properties. The properties are added with `addItemProperty()`, which takes a name and the property as parameters.

The following example demonstrates a typical case of collecting **ObjectProperty** properties in an item:

```
PropertysetItem item = new PropertysetItem();
item.addItemProperty("name", new ObjectProperty("Zaphod"));
item.addItemProperty("age", new ObjectProperty(42));

// Bind it to a component
Form form = new Form();
form.setItemDataSource(item);
```

9.3.2. Wrapping a Bean in a BeanItem

The **BeanItem** implementation of the **Item** interface is a wrapper for Java Bean objects. In fact, only the setters and getters are required while serialization and other bean features are not, so you can wrap almost any POJOs with minimal requirements.

```
// Here is a bean (or more exactly a POJO)
class Person {
    String name;
    int    age;

    public String getName() {
        return name;
    }

    public void setName(String name) {
        this.name = name;
    }

    public Integer getAge() {
        return age;
    }

    public void setAge(Integer age) {
        this.age = age.intValue();
    }
}

// Create an instance of the bean
Person bean = new Person();
```

```
// Wrap it in a BeanItem
BeanItem<Person> item = new BeanItem<Person>(bean);

// Bind it to a component
Form form = new Form();
form.setItemDataSource(item);
```

You can use the `getBean()` method to get a reference to the underlying bean.

Nested Beans

You may often have composite classes where one class "has a" another class. For example, consider the following **Planet** class which "has a" discoverer:

```
// Here is a bean with two nested beans
public class Planet implements Serializable {
    String name;
    Person discoverer;

    public Planet(String name, Person discoverer) {
        this.name = name;
        this.discoverer = discoverer;
    }

    ... getters and setters ...
}

...
// Create an instance of the bean
Planet planet = new Planet("Uranus",
                new Person("William Herschel", 1738));
```

When shown in a **Form**, for example, you would want to list the properties of the nested bean along the properties of the composite bean. You can do that by binding the properties of the nested bean individually with a **MethodProperty** or **NestedMethodProperty**. You should usually hide the nested bean from binding as a property by listing only the bound properties in the constructor.

```
// Wrap it in a BeanItem and hide the nested bean property
BeanItem<Planet> item = new BeanItem<Planet>(planet,
        new String[]{"name"});

// Bind the nested properties.
// Use NestedMethodProperty to bind using dot notation.
item.addItemProperty("discoverername",
    new NestedMethodProperty(planet, "discoverer.name"));

// The other way is to use regular MethodProperty.
item.addItemProperty("discovererborn",
```

```
new MethodProperty<Person>(planet.getDiscoverer(),
                            "born"));
```

The difference is that **NestedMethodProperty** does not access the nested bean immediately but only when accessing the property values, while when using **MethodProperty** the nested bean is accessed when creating the method property. The difference is only significant if the nested bean can be null or be changed later.

You can use such a bean item for example in a **Form** as follows:

```
// Bind it to a component
Form form = new Form();
form.setItemDataSource(item);

// Nicer captions
form.getField("discoverername").setCaption("Discoverer");
form.getField("discovererborn").setCaption("Born");
```

Name	Uranus
Discoverer	William Herschel
Born	1738

Figure 9.3. A Form with Nested Bean Properties

The **BeanContainer** and **BeanItemContainer** allow easy definition of nested bean properties with `addNestedContainerProperty()`, as described in the section called "Nested Properties".

9.4. Binding Fields to Items

Most applications in existence have forms of some sort. Forms contain fields, which you want to bind to a data source, an item in the Vaadin data model. **FieldGroup** provides an easy way to bind fields to the properties of an item. You can use it by first creating a layout with some fields, and then call it to bind the fields to the data source. You can also let the **FieldGroup** create the fields using a field factory. It can also handle commits. Notice that **FieldGroup** is not a user interface component, so you can not add it to a layout.

9.4.1. Simple Binding

Let us start with a data model that has an item with a couple of properties. The item could be any item type, as described earlier.

```
// Have an item
PropertysetItem item = new PropertysetItem();
item.addItemProperty("name", new ObjectProperty<String>("Zaphod"));
item.addItemProperty("age", new ObjectProperty<Integer>(42));
```

Next, you would design a form for editing the data. The **FormLayout** (Section 6.5, "**FormLayout**" is ideal for forms, but you could use any other layout as well.

```
// Have some layout and create the fields
FormLayout form = new FormLayout();

TextField nameField = new TextField("Name");
form.addComponent(nameField);

TextField ageField = new TextField("Age");
form.addComponent(ageField);
```

Then, we can bind the fields to the data as follows:

```
// Now create the binder and bind the fields
FieldGroup binder = new FieldGroup(item);
binder.bind(nameField, "name");
binder.bind(ageField, "age");
```

The above way of binding is not different from simply calling `setPropertyDataSource()` for the fields. It does, however, register the fields in the field group, which for example enables buffering or validation of the fields using the field group, as described in Section 9.4.4, "Buffering Forms".

Next, we consider more practical uses for a **FieldGroup**.

9.4.2. Using a `FieldFactory` to Build and Bind Fields

Using the `buildAndBind()` methods, **FieldGroup** can create fields for you using a `FieldGroupFieldFactory`, but you still have to add them to the correct position in your layout.

```
// Have some layout
FormLayout form = new FormLayout();

// Now create a binder that can also create the fields
// using the default field factory
```

```
FieldGroup binder = new FieldGroup(item);
form.addComponent(binder.buildAndBind("Name", "name"));
form.addComponent(binder.buildAndBind("Age", "age"));
```

9.4.3. Binding Member Fields

The `bindMemberFields()` method in **FieldGroup** uses reflection
to bind the properties of an item to field components that are
member variables of a class. Hence, if you implement a form as a
class with the fields stored as member variables, you can use this
method to bind them super-easy.

The item properties are mapped to the members by the property
ID and the name of the member variable. If you want to map a
property with a different ID to a member, you can use the `@Proper-`
`tyId` annotation for the member, with the property ID as the parameter.

For example:

```
// Have an item
PropertysetItem item = new PropertysetItem();
item.addItemProperty("name", new ObjectProperty<String>("Zaphod"));
item.addItemProperty("age", new ObjectProperty<Integer>(42));

// Define a form as a class that extends some layout
class MyForm extends FormLayout {
    // Member that will bind to the "name" property
    TextField name = new TextField("Name");

    // Member that will bind to the "age" property
    @PropertyId("age")
    TextField ageField = new TextField("Age");

    public MyForm() {
        // Customize the layout a bit
        setSpacing(true);

        // Add the fields
        addComponent(name);
        addComponent(ageField);
    }
}

// Create one
MyForm form = new MyForm();

// Now create a binder that can also creates the fields
// using the default field factory
FieldGroup binder = new FieldGroup(item);
binder.bindMemberFields(form);
```

```
// And the form can be used in an higher-level layout
layout.addComponent(form);
```

Encapsulating in CustomComponent

Using a **CustomComponent** can be better for hiding the implementation details than extending a layout. Also, the use of the **FieldGroup** can be encapsulated in the form class.

Consider the following as an alternative for the form implementation presented earlier:

```
// A form component that allows editing an item
class MyForm extends CustomComponent {
    // Member that will bind to the "name" property
    TextField name = new TextField("Name");

    // Member that will bind to the "age" property
    @PropertyId("age")
    TextField ageField = new TextField("Age");

    public MyForm(Item item) {
        FormLayout layout = new FormLayout();
        layout.addComponent(name);
        layout.addComponent(ageField);

        // Now use a binder to bind the members
        FieldGroup binder = new FieldGroup(item);
        binder.bindMemberFields(this);

        setCompositionRoot(layout);
    }
}

// And the form can be used as a component
layout.addComponent(new MyForm(item));
```

9.4.4. Buffering Forms

A **FieldGroup** handles buffering the form content so that it is written to the data model only when the commit() is called for the **FieldGroup**. Edits can be discarded, so that the underlying property value is reloaded, by calling discard(). Buffering is enabled by default, but can be set with the setBuffered() method in **FieldGroup**.

```
// Have an item of some sort
final PropertysetItem item = new PropertysetItem();
item.addItemProperty("name", new ObjectProperty<String>("Q"));
```

```
item.addItemProperty("age",  new ObjectProperty<Integer>(42));

// Have some layout and create the fields
Panel form = new Panel("Buffered Form");
form.setContent(new FormLayout());

// Build and bind the fields using the default field factory
final FieldGroup binder = new FieldGroup(item);
form.addComponent(binder.buildAndBind("Name", "name"));
form.addComponent(binder.buildAndBind("Age", "age"));

// Enable buffering (actually enabled by default)
binder.setBuffered(true);

// A button to commit the buffer
form.addComponent(new Button("OK", new ClickListener() {
    @Override
    public void buttonClick(ClickEvent event) {
        try {
            binder.commit();
            Notification.show("Thanks!");
        } catch (CommitException e) {
            Notification.show("You fail!");
        }
    }
}));

// A button to discard the buffer
form.addComponent(new Button("Discard", new ClickListener() {
    @Override
    public void buttonClick(ClickEvent event) {
        binder.discard();
        Notification.show("Discarded!");
    }
}));
```

9.4.5. Binding Fields to a Bean

The **BeanFieldGroup** makes it easier to bind fields to a bean. It also handles binding to nested beans properties. The build a field bound to a nested bean property, identify the property with dot notation. For example, if a **Person** bean has a `address` property with an **Address** type, which in turn has a `street` property, you could build a field bound to the property with `buildAndBind("Street", "address.street")`.

The input to fields bound to a bean can be validated using the Java Bean Validation API, as described in Section 9.4.6, "Bean Validation". The **BeanFieldGroup** automatically adds a **BeanValidator** to every field if a bean validation implementation is included in the classpath.

9.4.6. Bean Validation

Vaadin allows using the Java Bean Validation API 1.0 (JSR-303) for validating input from fields bound to bean properties before the values are committed to the bean. The validation is done based on annotations on the bean properties.

Using bean validation requires an implementation of the Bean Validation API, such as Hibernate Validator (`hibernate-validator-4.2.0.Final.jar` or later) or Apache Bean Validation. The implementation JAR must be included in the project classpath when using the bean validation, or otherwise an internal error is thrown.

Bean validation is especially useful when persisting entity beans with the Vaadin JPAContainer, described in Chapter 18, *Vaadin JPAContainer*.

Annotations

The validation constraints are defined as annotations. For example, consider the following bean:

```
// Here is a bean
public class Person implements Serializable {
    @NotNull
    @javax.validation.constraints.Size(min=2, max=10)
    String name;

    @Min(1)
    @Max(130)
    int age;

    // ... setters and getters ...
}
```

For a complete list of allowed constraints for different data types, please see the Bean Validation API documentation.

Validating the Beans

Validating a bean is done with a **BeanValidator**, which you initialize with the name of the bean property it should validate and add it the the editor field.

In the following example, we validate a single unbuffered field:

```
Person bean = new Person("Mung bean", 100);
BeanItem<Person> item = new BeanItem<Person> (bean);

// Create an editor bound to a bean field
TextField firstName = new TextField("First Name",
        item.getItemProperty("name"));

// Add the bean validator
firstName.addValidator(new BeanValidator(Person.class, "name"));

firstName.setImmediate(true);
layout.addComponent(firstName);
```

In this case, the validation is done immediately after focus leaves the field. You could do the same for the other field as well.

Bean validators are automatically created when using a **BeanField-Group**.

```
// Have a bean
Person bean = new Person("Mung bean", 100);

// Form for editing the bean
final BeanFieldGroup<Person> binder =
        new BeanFieldGroup<Person>(Person.class);
binder.setItemDataSource(bean);
layout.addComponent(binder.buildAndBind("Name", "name"));
layout.addComponent(binder.buildAndBind("Age", "age"));

// Buffer the form content
binder.setBuffered(true);
layout.addComponent(new Button("OK", new ClickListener() {
    @Override
    public void buttonClick(ClickEvent event) {
        try {
            binder.commit();
        } catch (CommitException e) {
        }
    }
}));
```

Locale Setting for Bean Validation

The validation error messages are defined in the bean validation implementation, in a `ValidationMessages.properties` file. The message is shown in the language specified with the locale setting for the form. The default language is English, but for example Hibernate Validator contains translations of the messages for a number of languages. If other languages are needed, you need to provide a translation of the properties file.

9.5. Collecting Items in Containers

Container is the highest-level of the data model interfaces supported by Vaadin. It provides a very flexible way of managing a set of items that share common properties. Contained items are identified by an *item identifier* or *IID*.

Items can be added to a container with the `addItem()` method. Notice that the actual item is not passed as a parameter to the method, only the item ID, as the interface assumes that the container implementation knows how to create the item. The parameterless version of the method uses an automatically generated item ID. Implementations can provide methods to add externally created items, or they can assume that the item ID is also the item itself.

Properties can be requested from container by first requesting an item with `getItem()` and then getting the properties from the item with `getItemProperty()`. You can also get a property directly by the item and property ids with `getContainerProperty()`.

The **Container** interface was designed with flexibility and efficiency in mind. It contains inner interfaces that containers can optionally implement for ordering the items sequentially, indexing the items, and accessing them hierarchically. Such ordering models provide the basis for the **Table**, **Tree**, and **Select** components. As with other data model interfaces, the **Container** supports events for notifying about changes made to their contents.

As containers can be unordered, ordered, indexed, or hierarchical, they can interface practically any kind of data representation. Vaadin includes data connectors for some common data sources, such as the simple tabular data, with **IndexedContainer**, and the filesystem, with **FilesystemContainer**.

In addition to generic container implementations, also many user interface components are containers as themselves, in addition to being properties. This is especially true for selection components, that is, those that implement **Select**, because they are containers that contain selectable items. Their property is the currently selected item. This is useful as it allows binding components to view and updating each others' data directly, and makes it easy to reuse already constructed data models, for example, a form could edit a row (item) of a table directly, and the table could use a database container as its underlying container. The fields of the form would correspond to the properties of the item, that is, the cells of the table row.

The library contains a set of utilities for converting between different container implementations by adding external ordering or hierarchy into existing containers. In-memory containers implementing indexed and hierarchical models provide easy-to-use tools for setting up in-memory data storages. Such default container implementations include **IndexedContainer**, which can be thought of as a generalization of a two-dimensional data table, and **BeanItemContainer**, which maps standard Java objects (beans) to items of an indexed container. In addition, the built-in containers include a hierarchical container for direct file system browsing.

9.5.1. BeanContainer

The **BeanContainer** is an in-memory container for JavaBean objects. Each contained bean is wrapped inside a **BeanItem** wrapper. The item properties are determined automatically by inspecting the getter and setter methods of the class. This requires that the bean class has public visibility, local classes for example are not allowed. Only beans of the same type can be added to the container.

The generic has two parameters: a bean type and an item identifier type. The item identifiers can be obtained by defining a custom resolver, using a specific item property for the IDs, or by giving item IDs explicitly. As such, it is more general than the **BeanItemContainer**, which uses the bean object itself as the item identifier, making the use usually simpler. Managing the item IDs makes **BeanContainer** more complex to use, but it is necessary in some cases where the `equals()` or `hashCode()` methods have been reimplemented in the bean.

```
// Here is a JavaBean
public class Bean implements Serializable {
    String name;
    double energy; // Energy content in kJ/100g

    public Bean(String name, double energy) {
        this.name   = name;
        this.energy = energy;
    }

    public String getName() {
```

```
        return name;
    }

    public void setName(String name) {
        this.name = name;
    }

    public double getEnergy() {
        return energy;
    }

    public void setEnergy(double energy) {
        this.energy = energy;
    }
}

void basic(VerticalLayout layout) {
    // Create a container for such beans with
    // strings as item IDs.
    BeanContainer<String, Bean> beans =
        new BeanContainer<String, Bean>(Bean.class);

    // Use the name property as the item ID of the bean
    beans.setBeanIdProperty("name");

    // Add some beans to it
    beans.addBean(new Bean("Mung bean",    1452.0));
    beans.addBean(new Bean("Chickpea",      686.0));
    beans.addBean(new Bean("Lentil",       1477.0));
    beans.addBean(new Bean("Common bean",   129.0));
    beans.addBean(new Bean("Soybean",      1866.0));

    // Bind a table to it
    Table table = new Table("Beans of All Sorts", beans);
    layout.addComponent(table);
}
```

To use explicit item IDs, use the methods addItem(Object, Object), addItemAfter(Object, Object, Object), and addItemAt(int, Object, Object).

It is not possible to add additional properties to the container, except properties in a nested bean.

Nested Properties

If you have a nested bean with a 1:1 relationship inside a bean type contained in a **BeanContainer** or **BeanItemContainer**, you can add its properties to the container by specifying them with addNestedContainerProperty(). The feature is defined at the level of **AbstractBeanContainer**.

As with a top-level bean in a bean container, also a nested bean must have public visibility or otherwise an access exception is thrown. Intermediary getters returning a nested bean must always return a non-null value.

For example, assume that we have the following two beans with the first one nested inside the second one.

```
/** Bean to be nested */
public class EqCoord implements Serializable {
    double rightAscension; /* In angle hours */
    double declination;    /* In degrees     */

    ... constructor and setters and getters for the properties ...
}

/** Bean containing a nested bean */
public class Star implements Serializable {
    String  name;
    EqCoord equatorial; /* Nested bean */

    ... constructor and setters and getters for the properties ...
}
```

After creating the container, you can declare the nested properties by specifying their property identifiers with the `addNestedContainerProperty()` in dot notation.

```
// Create a container for beans
final BeanItemContainer<Star> stars =
    new BeanItemContainer<Star>(Star.class);

// Declare the nested properties to be used in the container
stars.addNestedContainerProperty("equatorial.rightAscension");
stars.addNestedContainerProperty("equatorial.declination");

// Add some items
stars.addBean(new Star("Sirius",  new EqCoord(6.75, 16.71611)));
stars.addBean(new Star("Polaris", new EqCoord(2.52, 89.26417)));
```

If you bind such a container to a **Table**, you probably also need to set the column headers. Notice that the entire nested bean itself is still a property in the container and would be displayed in its own column. The `toString()` method is used for obtaining the displayed value, which is by default an object reference. You normally do not want this, so you can hide the column with `setVisibleColumns()`.

```
// Put them in a table
Table table = new Table("Stars", stars);
table.setColumnHeader("equatorial.rightAscension", "RA");
table.setColumnHeader("equatorial.declination",    "Decl");
```

```
table.setPageLength(table.size());

// Have to set explicitly to hide the "equatorial" property
table.setVisibleColumns(new Object[]{"name",
    "equatorial.rightAscension", "equatorial.declination"});
```

The resulting table is shown in Figure 9.4, "**Table** Bound to a **BeanContainer** with Nested Properties".

Stars

NAME	RA	DECL
Sirius	6.75	16.71611
Polaris	2.52	89.26417

Figure 9.4. Table Bound to a BeanContainer with Nested Properties

The bean binding in **AbstractBeanContainer** normally uses the **MethodProperty** implementation of the **Property** interface to access the bean properties using the setter and getter methods. For nested properties, the **NestedMethodProperty** implementation is used.

Defining a Bean ID Resolver

If a bean ID resolver is set using `setBeanIdResolver()` or `setBeanIdProperty()`, the methods `addBean()`, `addBeanAfter()`, `addBeanAt()` and `addAll()` can be used to add items to the container. If one of these methods is called, the resolver is used to generate an identifier for the item (must not return `null`).

Note that explicit item identifiers can also be used when a resolver has been set by calling the `addItem*()` methods - the resolver is only used when adding beans using the `addBean*()` or `addAll(Collection)` methods.

9.5.2. BeanItemContainer

BeanItemContainer is a container for JavaBean objects where each bean is wrapped inside a **BeanItem** wrapper. The item properties are determined automatically by inspecting the getter and setter methods of the class. This requires that the bean class has public visibility, local classes for example are not allowed. Only beans of the same type can be added to the container.

BeanItemContainer is a specialized version of the **BeanContainer** described in Section 9.5.1, "**BeanContainer**". It uses the bean itself as the item identifier, which makes it a bit easier to use than **BeanContainer** in many cases. The latter is, however, needed if the bean has reimplemented the `equals()` or `hashCode()` methods.

Let us revisit the example given in Section 9.5.1, "**BeanContainer**" using the **BeanItemContainer**.

```
// Create a container for the beans
BeanItemContainer<Bean> beans =
    new BeanItemContainer<Bean>(Bean.class);

// Add some beans to it
beans.addBean(new Bean("Mung bean",   1452.0));
beans.addBean(new Bean("Chickpea",     686.0));
beans.addBean(new Bean("Lentil",      1477.0));
beans.addBean(new Bean("Common bean",  129.0));
beans.addBean(new Bean("Soybean",     1866.0));

// Bind a table to it
Table table = new Table("Beans of All Sorts", beans);
```

It is not possible to add additional properties to a **BeanItemContainer**, except properties in a nested bean, as described in Section 9.5.1, "**BeanContainer**".

9.5.3. Iterating Over a Container

As the items in a **Container** are not necessarily indexed, iterating over the items has to be done using an **Iterator**. The `getItemIds()` method of **Container** returns a **Collection** of item identifiers over which you can iterate. The following example demonstrates a typical case where you iterate over the values of check boxes in a column of a **Table** component. The context of the example is the example used in Section 5.15, "**Table**".

```
// Collect the results of the iteration into this string.
String items = "";

// Iterate over the item identifiers of the table.
for (Iterator i = table.getItemIds().iterator(); i.hasNext();) {
    // Get the current item identifier, which is an integer.
    int iid = (Integer) i.next();
```

```
// Now get the actual item from the table.
Item item = table.getItem(iid);

// And now we can get to the actual checkbox object.
Button button = (Button)
        (item.getItemProperty("ismember").getValue());

// If the checkbox is selected.
if ((Boolean)button.getValue() == true) {
    // Do something with the selected item; collect the
    // first names in a string.
    items += item.getItemProperty("First Name")
            .getValue() + " ";
}
}

// Do something with the results; display the selected items.
layout.addComponent (new Label("Selected items: " + items));
```

Notice that the getItemIds() returns an *unmodifiable collection*,
so the **Container** may not be modified during iteration. You can
not, for example, remove items from the **Container** during iteration.
The modification includes modification in another thread. If the
Container is modified during iteration, a **ConcurrentModifica-
tionException** is thrown and the iterator may be left in an undefined
state.

9.5.4. Filterable Containers

Containers that implement the **Container.Filterable** interface can
be filtered. For example, the built-in **IndexedContainer** and the
bean item containers implement it. Filtering is typically used for
filtering the content of a **Table**.

Filters implement the **Filter** interface and you add them to a filterable container with the addContainerFilter() method. Container
items that pass the filter condition are kept and shown in the filterable component.

```
Filter filter = new SimpleStringFilter("name",
        "Douglas", true, false);
table.addContainerFilter(filter);
```

If multiple filters are added to a container, they are evaluated using
the logical AND operator so that only items that are passed by all
the filters are kept.

Atomic and Composite Filters

Filters can be classified as *atomic* and *composite*. Atomic filters, such as **SimpleStringFilter**, define a single condition, usually for a specific container property. Composite filters make filtering decisions based on the result of one or more other filters. The built-in composite filters implement the logical operators AND, OR, or NOT.

For example, the following composite filter would filter out items where the name property contains the name "Douglas" somewhere *and* where the age property has value less than 42. The properties must have **String** and **Integer** types, respectively.

```
filter = new Or(new SimpleStringFilter("name",
        "Douglas", true, false),
        new Compare.Less("age", 42));
```

Built-In Filter Types

The built-in filter types are the following:

SimpleStringFilter

Passes items where the specified property, that must be of **String** type, contains the given *filterString* as a substring. If *ignoreCase* is *true*, the search is case insensitive. If the *onlyMatchPrefix* is *true*, the substring may only be in the beginning of the string, otherwise it may be elsewhere as well.

IsNull

Passes items where the specified property has null value. For in-memory filtering, a simple == check is performed. For other containers, the comparison implementation is container dependent, but should correspond to the in-memory null check.

Equal, Greater, Less, GreaterOrEqual, and LessOrEqual

The comparison filter implementations compare the specified property value to the given constant and pass items for which the comparison result is true. The comparison operators are included in the abstract **Compare** class.

For the **Equal** filter, the `equals()` method for the property is used in built-in in-memory containers. In other types of containers, the comparison is container dependent and may use, for example, database comparison operations.

For the other filters, the property value type must implement the **Comparable** interface to work with the built-in in-memory containers. Again for the other types of containers, the comparison is container dependent.

And and Or

These logical operator filters are composite filters that combine multiple other filters.

Not

The logical unary operator filter negates which items are passed by the filter given as the parameter.

Implementing Custom Filters

A custom filter needs to implement the **Container.Filter** interface.

A filter can use a single or multiple properties for the filtering logic. The properties used by the filter must be returned with the `appliesToProperty()` method. If the filter applies to a user-defined property or properties, it is customary to give the properties as the first argument for the constructor of the filter.

```
class MyCustomFilter implements Container.Filter {
    protected String propertyId;
    protected String regex;

    public MyCustomFilter(String propertyId, String regex) {
        this.propertyId = propertyId;
        this.regex      = regex;
    }

    /** Tells if this filter works on the given property. */
    @Override
    public boolean appliesToProperty(Object propertyId) {
        return propertyId != null &&
               propertyId.equals(this.propertyId);
    }
```

The actual filtering logic is done in the `passesFilter()` method, which simply returns `true` if the item should pass the filter and `false` if it should be filtered out.

```
/** Apply the filter on an item to check if it passes. */
@Override
public boolean passesFilter(Object itemId, Item item)
        throws UnsupportedOperationException {
    // Acquire the relevant property from the item object
    Property p = item.getItemProperty(propertyId);

    // Should always check validity
    if (p == null || !p.getType().equals(String.class))
        return false;
    String value = (String) p.getValue();

    // The actual filter logic
    return value.matches(regex);
}
}
```

You can use such a custom filter just like any other:

```
c.addContainerFilter(
    new MyCustomFilter("Name", (String) tf.getValue()));
```

Chapter 10

Vaadin SQLContainer

Vaadin SQLContainer is a container implementation that allows easy and customizable access to data stored in various SQL-speaking databases.

SQLContainer supports two types of database access. Using **TableQuery**, the pre-made query generators will enable fetching, updating, and inserting data directly from the container into a database table - automatically, whereas **FreeformQuery** allows the developer to use their own, probably more complex query for fetching data and their own optional implementations for writing, filtering and sorting support - item and property handling as well as lazy loading will still be handled automatically.

In addition to the customizable database connection options, SQLContainer also extends the Vaadin **Container** interface to implement more advanced and more database-oriented filtering rules. Finally, the add-on also offers connection pool implementations for JDBC connection pooling and JEE connection pooling, as well as integrated transaction support; auto-commit mode is also provided.

The purpose of this section is to briefly explain the architecture and some of the inner workings of SQLContainer. It will also give the readers some examples on how to use SQLContainer in their own applications. The requirements, limitations and further development ideas are also discussed.

SQLContainer is available from the Vaadin Directory under the same unrestrictive Apache License 2.0 as the Vaadin Framework itself.

10.1. Architecture

The architecture of SQLContainer is relatively simple. **SQLContainer** is the class implementing the Vaadin **Container** interfaces and providing access to most of the functionality of this add-on. The standard Vaadin **Property** and **Item** interfaces have been implementd as the **ColumnProperty** and **RowItem** classes. Item IDs are represented by **RowId** and **TemporaryRowId** classes. The **RowId** class is built based on the primary key columns of the connected database table or query result.

In the connection package, the **JDBCConnectionPool** interface defines the requirements for a connection pool implementation. Two implementations of this interface are provided: **SimpleJDB-CConnectionPool** provides a simple yet very usable implementation to pool and access JDBC connections. **J2EEConnectionPool** provides means to access J2EE DataSources.

The query package contains the **QueryDelegate** interface, which defines everything the SQLContainer needs to enable reading and writing data to and from a database. As discussed earlier, two implementations of this interface are provided: **TableQuery** for automatic read-write support for a database table, and **Freeform-Query** for customizing the query, sorting, filtering and writing; this is done by implementing relevant methods of the **FreeformState-mentDelegate** interface.

The query package also contains **Filter** and **OrderBy** classes which have been written to provide an alternative to the standard Vaadin container filtering and make sorting non-String properties a bit more user friendly.

Finally, the generator package contains a **SQLGenerator** interface, which defines the kind of queries that are required by the **Table-Query** class. The provided implementations include support for HSQLDB, MySQL, PostgreSQL (**DefaultSQLGenerator**), Oracle (**OracleGenerator**) and Microsoft SQL Server (**MSSQLGenerator**). A new or modified implementations may be provided to gain compatibility with older versions or other database servers.

For further details, please refer to the SQLContainer API documentation.

10.2. Getting Started with SQLContainer

Getting development going with the SQLContainer is easy and quite straight-forward. The purpose of this section is to describe how to create the required resources and how to fetch data from and write data to a database table attached to the container.

10.2.1. Creating a connection pool

First, we need to create a connection pool to allow the SQLContainer to connect to a database. Here we will use the **SimpleJDBCConnectionPool**, which is a basic implementation of connection pooling with JDBC data sources. In the following code, we create a connection pool that uses the HSQLDB driver together with an in-memory database. The initial amount of connections is 2 and the maximum amount is set at 5. Note that the database driver, connection url, username, and password parameters will vary depending on the database you are using.

```
JDBCConnectionPool pool = new SimpleJDBCConnectionPool(
        "org.hsqldb.jdbc.JDBCDriver",
        "jdbc:hsqldb:mem:sqlcontainer", "SA", "", 2, 5);
```

10.2.2. Creating the TableQuery Query Delegate

After the connection pool is created, we'll need a query delegate for the SQLContainer. The simplest way to create one is by using the built-in **TableQuery** class. The **TableQuery** delegate provides access to a defined database table and supports reading and writing data out-of-the-box. The primary key(s) of the table may be anything that the database engine supports, and are found automatically by querying the database when a new **TableQuery** is instantiated. We create the **TableQuery** with the following statement:

```
TableQuery tq = new TableQuery("tablename", connectionPool);
```

In order to allow writes from several user sessions concurrently, we must set a version column to the **TableQuery** as well. The version column is an integer- or timestamp-typed column which will either be incremented or set to the current time on each modification of the row. **TableQuery** assumes that the database will take care of updating the version column; it just makes sure the column value is correct before updating a row. If another user has changed the row and the version number in the database does not match the version number in memory, an **OptimisticLockException** is thrown and you can recover by refreshing the container and allow the user to merge the data. The following code will set the version column:

```
tq.setVersionColumn("OPTLOCK");
```

10.2.3. Creating the Container

Finally, we may create the container itself. This is as simple as stating:

```
SQLContainer container = new SQLContainer(tq);
```

After this statement, the **SQLContainer** is connected to the table tablename and is ready to use for example as a data source for a Vaadin **Table** or a Vaadin **Form**.

10.3. Filtering and Sorting

Filtering and sorting the items contained in an SQLContainer is, by design, always performed in the database. In practice this

---

means that whenever the filtering or sorting rules are modified, at least some amount of database communication will take place (the minimum is to fetch the updated row count using the new filtering/sorting rules).

10.3.1. Filtering

Filtering is performed using the filtering API in Vaadin, which allows for very complex filtering to be easily applied. More information about the filtering API can be found in .

In addition to the filters provided by Vaadin, SQLContainer also implements the **Like** filter as well as the **Between** filter. Both of these map to the equally named WHERE-operators in SQL. The filters can also be applied on items that reside in memory, for example, new items that have not yet been stored in the database or rows that have been loaded and updated, but not yet stored.

The following is an example of the types of complex filtering that are possible with the new filtering API. We want to find all people named Paul Johnson that are either younger than 18 years or older than 65 years and all Johnsons whose first name starts with the letter "A":

```
mySQLContainer.addContainerFilter(
    new Or(new And(new Equal("NAME", "Paul"),
            new Or(new Less("AGE", 18),
                new Greater("AGE", 65))),
        new Like("NAME", "A%")));
mySQLContainer.addContainerFilter(
    new Equal("LASTNAME", "Johnson"));
```

This will produce the following WHERE clause:

```
WHERE (("NAME" = "Paul" AND ("AGE" < 18 OR "AGE" > 65)) OR
 "NAME" LIKE "A%") AND "LASTNAME" = "Johnson"
```

10.3.2. Sorting

Sorting can be performed using standard Vaadin, that is, using the sort method from the **Container.Sortable** interface. The *propertyId* parameter refers to column names.

```
public void sort(Object[] propertyId, boolean[] ascending)
```

In addition to the standard method, it is also possible to directly add an **OrderBy** to the container via the `addOrderBy()` method. This enables the developer to insert sorters one by one without providing the whole array of them at once.

All sorting rules can be cleared by calling the sort method with null or an empty array as the first argument.

10.4. Editing

Editing the items (**RowItem**s) of SQLContainer can be done similarly to editing the items of any Vaadin container. **ColumnProperties** of a **RowItem** will automatically notify SQLContainer to make sure that changes to the items are recorded and will be applied to the database immediately or on commit, depending on the state of the auto-commit mode.

10.4.1. Adding items

Adding items to an **SQLContainer** object can only be done via the `addItem()` method. This method will create a new **Item** based on the connected database table column properties. The new item will either be buffered by the container or committed to the database through the query delegate depending on whether the auto commit mode (see the next section) has been enabled.

When an item is added to the container it is impossible to precisely know what the primary keys of the row will be, or will the row insertion succeed at all. This is why the SQLContainer will assign an instance of **TemporaryRowId** as a **RowId** for the new item. We will later describe how to fetch the actual key after the row insertion has succeeded.

If auto-commit mode is enabled in the **SQLContainer**, the `addItem()` methot will return the final **RowId** of the new item.

10.4.2. Fetching generated row keys

Since it is a common need to fetch the generated key of a row right after insertion, a listener/notifier has been added into the **QueryDelegate** interface. Currently only the **TableQuery** class implements the **RowIdChangeNotifier** interface, and thus can notify interested objects of changed row IDs. The events fill be fired after

---

commit() in **TableQuery** has finished; this method is called by **SQLContainer** when necessary.

To receive updates on the row IDs, you might use the following code (assuming container is an instance of **SQLContainer**). Note that these events are not fired if auto commit mode is enabled.

```
app.getDbHelp().getCityContainer().addListener(
    new QueryDelegate.RowIdChangeListener() {
        public void rowIdChange(RowIdChangeEvent event) {
            System.err.println("Old ID: " + event.getOldRowId());
            System.err.println("New ID: " + event.getNewRowId());
        }
    });
```

10.4.3. Version column requirement

If you are using the **TableQuery** class as the query delegate to the **SQLContainer** and need to enable write support, there is an enforced requirement of specifying a version column name to the **TableQuery** instance. The column name can be set to the **TableQuery** using the following statement:

```
tq.setVersionColumn("OPTLOCK");
```

The version column is preferably an integer or timestamp typed column in the table that is attached to the **TableQuery**. This column will be used for optimistic locking; before a row modification the **TableQuery** will check before that the version column value is the same as it was when the data was read into the container. This should ensure that no one has modified the row inbetween the current user's reads and writes.

Note! **TableQuery** assumes that the database will take care of updating the version column by either using an actual VERSION column (if supported by the database in question) or by a trigger or a similar mechanism.

If you are certain that you do not need optimistic locking, but do want to enable write support, you may point the version column to, for example, a primary key column of the table.

10.4.4. Auto-commit mode

SQLContainer is by default in transaction mode, which means that actions that edit, add or remove items are recorded internally by the container. These actions can be either committed to the database by calling `commit()` or discarded by calling `rollback()`.

The container can also be set to auto-commit mode. When this mode is enabled, all changes will be committed to the database immediately. To enable or disable the auto-commit mode, call the following method:

```
public void setAutoCommit(boolean autoCommitEnabled)
```

It is recommended to leave the auto-commit mode disabled, as it ensures that the changes can be rolled back if any problems are noticed within the container items. Using the auto-commit mode will also lead to failure in item addition if the database table contains non-nullable columns.

10.4.5. Modified state

When used in the transaction mode it may be useful to determine whether the contents of the **SQLContainer** have been modified or not. For this purpose the container provides an `isModified()` method, which will tell the state of the container to the developer. This method will return true if any items have been added to or removed from the container, as well as if any value of an existing item has been modified.

Additionally, each **RowItem** and each **ColumnProperty** have `isModified()` methods to allow for a more detailed view over the modification status. Do note that the modification statuses of **RowItem** and **ColumnProperty** objects only depend on whether or not the actual **Property** values have been modified. That is, they do not reflect situations where the whole **RowItem** has been marked for removal or has just been added to the container.

10.5. Caching, Paging and Refreshing

To decrease the amount of queries made to the database, SQL-Container uses internal caching for database contents. The caching is implemented with a size-limited **LinkedHashMap** containing a mapping from **RowId**s to **RowItem**s. Typically developers do not need to modify caching options, although some fine-tuning can be done if required.

Chapter 10. Vaadin SQLContainer

10.5.1. Container Size

The **SQLContainer** keeps continuously checking the amount of rows in the connected database table in order to detect external addition or removal of rows. By default, the table row count is assumed to remain valid for 10 seconds. This value can be altered from code; with `setSizeValidMilliSeconds()` in **SQLContainer**.

If the size validity time has expired, the row count will be automatically updated on:

- A call to `getItemIds()` method
- A call to `size()` method
- Some calls to `indexOfId(Object itemId)` method
- A call to `firstItemId()` method
- When the container is fetching a set of rows to the item cache (lazy loading)

10.5.2. Page Length and Cache Size

The page length of the **SQLContainer** dictates the amount of rows fetched from the database in one query. The default value is 100, and it can be modified with the `setPageLength()` method. To avoid constant queries it is recommended to set the page length value to at least 5 times the amount of rows displayed in a Vaadin **Table**; obviously, this is also dependent on the cache ratio set for the **Table** component.

The size of the internal item cache of the **SQLContainer** is calculated by multiplying the page lenght with the cache ratio set for the container. The cache ratio can only be set from the code, and the default value for it is 2. Hence with the default page length of 100 the internal cache size becomes 200 items. This should be enough even for larger **Table**s while ensuring that no huge amounts of memory will be used on the cache.

10.5.3. Refreshing the Container

Normally, the **SQLContainer** will handle refreshing automatically when required. However, there may be situations where an implicit refresh is needed, for example, to make sure that the version column is up-to-date prior to opening the item for editing in a form. For this purpose a `refresh()` method is provided. This method simply clears all caches, resets the current item fetching offset and sets the container size dirty. Any item-related call after this will inevitably result into row count and item cache update.

Note that a call to the refresh method will not affect or reset the following properties of the container:

- The **QueryDelegate** of the container
- Auto-commit mode
- Page length
- Filters
- Sorting

10.5.4. Cache Flush Notification Mechanism

Cache usage with databases in multiuser applications always results in some kind of a compromise between the amount of queries we want to execute on the database and the amount of memory we want to use on caching the data; and most importantly, risking the cached data becoming stale.

SQLContainer provides an experimental remedy to this problem by implementing a simple cache flush notification mechanism. Due to its nature these notifications are disabled by default but can be easily enabled for a container instance by calling `enableCache-FlushNotifications()` at any time during the lifetime of the container.

The notification mechanism functions by storing a weak reference to all registered containers in a static list structure. To minimize the risk of memory leaks and to avoid unlimited growing of the reference list, dead weak references are collected to a reference queue and removed from the list every time a **SQLContainer** is added to the notification reference list or a container calls the notification method.

When a **SQLContainer** has its cache notifications set enabled, it will call the static `notifyOfCacheFlush()` method giving itself as a parameter. This method will compare the notifier-container to all the others present in the reference list. To fire a cache flush event, the target container must have the same type of **QueryDelegate** (either **TableQuery** or **FreeformQuery**) and the table name or query string must match with the container that fired the notification. If a match is found the `refresh()` method of the matching container is called, resulting in cache flushing in the target container.

*Note: Standard Vaadin issues apply; even if the **SQLContainer** is refreshed on the server side, the changes will not be reflected to the UI until a server round-trip is performed, or unless a push mechanism is used.*

10.6. Referencing Another SQLContainer

When developing a database-connected application, there is usually a need to retrieve data related to one table from one or more other tables. In most cases, this relation is achieved with a foreign key reference, where a column of the first table contains a primary key or candidate key of a row in another table.

SQLContainer offers limited support for this kind of referencing relation, although all referencing is currently done on the Java side so no constraints need to be made in the database. A new reference can be created by calling the following method:

```
public void addReference(SQLContainer refdCont,
                         String refingCol, String refdCol);
```

This method should be called on the source container of the reference. The target container should be given as the first parameter. The *refingCol* is the name of the 'foreign key' column in the source container, and the *refdCol* is the name of the referenced key column in the target container.

*Note: For any **SQLContainer**, all the referenced target containers must be different. You can not reference the same container from the same source twice.*

Handling the referenced item can be done through the three provided set/get methods, and the reference can be completely removed with the `removeReference()` method. Signatures of these methods are listed below:

```
public boolean setReferencedItem(Object itemId,
        Object refdItemId, SQLContainer refdCont)
public Object getReferencedItemId(Object itemId,
                            SQLContainer refdCont)
public Item getReferencedItem(Object itemId,
                        SQLContainer refdCont)
public boolean removeReference(SQLContainer refdCont)
```

The setter method should be given three parameters: *itemId* is the ID of the referencing item (from the source container), *refdItemId* is the referenced *itemID* (from the target container) and *refdCont* is a reference to the target container that identifies the reference. This method returns true if the setting of the referenced item was successful. After setting the referenced item you must normally call `commit()` on the source container to persist the changes to the database.

The `getReferencedItemId()` method will return the item ID of the referenced item. As parameters this method needs the item ID of the referencing item and a reference to the target container as an identifier. **SQLContainer** also provides a convenience method `getReferencedItem()`, which directly returns the referenced item from the target container.

Finally, the referencing can be removed from the source container by calling the `removeReference()` method with the target container as parameter. Note that this does not actually change anything in the database; it merely removes the logical relation that exists only on the Java-side.

10.7. Using FreeformQuery and FreeformStatementDelegate

In most cases, the provided **TableQuery** will be enough to allow a developer to gain effortless access to an SQL data source. However there may arise situations when a more complex query with, for example, join expressions is needed. Or perhaps you need to redefine how the writing or filtering should be done. The **FreeformQuery** query delegate is provided for this exact purpose. Out of the box the **FreeformQuery** supports read-only access to a database, but it can be extended to allow writing also.

Getting started

Getting started with the **FreeformQuery** may be done as shown in the following. The connection pool initialization is similar to the **TableQuery** example so it is omitted here. Note that the name(s) of the primary key column(s) must be provided to the **Freeform-Query** manually. This is required because depending on the query the result set may or may not contain data about primary key columns. In this example, there is one primary key column with a name 'ID'.

```
FreeformQuery query = new FreeformQuery(
        "SELECT * FROM SAMPLE", pool, "ID");
SQLContainer container = new SQLContainer(query);
```

Limitations

While this looks just as easy as with the **TableQuery**, do note that there are some important caveats here. Using **FreeformQuery** like this (without providing **FreeformQueryDelegate** or **Freeform-StatementDelegate** implementation) it can only be used as a read-only window to the resultset of the query. Additionally filtering, sorting and lazy loading features will not be supported, and the row count will be fetched in quite an inefficient manner. Bearing these limitations in mind, it becomes quite obvious that the developer is in reality meant to implement the **FreeformQueryDelegate** or **FreeformStatementDelegate** interface.

The **FreeformStatementDelegate** interface is an extension of the **FreeformQueryDelegate** interface, which returns **StatementHelper** objects instead of pure query **Strings**. This enables the developer to use prepared statemens instead of regular statements. It is highly recommended to use the **FreeformStatement-Delegate** in all implementations. From this chapter onwards, we will only refer to the **FreeformStatementDelegate** in cases where **FreeformQueryDelegate** could also be applied.

Creating your own FreeformStatementDelegate

To create your own delegate for **FreeformQuery** you must implement some or all of the methods from the **FreeformStatement-Delegate** interface, depending on which ones your use case requires. The interface contains eight methods which are shown below. For more detailed requirements, see the JavaDoc document-ation of the interface.

```
// Read-only queries
public StatementHelper getCountStatement()
public StatementHelper getQueryStatement(int offset, int limit)
public StatementHelper getContainsRowQueryStatement(Object... keys)

// Filtering and sorting
public void setFilters(List<Filter> filters)
public void setFilters(List<Filter> filters,
                       FilteringMode filteringMode)
public void setOrderBy(List<OrderBy> orderBys)

// Write support
public int storeRow(Connection conn, RowItem row)
public boolean removeRow(Connection conn, RowItem row)
```

A simple demo implementation of this interface can be found in the SQLContainer package, more specifically in the class **com.vaadin.addon.sqlcontainer.demo.DemoFreeformQuery-Delegate**.

10.8. Non-implemented methods of Vaadin container interfaces

Due to the database connection inherent to the SQLContainer, some of the methods from the container interfaces of Vaadin can not (or would not make sense to) be implemented. These methods are listed below, and they will throw an **UnsupportedOperationEx-ception** on invocation.

```
public boolean addContainerProperty(Object propertyId,
                                    Class<?> type,
                                    Object defaultValue)
public boolean removeContainerProperty(Object propertyId)
public Item addItem(Object itemId)
public Object addItemAt(int index)
public Item addItemAt(int index, Object newItemId)
public Object addItemAfter(Object previousItemId)
public Item addItemAfter(Object previousItemId, Object newItemId)
```

Additionally, the following methods of the **Item** interface are not supported in the **RowItem** class:

```
public boolean addItemProperty(Object id, Property property)
public boolean removeItemProperty(Object id)
```

About the getItemIds() method

To properly implement the Vaadin **Container** interface, a `getItemIds()` method has been implented in the **SQLContainer**. By definition, this method returns a collection of all the item IDs present in the container. What this means in the **SQLContainer** case is that the container has to query the database for the primary key columns of all the rows present in the connected database table.

It is obvious that this could potentially lead to fetching tens or even hundreds of thousands of rows in an effort to satisfy the method caller. This will effectively kill the lazy loading properties of **SQLContainer** and therefore the following warning is expressed here:

Warning

It is highly recommended not to call the `getitemIds()` method, unless it is known that in the use case in question the item ID set will always be of reasonable size.

10.9. Known Issues and Limitations

At this point, there are still some known issues and limitations affecting the use of SQLContainer in certain situations. The known issues and brief explanations are listed below:

- Some SQL data types do not have write support when using TableQuery:

  - All binary types

  - All custom types

  - CLOB (if not converted automatically to a **String** by the JDBC driver in use)

  - See **com.vaadin.addon.sqlcontainer.query.generator.StatementHelper** for details.

- When using Oracle or MS SQL database, the column name "*rownum*" can not be used as a column name in a table connected to **SQLContainer**.

  This limitation exists because the databases in question do not support limit/offset clauses required for paging. Instead, a generated column named 'rownum' is used to implement paging support.

The permanent limitations are listed below. These can not or most probably will not be fixed in future versions of SQLContainer.

- The `getItemIds()` method is very inefficient - avoid calling it unless absolutely required!

- When using **FreeformQuery** without providing a **FreeformStatementDelegate**, the row count query is very inefficient - avoid using **FreeformQuery** without implementing at least the count query properly.

- When using **FreeformQuery** without providing a **FreeformStatementDelegate**, writing, sorting and filtering will not be supported.

- When using Oracle database most or all of the numeric types are converted to **java.math.BigDecimal** by the Oracle JDBC Driver.

  This is a feature of how Oracle DB and the Oracle JDBC Driver handles data types.

# Chapter 11

Developing New Components

This chapter describes how you can create new client-side components (widgets) or JavaScript components and how you can integrate them with server-side components. The client-side implementations of all standard user interface components in Vaadin use the same client-side interfaces and patterns.

This edition is a draft. Many new features that will be included in Vaadin 7 are not yet covered in the draft and some of the content may in fact be outdated. For the most current version, please see the on-line edition available at http://vaadin.com/book.

On Terminology

Google Web Toolkit uses the term *widget* for user interface components. In this book, we use the term widget to refer to client-side components, while using the term *component* in a general sense and also in the special sense for server-side components.

11.1. Overview

Vaadin components consist of two parts: a server-side and a client-side component. The latter are also called *widgets* in Google Web Toolkit (GWT) parlance. A Vaadin application uses the API of the server-side component, which is "painted" as a client-side widget in the browser. As on the server-side, the client-side widgets form a hierarchy of layout widgets and regular widgets as the leaves.

The communication between a client-side widget and a server-side component is managed with a *connector* that handles syncronizing the widget state and events to and from the server-side.

When painting the user interface, a client-side widget is created for each server-side component. This mapping is defined in the connector class with a @Connect annotation.

The state of a server-side component is synchronized automatically to the client-side widget and back using a *shared state* object. A shared state object implements the ComponentState interface and it is used both in the server-side and the client-side component. On the client-side, a connector always has access to its state instance, as well to the state of its parent component state and the states of its children.

The state sharing assumes that state is defined with standard Java types, such as integers, doubles, ...

In addition to state, both server- and client-side can make remote procedure calls (RPC) on the other side. RPC is used foremost for event notifications. For example, when a client-side connector of a button receives a click, it sends the event to the server-side using RPC.

Integrating JavaScript Components

In addition to the GWT widget integration, Vaadin offers a simplified way to integrate pure JavaScript components. The JavaScript connector code is published from the server-side. As the JavaScript integration does not involve GWT programming, no widget set compilation is needed.

11.2. Starting It Simple With Eclipse

Let us first take the easy way and create a simple component with Eclipse. While you can develop new widgets with any IDE or even without, you may find Eclipse and the Vaadin Plugin for it useful, as it automates all the basic routines of widget development, most importantly the creation of new widgets.

11.2.1. Creating a Widget

1. Right-click the project in the Project Explorer and select **New → Other...**.

2. In the wizard selection, select **Vaadin → Vaadin Widget** and click **Next**.

3. In the **New Component Wizard**, make the following settins.

Source folder

> The root folder of the entire source tree. The default value is the default source tree of your project, and you should normally leave it unchanged unless you have a different project structure.

Package

The parent package under which the new server-side component should be created. If the project does not already have a widget set, one is created under this package in widgetset subpackage. The subpackage will contain the `.gwt.xml` descriptor that defines the widget set and the new widget stub under the widgetset.client subpackage.

Name

The class name of the new *server-side component*. The name of the client-side widget stub will be the same but with "**-Widget**" suffix, for example, **MycomponentWidget**. You can rename the classes afterwards.

Superclass

The superclass of the server-side component. It is **AbstractComponent** by default, but **com.vaadin.ui.AbstractField** or **com.vaadin.ui.AbstractSelect** are other commonly used superclasses. If you are extending an existing component, you should select it as the superclass. You can easily change the superclass later.

Template

Select which template to use. The default is **Full fledged**, which creates the server-side component, the client-side widget, the connector, a shared state object, and an RPC object. The **Connector only** leaves the shared state and RPC objects out.

Finally, click **Finish** to create the new component.

The wizard will:

- Create a server-side component stub in the base package

- If the project does not already have a widget set, the wizard creates a GWT module descriptor file (`.gwt.xml`) in the base package and modifies the `web.xml` deployment descriptor to specify the widget set class name parameter for the application

- Create a client-side widget stub (along with the connector and shared state and RPC stubs) in the `client.component-name` package under the base package

The structure of the server-side component and the client-side widget, and the serialization of component state between them, is explained in the subsequent sections of this chapter.

To compile the widget set, click the **Compile widget set** button in the Eclipse toolbar. See Section 11.2.2, "Compiling the Widget Set" for details. After the compilation finishes, you should be able to run your application as before, but using the new widget set. The compilation result is written under the `WebContent/VAADIN/widgetsets` folder. When you need to recompile the widget set in Eclipse, see Section 11.2.2, "Compiling the Widget Set". For detailed information on compiling widget sets, see Section 11.12, "Compiling a Client-Side Module".

The following setting is inserted in the `web.xml` deployment descriptor to enable the widget set:

```
<init-param>
    <description>Application widgetset</description>
    <param-name>widgetset</param-name>
    <param-value>com.example.myproject.widgetset.MyprojectApplica-
tionWidgetset</param-value>
</init-param>
```

You can refactor the package structure if you find need for it, but GWT compiler requires that the client-side code *must* always be stored under a package named "`client`".

11.2.2. Compiling the Widget Set

After you edit a widget, you need to compile the widget set. The Vaadin Plugin for Eclipse automatically suggests to compile the widget set in various situations, such as when you save a client-side source file. If this gets annoying, you can disable the automatic recompilation in the Vaadin category in project settings, by selecting the **Suspend automatic widgetset builds** option.

You can compile the widget set manually by clicking the **Compile widgetset** button in the Eclipse toolbar, shown in Figure 11.1, "The **Compile Widgetset** Button in Eclipse Toolbar", while the project is open and selected. If the project has multiple widget set definition files, you need to select the one to compile in the Project Explorer.

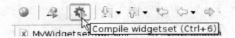

Figure 11.1. The Compile Widgetset Button in Eclipse Toolbar

The compilation progress is shown in the **Console** panel in Eclipse, illustrated in Figure 11.2, "Compiling a Widget Set". You should note especially the list of widget sets found in the class path.

The compilation output is written under the `WebContent/VAAD-IN/widgetsets` folder, in a widget set specific folder.

You can speed up the compilation significantly by compiling the widget set only for your browser during development. The generated `.gwt.xml` descriptor stub includes a disabled element that specifies the target browser. See Section 11.11, "Defining a Client-Side Module Descriptor" for more details on setting the `user-agent` property.

For more information on compiling widget sets, see Section 11.12, "Compiling a Client-Side Module". Should you compile a widget set outside Eclipse, you need to refresh the project by selecting it in **Project Explorer** and pressing **F5**.

11.3. Creating a Widget

Creating a new Vaadin component begins from a client-side widget, which is later integrated with a server-side counterpart to enable server-side development. In addition, you can also choose to make pure client-side widgets, a possibility which we also describe later in this section.

11.3.1. A Basic Widget

All widgets extend the GWT **Widget** class or some of its subclasses. You can extend any GWT or Vaadin widgets. The basic GWT widget component hierarchy is illustrated in Figure 11.3, "GWT Widget Base Class Hierarchy".

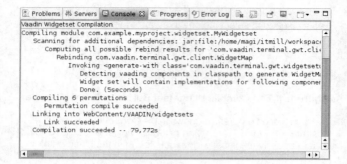

Figure 11.2. Compiling a Widget Set

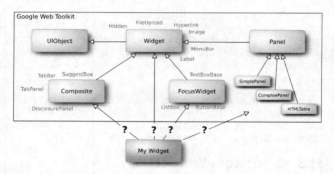

Figure 11.3. GWT Widget Base Class Hierarchy

For example, we could extend the GWT **Label** to display some custom text.

```
package com.example.myapp.client;

import com.google.gwt.user.client.ui.Label;

public class MyWidget extends Label {
    public static final String CLASSNAME = "mywidget";

    public MyWidget() {
        setStyleName(CLASSNAME);
        setText("This is MyWidget");
```

```
    }
}
```

The above example is largely what the Eclipse plugin generates as a widget stub. It is a good practice to set a style class for the widget, to allow styling it with CSS.

The client-side source code *must* be contained in a `client` package under the package of the descriptor file, which is covered later.

11.3.2. Creating a Pure Client-Side Application

Widgets can be used on their own in a pure client-side application, without a server-side Vaadin application. Such applications are useful when retrieving or storing data in a server is not necessary.

Even with regular server-side Vaadin applications, it may be useful to provide an off-line mode if the connection is closed. An off-line mode can persist data in a local store in the browser, thereby avoiding the need for server-side storage, and transmit the data to the server when the connection is again available. Such pattern is commonly used with Vaadin TouchKit, as described in Chapter 19, *Mobile Applications with TouchKit*.

Entry-Point

A client-side application requires an *entry-point* where the execution starts, much like an `init()` method in regular Vaadin applications.

```
package com.example.myapp.client;

import com.google.gwt.core.client.EntryPoint;
import com.google.gwt.event.dom.client.ClickEvent;
import com.google.gwt.event.dom.client.ClickHandler;
import com.google.gwt.user.client.ui.RootPanel;
import com.vaadin.terminal.gwt.client.ui.button.VButton;

public class MyEntryPoint implements EntryPoint {
    @Override
    public void onModuleLoad() {
        // Use the custom widget
        final MyWidget mywidget = new MyWidget();
        RootPanel.get().add(mywidget);

        // Add a Vaadin button
```

```
        VButton button = new VButton();
        button.setText("Click me!");
        button.addClickHandler(new ClickHandler() {
            @Override
            public void onClick(ClickEvent event) {
                mywidget.setText("Clicked!");
            }
        });

        RootPanel.get().add(button);
    }
}
```

Module Descriptor

The entry-point is defined, along with any other configuration, in a
GWT module descriptor. The descriptor is an XML file with suffix
.gwt.xml.

```
<?xml version="1.0" encoding="UTF-8"?>
<!DOCTYPE module PUBLIC
    "-//Google Inc.//DTD Google Web Toolkit 1.7.0//EN"
    "http://google-web-toolkit.googlecode.com/svn/tags/1.7.0/distro-
source/core/src/gwt-module.dtd">
<module>
    <!-- Inherit the core Vaadin and GWT widgets -->
    <inherits name="com.vaadin.Vaadin" />

    <!-- The entry-point for the client-side application -->
    <entry-point class="com.example.myapp.client.MyEntryPoint"/>
</module>
```

Any static resources, such as images or CSS stylesheets, must be
contained in a public folder (not a Java package) under the folder
of the descriptor file.

Compiling

The application needs to be compiled with the GWT Compiler into
JavaScript. We cover the details of the GWT compilation later, but
compiling pure client-side applications is a bit different as there is
no widget set.

Probably the easiest way to compile a client-side application is to
use the GWT Development Mode, which also allows debugging.
You need to execute the **com.google.gwt.dev.DevMode** class
in the Vaadin JAR with the following parameters:

```
-noserver -war warname com.example.myapp.MyModule
-startupUrl http://localhost:8080/myproject
warname -bindAddress 127.0.0.1
```

Executing

You can use the JavaScript code of a pure client-side application
in a HTML page for example as follows:

```
<html xmlns="http://www.w3.org/1999/xhtml">
  <head>
    <meta http-equiv="Content-Type"
          content="text/html; charset=UTF-8" />

    <title>Embedding a Vaadin Application in HTML Page</title>

    <!-- Load the Vaadin style sheet -->
    <link rel="stylesheet"
          type="text/css"
          href="/myproject/VAADIN/themes/reindeer/styles.css"/>
  </head>

  <body>
    <h1>A Pure Client-Side Application</h1>

    <script type="text/javascript" language="javascript"
          src="com.example.myapp.MyModule/com.example.myapp.MyMod-
ule.nocache.js"></script>
  </body>
</html>
```

The JavaScript module is loaded in a `<script>` element. The `src`
parameter should be a relative link from the page to the compiled
JavaScript module.

If the application uses Vaadin widgets, and not just GWT core
widgets, you need to include the Vaadin theme as was done in the
example. The exact path to the style file depends on your project
structure - the example is given for a regular Vaadin application
where themes are contained in the `VAADIN` folder in the WAR.

11.4. Creating a Server-Side Component

Normal server-side Vaadin applications interface with a server-side
component that is rendered on the client-side using the widget
counterpart. A server-side component must manage state synchronization between the widget on the client-side, in addition to any
server-side logic.

11.4.1. Basic Server-Side Component

The component state is usually managed by a *shared state*, described later in Section 11.6, "Sharing State".

```
public class MyComponent extends AbstractComponent {
    public MyComponent() {
        getState().setText("This is MyComponent");
    }

    @Override
    public MyComponentState getState() {
        return (MyComponentState) super.getState();
    }
}
```

11.5. Integrating the Two Sides with a Connector

A client-side widget is integrated with a server-side component with a *connector*. A connector is a client-side class that communicates changes to the widget state and events to the server-side.

11.5.1. A Basic Connector

The basic tasks of a connector is to hook up to the widget and handle events from user interaction and changes received from the server. A connector also has a number of routine infrastructure methods which need to be implemented.

```
@Connect(MyComponent.class)
public class MyComponentConnector
        extends AbstractComponentConnector {
    public MyComponentConnector() {
    }

    @Override
    protected Widget createWidget() {
        return GWT.create(MyComponentWidget.class);
    }

    @Override
    public MyComponentWidget getWidget() {
        return (MyComponentWidget) super.getWidget();
    }

    @Override
    public MyComponentState getState() {
        return (MyComponentState) super.getState();
    }

    @Override
```

```
public void onStateChanged(StateChangeEvent stateChangeEvent)
{
    super.onStateChanged(stateChangeEvent);

    // Do something useful
    final String text = getState().getText();
    getWidget().setText(text);
}
}
```

11.5.2. Communication with the Server-Side

The main task of a connector is to handle communicating user interaction to the server-side and receive state changes to be displayed to the user.

State changes are communicated to and from the server-side
through a *shared state* interface, as described in Section 11.6,
"Sharing State". The serialization of the state data is handled
completely transparently.

In addition, a connector can make remote procedure calls (RPC)
to the server-side and also the server-side component can make
RPC calls to the connector. For a thorough description of the RPC
mechanism, refer to Section 11.7, "RPC Calls Between Client- and
Server-Side".

11.6. Sharing State

The basic synchronization between the client-side widget and its
server-side counterpart is handled using a *shared state*. The shared
state is serialized transparently and communicated to the other
side.

A shared state object simply needs to extend the **Component-
State**. It should contain setters and getters for the properties that
are to be synchronized.

```
public class MyComponentState extends ComponentState {
    private String text;

    public String getText() {
        return text;
    }

    public void setText(String text) {
        this.text = text;
    }
}
```

11.6.1. Handling Shared State on Server-Side

A server-side component can access the shared state with the `getState()` method, which returns the **ComponentState** object of the shared state type of the component.

To prevent casting the shared state object every time, it is recommended that you override the base implementation with one that returns the proper shared state type, as follows:

```
@Override
public MyComponentState getState() {
    return (MyComponentState) super.getState();
}
```

You can then use the `getState()` to access the shared state object with the proper type.

```
public MyComponent() {
    getState().setText("This is the initial state");
    ....
}
```

After you make changes to the shared state object in the server-side component, you need to call `requestRepaint()` to inform the framework that the state has changed and the client-side widget needs to be repainted by synchronizing the state.

For example, the server-side component could offer a setter for a component property, which delegates the property to the shared state object and requests the repaint:

```
void setText(String text) {
    // update shared state
    getState().setText(text);
    requestRepaint();
}
```

11.6.2. Handing Shared State in a Connector

A connector can access the shared state with the `getState()` method. To prevent casting the shared state object every time, it is recommended that you override the base implementation with one that returns the proper shared state type, as follows:

```
@Override
public MyComponentState getState() {
    return (MyComponentState) super.getState();
}
```

State changes made on the server-side are communicated transparently to the client-side. When a state change occurs, the on-StateChanged() method in the connector is called. You should should always call the superclass method before anything else to handle changes to common component properties.

```
@Override
public void onStateChanged(StateChangeEvent stateChangeEvent) {
    super.onStateChanged(stateChangeEvent);

    // TODO do something useful
    final String text = getState().getText();
    getWidget().setText(text);
}
```

11.6.3. Referring to Components in Shared State

While you can pass any regular Java objects through a shared state, referring to another component requires special handling because on the server-side you can only refer to a server-side component, while on the client-side you only have widgets. References to components can be made by referring to their connectors, which are shared.

```
public class MyComponentState extends ComponentState {
    private Connector otherComponent;

    public Connector getOtherComponent() {
        return otherComponent;
    }

    public void setOtherComponent(Connector otherComponent) {
        this.otherComponent = otherComponent;
    }
}
```

You could then access the component on the server-side as follows:

```
public class MyComponent {
    public void MyComponent(Component otherComponent) {
        getState().setOtherComponent(otherComponent);
    }

    public Component getOtherComponent() {
        return (Component)getState().getOtherComponent();
    }
```

```
    // And the cast method
    @Override
    public MyComponentState getState() {
        return (MyComponentState) super.getState();
    }
}
```

On the client-side, you should cast it in a similar fashion to a **ComponentConnector**, or possibly to the specific connector type if it is known.

11.6.4. Sharing Resources

Resources, which commonly are references to icons or other images, are another case of objects that require special handling in sharing. A Resource object exists only on the server-side and on the client-side you have an URL to the resource. The shared state object needs to pass the reference as a **URLReference** object.

```
public class MyState extends ComponentState {
    private URLReference myIcon;

    public URLReference getMyIcon() {
        return icon;
    }

    public void setMyIcon(URLReference myIcon) {
        this.myIcon = myIcon;
    }
}
```

On the server-side, you can set the reference as a **ResourceReference** object, which creates the URL for the resource object given to the constructor as follows:

```
getState().setMyIcon(new ResourceReference(myResource));
```

It is normally meaningful only to set the resource on the server-side and then access it on the client-side. If you for some reason need to access it on the server-side, you need to cast the **URLReference** to the **ResourceReference** that exists on the server-side, and get the Resource object with getResource().

```
ResourceReference ref =
    ((ResourceReference) getState().getMyIcon());
if (ref != null) {
    Resource resource = ref.getResource();
```

```
    ...
}
```

The URL for the resource can be accessed on the client-side with the `getURL()` method.

```
String url = getState().getMyIcon().getURL();
```

11.7. RPC Calls Between Client- and Server-Side

Vaadin supports making Remote Procedure Calls (RPC) between a server-side component and its client-side widget counterpart. RPC calls are normally used for communicating stateless events, such as button clicks or other user interaction, in contrast to changing the shared state. Either party can make an RPC call to the other side. When a client-side widget makes a call, a server request is made. Calls made from the server-side to the client-side are communicated in the response of the server request during which the call was made.

If you use Eclipse and enable the "Full-Fledged" widget in the New Vaadin Widget wizard, it automatically creates a component with an RPC stub.

11.7.1. RPC Calls to the Server-Side

RPC calls from the client-side to the server-side are made through an RPC interface that extends the `ServerRpc` interface. A server RPC interface simply defines any methods that can be called through the interface.

For example:

```
public interface MyComponentServerRpc extends ServerRpc {
    public void clicked(MouseEventDetails mouseDetails);
}
```

The above example defines a single `clicks()` RPC call, which takes a **MouseEventDetails** object as the parameter. You can pass any serializable Java objects in RPC calls and Vaadin handles the serialization.

Making a Call

Before making a call, you need to instantiate the server RPC object with `RpcProxy.create()`. After that, you can make calls through the server RPC interface that you defined, for example as follows:

```
@Connect(MyComponent.class)
public class MyComponentConnector
        extends AbstractComponentConnector {

    MyComponentServerRpc rpc = RpcProxy
            .create(MyComponentServerRpc.class, this);

    public MyComponentConnector() {
        getWidget().addClickHandler(new ClickHandler() {
            public void onClick(ClickEvent event) {
                final MouseEventDetails mouseDetails =
                    MouseEventDetailsBuilder
                        .buildMouseEventDetails(
                            event.getNativeEvent(),
                            getWidget().getElement());

                // Make the call
                rpc.clicked(mouseDetails);
            }
        });
    }
}
```

Handling a Call

RPC calls are handled in a server-side implementation of the server RPC interface. The call and its parameters are serialized and passed to the server in an RPC request transparently.

```
public class MyComponent extends AbstractComponent {
    private MyComponentServerRpc rpc =
    new MyComponentServerRpc() {
        private int clickCount = 0;

        public void clicked(MouseEventDetails mouseDetails) {
            Notification.show("Click from the client!");
        }
    };

    public MyComponent() {
        ...
        registerRpc(rpc);
    }
}
```

11.8. Component and Root Extensions

Adding features to existing components by extending them by inheritance creates a problem when you want to combine such features. For example, one add-on could add spell-check to a **TextField**, while another could add client-side validation. Combining such add-on features would be difficult if not impossible. You might also want to add a feature to several or even to all components, but extending all of them by inheritance is not really an option. Vaadin includes a component plug-in mechanism for these purposes. Such plug-ins are simply called *extensions*.

Also a root can be extended in a similar fashion. In fact, some Vaadin features such as notifications are root extensions.

Implementing an extension requires defining a server-side extension class and a client-side connector. An extension can have a shared state with the connector and use RPC, just like a component could.

11.8.1. Server-Side Extension API

The server-side API for an extension consists of class that extends (in the Java sense) the **AbstractExtension** class. It needs to have an *extend()* method that takes the extended component or root as a parameter and passes it to the *super.extend()*.

For example, let us have a trivial example with an extension that takes no special parameters:

```
public class CapsLockWarning extends AbstractExtension {
    public void extend(PasswordField field) {
        super.extend(field);
    }
}
```

The extension can then be added to a component as follows:

```
PasswordField password = new PasswordField("Give it");
new CapsLockWarning().extend(password);
layout.addComponent(password);
```

Adding a feature in such a "reverse" way is a bit unusual in the Vaadin API, but allows type safety for extensions, as the method can limit the target type to which the extension can be applied, and whether it is a component or root.

11.8.2. Extension Connectors

An extension does not have a corresponding widget on the client-side, but only an extension connector that extends the **AbstractExtensionConnector** class. The server-side extension class is specified with a `@Connect` annotation, just like in component connectors.

An extension connector needs to implement the `extend()` method, which allows hooking to the extended component. The normal extension mechanism is to modify the extended component as needed and add event handlers to it to handle user interaction. A connector can share a state with the server-side extension as well as make RPC calls just like with normal components.

In the following example, we implement a "Caps Lock warning" extension. It listens for changes in the Caps Lock state and displays a floating warning element over the extended component if the Caps Lock is on.

```
@Connect(CapsLockWarning.class)
public class CapsLockWarningConnector
        extends AbstractExtensionConnector {

    @Override
    protected void extend(ServerConnector target) {
        // Get the extended widget
        final Widget passwordWidget =
                ((ComponentConnector) target).getWidget();

        // Preparations for the added feature
        final VOverlay warning = new VOverlay();
        warning.add(new HTML("Caps Lock is enabled!"));

        // Add an event handler
        pw.addDomHandler(new KeyPressHandler() {
            public void onKeyPress(KeyPressEvent event) {
                if (isEnabled() && isCapsLockOn(event)) {
                    warning.showRelativeTo(passwordWidget);
                } else {
                    warning.hide();
                }
            }
        }, KeyPressEvent.getType());
    }

    private boolean isCapsLockOn(KeyPressEvent e) {
        return e.isShiftKeyDown() ^
```

```
                Character.isUpperCase(e.getCharCode());
    }
}
```

The `extend()` method gets the connector of the extended component as the parameter, in the above example a **PasswordFieldConnector**. It can access the widget with the `getWidget()`.

An extension connector needs to be included in a widget set. The class must therefore be defined under the `client` package of a widget set, just like with component connectors.

11.9. Styling a Widget

To make your widget look stylish, you need to style it. There are two basic ways to define CSS styles for a component: in the widget sources and in a theme. A default style should be defined in the widget sources, and different themes can then modify the style.

11.9.1. Determining the CSS Class

The CSS class of a widget element is normally defined in the widget class and set with `setStyleName()`. A widget should set the styles for its sub-elements as it desires.

For example, you could style a composite widget with an overall style and with separate styles for the sub-widgets as follows:

```
public class MyPickerWidget extends ComplexPanel {
    public static final String CLASSNAME = "mypicker";

    private final TextBox textBox = new TextBox();
    private final PushButton button = new PushButton("...");

    public MyPickerWidget() {
        setElement(Document.get().createDivElement());
        setStylePrimaryName(CLASSNAME);

        textBox.setStylePrimaryName(CLASSNAME + "-field");
        button.setStylePrimaryName(CLASSNAME + "-button");

        add(textBox, getElement());
        add(button, getElement());

        button.addClickHandler(new ClickHandler() {
            public void onClick(ClickEvent event) {
                Window.alert("Calendar picker not yet supported!");
            }
        });
```

```
      }
   }
```

In addition, all Vaadin components get the `v-connector` class. If it extends an existing Vaadin or GWT widget, it will inherit CSS classes from that as well.

11.9.2. Default Stylesheet

A client-side module, which is normally a widget set, can include stylesheets. They must be placed under the `public` folder under the folder of the widget set, a described in Section 11.11.1, "Specifying a Stylesheet".

For example, you could style the widget described above as follows:

```
.mypicker {
 white-space: nowrap;
}

.mypicker-button {
 display: inline-block;
 border: 1px solid black;
 padding: 3px;
 width: 15px;
 text-align: center;
}
```

Notice that some size settings may require more complex handling and calculating the sizes dynamically.

11.10. Component Containers

Component containers, such as layout components, are a special group of components that require some consideration. In addition to handling state, they need to manage the serialization of their contained components to the other side.

The easiest way to implement a component container is extend the **AbstractComponentContainer**, which handles the serialization of the container server-side components to the client-side.

11.11. Defining a Client-Side Module Descriptor

Widget sets and other client-side modules are defined in a GWT *module descriptor*, which is an XML file with `.gwt.xml` suffix. The only necessary task is to inherit a base widget set. If you are developing a regular widget set, you should normally inherit the **DefaultWidgetSet**.

```
<?xml version="1.0" encoding="UTF-8"?>
<!DOCTYPE module PUBLIC
  "-//Google Inc.//DTD Google Web Toolkit 1.7.0//EN"
  "http://google-web-toolkit.googlecode.com/svn/tags/1.7.0/distro-
source/core/src/gwt-module.dtd">

<module>
    <!-- Inherit the default widget set -->
    <inherits name="com.vaadin.terminal.gwt.DefaultWidgetSet" />
</module>
```

If you are developing a pure client-side application, you should instead inherit **com.vaadin.Vaadin**, as described in Section 11.3.2, "Creating a Pure Client-Side Application". In that case, the module descriptor also needs an entry-point.

If you are using the Eclipse IDE, the New Vaadin Widget wizard will automatically create the GWT module descriptor. See Section 11.2.1, "Creating a Widget" for detailed instructions.

11.11.1. Specifying a Stylesheet

Widgets can have CSS stylesheets. These stylesheets are compiled into the widget set. In the module descriptor, define a `stylesheet` element as follows:

```
<!-- The default theme of this widget set -->
<stylesheet src="mycomponent/styles.css"/>
```

The specified path is relative to the *public* folder under the folder of the module descriptor.

11.11.2. Limiting Compilation Targets

Compiling widget sets takes considerable time. You can reduce the compilation time significantly by compiling the widget sets only for your browser, which is useful during development. You can do this by setting the *user.agent* property in the module descriptor.

```
<set-property name="user.agent" value="gecko1_8"/>
```

The *value* attribute should match your browser. The browsers supported by GWT depend on the GWT version, below is a list of browser identifiers supported by GWT 2.0.

Table 11.1. GWT User Agents

Identifier	Name
gecko1_8	Mozilla Firefox 1.5 and later
gecko	Mozilla Firefox 1.0 (*obsolete*)
ie6	Internet Explorer 6
ie8	Internet Explorer 8
safari	Apple Safari and other Webkit-based browsers including Google Chrome
opera	Opera

For more information about the GWT Module XML Format, please see Google Web Toolkit Developer Guide.

11.12. Compiling a Client-Side Module

A client-side module, either a widget set or a pure client-side module, must be compiled to JavaScript using the GWT Compiler.

As most Vaadin add-ons include widgets, widget set compilation is usually needed when using add-ons. In that case, the widget sets from different add-ons are compiled into a *project widget set*, as described in Section 15.3, "Compiling Add-on Widget Sets".

11.12.1. GWT Compiler Overview

The GWT Compiler compiles Java to JavaScript. It is included in the Vaadin JAR as **com.google.gwt.dev.Compiler**, together with the core GWT and Vaadin widgets.

The compiler compiles a *client module*, which can be either a pure client-side module or a Vaadin widget set, that is, the Vaadin Client-Side Engine that includes the widgets used in the application. The client module is defined with a module descriptor, which was described in Section 11.11, "Defining a Client-Side Module Descriptor".

The compiler writes the compilation result to a target folder that will include the compiled JavaScript with any static resources included in the module.

11.12.2. Compiling in Eclipse

For compiling a widget set or other client-side module in Eclipse, see Section 11.2.2, "Compiling the Widget Set". To put it short, when the Vaadin Plugin is installed in Eclipse, you can simply click the **Compile Vaadin widgets** button in the toolbar. It will compile the widget set it finds from the project. If the project has multiple widget sets, such as one for custom widgets and another one for the project, you need to select the module descriptor of the widget set to compile before clicking the button.

11.12.3. Compiling with Ant

You can find a script template for compiling widget sets with Ant at the URL https://vaadin.com/download/misc/build-widgetset-vaadin7.xml. You can copy the build script to your project and, once configured, use it by entering:

```
$ ant -f build-widgetset-vaadin7.xml
```

11.12.4. Compiling with Maven

You can compile the widget set with the `gwt:compile` goal as follows:

```
$ mvn gwt:compile
```

11.13. Debugging Client-Side Code

Vaadin includes two application execution modes for debugging client-side code. The Development Mode compiles the client-side module and runs it in the browser, using a browser plugin to communicate with the debugger. The "SuperDevMode" allows debugging the code right in the browser, without even need to install a plugin.

11.13.1. Launching Development Mode

The Development Mode compiles the client-side module (or widget set), launches the application in the browser, and allows debugging the client-side code in Eclipse. You can launch the Development Mode by running the **com.google.gwt.dev.DevMode** class. It requires some parameters, as described later.

The Vaadin Plugin for Eclipse can create a launch configuration for the Development Mode. In the Vaadin section of project properties, click the **Create development mode launch** button. This creates a new launch configuration in the project. You can edit the launch configuration in **Run → Run Configurations**.

```
-noserver -war WebContent/VAADIN/widgetsets com.example.myproject.wid-
getset.MyWidgetSet -startupUrl http://localhost:8080/myproject -
bindAddress 127.0.0.1
```

The parameters are as follows:

-noserver
> Normally, the Development Mode launches its own server for hosting the content. As we are developing the application under an IDE that deploys it to a server, we can disable the Development Mode server with this option.

-war
> Specifies path to the location where the JavaScript is to be compiled. When developing pure client-side widgets, this could be the `WebContent` folder, or some other folder. When compiling widget sets, it must be `WebContent/VAADIN/widgetsets`.

-startupUrl
> Specifies the address of the loader page for the application. For server-side Vaadin applications, this should be the path to the Vaadin application servlet, as defined in the deployment. For pure client-side widgets, it should be the page where the application is included.

```
-bindAddress
```
This is the IP address of the host in which the Development Mode runs. Normally it is the local host, that is, `127.0.0.1`.

11.13.2. Launching SuperDevMode

The SuperDevMode is much like the regular Development Mode, except that it does not require a browser plugin. Compilation from Java to JavaScript is done incrementally, reducing the compilation time significantly. It also allows debugging JavaScript and even Java right in the browser (currently only supported in Chrome).

You can enable SuperDevMode as follows:

1. You need to set a redirect property in the `.gwt.xml` module descriptor as follows:

   ```
   <set-configuration-property name="devModeRedirectEnabled"
   value="true" />
   ```

   In addition, you need the `xsiframe` linker. It is included in the **com.vaadin.terminal.gwt.DefaultWidgetSet** as well as in the **com.vaadin.Vaadin** module. Otherwise, you need to include it with:

   ```
   <add-linker name="xsiframe" />
   ```

2. Compile the module (that is, the widget set), for example by clicking the button in Eclipse.

3. If you are using Eclipse, create a launch configuration for the SuperDevMode by clicking the **Create SuperDevMode launch** in the **Vaadin** section of the project properties.

   a. The main class to execute should be **com.google.gwt.dev.codeserver.CodeServer**.

   b. The application takes the fully-qualified class name of the module (or widget set) as parameter, for example, **com.example.myproject.widgetset.MyprojectWidget-set**.

   c. Add project sources to the class path of the launch if they are not in the project class path.

The above configuration only needs to be once to enable the SuperDevMode. After that, you can launch the mode as follows:

1. Run the SuperDevMode Code Server with the launch configuration that you created above. This perfoms the initial compilation of your module or widget set.

2. Launch the servlet container for your application, for example, Tomcat.

3. Open your browser with the application URL and add `?superdevmode` parameter to the URL (see the notice below if you are not extending **DefaultWidgetSet**). This recompiles the code, after which the page is reloaded with the SuperDevMode. You can also use the `?debug` parameter and then click the **SDev** button in the debug console.

If you make changes to the client-side code and refresh the page in the browser, the client-side is recompiled and you see the results immediately.

The Step 3 above assumes that you extend **DefaultWidgetSet** in your module. If that is not the case, you need to add the following at the start of the `onModuleLoad()` method of the module:

```
if (SuperDevMode.enableBasedOnParameter()) { return; }
```

Alternatively, you can use the bookmarklets provided by the code server. Go to `http://localhost:9876/` and drag the bookmarklets "**Dev Mode On**" and "**Dev Mode Off**" to the bookmarks bar

Debugging Java Code in Chrome

Chrome supports source maps, which allow debugging Java source code from which the JavaScript was compiled.

Open the Chrome Inspector by right-clicking and selecting **Inspect Element**. Click the settings icon in the lower corner of the window and check the **Scripts → Enable source maps** option. Refresh the page with the Inspector open, and you will see Java code instead of JavaScript in the scripts tab.

11.14. Creating Add-ons

11.14.1. Packaging an Add-On JAR

The widget set build script template, which you can find at the URL
https://vaadin.com/download/misc/build-widgetset-vaadin7.xml,
includes an example `package-jar` target for building a JAR. You
can use the example as it is or modify it as you need.

You need to make the JAR packaging specific configuration in the
`configure-jar` target. Change to property values to reflect your
widget set.

```
<target name="configure-jar">
    <!-- The compiled JAR name -->
    <property name="jar-destination"
            value="${base}colorpicker.jar"/>

    <!-- Title of the widget set (for JAR) -->
    <property name="widgetset-title"
            value="ColorPicker"/>

    <!-- Version of the widget set (for JAR) -->
    <property name="widgetset-version" value="1.0"/>

    <!-- Vendor of the widget set (for JAR) -->
    <property name="widgetset-vendor"
            value="IT Mill Oy"/>
</target>
```

You may want to check also the `package-jar` target if you want to
use other license information or otherwise customize the package
content.

Assuming that you have otherwise configured the build script for
your project as described in Section 11.12.3, "Compiling with Ant",
you can build the JAR package with the following command:

```
$ ant -f build-widgetset-vaadin7.xml package-jar
```

Notice that the `package-jar` target *does not* depend on the `com-
pile-widgetset` target, as the compiled widget set is not included
in the package. If you really wish to do so, add the dependency
and include the compiled files as a fileset for the package.

11.15. Migrating from Vaadin 6

The client-side architecture was redesigned almost entirely in Vaadin 7. In Vaadin 6, state synchronization was done explicitly by serializing and deserializing the state on the server- and client-side. In Vaadin 7, the serialization is handled automatically by the framework using state objects.

In Vaadin 6, a server-side component serialized its state to the client-side using the `Paintable` interface and deserialized the state through the `VariableOwner` interface. In Vaadin 7, these are done through the `ClientConnector` interface.

On the client-side, a widget deserialized its state through the `Paintable` interface and sent state changes through the `ApplicationConnection` object. In Vaadin 7, these are replaced with the `ServerConnector`.

In addition to state synchronization, Vaadin 7 has an RPC mechanism that can be used for communicating events. They are especially useful for events that are not associated with a state change, such as a button click.

The framework ensures that the connector hierarchy and states are up-to-date when listeners are called.

11.15.1. Quick (and Dirty) Migration

Vaadin 7 has a compatibility layer that allows quick conversion of a widget.

1. Create a connector class, such as **MyConnector**, that extends **Vaadin6Connector**. Implement the `createWidget()` method as `GWT.create(MyWidget.class)`.

2. Move the `@ClientWidget(MyWidget.class)` from the server-side component, say **MyComponent**, to the **MyConnector** class and make it `@Connect(MyComponent.class)`.

3. Have the server-side component implement the Vaadin6Component interface to enable compatibility handling.

4. Remove any calls to `super.paintContent()`

11.16. Integrating JavaScript Components

Vaadin allows simplified integration of pure JavaScript components. The JavaScript connector code is published from the server-side. As the JavaScript integration does not involve GWT programming, no widget set compilation is needed.

11.16.1. Defining a JavaScript Connector

A JavaScript connector is a function that handles communication between the server-side code and the integrated JavaScript code. The connector functions are added in the `window` object.

Chapter 12

Advanced Web Application Topics

This chapter covers various features and topics often needed in applications.

This edition is a draft. Many new features that will be included in Vaadin 7 are not yet covered in this chapter and some of the content may in fact be outdated. For the most current version, please see the on-line edition available at `http://vaadin.com/book`.

12.1. Handling Browser Windows

*This section is not yet updated for Vaadin 7. The **Window** class in Vaadin 6 has largely been replaced by **Root** in Vaadin 7. In Vaadin 7, a **Window** refers only to a sub-window. However, much of the old window functionality is not yet implemented for roots.*

Vaadin supports two types of windows: *browser windows* and *sub-windows*. A browser window displays a web page, represented by a **Page** object. Sub-windows, on the other hand, are freely floating HTML windows inside a browser window, as described in Section 6.7, "Sub-Windows".

Application-level windows of the same application use the same **Application** object and therefore share the same session. Each window is identified with a URL that is used to access it. This makes it possible to bookmark application-level windows. Such windows can even be created dynamically based on the URLs.

Application-level windows allow several common use cases for browser-based applications.

- *Native popup windows*. An application can open popup windows for sub-tasks.

- *Page-based browsing*. The application can allow the user to open certain content to different windows. For example, in a messaging application, it can be useful to open different messages to different windows so that the user can browse through them while writing a new message.

- *Bookmarking*. Bookmarks in the web browser can provide an entry-point to some content provided by an application.

- *Embedding windows*. Windows can be embedded in web pages, thus making it possible to provide different views to an application from different pages or even from the same page, while keeping the same session. See Section 12.2, "Embedding Applications in Web Pages".

Because of the special nature of AJAX applications, these uses require some caveats. We will go through them later in Section 12.1.5, "Caveats in Using Multiple Windows".

12.1.1. Creating New Application-Level Windows

Creating a new application-level window is much like creating a sub-window (see Section 6.7, "Sub-Windows"), except that the window is added with `addWindow()` to the application object instead of the main window.

```
public class WindowTestApplication extends Application {
    public void init() {
        // First create the main window.
        final Window main = new Window ("My Test Application");
        setMainWindow(main);

        // Create another application-level window.
        final Window mywindow = new Window("Second Window");

        // Manually set the name of the window.
        mywindow.setName("mywindow");

        // Add some content to the window.
        mywindow.addComponent(new Label("Has content."));

        // Add the window to the application.
        addWindow(mywindow);
    }
}
```

This creates the window object that a user can view by opening a URL in a browser. Creating an application-level window object does not open a new browser window automatically to view the object, but if you wish to open one, you have to do it explicitly as shown below. An application-level window has a unique URL, which is based on the application URL and the name of the window given with the `setName()` method. For example, if the application URL is `http://localhost:8080/myapp/` and the window name is `mywindow`, the URL for the window will be `http://localhost:8080/myapp/mywindow/`. If the name of a window is not explicitly set with `setName()`, an automatically generated name will be used. The name can be retrieved with the `getName()` method and the entire URL with `getURL()`.

There are three typical ways to open a new window: using the `open()` method of **Window** class, a **Link**, or referencing it from HTML or JavaScript code written inside a **Label** component.

The **Window** `open()` method takes as parameters a resource to open and the target name. You can use **ExternalResource** to

---

open a specific URL, which you get from the window to be opened
with the `getURL()` method.

```
/* Create a button to open a new window. */
main.addComponent(new Button("Click to open new window",
                  new Button.ClickListener() {
    public void buttonClick(ClickEvent event) {
        // Open the window.
        main.open(new ExternalResource(mywindow.getURL()),
                  "_new");
    }
}));
```

The target name is one of the default HTML target names (_new,
_blank, _top, etc.) or a custom target name. How the window is
exactly opened depends on the browser. Browsers that support
tabbed browsing can open the window in another tab, depending
on the browser settings.

Another typical way to open windows is to use a **Link** component
with the window URL as an **ExternalResource**.

```
/* Add a link to the second window. */
Link link = new Link("Click to open second window",
                     new ExternalResource(mywindow.getURL()));
link.setTargetName("second");
link.setTargetHeight(300);
link.setTargetWidth(300);
link.setTargetBorder(Link.TARGET_BORDER_DEFAULT);
main.addComponent(link);
```

Using a **Link** allows you to specify parameters for the window that
opens by clicking on the link. Above, we set the dimensions of the
window and specify what window controls the window should
contain. The `Link.TARGET_BORDER_DEFAULT` specifies to use the
default, which includes most of the usual window controls, such
as the menu, the toolbar, and the status bar.

Another way to allow the user to open a window is to insert the
URL in HTML code inside a **Label**. This allows even more flexibility
in specifying how the window should be opened.

```
// Add the link manually inside a Label.
main.addComponent(
    new Label("Second window: <a href='" + mywindow.getURL()
              + "' target='second'>click to open</a>",
              Label.CONTENT_XHTML));
main.addComponent(
    new Label("The second window can be accessed through URL: "
              + mywindow.getURL()));
```

When an application-level window is closed in the browser the `close()` method is normally called just like for a child window and the **Window** object is purged from the application. However, there are situations where `close()` might not be called. See Section 12.1.4, "Closing Windows" for more information.

12.1.2. Creation of Windows When Requested

You can create a window object dynamically by its URL sub-path when it is first requested by overriding the `getWindow()` method of the **Application** class. The method gets a window name as its parameter and must return the corresponding **Window** object. The window name is determined from the first URL path element after the application URL (the name may not contain slashes). See the notes below for setting the actual name of the dynamically created windows below.

The following example allows opening windows with a window name that begins with `"planet-"` prefix. Since the method is called for *every* browser request for the application, we filter only the requests where a window with the given name does not yet exist.

```
public class WindowTestApplication extends Application {
    ...

    @Override
    public Window getWindow(String name) {
        // If a dynamically created window is requested, but
        // it does not exist yet, create it.
        if (name.startsWith("planet-") &&
                super.getWindow(name) == null) {
            String planetName =
                    name.substring("planet-".length());

            // Create the window object.
            Window newWindow =
                    new Window("Window about " + planetName);

            // DANGEROUS: Set the name explicitly. Otherwise,
            // an automatically generated name is used, which
            // is usually safer.
            newWindow.setName(name);

            // Put some content in it.
            newWindow.addComponent(
                new Label("This window contains details about " +
                        planetName + "."));

            // Add it to the application as a regular
            // application-level window.
            addWindow(newWindow);
```

```
        return newWindow;
    }

    // Otherwise the Application object manages existing
    // windows by their name.
    return super.getWindow(name);
}
```

The window name must be a unique indentifier for each **Window**
object instance. If you use `setName()` to set the window name explicitly, as we did above, any browser window that has the same
URL (within the same browser) would open the *same* window object. This is dangerous and *generally not recommended*, because
the browser windows would share the same window object.
Opening two windows with the same static name would immediately
lead to a synchronization error, as is shown in Figure 12.1, "Synchronization Error Between Windows with the Same Name" below.
(While also the window captions are same, they are irrelevant for
this problem.)

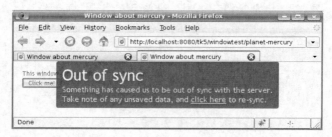

**Figure 12.1. Synchronization Error Between Windows with
the Same Name**

There are some cases where setting the name explicitly is useful.
The launch application below is one example, as it always opens
the other windows in a window target that is specific to the window
name, thereby never creating two windows with the same URL.
Similarly, if you had embedded the application in a browser frame
and the link would open the window in a frame, you would not have
problems. Having a single window instance for a URL is also useful
if the browser crashes and the user opens the window again, as
it will have kept its previous (server-side) state.

12.1.3. Dynamic Multi-Window Applications

Having multiple browser windows or tabs open in the same website and even the same page is one of the basic use cases of web browsing. The creation of **Window** objects described in the previous section allows opening multiple special-purpose windows with different URLs, but how to open multiple windows with the same URL? The solution is based on the fact that Vaadin doesn't identify windows only by their URL subpath, but also by an invisible window name.

Leaving the window name to be automatically generated allows opening multiple windows with the same URL, while each of the windows will have a separate state. The URL in the location bar stays unchanged and the generated window name is used only for the Ajax communications to identify the window object. A generated name is a string representation of a unique random number, such as "1928676448". You should be aware of the generated window names when overriding the getWindow() method (and not unintentionally create a new window instance dynamically for each such request). The condition in the above example would also filter out the requests for an already existing window with a generated name.

Figure 12.2, "A Dynamically Created Window" shows a dynamically created application-level window with the URL shown in the address bar. The URL for the application is here http://local-host:8080/book-examples/windowexample/, including the application context, application path. The dynamically created window's name is planet-mars.

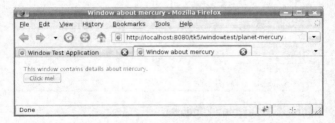

Figure 12.2. A Dynamically Created Window

The application knows the windows it already has and can return them after the creation. The application also handles closing and destruction of application-level window objects, as discussed in Section 12.1.4, "Closing Windows".

Such dynamic windows could be opened as in the following example:

```
public void init() {
    final Window main = new Window("Window Test");
    setMainWindow(main);

    // Have some IDs for the dynamically creatable windows.
    final String[] items = new String[] { "mercury", "venus",
            "earth", "mars", "jupiter", "saturn", "uranus",
            "neptune" };

    // Create a list of links to each of the available window.
    for (int i = 0; i < items.length; i++) {
        // Create a URL for the window.
        String windowUrl = getURL() + "planet-" + items[i];

        // Create a link to the window URL. Using the
        // item ID for the target also opens it in a new
        // browser window (or tab) unique to the window name.
        main.addComponent(
            new Link("Open window about " + items[i],
                    new ExternalResource(windowUrl),
                    items[i], -1, -1, Window.BORDER_DEFAULT));
    }
}
```

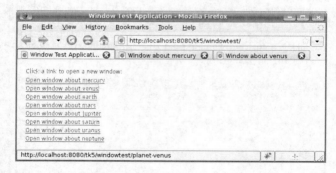

Figure 12.3. Opening Windows

12.1.4. Closing Windows

When the user closes an application-level window, the Client-Side Engine running in the browser will report the event to the server before the page is actually removed. You can catch the event with a **Window.CloseListener**, as is done in the example below.

```
newWindow.addListener(new Window.CloseListener() {
    @Override
    public void windowClose(CloseEvent e) {
        // Do something.
        System.out.println(e.getWindow().getName() +
                " was closed");

        // Add a text to the main window about closing.
        // (This does not update the main window.)
        getMainWindow().addComponent(
            new Label("Window '" + e.getWindow().getName() +
                "' was closed."));
    }
});
```

Notice that the change to the server-side state of the main window (or another application-level window) does not refresh the window in the browser, so the change will be unseen until user interaction or polling refreshes the window. This problem and its dangers are discussed in Section 12.1.5, "Caveats in Using Multiple Windows" below.

The close event does not occur if the browser crashes or the connection is otherwise severed violently. In such a situation, the window object will be left hanging, which could become a resource problem if you allow the users to open many such application-level windows. The positive side is that the user can reconnect to the window using the window URL.

12.1.5. Caveats in Using Multiple Windows

Communication Between Windows

For cases where you need communication between windows, we recommend using floating child windows. In Vaadin Release 5, an application window can not update the data in other windows. The contents of a window can only be updated when the particular window makes a request to the server. The request can be caused by user input or through polling.

Changing the server-side state of a window while processing a user event from another window can potentially cause serious problems. Changing the client-side state of a window does not always immediately communicate the changes to the server. The server-side state can therefore be out of sync with the client-side state.

Figure 12.4. Communication Between Two Application-Level Windows

The following example creates a second window that changes the contents of the main window, as illustrated in the figure above. In this simple case, changing the main window contents is safe.

```
// Create a table in the main window to hold items added
// in the second window
final Table table = new Table();
table.setPageLength(5);
table.getSize().setWidth(100, Size.UNITS_PERCENTAGE);
table.addContainerProperty("Name", String.class, "");
main.addComponent(table);

// Create the second window
final Window adderWindow = new Window("Add Items");
adderWindow.setName("win-adder");
main.getApplication().addWindow(adderWindow);

// Create selection component to add items to the table
final NativeSelect select = new NativeSelect("Select item to add");
select.setImmediate(true);
adderWindow.addComponent(select);
```

```
// Add some items to the selection
String items[] = new String[]{"- Select -", "Mercury", "Venus",
        "Earth", "Mars", "Jupiter", "Saturn", "Uranus", "Neptune"};
for (int i=0; i<items.length; i++)
    select.addItem(items[i]);
select.setNullSelectionItemId(items[0]);

// When an item is selected in the second window, add
// table in the main window
select.addListener(new ValueChangeListener() {
    public void valueChange(ValueChangeEvent event) {
        // If the selected value is something else
        // but a null selection item.
        if (select.getValue() != null) {
            // Add the selected item to the table
            // in the main window
            table.addItem(new Object[]{select.getValue()},
                        new Integer(table.size()));
        }
    }
});

// Link to open the selection window
Link link = new Link("Click to open second window",
                    new ExternalResource(adderWindow.getURL()),
                    "_new", 50, 200,
                    Link.TARGET_BORDER_DEFAULT);
main.addComponent(link);

// Enable polling to update the main window
ProgressIndicator poller = new ProgressIndicator();
poller.addStyleName("invisible");
main.addComponent(poller);
```

The example uses an invisible **ProgressIndicator** to implement polling. This is sort of a trick and a more proper API for polling is under design. Making the progress indicator invisible requires the following CSS style definition:

```
.v-progressindicator-invisible {
    display: none;
}
```

12.2. Embedding Applications in Web Pages

Many web sites are not all Ajax, but Ajax is used only for specific functionalities. In practice, many web applications are a mixture of dynamic web pages and Ajax applications embedded in such pages.

Embedding Vaadin applications is easy and there are several different ways to embed them. One is to have a `<div>` placeholder for the web application and load the Vaadin Client-Side Engine with a simple JavaScript code. Another method is even easier, which is to simply use the `<iframe>` element. Both of these methods have advantages and disadvantages. The `<div>` method can only embed one application in a page, while the `<iframe>` method can embed as many as needed. One disadvantage of the `<iframe>` method is that the size of the `<iframe>` element is not flexible according to the content while the `<div>` method allows such flexibility. The following sections look closer into these two embedding methods. Additionally, the Vaadin XS add-on allows embedding Vaadin applications in websites running in another server.

12.2.1. Embedding Inside a `div` Element

You can embed a Vaadin application inside a web page with a method that is equivalent to loading the initial page content from the application servlet in a non-embedded application. Normally, the **ApplicationServlet** servlet generates an initial page that contains the correct parameters for the specific application. You can easily configure it to load multiple Vaadin applications on the same page, assuming that they use the same widget set.

You can view the initial page for your application easily simply by opening the application in a web browser and viewing the HTML source code. You could just copy and paste the embedding code from the default initial page. It has, however, some extra functionality that is not normally needed: it generates some of the script content with `document.write()` calls, which is useful only when you are running the application as a portlet in a portal. The method outlined below is much simpler.

Embedding requires four elements inside the HTML document:

1. In the `<head>` element, you need to define the application URI and parameters and load the Vaadin Client-Side Engine. The `vaadin` variable is an associative map that can contain various runtime data used by the Client-Side Engine of Vaadin. The `vaadinConfigurations` item is itself an associate map that contains parameters for each of the applications embedded in the page. The map must contain the following items:

---

appUri

> The application URI consists of the context and the application path. If the context is `/mycontext` and the application path is `myapp`, the *appUri* would be `/mycontext/myapp`.

pathInfo

> The `PATHINFO` parameter for the Servlet.

themeUri (optional)

> URI of the application theme. The URI must include application context and the path to the theme directory. Themes are, by default, stored under the `/VAADIN/themes/` path.

versionInfo

> This parameter is itself an associative map that contains two parameters: *vaadinVersion* contains the version number of the Vaadin version used by the application. The *applicationVersion* parameter contains the version of the particular application. The contained parameters are optional, but the *versionInfo* parameter itself is not.

The following example defines two applications to run in the same window: the Calculator and Hello World examples. In the example, the application context is `/mycontext`.

```
<script type="text/javascript">
  var vaadin = {
    vaadinConfigurations: {
      'calc': {
        appUri:'/mycontext/Calc',
        pathInfo: '/',
        themeUri: '/mycontext/VAADIN/themes/example',
        versionInfo : {
          vaadinVersion: "6.7.6",
          applicationVersion: "NONVERSIONED"
        }
      },
      'hello': {
        appUri:'/mycontext/HelloWorld',
        pathInfo: '/',
        themeUri: '/mycontext/VAADIN/themes/example',
        versionInfo : {}
      }
    }};
</script>
```

2. Loading the Vaadin Client-Side Engine, that is, the widget set, is done with the following kind of line in the `<head>` element:

```
<script language='javascript' src='/mycontext/VAADIN/widget-
sets/com.vaadin.terminal.gwt.DefaultWidgetSet/com.vaadin.ter-
minal.gwt.DefaultWidgetSet.nocache.js'></script>
```

The engine URI consists of the context of the web application, `mycontext` above, followed by the path to the JavaScript (`.js`) file of the widget set, relative to the web application root (the `WebContent` directory in Eclipse). The line above assumes the use of the default widget set in Vaadin. If you have made custom widgets that are defined in a custom widget set, you need to use the path to the compiled widget set file. Widget sets must be compiled under the `WebContent/VAADIN/widgetsets` directory.

3. In the `<html>` element, you need to do a routine inclusion of GWT history `iframe` element as follows:

```
<iframe id="__gwt_historyFrame"
        style="width:0;height:0;border:0"></iframe>
```

4. The location of the Vaadin application is defined with a `div` placeholder element having `id="calc"`, where the identifier is the same as in the *vaadinConfigurations* parameter, as follows:

```
<div id="calc"></div>
```

The embedding element should not be self-closing.

Below is a complete example of embedding an application.

```
<?xml version="1.0" encoding="UTF-8" ?>
<!DOCTYPE html PUBLIC "-//W3C//DTD XHTML 1.0 Strict//EN"
        "http://www.w3.org/TR/xhtml1/DTD/xhtml1-strict.dtd">
<html xmlns="http://www.w3.org/1999/xhtml">
<head>
  <meta http-equiv="Content-Type"
        content="text/html; charset=UTF-8" />

  <title>Embedding a Vaadin Application in HTML Page</title>

  <!-- Define the application configuration -->
  <script type="text/javascript">
    var vaadin = {
      vaadinConfigurations: {
        helloworld: {
```

```
          appUri:'/book-examples/helloworld',
          pathInfo: '/',
          themeUri:'/book-examples/VAADIN/themes/book-examples',
          versionInfo : {}}
      }};
  </script>

  <!-- Load the widget set, that is, the Client-Side Engine -->
  <script language='javascript' src='/book-examples/VAADIN/widget-
sets/com.vaadin.book.widgetset.BookExamplesWidgetSet/com.vaad-
in.book.widgetset.BookExamplesWidgetSet.nocache.js'></script>

  <!-- Load the style sheet -->
  <link rel="stylesheet"
        type="text/css"
        href="/book-examples/VAADIN/themes/book-ex-
amples/styles.css"/>
</head>

<body>
  <!-- GWT requires an invisible history frame is needed for -->
  <!-- page/fragment history in the browser                  -->
  <iframe tabIndex="-1" id="__gwt_historyFrame" style="position:ab-
solute;width:0;height:0;border:0;overflow:hidden;" src="javas-
cript:false"></iframe>

  <h1>Embedding a Vaadin Application</h1>

  <p>This is a static web page that contains an embedded Vaadin
     application. It's here:</p>

  <!-- So here comes the div element in which the Vaadin -->
  <!-- application is embedded.                          -->
  <div id="helloworld" style="border: 2px solid green;"></div>

  <p>Please view the page source to see how embedding works.</p>

  <noscript>You have to enable javascript in your browser to
            use an application built with Vaadin.</noscript>
</body>
</html>
```

You can style the embedded application with themes, as described
in Chapter 8, *Themes*. The Client-Side Engine loads the theme required by the application. In addition, you can do styling with CSS
in the embedding page. In the above example, we added some
styling directly to the element.

12.2.2. Embedding Inside an `iframe` Element

Embedding a Vaadin application inside an `<iframe>` element is
even easier than the method described above, as it does not require definition of any Vaadin specific definitions. The use of

`<iframe>` makes it possible to embed multiple web applications or two different views to the same application on the same page.

You can embed an application with an element such as the following:

```
<iframe src="/vaadin-examples/Calc"></iframe>
```

The problem with `<iframe>` elements is that their size of is not flexible depending on the content of the frame, but the content must be flexible to accommodate in the frame. You can set the size of an `<iframe>` element with `height` and `width` attributes.

Below is a complete example of using the `<iframe>` to embed two applications in a web page.

```
<!DOCTYPE html PUBLIC "-//W3C//DTD XHTML 1.0 Transitional//EN"
     "http://www.w3.org/TR/xhtml1/DTD/xhtml1-transitional.dtd">
<html xmlns="http://www.w3.org/1999/xhtml" >
  <head>
    <title>Embedding in IFrame</title>
  </head>

  <body style="background: #d0ffd0;">
    <h1>This is a HTML page</h1>
    <p>Below are two Vaadin applications embedded inside
       a table:</p>

    <table align="center" border="3">
      <tr>
        <th>The Calculator</th>
        <th>The Color Picker</th>
      </tr>
      <tr valign="top">
        <td>
          <iframe src="/vaadin-examples/Calc" height="200"
                  width="150" frameborder="0"></iframe>
        </td>
        <td>
          <iframe src="/vaadin-examples/colorpicker"
                  height="330" width="400"
                  frameborder="0"></iframe>
        </td>
      </tr>
    </table>
  </body>
</html>
```

The page will look as shown in Figure 12.5, "Vaadin Applications Embedded Inside IFrames" below.

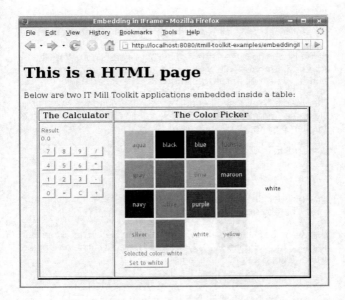

Figure 12.5. Vaadin Applications Embedded Inside IFrames

You can embed almost anything in an iframe, which essentially acts as a browser window. However, this creates various problems. The iframe must have a fixed size, inheritance of CSS from the embedding page is not possible, and neither is interaction with JavaScript, which makes mashups impossible, and so on. Even bookmarking with URI fragments will not work.

Note also that websites can forbid iframe embedding by specifying an X-Frame-Options: SAMEORIGIN header in the HTTP response.

12.2.3. Cross-Site Embedding with the Vaadin XS Add-on

In the previous sections, we described the two basic methods for embedding Vaadin applications: in a `<div>` element and in an `<iframe>`. One problem with div embedding is that it does not work between different Internet domains, which is a problem if you want to have your website running in one server and your Vaadin application in another. The security model in browsers effectively prevents such cross-site embedding of Ajax applications by enforcing the *same origin policy* for XmlHttpRequest calls, even if the server is running in the same domain but different port. While iframe is more permissive, allowing embedding almost anything in anywhere, it has many disadvantages, as described earlier.

The Vaadin XS (Cross-Site) add-on works around the limitation in div embedding by using JSONP-style communication instead of the standard XmlHttpRequests.

Embedding is done simply with:

```
<script src="http://demo.vaadin.com/xsembed/getEmbedJs"
        type="text/javascript"></script>
```

This includes an automatically generated embedding script in the page, thereby making embedding effortless.

This assumes that the main layout of the application has undefined height. If the height is 100%, you have to wrap it inside an element with a defined height. For example:

```
<div style="height: 500px;">
 <script src="http://demo.vaadin.com/xsembed/getEmbedJs"
        type="text/javascript"></script>
</div>
```

It is possible to restrict where the application can be embedded by using a whitelist. The add-on also encrypts the client-server communication, which is more important for embedded applications than usual.

You can get the Vaadin XS add-on from Vaadin Directory. It is provided as a Zip package. Download and extract the installation package to a local folder. Instructions for installation and further information is given in the README.html file in the package.

Some restrictions apply. You can have only one embedded application in one page. Also, some third-party libraries may interfere with the communication. Other notes are given in the README.

12.2.4. Embedding Into JSP and JSF Applications

12.3. Debug and Production Mode

Vaadin applications can be run in two modes: *debug mode* and *production mode*. The debug mode, which is on by default, enables a number of built-in debug features for the developers. The features include:

- Debug Window for accessing debug functionalities

- Display debug information in the Debug Window and server console.

- **Analyze layouting** button that analyzes the layout for possible problems.

All applications are run in the debug mode by default (since IT Mill Toolkit version 5.3.0). The production mode can be enabled, and debug mode thereby disabled, by adding a `productionMode=true` parameter to the servlet context in the `web.xml` deployment descriptor:

```
<context-param>
  <description>Vaadin production mode</description>
  <param-name>productionMode</param-name>
  <param-value>true</param-value>
</context-param>
```

Enabling the production mode disables the debug features, thereby preventing users from easily inspecting the inner workings of the application from the browser.

12.3.1. Debug Mode

Running an application in the debug mode enables the client-side Debug Window in the browser. You can open the Debug Window by adding "?debug" to the application URL, for example, `http://localhost:8080/myapp/?debug`. The Debug Window, shown in Figure 12.6, "Debug Window", consists of buttons controlling the debugging features and a scrollable log of debug messages.

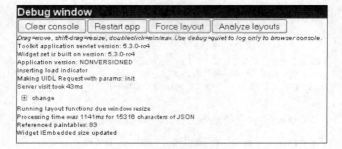

Figure 12.6. Debug Window

Clear console
> Clears the log in the Debug Window.

Restart app
> Restarts the application.

Force layout
> Causes all currently visible layouts to recalculate their appearance. Layout components calculate the space required by all child components, so the layout appearance must be recalculated whenever the size of a child component is changed. In normal applications, this is done automatically, but when you do themeing or alter the CSS with Firebug, you may need to force all layouts to recalculate themselves, taking into account the recently made changes.

Analyze layouts
> This is described in the following section.

If you use the Firebug plugin in Mozilla Firefox, the log messages will also be printed to the Firebug console. In such a case, you may want to enable client-side debugging without showing the Debug Window with "`?debug=quiet`" in the URL. In the quiet debug mode, log messages will only be printed to the Firebug console.

12.3.2. Analyzing Layouts

The **Analyze layouts** button analyzes the currently visible layouts and makes a report of possible layout related problems. All detected layout problems are displayed in the log and also printed to the console.

The most common layout problem is caused by placing a component that has a relative size inside a container (layout) that has undefined size, for example, adding a 100% wide **Panel** inside a **HorizontalLayout** with no width specification. In such a case, the error will look as shown below:

```
Vaadin DEBUG
- Window/1a8bd74 "My window" (width: MAIN WINDOW)
  - HorizontalLayout/1cf243b (width: UNDEFINED)
    - Panel/12e43f1 "My panel" (width: RELATIVE, 100.0 %)
Layout problem detected: Component with relative width inside a Ho-
rizontalLayout with no width defined
Relative sizes were replaced by undefined sizes, components may not
  render as expected.
```

This particular error tells that the **Panel** "My panel" is 100% wide while the width of the containing **HorizontalLayout** is undefined. The components will be rendered as if the the width of the contained **Panel** was undefined, which might not be what the developer wanted. There are two possible fixes for this case: if the **Panel** should fill the main window horizontally, set a width for the **HorizontalLayout** (for example 100% wide), or set the width of the **Panel** to "undefined" to render the it as it is currently rendered but avoiding the warning message.

The same error is shown in the Debug Window in a slightly different form and with an additional feature (see Figure 12.7, "Debug Window Showing the Result of **Analyze layouts**."). Checking the **Emphasize component in UI** box will turn red the background of the component that caused a warning, making it easy for the developer to figure out which component each warning relates to. The messages will also be displayed hierarchically, as a warning from a containing component often causes more warnings from its child components. A good rule of thumb is to work on the upper-level problems first and only after that worry about the warnings from the children.

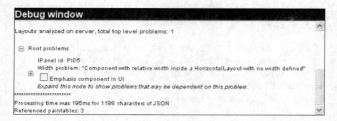

Figure 12.7. Debug Window Showing the Result of Analyze layouts.

12.3.3. Custom Layouts

CustomLayout components can not be analyzed in the same way as other layouts. For custom layouts, the **Analyze layouts** button analyzes all contained relative-sized components and checks if any relative dimension is calculated to zero so that the component will be invisible. The error log will display a warning for each of these invisible components. It would not be meaningful to emphasize the component itself as it is not visible, so when you select such an error, the parent layout of the component is emphasized if possible.

12.3.4. Debug Functions for Component Developers

You can take advantage of the debug mode when developing client-side components. The static function `ApplicationConnection.getConsole()` will return a reference to a **Console** object which contains logging methods such as `log(String msg)` and `error(String msg)`. These functions will print messages to the Debug Window and Firebug console in the same way as other debugging functionalities of Vaadin do. No messages will be printed if the Debug Window is not open or if the application is running in production mode.

12.4. Request Handlers

You may need to handle pure HTTP requests for some purposes, typically for generating some dynamic HTML, image, PDF, or other content. You can provide HTTP content easily with resources, as described in Section 4.3, "Referencing Resources", including dynamic content with **StreamResource**. The resources, however, are only usable from within a Vaadin application, such as with the **Embedded** component. Request handlers allow responding to HTTP requests made with the application URL, including GET or POST parameters.

To handle requests, you need to implement a `RequestHandler`. The `handleRequest()` method gets the application, request, as well as a response object as parameters.

If the handler writes a response, it must return `true`. This stops running other possible request handlers. Otherwise, it should return `false` so that another handler could return a response.

12.5. Shortcut Keys

Vaadin provides simple ways for defining shortcut keys for field components and a default button, and a lower-level generic shortcut key binding API based on actions.

12.5.1. Click Shortcuts for Default Buttons

You can add or set a *click shortcut* to a button to set it as "default" button; pressing the defined key, typically **Enter**, in any component in the window causes a click event for the button.

You can define a click shortcut with the `setClickShortcut()` shorthand method:

```
// Have an OK button and set it as the default button
Button ok = new Button("OK");
ok.setClickShortcut(KeyCode.ENTER);
ok.addStyleName("primary");
```

The `primary` style name highlights a button to show the default button status; usually with a bolder font than usual, depending on the theme. The result can be seen in Figure 12.8, "Default Button with Click Shortcut".

Name of the Field Agent

OK   Cancel

Figure 12.8. Default Button with Click Shortcut

12.5.2. Field Focus Shortcuts

You can define a shortcut key that sets the focus to a field component (any component that inherits **AbstractField**) by adding a **FocusShortcut** as a shortcut listener to the field.

```
// A field with Alt+N bound to it
TextField name = new TextField("Name (Alt+N)");
name.addShortcutListener(
        new AbstractField.FocusShortcut(name, KeyCode.N,
                                        ModifierKey.ALT));
layout.addComponent(name);

// A field with Alt+A bound to it
TextField address = new TextField("Address (Alt+A)");
address.addShortcutListener(
        new AbstractField.FocusShortcut(address, KeyCode.A,
                                        ModifierKey.ALT));
layout.addComponent(address);
```

The constructor of the **FocusShortcut** takes the field component as its first parameter, followed by the key code, and an optional list of modifier keys, as listed in Section 12.5.4, "Supported Key Codes and Modifier Keys".

12.5.3. Generic Shortcut Actions

Shortcut keys can be defined as *actions* using the **ShortcutAction** class. ShortcutAction extends the generic **Action** class that is used for example in **Tree** and **Table** for context menus. Currently, the only classes that accept **ShortcutAction**s are **Window** and **Panel**.

To handle key presses, you need to define an action handler by implementing the **Handler** interface. The interface has two methods that you need to implement: getActions() and handleAction().

The getActions() method must return an array of **Action** objects for the component, specified with the second parameter for the method, the *sender* of an action. For a keyboard shortcut, you use a **ShortcutAction**. The implementation of the method could be following:

```
// Have the unmodified Enter key cause an event
Action action_ok = new ShortcutAction("Default key",
        ShortcutAction.KeyCode.ENTER, null);

// Have the C key modified with Alt cause an event
Action action_cancel = new ShortcutAction("Alt+C",
        ShortcutAction.KeyCode.C,
        new int[] { ShortcutAction.ModifierKey.ALT });

Action[] actions = new Action[] {action_cancel, action_ok};

public Action[] getActions(Object target, Object sender) {
    if (sender == myPanel)
        return actions;

    return null;
}
```

The returned **Action** array may be static or you can create it dynamically for different senders according to your needs.

The constructor of **ShortcutAction** takes a symbolic caption for the action; this is largely irrelevant for shortcut actions in their current implementation, but might be used later if implementors use them both in menus and as shortcut actions. The second parameter is the key code and the third a list of modifier keys, which are listed in Section 12.5.4, "Supported Key Codes and Modifier Keys".

The following example demonstrates the definition of a default button for a user interface, as well as a normal shortcut key, **Alt**+**C** for clicking the **Cancel** button.

```
public class DefaultButtonExample extends CustomComponent
                                  implements Handler {
    // Define and create user interface components
    Panel panel = new Panel("Login");
    FormLayout formlayout = new FormLayout();
    TextField username = new TextField("Username");
    TextField password = new TextField("Password");
    HorizontalLayout buttons = new HorizontalLayout();

    // Create buttons and define their listener methods.
    Button ok = new Button("OK", this, "okHandler");
    Button cancel = new Button("Cancel", this, "cancelHandler");

    // Have the unmodified Enter key cause an event
    Action action_ok = new ShortcutAction("Default key",
            ShortcutAction.KeyCode.ENTER, null);

    // Have the C key modified with Alt cause an event
```

```
    Action action_cancel = new ShortcutAction("Alt+C",
            ShortcutAction.KeyCode.C,
            new int[] { ShortcutAction.ModifierKey.ALT });

public DefaultButtonExample() {
    // Set up the user interface
    setCompositionRoot(panel);
    panel.addComponent(formlayout);
    formlayout.addComponent(username);
    formlayout.addComponent(password);
    formlayout.addComponent(buttons);
    buttons.addComponent(ok);
    buttons.addComponent(cancel);

    // Set focus to username
    username.focus();

    // Set this object as the action handler
    System.out.println("adding ah");
    panel.addActionHandler(this);

    System.out.println("start done.");
}

/**
 * Retrieve actions for a specific component. This method
 * will be called for each object that has a handler; in
 * this example just for login panel. The returned action
 * list might as well be static list.
 */
public Action[] getActions(Object target, Object sender) {
    System.out.println("getActions()");
    return new Action[] { action_ok, action_cancel };
}

/**
 * Handle actions received from keyboard. This simply directs
 * the actions to the same listener methods that are called
 * with ButtonClick events.
 */
public void handleAction(Action action, Object sender,
                         Object target) {
    if (action == action_ok) {
        okHandler();
    }
    if (action == action_cancel) {
        cancelHandler();
    }
}

public void okHandler() {
    // Do something: report the click
    formlayout.addComponent(new Label("OK clicked. "
            + "User=" + username.getValue() + ", password="
            + password.getValue()));
}
```

```
public void cancelHandler() {
    // Do something: report the click
    formlayout.addComponent(new Label("Cancel clicked. User="
            + username.getValue() + ", password="
            + password.getValue()));
}
}
```

Notice that the keyboard actions can currently be attached only to **Panel**s and **Window**s. This can cause problems if you have components that require a certain key. For example, multi-line **TextField** requires the **Enter** key. There is currently no way to filter the shortcut actions out while the focus is inside some specific component, so you need to avoid such conflicts.

12.5.4. Supported Key Codes and Modifier Keys

The shortcut key definitions require a key code to identify the pressed key and modifier keys, such as Shift, Alt, or Ctrl, to specify a key combination.

The key codes are defined in the **ShortcutAction.KeyCode** interface and are:

Keys *A* to *Z*
    Normal letter keys

F1 to *F12*
    Function keys

BACKSPACE, *DELETE*, *ENTER*, *ESCAPE*, *INSERT*, *TAB*
    Control keys

NUM0 to *NUM9*
    Number pad keys

ARROW_DOWN, *ARROW_UP*, *ARROW_LEFT*, *ARROW_RIGHT*
    Arrow keys

HOME, *END*, *PAGE_UP*, *PAGE_DOWN*
    Other movement keys

Modifier keys are defined in **ShortcutAction.ModifierKey** and are:

```
ModifierKey.ALT
```
Alt key

```
ModifierKey.CTRL
```
Ctrl key

```
ModifierKey.SHIFT
```
Shift key

All constructors and methods accepting modifier keys take them as a variable argument list following the key code, separated with commas. For example, the following defines a **Ctrl+Shift+N** key combination for a shortcut.

```
TextField name = new TextField("Name (Ctrl+Shift+N)");
name.addShortcutListener(
        new AbstractField.FocusShortcut(name, KeyCode.N,
                                        ModifierKey.CTRL,
                                        ModifierKey.SHIFT));
```

Supported Key Combinations

The actual possible key combinations vary greatly between browsers, as most browsers have a number of built-in shortcut keys, which can not be used in web applications. For example, Mozilla Firefox allows binding almost any key combination, while Opera does not even allow binding Alt shortcuts. Other browsers are generally in between these two. Also, the operating system can reserve some key combinations and some computer manufacturers define their own system key combinations.

12.6. Printing

Vaadin does not currently have any special support for printing. Printing on the server-side is, in any case, largely independent from the web UI of an application. You just have to take care that the printing does not block server requests, possibly by running printing in another thread.

For client-side printing, most browsers support printing the web page. Vaadin does not explicitly support launching the printing in browser, but you can easily use the JavaScript `print()` method that opens the print window of the browser.

```
final Button print = new Button("Print This Page");
print.addListener(new ClickListener() {
```

```
    public void buttonClick(ClickEvent event) {
        print.getWindow().executeJavaScript("print();");
    }
});
```

This button would print the current page, including the button itself.
Often, you want to be able to print a report or receipt and it should
not have any visible UI components. In such a case, you could
offer it as a PDF resource, or you could open a new window, as is
done below, and automatically launch printing.

```
// A button to open the printer-friendly page.
Button print = new Button("Click to Print");

print.addListener(new Button.ClickListener() {
 public void buttonClick(ClickEvent event) {
        // Create a window that contains what you want to print
        Window window = new Window("Window to Print");

        // Have some content to print
        window.addComponent(new Label(
                "<h1>Here's some dynamic content</h1>\n" +
                "<p>This is to be printed to the printer.</p>",
                Label.CONTENT_XHTML));

        // Add the printing window as a new application-level
        // window
        getApplication().addWindow(window);

        // Open it as a popup window with no decorations
        getWindow().open(new ExternalResource(window.getURL()),
                "_blank", 500, 200, // Width and height
                Window.BORDER_NONE); // No decorations

        // Print automatically when the window opens.
        // This call will block until the print dialog exits!
        window.executeJavaScript("print();");

        // Close the window automatically after printing
        window.executeJavaScript("self.close();");
    }
});
```

How the browser opens the window, as an actual (popup) window
or just a tab, depends on the browser. Notice that calling the
print() method in the window will block the entire application
until the print dialog exits. After printing, we automatically close
the window with another JavaScript call, as there is no close()
method in **Window**.

Printing as PDF would not require creating a **Window** object, but
you would need to provide the content as a static or a dynamic
resource for the open() method. Printing a PDF file would obviously

require a PDF viewer cabability (such as Adobe Reader) in the browser.

12.7. Google App Engine Integration

Vaadin includes support to run Vaadin applications in the Google App Engine (GAE). The most essential requirement for GAE is the ability to serialize the application state. Vaadin applications are serializable through the **java.io.Serializable** interface.

To run as a GAE application, an application must use **GAEApplicationServlet** instead of **ApplicationServlet** in `web.xml`, and of course implement the **java.io.Serializable** interface for all persistent classes. You also need to enable session support in `appengine-web.xml` with:

```
<sessions-enabled>true</sessions-enabled>
```

The Vaadin Project wizard can create the configuration files needed for GAE deployment. See Section 2.3.1, "Creating the Project". When the Google App Engine deployment configuration is selected, the wizard will create the project structure following the GAE Servlet convention instead of the regular Servlet convention. The main differences are:

- Source directory: `src/main/java`

- Output directory: `war/WEB-INF/classes`

- Content directory: `war`

Rules and Limitations

Running Vaadin applications in Google App Engine has the following rules and limitations:

- Avoid using the session for storage, usual App Engine limitations apply (no synchronization, that is, it is unreliable).

- Vaadin uses memcache for mutex, the key is of the form `_vmutex<sessionid>`.

- The Vaadin **WebApplicationContext** class is serialized separately into memcache and datastore; the memcache

---

key is _vac<sessionid> and the datastore entity kind is
_vac with identifiers of the type _vac<sessionid>.

- *Do not* update the application state when serving an **ApplicationResource** (such as **ClassResource**.getStream()).

- *Avoid* (or be very careful when) updating application state in a **TransactionListener** - it is called even when the application is not locked and won't be serialized (such as with **ApplicationResource**), and changes can therefore be lost (it should be safe to update things that can be safely discarded later, that is, valid only for the current request).

- The application remains locked during uploads - a progress bar is not possible.

12.8. Common Security Issues

12.8.1. Sanitizing User Input to Prevent Cross-Site Scripting

You can put raw XHTML content in many components, such as the **Label** and **CustomLayout**, as well as in tooltips and notifications. In such cases, you should make sure that if the content has any possibility to come from user input, the input is well sanitized before displaying it. Otherwise, a malicious user can easily make a cross-site scripting attack by injecting offensive JavaScript code in such components.

Offensive code can easily be injected with <script> markup or in tag attributes as events, such as onLoad. Cross-site scripting vulnerabilities are browser dependent, depending on the situations in which different browsers execute scripting markup.

There is no generic way to sanitize user input as different applications can allow different kinds of input. Pruning (X)HTML tags out is somewhat simple, but some applications may need to allow (X)HTML. It is therefore the responsibility of the application to sanitize the input.

Character encoding can make sanitization more difficult, as offensive tags can be encoded so that they are not recognized by a sanitizer. This can be done, for example, with HTML character entities and with variable-width encodings such as UTF-8 or various CJK encodings, by abusing multiple representations of a character. Most trivially, you could input < and > with < and >, respectively. The input could also be malformed and the sanitizer must be able to interpret it exactly as the browser would, and different browsers can interpret malformed HTML and variable-width character encodings differently.

Notice that the problem applies also to user input from a **RichTextArea** is transmitted as XHTML from the browser to server-side and is not sanitized. As the entire purpose of the **RichTextArea** component is to allow input of formatted text, you can not just remove all HTML tags. Also many attributes, such as *style*, should pass through the sanitization.

12.9. URI Fragment and History Management with UriFragmentUtility

*This section is not yet updated for Vaadin 7. The **UriFragmentUtility** is obsolete in Vaadin 7 and URI fragment changes are handled with a* FragmentChangedListener *and* setFragment() *in the **Page** class, for example:* Page.getCurrent().setFragment("foo").

A major issue in AJAX applications is that as they run in a single web page, bookmarking the application URL (or more generally the *URI*) can only bookmark the application, not an application state. This is a problem for many applications such as product catalogs and forums, in which it would be good to provide links to specific products or messages. Consequently, as browsers remember the browsing history by URI, the history and the **Back** button do not normally work. The solution is to use the *fragment* part of the URI, which is separated from the primary part (address + path + optional query parameters) of the URI with the hash (#) character. For example:

```
http://example.com/path#myfragment
```

The exact syntax of the fragment part is defined in RFC 3986 (Internet standard STD 66) that defines the URI syntax. A fragment may only contain the regular URI *path characters* (see the standard) and additionally the slash and the question mark.

The **UriFragmentUtility** is a special-purpose component that manages the URI fragment; it allows setting the fragment and to handle user-made changes to it. As it is a regular component, though invisible, you must add it to a layout in an application window with the `addComponent()`, as usual.

```
public void init() {
    Window main = new Window("URI Fragment Example");
    setMainWindow(main);

    // Create the URI fragment utility
    final UriFragmentUtility urifu = new UriFragmentUtility();
    main.addComponent(urifu);
```

Notice that the utility component can work only when it is attached to the window, so in practice it must be added in the `init()` method of the application and must afterwards always remain in the application's user interface.

You can set the URI fragment with the `setFragment()` method of the **UriFragmentUtility** object. The method takes the fragment as a string parameter. In the following example, we have a menu, from which the user can select the URI fragment.

```
// Application state menu
final ListSelect menu = new ListSelect("Select a URI Fragment");
menu.addItem("mercury");
menu.addItem("venus");
menu.addItem("earth");
menu.addItem("mars");
menu.setImmediate(true);
main.addComponent(menu);

// Set the URI Fragment when menu selection changes
menu.addListener(new Property.ValueChangeListener() {
    public void valueChange(ValueChangeEvent event) {
        String itemid = (String) event.getProperty().getValue();
        urifu.setFragment(itemid);
    }
});
```

The URI fragment and any changes to it are passed to an application as **FragmentChangedEvent**s, which you can handle with a **FragmentChangedListener**. You can get the new fragment value with the `getFragment()` method from the URI fragment utility component.

```
// When the URI fragment is given, use it to set menu selection
urifu.addListener(new FragmentChangedListener() {
    public void fragmentChanged(FragmentChangedEvent source) {
        String fragment =
                source.getUriFragmentUtility().getFragment();
```

```
        if (fragment != null)
            menu.setValue(fragment);
    }
});
```

Figure 12.9, "Application State Management with URI Fragment Utility" shows an application that allows specifying the menu selection with a URI fragment and correspondingly sets the fragment when the user selects a menu item, as done in the code examples above.

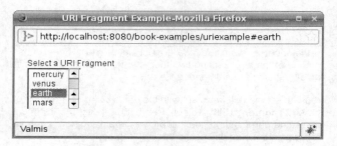

Figure 12.9. Application State Management with URI Fragment Utility

12.10. Navigating in an Application

Plain Vaadin applications do not have normal web page navigation as they usually run on a single page, as all Ajax applications do. Quite commonly, however, applications have different views between which the user should be able to navigate. The **Navigator** in Vaadin can be used for most cases of navigation. Views managed by the navigator automatically get a distinct URI fragment, which can be used to be able to bookmark the views and their states and to go back and forward in the browser history.

12.10.1. Setting Up for Navigation

The **Navigator** class manages a collection of *views* that implement the `View` interface. The views can be either registered beforehand or acquired from a *view provider*. When registering, the views must have a name identifier and be added to a navigator with `addView()`.

You can register new views at any point. Once registered, you can navigate to them with `navigateTo()`.

The views managed by the **Navigator** are displayed in a `ViewDisplay`. The framework includes a **SimpleViewDisplay** component, which can be used in most cases to display views.

Let us consider the following application with two views: start and main. Here, we define their names with enums to be typesafe.

```
public class NavigatorRoot extends Root {
    Navigator  navigator;

    enum Views {START, MAIN};

    @Override
    protected void init(WrappedRequest request) {
        getPage().setTitle("Navigation Example");

        // Fill the page with a view display
        SimpleViewDisplay viewDisplay = new SimpleViewDisplay();
        viewDisplay.setSizeFull();
        setContent(viewDisplay);

        // Create the navigator to control the page
        navigator = new Navigator(Page.getCurrent(),
                                  viewDisplay);

        // Create and register the views
        navigator.addView(Views.START.name(), new StartView());
        navigator.addView(Views.MAIN.name(), new MainView());

        // Navigate to the start view
        navigator.navigateTo(Views.START.name());
    }
}
```

The **Navigator** automatically sets the URI fragment of the application URL. It also registers a `FragmentChangeListener` in the page (see Section 12.9, "URI Fragment and History Management with **UriFragmentUtility**") to show the view identified by the URI fragment if entered or navigated to in the browser. This also enables browser navigation history in the application.

View Providers

You can create new views dynamically using a *view provider* that implement the `ViewProvider` interface. A provider is registered in **Navigator** with `registerProvider()`.

The ClassBasedViewProvider is a view provider that can dynamically create new instances of a specified view class based on the view name.

The StaticViewProvider returns an existing view instance based on the view name. The addView() in **Navigator** is actually just a shorthand for creating a static view provider for each registered view.

View Change Listeners

You can handle view changes also by implementing a ViewChangeListener and adding it to a **Navigator**. When a view change occurs, a listener receives a **ViewChangeEvent** object, which has references to the old and the activated view, the name of the activated view, as well as the fragment parameters.

12.10.2. Implementing a View

Views can be any objects that implement the View interface. When the navigateTo() is called for the navigator, or the application is opened with the URI fragment associated with the view, it switches to the view and calls its navigateTo() method.

To continue with the example, consider the following simple view just lets the user to navigate to the other view. It doesn't do anything special when the user navigates to it.

```
/** A start view for navigating to the main view */
public class StartView extends VerticalLayout implements View {
    public StartView() {
        setSizeFull();

        Button button = new Button("Go to Main View",
                new Button.ClickListener() {
            @Override
            public void buttonClick(ClickEvent event) {
                navigator.navigateTo(Views.MAIN.name());
            }
        });
        addComponent(button);
        setComponentAlignment(button, Alignment.MIDDLE_CENTER);
    }

    @Override
    public void navigateTo(String fragmentParameters) {
        // Nothing to do here really
    }
}
```

12.10.3. Handling URI Fragment Path

URI fragments can be used with **Navigator** in two ways: for navigating to a specific view and for navigating to a state within the view. The URI fragment accepted by navigateTo() can have the view name at the root, followed by fragment parameters after a slash ("/"). These parameters are passed to the navigateTo() method in the View.

In the following example, we implement within-view navigation.

```
/** Main view with a menu */
public class MainView extends VerticalLayout implements View {

    // Menu navigation button listener
    class ButtonListener implements Button.ClickListener {
        String menuitem;
        public ButtonListener(String menuitem) {
            this.menuitem = menuitem;
        }

        @Override
        public void buttonClick(ClickEvent event) {
            // Navigate to a specific state
            navigator.navigateTo(Views.MAIN.name() +
                                 "/" + menuitem);
        }
    }

    public MainView() {
        setSizeFull();

        // Layout with menu on left and view area on right
        HorizontalLayout hLayout = new HorizontalLayout();
        hLayout.setSizeFull();

        // Have a menu on the left side of the screen
        Panel menu = new Panel("Menu");
        menu.addComponent(new Button("Cat",
                new ButtonListener("cat")));
        menu.addComponent(new Button("Dog",
                new ButtonListener("dog")));
        menu.addComponent(new Button("Reindeer",
                new ButtonListener("reindeer")));
        menu.addComponent(new Button("Penguin",
                new ButtonListener("penguin")));
        menu.addComponent(new Button("Sheep",
                new ButtonListener("sheep")));
        menu.setHeight("100%");
        menu.setWidth(null);
        menu.getContent().setWidth(null);
        hLayout.addComponent(menu);

        // Have a panel that contains a content area on the right
        panel = new Panel("Content Panel");
```

```
        panel.setSizeFull();
        hLayout.addComponent(panel);
        hLayout.setExpandRatio(panel, 1.0f);

        addComponent(hLayout);
        setExpandRatio(hLayout, 1.0f);

        // Allow going back to the start
        Button logout = new Button("Logout",
                new Button.ClickListener() {
            @Override
            public void buttonClick(ClickEvent event) {
                navigator.navigateTo(Views.START.name());
            }
        });
        addComponent(logout);
    }

    @Override
    public void navigateTo(String fragmentParameters) {
        panel.removeAllComponents();

        if (fragmentParameters == null) {
            panel.addComponent(
                new Label("Nothing to see here, " +
                        "just pass along."));
            return;
        }

        // Display some content
        panel.addComponent(
            new Label("You are currently watching a " +
                    fragmentParameters));
        panel.addComponent(new Embedded(null,
            new ThemeResource("img/" + fragmentParameters +
                    "-128px.png")));
    }
}
```

The main view is shown in Figure 12.10, "Navigator Main View".
At this point, the URL would be http://local-
host:8080/myapp#MAIN/reindeer.

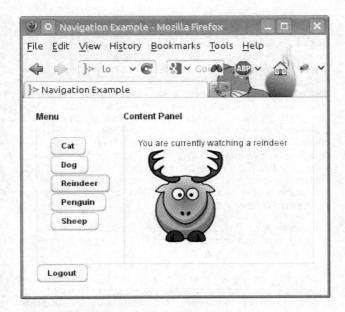

Figure 12.10. Navigator Main View

12.11. Drag and Drop

Dragging an object from one location to another by grabbing it with mouse, holding the mouse button pressed, and then releasing the button to "drop" it to the other location is a common way to move, copy, or associate objects. For example, most operating systems allow dragging and dropping files between folders or dragging a document on a program to open it. In Vaadin, it is possible to drag and drop components and parts of certain components.

Dragged objects, or *transferables*, are essentially data objects. You can drag and drop rows in **Table** and nodes in **Tree** components, either within or between the components. You can also drag entire components by wrapping them inside **DragAndDropWrapper**.

Dragging starts from a *drag source*, which defines the transferable. Transferables implement the **Transferable** interfaces. For trees and tables, which are bound to **Container** data sources, a node or row transferable is a reference to an **Item** in the Vaadin Data Model. Dragged components are referenced with a **WrapperTransferable**. Starting dragging does not require any client-server communication, you only need to enable dragging. All drag and drop logic occurs in two operations: determining (*accepting*) where dropping is allowed and actually dropping. Drops can be done on a *drop target*, which implements the **DropTarget** interface. Three components implement the interface: **Tree**, **Table**, and **DragAndDropWrapper**. These accept and drop operations need to be provided in a *drop handler*. Essentially all you need to do to enable drag and drop is to enable dragging in the drag source and implement the `getAcceptCriterion()` and `drop()` methods in the **DropHandler** interface.

The client-server architecture of Vaadin causes special requirements for the drag and drop functionality. The logic for determining where a dragged object can be dropped, that is, *accepting* a drop, should normally be done on the client-side, in the browser. Server communications are too slow to have much of such logic on the server-side. The drag and drop feature therefore offers a number of ways to avoid the server communications to ensure a good user experience.

12.11.1. Handling Drops

Most of the user-defined drag and drop logic occurs in a *drop handler*, which is provided by implementing the `drop()` method in the **DropHandler** interface. A closely related definition is the drop accept criterion, which is defined in the `getAcceptCriterion()` method in the same interface. It is described in Section 12.11.4, "Accepting Drops" later.

The `drop()` method gets a **DragAndDropEvent** as its parameters. The event object provides references to two important object: **Transferable** and **TargetDetails**.

A **Transferable** contains a reference to the object (component or data item) that is being dragged. A tree or table item is represented as a **TreeTransferable** or **TableTransferable** object, which carries the item identifier of the dragged tree or table item. These special transferables, which are bound to some data in a container, are **DataBoundTransferable**. Dragged components are represented as **WrapperTransferable** objects, as the components are wrapped in a **DragAndDropWrapper**.

The **TargetDetails** object provides information about the exact location where the transferable object is being dropped. The exact class of the details object depends on the drop target and you need to cast it to the proper subclass to get more detailed information. If the target is selection component, essentially a tree or a table, the **AbstractSelectTargetDetails** object tells the item on which the drop is being made. For trees, the **TreeTargetDetails** gives some more details. For wrapped components, the information is provided in a **WrapperDropDetails** object. In addition to the target item or component, the details objects provide a *drop location*. For selection components, the location can be obtained with the `getDropLocation()` and for wrapped components with `verticalDropLocation()` and `horizontalDropLocation()`. The locations are specified as either **VerticalDropLocation** or **HorizontalDropLocation** objects. The drop location objects specify whether the transferable is being dropped above, below, or directly on (at the middle of) a component or item.

Dropping on a **Tree**, **Table**, and a wrapped component is explained further in the following sections.

12.11.2. Dropping Items On a Tree

You can drag items from, to, or within a **Tree**. Making tree a drag source requires simply setting the drag mode with `setDragMode()`. **Tree** currently supports only one drag mode, `TreeDragMode.NODE`, which allows dragging single tree nodes. While dragging, the dragged node is referenced with a **TreeTransferable** object, which is a **DataBoundTransferable**. The tree node is identified by the item ID of the container item.

When a transferable is dropped on a tree, the drop location is stored in a **TreeTargetDetails** object, which identifies the target location by item ID of the tree node on which the drop is made. You can get the item ID with `getItemIdOver()` method in **AbstractSelectTargetDetails**, which the **TreeTargetDetails** inherits. A drop can occur directly on or above or below a node; the exact location is a **VerticalDropLocation**, which you can get with the `getDropLocation()` method.

In the example below, we have a **Tree** and we allow reordering the tree items by drag and drop.

```
final Tree tree = new Tree("Inventory");
tree.setContainerDataSource(TreeExample.createTreeContent());
layout.addComponent(tree);

// Expand all items
for (Iterator<?> it = tree.rootItemIds().iterator(); it.hasNext();)

    tree.expandItemsRecursively(it.next());

// Set the tree in drag source mode
tree.setDragMode(TreeDragMode.NODE);

// Allow the tree to receive drag drops and handle them
tree.setDropHandler(new DropHandler() {
    public AcceptCriterion getAcceptCriterion() {
        return AcceptAll.get();
    }

    public void drop(DragAndDropEvent event) {
        // Wrapper for the object that is dragged
        Transferable t = event.getTransferable();

        // Make sure the drag source is the same tree
        if (t.getSourceComponent() != tree)
            return;

        TreeTargetDetails target = (TreeTargetDetails)
            event.getTargetDetails();

        // Get ids of the dragged item and the target item
        Object sourceItemId = t.getData("itemId");
        Object targetItemId = target.getItemIdOver();

        // On which side of the target the item was dropped
        VerticalDropLocation location = target.getDropLocation();

        HierarchicalContainer container = (HierarchicalContainer)
        tree.getContainerDataSource();

        // Drop right on an item -> make it a child
        if (location == VerticalDropLocation.MIDDLE)
            tree.setParent(sourceItemId, targetItemId);

        // Drop at the top of a subtree -> make it previous
        else if (location == VerticalDropLocation.TOP) {
            Object parentId = container.getParent(targetItemId);
            container.setParent(sourceItemId, parentId);
            container.moveAfterSibling(sourceItemId, targetItemId);

            container.moveAfterSibling(targetItemId, sourceItemId);
```

```
            }

            // Drop below another item -> make it next
            else if (location == VerticalDropLocation.BOTTOM) {
                Object parentId = container.getParent(targetItemId);
                container.setParent(sourceItemId, parentId);
                container.moveAfterSibling(sourceItemId, targetItemId);

            }
        }
});
```

Accept Criteria for Trees

Tree defines some specialized accept criteria for trees.

TargetInSubtree (client-side)

Accepts if the target item is in the specified sub-tree. The sub-tree is specified by the item ID of the root of the sub-tree in the constructor. The second constructor includes a depth parameter, which specifies how deep from the given root node are drops accepted. Value –1 means infinite, that is, the entire sub-tree, and is therefore the same as the simpler constructor.

TargetItemAllowsChildren (client-side)

Accepts a drop if the tree has `setChildrenAllowed()` enabled for the target item. The criterion does not require parameters, so the class is a singleton and can be acquired with `Tree.TargetItemAllowsChildren.get()`. For example, the following composite criterion accepts drops only on nodes that allow children, but between all nodes:

```
return new Or (Tree.TargetItemAllowsChildren.get(), new
Not(VerticalLocationIs.MIDDLE));
```

TreeDropCriterion (server-side)

Accepts drops on only some items, which as specified by a set of item IDs. You must extend the abstract class and implement the `getAllowedItemIds()` to return the set. While the criterion is server-side, it is lazy-loading, so that the list of accepted target nodes is loaded only once from the server for each drag operation. See Section 12.11.4, "Accepting Drops" for an example.

In addition, the accept criteria defined in **AbstractSelect** are available for a **Tree**, as listed in Section 12.11.4, "Accepting Drops".

12.11.3. Dropping Items On a Table

You can drag items from, to, or within a **Table**. Making table a drag source requires simply setting the drag mode with `setDragMode()`. **Table** supports dragging both single rows, with `TableDragMode.ROW`, and multiple rows, with `TableDragMode.MULTIROW`. While dragging, the dragged node or nodes are referenced with a **TreeTransferable** object, which is a **DataBoundTransferable**. Tree nodes are identified by the item IDs of the container items.

When a transferable is dropped on a table, the drop location is stored in a **AbstractSelectTargetDetails** object, which identifies the target row by its item ID. You can get the item ID with `getItemIdOver()` method. A drop can occur directly on or above or below a row; the exact location is a **VerticalDropLocation**, which you can get with the `getDropLocation()` method from the details object.

Accept Criteria for Tables

Table defines one specialized accept criterion for tables.

TableDropCriterion (server-side)
Accepts drops only on (or above or below) items that are specified by a set of item IDs. You must extend the abstract class and implement the `getAllowedItemIds()` to return the set. While the criterion is server-side, it is lazy-loading, so that the list of accepted target items is loaded only once from the server for each drag operation.

12.11.4. Accepting Drops

You can not drop the objects you are dragging around just anywhere. Before a drop is possible, the specific drop location on which the mouse hovers must be *accepted*. Hovering a dragged object over an accepted location displays an *accept indicator*, which allows the user to position the drop properly. As such checks have to be done all the time when the mouse pointer moves around the drop targets, it is not feasible to send the accept requests to the server-side, so drops on a target are normally accepted by a client-side *accept criterion*.

A drop handler must define the criterion on the objects which it accepts to be dropped on the target. The criterion needs to be provided in the **getAcceptCriterion()** method of the **DropHandler** interface. A criterion is represented in an **AcceptCriterion** object, which can be a composite of multiple criteria that are evaluated using logical operations. There are two basic types of criteria: *client-side* and *server-side criteria*. The various built-in criteria allow accepting drops based on the identity of the source and target components, and on the *data flavor* of the dragged objects.

To allow dropping any transferable objects, you can return a universal accept criterion, which you can get with `AcceptAll.get()`.

```
tree.setDropHandler(new DropHandler() {
    public AcceptCriterion getAcceptCriterion() {
        return AcceptAll.get();
    }
    ...
```

Client-Side Criteria

The *client-side criteria*, which inherit the **ClientSideCriterion**, are verified on the client-side, so server requests are not needed for verifying whether each component on which the mouse pointer hovers would accept a certain object.

The following client-side criteria are define in com.vaadin.event.dd.acceptcriterion:

AcceptAll
Accepts all transferables and targets.

And
Logical AND operation on two client-side criterion; accepts the transferable if all the defined sub-criteria accept it.

ContainsDataFlavour
The transferable must contain the defined data flavour.

Not
Logical NOT operation on two client-side criterion; accepts the transferable if and only if the sub-criterion does not accept it.

Or

> Logical OR operation on two client-side criterion; accepts the transferable if any of the defined sub-criteria accept it.

SourceIs

> Accepts all transferables from any of the given source components

SourceIsTarget

> Accepts the transferable only if the source component is the same as the target. This criterion is useful for ensuring that items are dragged only within a tree or a table, and not from outside it.

TargetDetailIs

> Accepts any transferable if the target detail, such as the item of a tree node or table row, is of the given data flavor and has the given value.

In addition, target components such as **Tree** and **Table** define some component-specific client-side accept criteria. See Section 12.11.2, "Dropping Items On a **Tree**" for more details.

AbstractSelect defines the following criteria for all selection components, including **Tree** and **Table**.

AcceptItem

> Accepts only specific items from a specific selection component. The selection component, which must inherit **AbstractSelect**, is given as the first parameter for the constructor. It is followed by a list of allowed item identifiers in the drag source.

AcceptItem.ALL

> Accepts all transferables as long as they are items.

TargetItemIs

> Accepts all drops on the specified target items. The constructor requires the target component (**AbstractSelect**) followed by a list of allowed item identifiers.

VerticalLocationIs.MIDDLE, **TOP**, and **BOTTOM**

The three static criteria accepts drops on, above, or below an item. For example, you could accept drops only in between items with the following:

```
public AcceptCriterion getAcceptCriterion() {
    return new Not(VerticalLocationIs.MIDDLE);
}
```

Server-Side Criteria

The *server-side criteria* are verified on the server-side with the `accept()` method of the **ServerSideCriterion** class. This allows fully programmable logic for accepting drops, but the negative side is that it causes a very large amount of server requests. A request is made for every target position on which the pointer hovers. This problem is eased in many cases by the component-specific lazy loading criteria **TableDropCriterion** and **TreeDropCriterion**. They do the server visit once for each drag and drop operation and return all accepted rows or nodes for current **Transferable** at once.

The `accept()` method gets the drag event as a parameter so it can perform its logic much like in `drop()`.

```
public AcceptCriterion getAcceptCriterion() {
    // Server-side accept criterion that allows drops on any other
    // location except on nodes that may not have children
    ServerSideCriterion criterion = new ServerSideCriterion() {
        public boolean accept(DragAndDropEvent dragEvent) {
            TreeTargetDetails target = (TreeTargetDetails)
                dragEvent.getTargetDetails();

            // The tree item on which the load hovers
            Object targetItemId = target.getItemIdOver();

            // On which side of the target the item is hovered
            VerticalDropLocation location = target.getDropLocation();

            if (location == VerticalDropLocation.MIDDLE)
                if (! tree.areChildrenAllowed(targetItemId))
                    return false; // Not accepted

            return true; // Accept everything else
        }
    };
    return criterion;
}
```

The server-side criteria base class **ServerSideCriterion** provides a generic `accept()` method. The more specific **TableDropCri-**

terion and **TreeDropCriterion** are conveniency extensions that allow defining allowed drop targets as a set of items. They also provide some optimization by lazy loading, which reduces server communications significantly.

```
public AcceptCriterion getAcceptCriterion() {
    // Server-side accept criterion that allows drops on any
    // other tree node except on node that may not have children
    TreeDropCriterion criterion = new TreeDropCriterion() {
        @Override
        protected Set<Object> getAllowedItemIds(
                DragAndDropEvent dragEvent, Tree tree) {
            HashSet<Object> allowed = new HashSet<Object>();
            for (Iterator<Object> i =
                    tree.getItemIds().iterator(); i.hasNext();) {
                Object itemId = i.next();
                if (tree.hasChildren(itemId))
                    allowed.add(itemId);
            }
            return allowed;
        }
    };
    return criterion;
}
```

Accept Indicators

When a dragged object hovers on a drop target, an *accept indicator* is displayed to show whether or not the location is accepted. For *MIDDLE* location, the indicator is a box around the target (tree node, table row, or component). For vertical drop locations, the accepted locations are shown as horizontal lines, and for horizontal drop locations as vertical lines.

For **DragAndDropWrapper** drop targets, you can disable the accept indicators or *drag hints* with the `no-vertical-drag-hints`, `no-horizontal-drag-hints`, and `no-box-drag-hints` styles. You need to add the styles to the *layout that contains* the wrapper, not to the wrapper itself.

```
// Have a wrapper
DragAndDropWrapper wrapper = new DragAndDropWrapper(c);
layout.addComponent(wrapper);

// Disable the hints
layout.addStyleName("no-vertical-drag-hints");
layout.addStyleName("no-horizontal-drag-hints");
layout.addStyleName("no-box-drag-hints");
```

12.11.5. Dragging Components

Dragging a component requires wrapping the source component within a **DragAndDropWrapper**. You can then allow dragging by putting the wrapper (and the component) in drag mode with `set-DragStartMode()`. The method supports two drag modes: `DragStartMode.WRAPPER` and `DragStartMode.COMPONENT`, which defines whether the entire wrapper is shown as the drag image while dragging or just the wrapped component.

```
// Have a component to drag
final Button button = new Button("An Absolute Button");

// Put the component in a D&D wrapper and allow dragging it
final DragAndDropWrapper buttonWrap = new DragAndDropWrapper(button);
buttonWrap.setDragStartMode(DragStartMode.COMPONENT);

// Set the wrapper to wrap tightly around the component
buttonWrap.setSizeUndefined();

// Add the wrapper, not the component, to the layout
layout.addComponent(buttonWrap, "left: 50px; top: 50px;");
```

The default height of **DragAndDropWrapper** is undefined, but the default width is 100%. If you want to ensure that the wrapper fits tightly around the wrapped component, you should call `set-SizeUndefined()` for the wrapper. Doing so, you should make sure that the wrapped component does not have a relative size, which would cause a paradox.

Dragged components are referenced in the **WrapperTransferable**. You can get the reference to the dragged component with `getDraggedComponent()`. The method will return `null` if the transferable is not a component. Also HTML 5 drags (see later) are held in wrapper transferables.

12.11.6. Dropping on a Component

Drops on a component are enabled by wrapping the component in a **DragAndDropWrapper**. The wrapper is an ordinary component; the constructor takes the wrapped component as a parameter. You just need to define the **DropHandler** for the wrapper with `setDropHandler()`.

In the following example, we allow moving components in an absolute layout. Details on the drop handler are given later.

```
// A layout that allows moving its contained components
// by dragging and dropping them
final AbsoluteLayout absLayout = new AbsoluteLayout();
absLayout.setWidth("100%");
absLayout.setHeight("400px");

... put some (wrapped) components in the layout ...

// Wrap the layout to allow handling drops
DragAndDropWrapper layoutWrapper =
        new DragAndDropWrapper(absLayout);

// Handle moving components within the AbsoluteLayout
layoutWrapper.setDropHandler(new DropHandler() {
    public AcceptCriterion getAcceptCriterion() {
        return AcceptAll.get();
    }

    public void drop(DragAndDropEvent event) {
        ...
    }
});
```

Target Details for Wrapped Components

The drop handler receives the drop target details in a **Wrapper-
TargetDetails** object, which implements the **TargetDetails** interface.

```
public void drop(DragAndDropEvent event) {
    WrapperTransferable t =
        (WrapperTransferable) event.getTransferable();
    WrapperTargetDetails details =
        (WrapperTargetDetails) event.getTargetDetails();
```

The wrapper target details include a **MouseEventDetails** object,
which you can get with getMouseEvent(). You can use it to get
the mouse coordinates for the position where the mouse button
was released and the drag ended. Similarly, you can find out the
drag start position from the transferable object (if it is a **Wrapper-
Transferable**) with getMouseDownEvent().

```
// Calculate the drag coordinate difference
int xChange = details.getMouseEvent().getClientX()
            - t.getMouseDownEvent().getClientX();
int yChange = details.getMouseEvent().getClientY()
            - t.getMouseDownEvent().getClientY();

// Move the component in the absolute layout
ComponentPosition pos =
    absLayout.getPosition(t.getSourceComponent());
pos.setLeftValue(pos.getLeftValue() + xChange);
pos.setTopValue(pos.getTopValue() + yChange);
```

You can get the absolute x and y coordinates of the target wrapper with `getAbsoluteLeft()` and `getAbsoluteTop()`, which allows you to translate the absolute mouse coordinates to coordinates relative to the wrapper. Notice that the coordinates are really the position of the wrapper, not the wrapped component; the wrapper reserves some space for the accept indicators.

The `verticalDropLocation()` and `horizontalDropLocation()` return the more detailed drop location in the target.

12.11.7. Dragging Files from Outside the Browser

The **DragAndDropWrapper** allows dragging files from outside the browser and dropping them on a component wrapped in the wrapper. Dropped files are automatically uploaded to the application and can be acquired from the wrapper with `getFiles()`. The files are represented as **Html5File** objects as defined in the inner class. You can define an upload **Receiver** to receive the content of a file to an **OutputStream**.

Dragging and dropping files to browser is supported in HTML 5 and requires a compatible browser, such as Mozilla Firefox 3.6 or newer.

12.12. Logging

You can do logging in Vaadin application using the standard java.util.logging facilities. Configuring logging is as easy as putting a file named `logging.properties` in the default package of your Vaadin application (`src` in an Eclipse project or `src/main/java` or `src/main/resources` in a Maven project). This file is read by the **Logger** class when a new instance of it is initialize.

Logging in Apache Tomcat

For logging Vaadin applications deployed in Apache Tomcat, you do not need to do anything special to log to the same place as Tomcat itself. If you need to write the Vaadin application related messages elsewhere, just add a custom `logging.properties` file to the default package of your Vaadin application.

If you would like to pipe the log messages through another logging solution, see the section called "Piping to Log4j using SLF4J" below.

Logging in Liferay

Liferay mutes logging through java.util.logging by default. In order to enable logging, you need to add a `logging.properties` file of your own to the default package of your Vaadin application. This file should define at least one destination where to save the log messages.

You can also log through SLF4J, which is used in and bundled with Liferay. Follow the instructions in the section called "Piping to Log4j using SLF4J".

Piping to Log4j using SLF4J

Piping output from java.util.logging to Log4j is easy with SLF4J (http://slf4j.org/). The basic way to go about this is to add the SLF4J JAR file as well as the `jul-to-slf4j.jar` file, which implements the bridge from java.util.logging, to SLF4J. You will also need to add a third logging implementation JAR file, that is, `slf4j-log4j12-x.x.x.jar`, to log the actual messages using Log4j. For more info on this, please visit the SLF4J site.

In order to get the java.util.logging to SLF4J bridge installed, you need to add the following snippet of code to your **Application** class at the very top:

```
static {
   SLF4JBridgeHandler.install();
}
```

This will make sure that the bridge handler is installed and working before Vaadin starts to process any logging calls.

Please note!

This can seriously impact on the cost of disabled logging statements (60-fold increase) and a measurable impact on enabled log statements (20% overall increase). However, Vaadin doesn't log very much, so the effect on performance will be negligible.

Using Logger

You can do logging with a simple pattern where you register a static logger instance in each class that needs logging, and use this logger wherever logging is needed in the class. For example:

```
public class MyClass {
  private final static Logger logger =
        Logger.getLogger(MyClass.class.getName());

  public void myMethod() {
    try {
      // do something that might fail
    } catch (Exception e) {
      logger.log(Level.SEVERE, "FAILED CATASTROPHICALLY!", e);
    }
  }
}
```

Having a `static` logger instance for each class needing logging saves a bit of memory and time compared to having a logger for every logging class instance. However, it could cause the application to leak PermGen memory with some application servers when redeploying the application. The problem is that the **Logger** may maintain hard references to its instances. As the **Logger** class is loaded with a classloader shared between different web applications, references to classes loaded with a per-application classloader would prevent garbage-collecting the classes after redeploying, hence leaking memory. As the size of the PermGen memory where class object are stored is fixed, the leakage will lead to a server crash after many redeployments. The issue depends on the way how the server manages classloaders, on the hardness of the back-references, and may also be different between Java 6 and 7. So, if you experience PermGen issues, or want to play it on the safe side, you should consider using non-static **Logger** instances.

12.13. JavaScript Interaction

Vaadin supports two-direction JavaScript calls from and to the server-side. This allows interfacing with JavaScript code without writing client-side integration code.

12.13.1. Calling JavaScript

You can make JavaScript calls from the server-side with the `executeJavascript()` method in the **Root** object.

12.13.2. Handling JavaScript Calls

You can register JavaScript call-back methods from the server-side. You need to implement and register a **JavaScriptCallback** and its `call()` method. Parameters passed to the JavaScript method on the client-side are provided in the first **JSONObject** object in the array passed to the `call()` method.

12.14. Advanced Application Architectures

In this section, we discuss some architectural patterns used with Vaadin.

12.14.1. Layered Architectures

Layered architectures, where each layer has a clearly distinct responsibility, are probably the most common architectures. Typically, applications follow at least a three-layer architecture:

- User interface (or presentation) layer

- Domain layer

- Data store layer

Such an architecture starts from a *domain model*, which defines the data model and the "business logic" of the application, typically as POJOs. A user interface is built on top of the domain model, in our context with the Vaadin Framework. The Vaadin user interface could be bound directly to the data model through the Vaadin Data Model, described in Chapter 9, *Binding Components to Data*. Beneath the domain model lies a data store, such as a relational database. The dependencies between the layers are restricted so that a higher layer may depend on a lower one, but never the other way around.

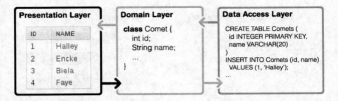

Figure 12.11. Three-Layer Architecture

An *application layer* (or *service layer*) is often distinguished from the domain layer, offering the domain logic as a service, which can be used by the user interface layer, as well as for other uses. In Java EE development, Enterprise JavaBeans (EJBs) are typically used for building this layer.

An *infrastructure layer* (or *data access layer*) is often distinguished from the data store layer, with a purpose to abstract the data store. For example, it could involve a persistence solution such as JPA and an EJB container. This layer becomes relevant with Vaadin when binding Vaadin components to data with the JPAContainer, as described in Chapter 18, *Vaadin JPAContainer*.

12.14.2. Model-View-Presenter Pattern

The Model-View-Presenter (MVP) pattern is one of the most common patterns in developing large applications with Vaadin. It is similar to the older Model-View-Controller (MVC) pattern, which is not as meaningful in Vaadin development. Instead of an implementation-aware controller, there is an implementation-agnostic presenter that operates the view through an interface. The view does not interact directly with the model. This isolates the view implementation better than in MVC and allows easier unit testing of the presenter and model.

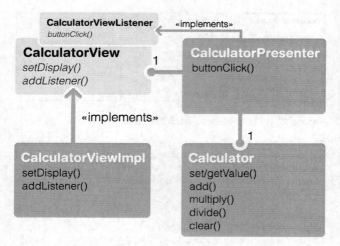

Figure 12.12. Model-View-Presenter Pattern

Figure 12.12, "Model-View-Presenter Pattern" illustrates the MVP pattern with a simple calculator. The domain model is realized in the **Calculator** class, which includes a data model and some model logic operations. The **CalculatorViewImpl** is a Vaadin implementation of the view, defined in the CalculatorView interface. The **CalculatorPresenter** handles the user interface logic. User interaction events received in the view are translated into implementation-independent events for the presenter to handle (the view implementation could also just call the presenter).

Let us first look how the model and view are bound together by the presenter in the following example:

```
// Create the model and the Vaadin view implementation
CalculatorModel    model = new CalculatorModel();
CalculatorViewImpl view  = new CalculatorViewImpl();

// The presenter binds the model and view together
new CalculatorPresenter(model, view);

// The view implementation is a Vaadin component
layout.addComponent(view);
```

You could add the view anywhere in a Vaadin application, as it is a composite component.

The Model

Our business model is quite simple, with one value and a number of operations for manipulating it.

```
/** The model **/
class CalculatorModel {
    private double value = 0.0;

    public void clear() {
        value = 0.0;
    }

    public void add(double arg) {
        value += arg;
    }

    public void multiply(double arg) {
        value *= arg;
    }

    public void divide(double arg) {
        if (arg != 0.0)
            value /= arg;
    }

    public double getValue() {
        return value;
    }

    public void setValue(double value) {
        this.value = value;
    }
}
```

The View

The purpose of the view in MVP is to display data and receive user interaction. It relays the user interaction to the presenter in an fashion that is independent of the view implementation, that is, no Vaadin events. It is defined as a UI framework interface that can have multiple implementations.

```
interface CalculatorView {
    public void setDisplay(double value);

    interface CalculatorViewListener {
        void buttonClick(char operation);
    }
    public void addListener(CalculatorViewListener listener);
}
```

The are design alternatives for the view. It could receive the listener in its constructor, or it could just know the presenter. Here, we forward button clicks as an implementation-independent event.

As we are using Vaadin, we make a Vaadin implementation of the interface as follows:

```
class CalculatorViewImpl extends CustomComponent
        implements CalculatorView, ClickListener {
    private Label display = new Label("0.0");

    public CalculatorViewImpl() {
        GridLayout layout = new GridLayout(4, 5);

        // Create a result label that spans over all
        // the 4 columns in the first row
        layout.addComponent(display, 0, 0, 3, 0);

        // The operations for the calculator in the order
        // they appear on the screen (left to right, top
        // to bottom)
        String[] operations = new String[] {
            "7", "8", "9", "/", "4", "5", "6",
            "*", "1", "2", "3", "-", "0", "=", "C", "+" };

        // Add buttons and have them send click events
        // to this class
        for (String caption: operations)
            layout.addComponent(new Button(caption, this));

        setCompositionRoot(layout);
    }

    public void setDisplay(double value) {
        display.setValue(Double.toString(value));
    }

    /* Only the presenter registers one listener... */
    List<CalculatorViewListener> listeners =
            new ArrayList<CalculatorViewListener>();

    public void addListener(CalculatorViewListener listener) {
        listeners.add(listener);
    }

    /** Relay button clicks to the presenter with an
     *  implementation-independent event */
    @Override
    public void buttonClick(ClickEvent event) {
        for (CalculatorViewListener listener: listeners)
            listener.buttonClick(event.getButton()
                                .getCaption().charAt(0));
    }
}
```

The Presenter

The presenter in MVP is a middle-man that handles all user inter-action logic, but in an implementation-independent way, so that it doesn't actually know anything about Vaadin. It shows data in the view and receives user interaction back from it.

```java
class CalculatorPresenter
        implements CalculatorView.CalculatorViewListener {
    CalculatorModel model;
    CalculatorView  view;

    private double current = 0.0;
    private char   lastOperationRequested = 'C';

    public CalculatorPresenter(CalculatorModel model,
                               CalculatorView  view) {
        this.model = model;
        this.view  = view;

        view.setDisplay(current);
        view.addListener(this);
    }

    @Override
    public void buttonClick(char operation) {
        // Handle digit input
        if ('0' <= operation && operation <= '9') {
            current = current * 10
                    + Double.parseDouble("" + operation);
            view.setDisplay(current);
            return;
        }

        // Execute the previously input operation
        switch (lastOperationRequested) {
        case '+':
            model.add(current);
            break;
        case '-':
            model.add(-current);
            break;
        case '/':
            model.divide(current);
            break;
        case '*':
            model.multiply(current);
            break;
        case 'C':
            model.setValue(current);
            break;
        } // '=' is implicit

        lastOperationRequested = operation;

        current = 0.0;
```

```
        if (operation == 'C')
            model.clear();
        view.setDisplay(model.getValue());
    }
}
```

In the above example, we held some state information in the presenter. Alternatively, we could have had an intermediate controller between the presenter and the model to handle the low-level button logic.

12.15. Accessing Session-Global Data

Applications typically need to access some objects from practically all user interface code, such as a user object, a business data model, or a database connection. This data is typically initialized and managed in the application class. Some such data is built-in into the **Application** class, such as the locale.

You can access the application object from any user interface component using the `getApplication()` method. For example:

```
class MyApplication extends Application {
    UserData userData;

    public void init() {
        userData = new UserData();
    }

    public UserData getUserData() {
        return userData;
    }
}

...
data = ((MyApplication)component.getApplication()).getUserData();
```

The Problem

The basic problem in accessing session-global data is that the `getApplication()` method works only after the component has been attached to the application. Before that, it returns *null*. This is the case in constructors of components, such as a **CustomComponent**:

```
class MyComponent extends CustomComponent {
    public MyComponent() {
        // This fails with NullPointerException
        Label label = new Label("Country: " +
            getApplication().getLocale().getCountry());
```

```
            setCompositionRoot(label);
    }
}
```

Using a static variable or a singleton implemented with such to give a global access to user session data is not possible, because static variables are global in the entire web application, not just the user session. This can be handy for communicating data between the concurrent sessions, but creates a problem within a session.

For example, the following would not work:

```
class MyApplication extends Application {
    static UserData userData;

    public void init() {
        userData = new UserData();
    }

    public static UserData getUserData() {
        return userData;
    }
}
```

The data would be shared by all users and be reinitialized every time a new user opens the application.

Overview of Solutions

To get the application object or any other global data, you have the following solutions:

- Pass a reference to the global data as a parameter.

- Initialize components in `attach()` method.

- Store a reference to global data using the *ThreadLocal Pattern*.

Each solution is described in the following sections.

12.15.1. Passing References Around

You can pass references to objects as parameters. This is the normal way in object-oriented programming.

```
class MyApplication extends Application {
    UserData userData;

    public void init() {
        Window mainWindow = new Window("My Window");
        setMainWindow(mainWindow);

        userData = new UserData();

        mainWindow.addComponent(new MyComponent(this));
    }

    public UserData getUserData() {
        return userData;
    }
}

class MyComponent extends CustomComponent {
    public MyComponent(MyApplication app) {
        Label label = new Label("Name: " +
            app.getUserData().getName());

        setCompositionRoot(label);
    }
}
```

If you need the reference in other methods, you either have to pass it again as a parameter or store it in a member variable.

The problem with this solution is that practically all constructors in the application need to get a reference to the application object, and passing it further around in the classes is another hard task.

12.15.2. Overriding `attach()`

The `attach()` method is called when the component is attached to the application component through containment hierarchy. The `getApplication()` method always works.

```
class MyComponent extends CustomComponent {
    public MyComponent() {
        // Must set a dummy root in constructor
        setCompositionRoot(new Label(""));
    }

    @Override
    public void attach() {
        Label label = new Label("Name: " +
            ((MyApplication) component.getApplication())
                .getUserData().getName());

        setCompositionRoot(label);
    }
}
```

While this solution works, it is slightly messy. You may need to do some initialization in the constructor, but any construction requiring the global data must be done in the `attach()` method. Especially, **CustomComponent** requires that the `setCompositionRoot()` method is called in the constructor. If you can't create the actual composition root component in the constructor, you need to use a temporary dummy root, as is done in the example above.

Using `getApplication()` also needs casting if you want to use methods defined in your application class.

12.15.3. ThreadLocal Pattern

Vaadin uses the ThreadLocal pattern for allowing global access to the **Application**, **Root**, and **Page** objects of the currently processed server request with a static `getCurrent()` method in all the respective classes. This section explains why the pattern is used in Vaadin and how it works. The explanation is given as an implementation, if you find a need to reimplement the pattern for some reason.

The ThreadLocal pattern gives a solution to the global access problem by solving two sub-problems of static variables.

As the first problem, assume that the servlet container processes requests for many users (sessions) sequentially. If a static variable is set in a request belonging one user, it could be read or re-set by the next incoming request belonging to another user. This can be solved by setting the global reference at the beginning of each HTTP request to point to data of the current user, as illustrated in Figure 12.13.

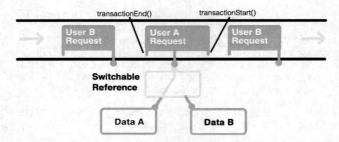

Figure 12.13. Switching a static (or ThreadLocal) reference during sequential processing of requests

It is possible to implement such switching either with the **TransactionListener** or **HttpServletRequestListener** interface by setting the reference in `transactionStart()` or `onRequestStart()`, respectively. We use the former interface in the example code in this section, as the latter interface has to be implemented in the application class.

The second problem is that servlet containers typically do thread pooling with multiple worker threads that process requests. Therefore, setting a static reference would change it in all threads running concurrently, possibly just when another thread is processing a request for another user. The solution is to store the reference in a thread-local variable instead of a static. You can do so by using the **ThreadLocal** class in Java for the switch reference.

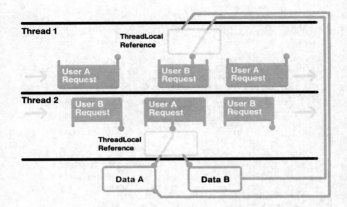

Figure 12.14. Switching ThreadLocal references during concurrent processing of requests

Notice that if you use a **TransactionListener**, the listeners are attached to the web application context (in practice a user session), not the application instance. The problem is that an application context can have multiple different Vaadin applications that share the same user session. If two of these applications add a transaction listener to the context to listen for requests, both are called and without any checks they would both set the reference to themselves. Therefore, the application data object needs to know which application it belongs to and check that when the transaction begins and ends. Using the **HttpServletRequestListener** frees you from these checks.

While you may not absolutely need to clear the reference in transactionEnd(), you are probably on the safer side if you do. Setting such unneeded references to null can help avoid memory leaks and it could also be a good security precaution not to leave a reference to session data so that it could be seen by another user session in the next request.

We end up with the following code. As we put the application data to a class separate from the application class, we have to make it a **TransactionListener**.

```
/** Holds data for one user session. */
public class AppData
```

```java
        implements TransactionListener, Serializable {
    private ResourceBundle bundle;
    private Locale locale;   // Current locale
    private String userData; // Trivial data model for the user

    private Application app; // For distinguishing between apps

    private static ThreadLocal<AppData> instance =
        new ThreadLocal<AppData>();

    public AppData(Application app) {
        this.app = app;

        // It's usable from now on in the current request
        instance.set(this);
    }

    @Override
    public void transactionStart(Application application,
                                 Object transactionData) {
        // Set this data instance of this application
        // as the one active in the current thread.
        if (this.app == application)
            instance.set(this);
    }

    @Override
    public void transactionEnd(Application application,
                               Object transactionData) {
        // Clear the reference to avoid potential problems
        if (this.app == application)
            instance.set(null);
    }

    public static void initLocale(Locale locale,
                                   String bundleName) {
        instance.get().locale = locale;
        instance.get().bundle =
            ResourceBundle.getBundle(bundleName, locale);
    }

    public static Locale getLocale() {
        return instance.get().locale;
    }

    public static String getMessage(String msgId) {
        return instance.get().bundle.getString(msgId);
    }

    public static String getUserData() {
        return instance.get().userData;
    }

    public static void setUserData(String userData) {
        instance.get().userData = userData;
    }
}
```

We can then use it in the application as follows. Observe that we do not have a reference to the application object in the constructor of the **MyComponent** class.

```
/**
 * We can now nicely access the session-global data
 * in the constuctor of this class.
 */
class MyComponent extends CustomComponent {
    public MyComponent() {
        VerticalLayout layout = new VerticalLayout();

        // Get stuff from the application data object
        layout.addComponent(new Label("Hello, " +
            AppData.getUserData()));

        layout.addComponent(new Label("Your locale is " +
            AppData.getLocale().getDisplayLanguage()));

        layout.addComponent(new Button(
            AppData.getMessage(MyAppCaptions.CancelKey)));

        setCompositionRoot(layout);
    }
}

/** The application class. */
public class ThreadLocalApplication extends Application {
    public void init() {
        Window main = new Window("Hello window");
        setMainWindow(main);

        // Create the application data instance
        AppData sessionData = new AppData(this);

        // Register it as a listener in the application context
        getContext().addTransactionListener(sessionData);

        // Initialize the session-global data
        AppData.initLocale(getLocale(),
                           MyAppCaptions.class.getName());

        // Also set the user data model
        AppData.setUserData("Billy");

        // Now, we do not pass this application object
        // in the constructor, so it couldn't access the
        // app data otherwise.
        main.addComponent(new MyComponent());
    }
}
```

Chapter 13

Portal Integration

Vaadin supports running applications as portlets, as defined in the JSR-168 (Java Portlet API) and JSR-286 (Java Portlet API 2.0) standards. While providing generic support for all portals implementing the standards, Vaadin especially supports the Liferay portal and the needed portal-specific configuration is given below for Liferay.

You can deploy the Vaadin demo package WAR (available from the download site) directly to a portal such as Liferay. It contains all the necessary portlet configuration files. For optimal performance with Liferay, you can install the Vaadin library and other needed resources in Liferay as described later in this section.

You can find more documentation and examples from the Vaadin Developer's Site at http://dev.vaadin.com/.

13.1. Deploying to a Portal

Deploying a Vaadin application as a portlet is essentially just as easy as deploying a regular application to an application server. You do not need to make any changes to the application itself, but only the following:

- Application packaged as a WAR
  - `WEB-INF/portlet.xml` descriptor
  - `WEB-INF/web.xml` descriptor for Portlet 1.0 portlets
  - `WEB-INF/liferay-portlet.xml` descriptor for Liferay
  - `WEB-INF/liferay-display.xml` descriptor for Liferay
  - `WEB-INF/liferay-plugin-package.properties` for Liferay
- Widget set installed to portal (optional)
- Themes installed to portal (optional)
- Vaadin library installed to portal (optional)
- Portal configuration settings (optional)

Installing the widget set and themes to the portal is required for running two or more Vaadin portlets simultaneously in a single portal page. As this situation occurs quite easily, we recommend installing them in any case.

In addition to the Vaadin library, you will need to copy the `portlet.jar` to your project. Notice that you must *not* put the `portlet.jar` in the same `WebContent/WEB-INF/lib` directory as the Vaadin JAR or otherwise include it in the WAR to be deployed, because it would create a conflict with the internal portlet library of the portal. The conflict would cause errors such as `"ClassCastException: ...ApplicationPortlet2 cannot be cast to javax.portlet.Portlet"`.

How you actually deploy a WAR package depends on the portal. In Liferay, you simply drop it to the `deploy` subdirectory under the Liferay installation directory. The deployment depends on the application server under which Liferay runs; for example, if you use Liferay bundled with Tomcat, you will find the extracted package in the `webapps` directory under the Tomcat installation directory included in Liferay.

13.2. Creating a Portal Application Project in Eclipse

While you can create the needed deployment descriptors manually for any existing Vaadin application, as described in subsequent sections, the Vaadin Plugin for Eclipse provides a wizard for easy creation of portal application projects.

Creation of a portal application project is almost identical to the creation of a regular application project. For a full treatment of the New Project Wizard and the possible options, please see Section 2.3.1, "Creating the Project".

1. Start creating a new project by selecting from the menu **File → New → Project...**.

2. In the **New Project** window that opens, select **Web → Vaadin Project** and click **Next**.

3. In the **Vaadin Project** step, you need to set the basic web project settings. You need to give at least the project name, the runtime, and select **Generic Portlet** for the deployment configuration; the default values should be good for the other settings.

You can click **Finish** here to use the defaults for the rest of the settings, or click **Next**.

4. The settings in the **Web Module** step define the basic servlet-related settings and the structure of the web application project. All the settings are pre-filled, and you should normally accept them as they are and click **Next**.

5. The **Vaadin project** step page has various Vaadin-specific application settings. These are largely the same as for regular applications. You should not need to change anything as you can change the application titles and other details afterwards. The **Create portlet template** option should be automatically selected. You can give another portlet title of you want. You can change most of the settings afterward.

Create project template
    Creates an application class and all the needed portlet deployment descriptors.

Application name

The application name is used in the title of the main window (which is usually invisible in portlets) and as an identifier, either as is or with a suffix, in various deployment descriptors.

Base package name

Java package for the application class.

Application class name

Name of the application class. The default is derived from the project name.

Portlet version

Same as in the project settings.

Portlet title

The portlet title, defined in `portlet.xml`, can be used as the display name of the portlet (at least in Liferay). The default value is the project name. The title is also used as a short description in `liferay-plugin-package.properties`.

Vaadin version

Same as in the project settings.

Finally, click **Finish** to create the project.

6. Eclipse may ask you to switch to J2EE perspective. A Dynamic Web Project uses an external web server and the J2EE perspective provides tools to control the server and manage application deployment. Click **Yes**.

13.3. Portlet Deployment Descriptors

To deploy a portlet WAR in a portal, you need to provide the basic `portlet.xml` descriptor specified in the Java Portlet standard. In addition, you may need to include possible portal vendor specific deployment descriptors. The ones required by Liferay are described below.

Portlet 2.0 Deployment Descriptor

The portlet WAR must include a portlet descriptor located at `Web-Content/WEB-INF/portlet.xml`. A portlet definition includes the portlet name, mapping to a servlet in `web.xml`, modes supported by the portlet, and other configuration. Below is an example of a simple portlet definition in `portlet.xml` descriptor.

```xml
<?xml version="1.0" encoding="UTF-8" standalone="no"?>
<portlet-app
  xmlns="http://java.sun.com/xml/ns/portlet/portlet-app_2_0.xsd"
  xmlns:xsi="http://www.w3.org/2001/XMLSchema-instance"
  version="2.0"
  xsi:schemaLocation=
    "http://java.sun.com/xml/ns/portlet/portlet-app_2_0.xsd
     http://java.sun.com/xml/ns/portlet/portlet-app_2_0.xsd">

  <portlet>
    <portlet-name>Portlet Example portlet</portlet-name>
    <display-name>Vaadin Portlet Example</display-name>

    <!-- Map portlet to a servlet. -->
    <portlet-class>
      com.vaadin.terminal.gwt.server.ApplicationPortlet2
    </portlet-class>
    <init-param>
      <name>application</name>

      <!-- The application class with package name. -->
      <value>com.example.myportlet.MyportletApplication</value>
    </init-param>

    <!-- Supported portlet modes and content types. -->
    <supports>
      <mime-type>text/html</mime-type>
      <portlet-mode>view</portlet-mode>
      <portlet-mode>edit</portlet-mode>
      <portlet-mode>help</portlet-mode>
    </supports>

    <!-- Not always required but Liferay requires these. -->
    <portlet-info>
      <title>Vaadin Portlet Example</title>
      <short-title>Portlet Example</short-title>
    </portlet-info>
  </portlet>
</portlet-app>
```

Listing supported portlet modes in `portlet.xml` enables the corresponding portlet controls in the portal user interface that allow changing the mode, as described later.

Portlet 1.0 Deployment Descriptor

The portlet deployment descriptor for Portlet 1.0 API is largely the same as for Portlet 2.0. The main differences are:

1. XML namespace and schema names

2. Portlet-class: **ApplicationPortlet** vs **ApplicationPortlet2**

3. The `application` parameter is a name of the servlet (defined in `web.xml` in Portlet 1.0, but name of the application class in Portlet 2.0. There is no longer a separate `web.xml` file in Servlet 2.0.

4. The `portlet-name` must not be same as the servlet name in Portlet 1.0; in Portlet 2.0 this does not matter.

Below is an example of a complete deployment descriptor for Portlet 1.0:

```
<?xml version="1.0" encoding="UTF-8"?>
<portlet-app
  version="1.0"
  xmlns="http://java.sun.com/xml/ns/portlet/portlet-app_1_0.xsd"
  xmlns:xsi="http://www.w3.org/2001/XMLSchema-instance"
  xsi:schemaLocation=
      "http://java.sun.com/xml/ns/portlet/portlet-app_1_0.xsd
       http://java.sun.com/xml/ns/portlet/portlet-app_1_0.xsd">

  <portlet>
    <!-- Must not be the same as servlet name. -->
    <portlet-name>Portlet Example portlet</portlet-name>
    <display-name>Vaadin Portlet Example</display-name>

    <!-- Map portlet to a servlet. -->
    <portlet-class>
      com.vaadin.terminal.gwt.server.ApplicationPortlet
    </portlet-class>
    <init-param>
      <name>application</name>

      <!-- Must match the servlet URL mapping in web.xml. -->
      <value>portletexample</value>
    </init-param>

    <!-- Supported portlet modes and content types. -->
    <supports>
      <mime-type>text/html</mime-type>
      <portlet-mode>view</portlet-mode>
      <portlet-mode>edit</portlet-mode>
      <portlet-mode>help</portlet-mode>
    </supports>
```

```
    <!-- Not always required but Liferay requires these. -->
    <portlet-info>
      <title>Vaadin Portlet Example</title>
      <short-title>Portlet Example</short-title>
    </portlet-info>
  </portlet>
</portlet-app>
```

The value of the application parameter must match the context in the `<url-pattern>` element in the `<servlet-mapping>` in the web.xml deployment descriptor, without the path qualifiers in the pattern. The above example would match the following servlet mapping in web.xml:

```
<servlet-mapping>
    <servlet-name>Portlet Example</servlet-name>
    <url-pattern>/portletexample/*</url-pattern>
</servlet-mapping>
```

In fact, it would also match the /* mapping.

Using a Single Widget Set

If you have just one Vaadin application that you ever need to run in your portal, you can just deploy the WAR as described above and that's it. However, if you have multiple applications, especially ones that use different custom widget sets, you run into problems, because a portal window can load only a single Vaadin widget set at a time. You can solve this problem by combining all the different widget sets in your different applications into a single widget set using inheritance or composition.

For example, the portal demos defined in the portlet.xml in the demo WAR have the following setting for all portlets so that they will all use the same widget set:

```
<portlet>
  ...
  <!-- Use the portal default widget set for all portal demos. -->
  <init-param>
    <name>widgetset</name>
    <value>com.vaadin.portal.gwt.PortalDefaultWidgetSet</value>
  </init-param>
  ...
```

The **PortalDefaultWidgetSet** extends **SamplerWidgetSet**, which extends the **DefaultWidgetSet**. The **DefaultWidgetSet** is therefore essentially a subset of **PortalDefaultWidgetSet**, which contains also the widgets required by the Sampler demo. Other applications that would otherwise require only the regular **DefaultWidgetSet**, and do not define their own widgets, can just as well use the larger set, making them compatible with the demos. The **PortalDefaultWidgetSet** will also be the default Vaadin widgetset bundled in Liferay 5.3 and later.

If your portlets are contained in multiple WARs, which can happen quite typically, you need to install the widget set and theme portalwide so that all the portlets can use them. See Section 13.5, "Installing Vaadin in Liferay" on configuring the widget sets in the portal itself.

Liferay Portlet Descriptor

Liferay requires a special `liferay-portlet.xml` descriptor file that defines Liferay-specific parameters. Especially, Vaadin portlets must be defined as "*instanceable*", but not "*ajaxable*".

Below is an example descriptor for the earlier portlet example:

```
<?xml version="1.0" encoding="UTF-8"?>
<!DOCTYPE liferay-portlet-app PUBLIC
  "-//Liferay//DTD Portlet Application 4.3.0//EN"
  "http://www.liferay.com/dtd/liferay-portlet-app_4_3_0.dtd">

<liferay-portlet-app>
    <portlet>
        <!-- Matches definition in portlet.xml.        -->
        <!-- Note: Must not be the same as servlet name. -->
        <portlet-name>Portlet Example portlet</portlet-name>

        <instanceable>true</instanceable>
        <ajaxable>false</ajaxable>
    </portlet>
</liferay-portlet-app>
```

See Liferay documentation for further details on the `liferay-portlet.xml` deployment descriptor.

Liferay Display Descriptor

The `WEB-INF/liferay-display.xml` file defines the portlet category under which portlets are located in the **Add Application** window in Liferay. Without this definition, portlets will be organized under the "Undefined" category.

The following display configuration, which is included in the demo WAR, puts the Vaadin portlets under the "Vaadin" category, as shown in Figure 13.1, "Portlet Categories in Add Application Window".

```xml
<?xml version="1.0"?>
<!DOCTYPE display PUBLIC
  "-//Liferay//DTD Display 4.0.0//EN"
  "http://www.liferay.com/dtd/liferay-display_4_0_0.dtd">

<display>
    <category name="Vaadin">
        <portlet id="Portlet Example portlet" />
    </category>
</display>
```

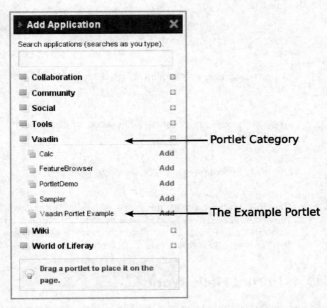

Figure 13.1. Portlet Categories in Add Application Window

See Liferay documentation for further details on how to configure the categories in the `liferay-display.xml` deployment descriptor.

Liferay Plugin Package Properties

The `liferay-plugin-package.properties` file defines a number of settings for the portlet, most importantly the Vaadin JAR to be used.

```
name=Portlet Example portlet
short-description=myportlet
module-group-id=Vaadin
module-incremental-version=1
#change-log=
#page-uri=
#author=
license=Proprietary
portal-dependency-jars=\
    vaadin.jar
```

name
> The plugin name must match the portlet name.

short-description
> A short description of the plugin. This is by default the project name.

module-group-id
> The application group, same as the category id defined in `liferay-display.xml`.

license
> The plugin license type; "proprietary" by default.

portal-dependency-jars
> The JAR libraries on which this portlet depends. This should have value `vaadin.jar`, unless you need to use a specific version. The JAR must be installed in the portal, for example, in Liferay bundled with Tomcat to `tomcat-x.x.x/webapps/ROOT/WEB-INF/lib/vaadin.jar`.

13.4. Portlet Hello World

The Hello World program that runs as a portlet is no different from a regular Vaadin application, as long as it doesn't need to handle portlet actions, mode changes, and so on.

```
import com.vaadin.Application;
import com.vaadin.ui.*;
```

```
public class PortletExample extends Application {
    @Override
    public void init() {
        Window mainWindow = new Window("Portlet Example");

        Label label = new Label("Hello Vaadin user");
        mainWindow.addComponent(label);
        setMainWindow(mainWindow);
    }
}
```

In addition to the application class, you need the descriptor files, libraries, and other files as described earlier. Figure 13.2, "Portlet Project Structure in Eclipse" shows the complete project structure under Eclipse.

Installed as a portlet in Liferay from the **Add Application** menu, the application will show as illustrated in Figure 13.3, "Hello World Portlet".

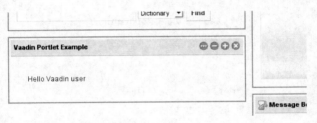

Figure 13.3. Hello World Portlet

13.5. Installing Vaadin in Liferay

Loading widget sets, themes, and the Vaadin JAR from a portlet is possible as long as you have a single portlet, but causes a problem if you have multiple portlets. To solve this, Vaadin portlets need to use a globally installed widget set, themes, and Vaadin JAR. They, and all the required configuration, are bundled with Liferay 5.3 and later, but if you are using an earlier version of Liferay or use a custom widget set, custom themes, or a later version of Vaadin, you need to install them in Liferay.

The easiest way to install or upgrade Vaadin or compile the widget set in Liferay is to use the Vaadin Control Panel for Liferay, as de-

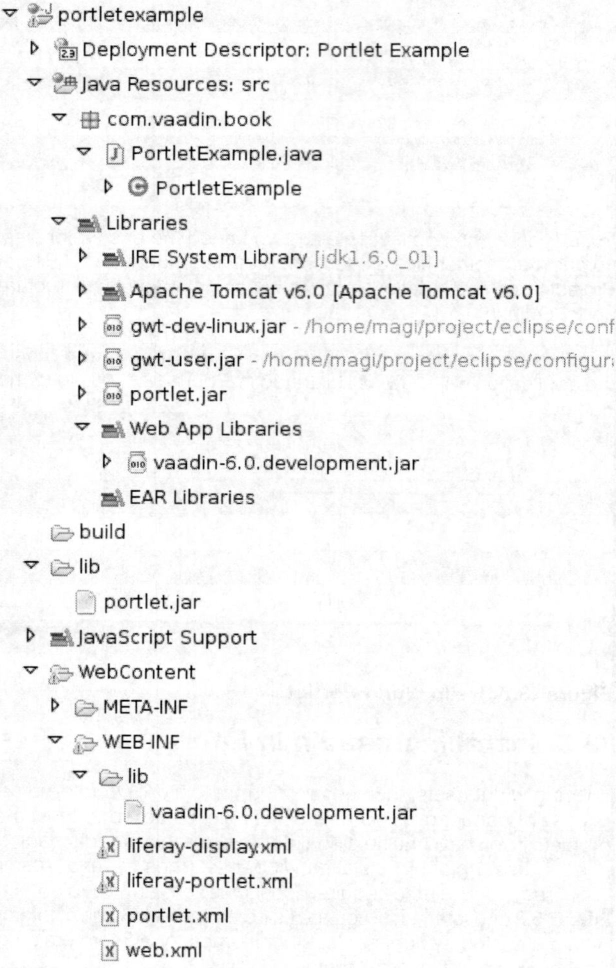

- ▽ portletexample
  - ▷ Deployment Descriptor: Portlet Example
  - ▽ Java Resources: src
    - ▽ com.vaadin.book
      - ▽ PortletExample.java
        - ▷ PortletExample
  - ▽ Libraries
    - ▷ JRE System Library [jdk1.6.0_01]
    - ▷ Apache Tomcat v6.0 [Apache Tomcat v6.0]
    - ▷ gwt-dev-linux.jar - /home/magi/project/eclipse/conf
    - ▷ gwt-user.jar - /home/magi/project/eclipse/configura
    - ▷ portlet.jar
    - ▽ Web App Libraries
      - ▷ vaadin-6.0.development.jar
      - EAR Libraries
  - build
  - ▽ lib
    - portlet.jar
  - ▷ JavaScript Support
  - ▽ WebContent
    - ▷ META-INF
    - ▽ WEB-INF
      - ▽ lib
        - vaadin-6.0.development.jar
      - liferay-display.xml
      - liferay-portlet.xml
      - portlet.xml
      - web.xml

Figure 13.2. Portlet Project Structure in Eclipse

scribed in Section 13.9, "Vaadin Control Panel for Liferay". If you need to make the installation or compilation manually, read ahead.

In these instructions, we assume that you use Liferay bundled with Apache Tomcat, although you can use almost any other application server with Liferay just as well. The Tomcat installation is included in the Liferay installation package, under the `tomcat-x.x.x` directory.

The Vaadin JAR should be put in `tomcat-x.x.x/webapps/ROOT/WEB-INF/lib/vaadin.jar`. The Vaadin version number should normally be left out from the JAR.

The widget set needs to be located at `/html/VAADIN/widgetsets/` and themes at `/html/VAADIN/themes/` path under the portal context. You simply need to copy the contents from under your `WebContent/VAADIN` directory to the `tomcat-x.x.x/webapps/ROOT/html/VAADIN` directory under the Liferay installation directory. If you use a built-in widget set or theme included in the Vaadin JAR, such as the **PortalDefaultWidgetSet**, you should extract it from the JAR, from under `VAADIN/widgetsets`. The default themes are located under `VAADIN/themes` in the JAR.

You need to define the widget set, the theme, and the JAR in the `portal-ext.properties` configuration file for Liferay, as described earlier. The file should normally be placed in the Liferay installation directory. See Liferay documentation for details on the configuration file.

Below is an example of a `portal-ext.properties` file:

```
# Path under which the VAADIN directory is located.
# (/html is the default so it is not needed.)
# vaadin.resources.path=/html

# Portal-wide widget set
vaadin.widgetset=com.vaadin.portal.gwt.PortalDefaultWidgetSet

# Theme to use
vaadin.theme=reindeer
```

The allowed parameters are:

> *vaadin.resources.path*
> Specifies the resource root path under the portal context. This is `/html` by default. Its actual location depends on the

portal and the application server; in Liferay with Tomcat it would be located at `webapps/ROOT/html` under the Tomcat installation directory.

vaadin.widgetset
> The widget set class to use. Give the full path to the class name in the dot notation. If the parameter is not given, the default widget set is used.

vaadin.theme
> Name of the theme to use. If the parameter is not given, the default theme is used, which is `reindeer` in Vaadin 6.

You will need to restart Liferay after creating or modifying the `portal-ext.properties` file.

13.6. Handling Portlet Requests

Portals such as Liferay are not AJAX applications but reload the page every time a user interaction requires data from the server. They consider a Vaadin application to be a regular web application that works by HTTP requests. All the AJAX communications required by the Vaadin application are done by the Vaadin Client-Side Engine (the widget set) past the portal, so that the portal is unaware of the communications.

The only way a portal can interact with an application is to load it with a HTTP request; reloading does not reset the application. The Portlet 2.0 API supports four types of requests: *render*, *action*, *resource*, and *event* requests. The old Portlet 1.0 API supports only the render and action requests. Requests can be caused by user interaction with the portal controls or by clicking action URLs displayed by the portlet. You can handle portlet requests by implementing the **PortletListener** interface and the handler methods for each of the request types. You can use the request object passed to the handler to access certain portal data, such as user information, the portlet mode, etc.

The **PortletListener** interface is defined in the **PortletApplicationContext2** for Portlet 2.0 API and **com.vaadin.terminal.gwt.server.PortletApplicationContext** class for the old Portlet 1.0 API. You can get the portlet application context with `getContext()` method of the application class.

You need to have the `portlet.jar` in your class path during development. However, you must *not* deploy the `portlet.jar` with the portlet, because it would create a conflict with the internal portlet library of the portal. You should put it in a directory that is not deployed with the portlet, for example, if you are using Eclipse, under the `lib` directory under the project root, not under `WebContent/WEB-INF/lib`, for example.

You can also define portal actions that you can handle in the `handleActionRequest()` method of the interface.

You add your portlet request listener to the application context of your application, which is a **PortletApplicationContext** when (and only when) the application is being run as a portlet.

```
// Check that we are running as a portlet.
if (getContext() instanceof PortletApplicationContext2) {
    PortletApplicationContext2 ctx =
            (PortletApplicationContext2) getContext();

    // Add a custom listener to handle action and
    // render requests.
    ctx.addPortletListener(this, new MyPortletListener());
} else {
    Notification.show("Not initialized via Portal!",
                    Notification.TYPE_ERROR_MESSAGE);
}
```

The handler methods receive references to request and response objects, which are defined in the Java Servlet API. Please refer to the Servlet API documentation for further details.

The PortletDemo application included in the demo WAR package includes examples of processing mode and portlet window state changes in a portlet request listener.

13.7. Handling Portlet Mode Changes

Portals support three portlet modes defined in the Portlet API: *view*, *edit*, and *help* modes. The *view* mode is the default and the portal can have buttons to switch the portlet to the other modes. In addition to the three predefined modes, the Portlet API standards allow custom portlet modes, although portals may support custom modes to a varying degree.

You need to define which portlet modes are enabled in the `port-let.xml` deployment descriptor as follows.

```
<!-- Supported portlet modes and content types. -->
<supports>
    <mime-type>text/html</mime-type>
    <portlet-mode>view</portlet-mode>
    <portlet-mode>edit</portlet-mode>
    <portlet-mode>help</portlet-mode>
</supports>
```

Changes in the portlet mode are received as resource requests, which you can handle with a `handleResourceRequest()`, defined in the **PortletListener** interface. The current portlet mode can be acquired with `getPortletMode()` from the request object.

The following complete example (for Portlet 2.0) shows how to handle the three built-modes in a portlet application.

```
// Use Portlet 2.0 API
import com.vaadin.terminal.gwt.server.PortletApplicationContext2;
import com.vaadin.terminal.gwt.server.PortletApplicationContext2.Port-
letListener;

public class PortletModeExample extends Application
                                implements PortletListener {
    Window          mainWindow;
    ObjectProperty data; // Data to view and edit
    VerticalLayout viewContent  = new VerticalLayout();
    VerticalLayout editContent  = new VerticalLayout();
    VerticalLayout helpContent  = new VerticalLayout();

    @Override
    public void init() {
        mainWindow = new Window("Myportlet Application");
        setMainWindow(mainWindow);

        // Data model
        data = new ObjectProperty("<h1>Heading</h1>"+
                    "<p>Some example content</p>");

        // Prepare views for the three modes (view, edit, help)
        // Prepare View mode content
        Label viewText = new Label(data, Label.CONTENT_XHTML);
        viewContent.addComponent(viewText);

        // Prepare Edit mode content
        RichTextArea editText = new RichTextArea();
        editText.setCaption("Edit the value:");
        editText.setPropertyDataSource(data);
        editContent.addComponent(editText);

        // Prepare Help mode content
        Label helpText = new Label("<h1>Help</h1>" +
                        "<p>This helps you!</p>",
```

```
                         Label.CONTENT_XHTML);
        helpContent.addComponent(helpText);

        // Start in the view mode
        mainWindow.setContent(viewContent);

        // Check that we are running as a portlet.
        if (getContext() instanceof PortletApplicationContext2) {
            PortletApplicationContext2 ctx =
                (PortletApplicationContext2) getContext();

            // Add a custom listener to handle action and
            // render requests.
            ctx.addPortletListener(this, this);
        } else {
            Notification.show("Not running in portal",
                              Notification.TYPE_ERROR_MESSAGE);
        }
    }


    // Dummy implementations for the irrelevant request types
    public void handleActionRequest(ActionRequest request,
                                    ActionResponse response,
                                    Window window) {
    }
    public void handleRenderRequest(RenderRequest request,
                                    RenderResponse response,
                                    Window window) {
    }
    public void handleEventRequest(EventRequest request,
                                   EventResponse response,
                                   Window window) {
    }

    public void handleResourceRequest(ResourceRequest request,
                                      ResourceResponse response,
                                      Window window) {
        // Switch the view according to the portlet mode
        if (request.getPortletMode() == PortletMode.EDIT)
            window.setContent(editContent);
        else if (request.getPortletMode() == PortletMode.VIEW)
            window.setContent(viewContent);
        else if (request.getPortletMode() == PortletMode.HELP)
            window.setContent(helpContent);
    }
}
```

Figure 13.4, "Portlet Modes in Action" shows the resulting portlet in the three modes: view, edit, and help. In Liferay, the edit mode is shown in the popup menu as a **Preferences** item.

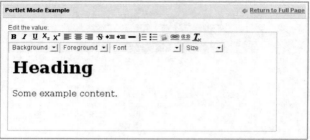

Figure 13.4. Portlet Modes in Action

13.8. Non-Vaadin Portlet Modes

In some cases, it can be useful to implement certain modes of a portlet as pure HTML or JSP pages instead of running the full Vaadin application user interface in them. Common reasons for this are static pages (for example, a simple help mode), integrating legacy content to a portlet (for example, a JSP configuration interface), and providing an ultra-lightweight initial view for a portlet (for users behind slow connections).

Fully static modes that do not require the Vaadin server side application to be running can be implemented by subclassing the portlet class **ApplicationPortlet2** (Portlet 2.0). The subclass can either create the HTML content directly or dispatch the request to, for example, a HTML or JSP page via the portal. When using this approach, any Vaadin portlet and portlet request listeners are not called.

Customizing the content for the standard modes (*view*, *edit*, and *help*) can be performed by overriding the methods `doView`, `doEdit` and `doHelp`, respectively. Custom modes can be handled by implementing similar methods with the **@javax.portlet.Render-Mode(name = "mymode")** annotation.

You need to define which portlet modes are enabled in the `portlet.xml` deployment descriptor as described in Section 13.7, "Handling Portlet Mode Changes". Also, the portlet class in `portlet.xml` should point to the customized subclass of **ApplicationPortlet2**.

The following example (for Portlet 2.0) shows how to create a static help page for the portlet.

`portlet.xml`:

```
<!-- Supported portlet modes and content types. -->
<supports>
    <mime-type>text/html</mime-type>
    <portlet-mode>view</portlet-mode>
    <portlet-mode>help</portlet-mode>
</supports>
```

`HtmlHelpPortlet.java:`:

```
// Use Portlet 2.0 API
import com.vaadin.terminal.gwt.server.ApplicationPortlet2;

public class HtmlHelpPortlet extends ApplicationPortlet2 {
    // Override the help mode, let the Vaadin
    // application handle the view mode
    @Override
    protected void doHelp(RenderRequest request,
                          RenderResponse response)
            throws PortletException, IOException {
        // Bypass the Vaadin application entirely
        response.setContentType("text/html");
        response.getWriter().println(
                "This is the help text as plain HTML.");

        // Alternatively, you could use the dispatcher for,
        // for example, JSP help pages as follows:
        // PortletRequestDispatcher dispatcher = getPortletContext()

        // .getRequestDispatcher("/html/myhelp.jsp");
        // dispatcher.include(request, response);
```

```
        }
    }
```

To produce pure HTML portlet content from a running Vaadin application instead of statically outside an application, the **ApplicationPortlet2** method `writeAjaxPage` should be overridden. This approach allows using the application state in HTML content generation, and all relevant Vaadin portlet request and portlet listeners are called around the portlet content generation. However, the client side engine (widgetset) is not loaded by the browser, which can shorten the initial page display time.

```
<portlet-class>com.vaadin.demo.portlet.HtmlModePortlet</portlet-
class>
<supports>
    <mime-type>text/html</mime-type>
    <portlet-mode>view</portlet-mode>
    <portlet-mode>help</portlet-mode>
</supports>

public class CountApplication extends Application {
    private int count = 0;

    public void init() {
        Window w = new Window("Portlet mode example");
        w.addComponent(new Label("This is the Vaadin app."));
        w.addComponent(new Label("Try opening the help mode."));
        setMainWindow(w);
    }

    public int incrementCount() {
        return ++count;
    }
}

// Use Portlet 2.0 API
public class HtmlModePortlet extends AbstractApplicationPortlet {

    @Override
    protected void writeAjaxPage(RenderRequest request,
            RenderResponse response, Window window,
            Application app)
                throws PortletException, IOException {
        if (PortletMode.HELP.equals(request.getPortletMode())) {
            CountApplication capp = (CountApplication) app;
            response.setContentType("text/html");
            response.getWriter().println(
                "This is the HTML help, shown "
                + capp.incrementCount() + " times so far.");
        } else {
            super.writeAjaxPage(request, response, window, app);
        }
    }

    @Override
    protected Class<? extends Application> getApplicationClass(){
```

```
        return CountApplication.class;
    }
}
```

The user can freely move between Vaadin and non-Vaadin portlet modes with the user interface provided by the portal (for standard modes) or the portlet (for example, action links). Once the server side application has been started, it continues to run as long as the session is alive. If necessary, specific portlet mode transitions can be disallowed in `portlet.xml`.

In the case of Portlet 1.0, both a portlet and a servlet are involved. A render request is received by **ApplicationPortlet** when the portlet mode is changed, and serving pure HTML in some modes can be achieved by overriding the method `render` and handling the modes of interest separately while calling `super.render()` for other modes. As always, when extending the portlet, the reference to the portlet class in `portlet.xml` needs to be updated.

To serve HTML-only content in the Portlet 1.0 case after starting the server side application and calling the relevant listeners, the servlet class **ApplicationServlet** should be subclassed instead of the portlet. The method `writeAjaxPage` can be overridden to produce custom HTML content for certain modes. However, it should be noted that some HTML content (for example, loading the portal-wide Vaadin theme) is created by the portlet and not the servlet.

13.9. Vaadin Control Panel for Liferay

Vaadin portlets, just as all Vaadin applications, use a *widget set* to render the user interface in the browser and to handle the Ajax communication with the server-side application. While regular Vaadin applications use a widget set for each application, in portals the widget set is shared by all Vaadin portlets running in the portal. Liferay actually comes preinstalled with a precompiled version of the default portal widget set. However, many add-on components come with their own widget set, which needs to be compiled into the portal widget set. The Vaadin Control Panel for Liferay automates this compilation. You can also use it to just install a new version of the Vaadin library.

13.9.1. Installing

Vaadin Control Panel for Liferay is available for download from Vaadin Directory. It is a WAR package, which you need to simply drop into Liferay's `deploy` folder. Once the deployment is done, the Vaadin Control Panel should show up in the Liferay Control Panel.

13.9.2. Using the Control Panel

Open the **Vaadin** section in the Liferay Control Panel. The initial state with is illustrated in Figure 13.5, "Initial State of Vaadin Control Panel for Liferay".

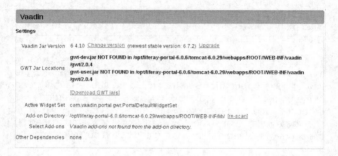

Figure 13.5. Initial State of Vaadin Control Panel for Liferay

Upgrading Vaadin

Liferay comes with Vaadin preinstalled. To upgrade the preinstalled version to a newer one, follow the following steps. Notice that the Vaadin library is upgraded for *all* Vaadin portlets, so they must all be compatible with the new version.

1. Click **Upgrade** in the **Vaadin Jar Version**.

2. In the warning dialog that appears, read the message and if you want to go on with the upgrade, click **Change version** to proceed.

3. Recompile the widget set as instructed below.

4. Redeploy all Vaadin portlets in Liferay, that is, copy the WARs to the `deploy` folder in Liferay.

The Google Web Toolkit (GWT) libraries required for the widget set compilation are also upgraded automatically.

Compiling Widget Set

When you need to compile the widget set, follow the following steps:

1. Place any add-on Jars containing widget sets, such as add-on Jars, in the `WEB-INF/lib` folder of Liferay. Its exact location depends on the used server; for example in Tomcat it is under the `webapps/ROOT` folder.

2. Click **re-scan** in the **Add-on Directory** to detect any new add-on libraries.

3. Select the add-ons which you wish to compile into the widget set.

4. Click **Manage Additional Dependencies** if the libraries require any special libraries and add them.

5. Click **Compile Widget Set** to compile the widget set. The compilation can take several minutes.

The compiled widget set is copied automatically to the proper folder and taken into use.

13.10. Vaadin IPC for Liferay

Portlets rarely live alone. A page can contain multiple portlets and when the user interacts with one portlet, you may need to have the other portlets react to the change immediately. This is not normally possible with Vaadin portlets, as Vaadin applications need to get an Ajax request from the client-side to change their user interface. On the other hand, the regular inter-portlet communication (IPC) mechanism in Portlet 2.0 Specification requires a complete page reload, but that is not appropriate with Vaadin or in general Ajax applications, which do not require a page reload. One solution is to communicate between the portlets on the server-side and then use a server-push mechanism to update the client-side.

The Vaadin IPC for Liferay Add-on takes another approach by communicating between the portlets through the client-side. Events (messages) are sent through the **LiferayIPC** component and the client-side widget relays them to the other portlets, as illustrated in Figure 13.6, "Vaadin IPC for Liferay Architecture".

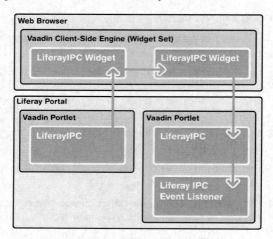

Figure 13.6. Vaadin IPC for Liferay Architecture

Vaadin IPC for Liferay uses the Liferay JavaScript event API for client-side inter-portlet communication, so you can communicate just as easily with other Liferay portlets.

Notice that you can use this communication only between portlets on the same page.

Figure 13.7, "Vaadin IPC Add-on Demo with Two Portlets" shows Vaadin IPC for Liferay in action. Entering a new item in one portlet is updated interactively in the other.

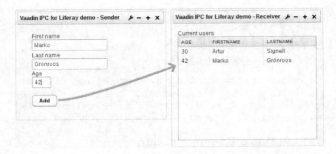

Figure 13.7. Vaadin IPC Add-on Demo with Two Portlets

13.10.1. Installing the Add-on

The Vaadin IPC for Liferay add-on is available from the Vaadin Directory as well as from a Maven repository, as described in Chapter 15, *Using Vaadin Add-ons*.

The contents of the installation package are as follows:

`vaadin-ipc-for-liferay-x.x.x.jar`
> The add-on JAR in the installation package must be installed in the `WEB-INF/lib` directory under the root context. The location depends on the server - for example in Liferay running in Tomcat it is located under the `webapps/ROOT` folder of the server.

`doc`
> The documentation folder includes a `README.TXT` file that describes the contents of the installation package briefly, and `licensing.txt` and `license-asl-2.0.txt`, which describe the licensing under the Apache License 2.0. Under the `doc/api` folder is included the complete JavaDoc API documentation for the add-on.

`vaadin-ipc-for-liferay-x.x.x-demo.war`
> A WAR containing demo portlets. After installing the add-on library and compiling the widget set, as described below, you can deploy the WAR to Liferay and add the two demo portlets to a page, as shown in Figure 13.7, "Vaadin IPC Add-on Demo with Two Portlets". The source of the demo

is available at dev.vaadin.com/svn/addons/IP-CforLiferay/trunk/.

Compiling the Widget Set

The add-on contains a widget set, which you must compile into the Vaadin widget set installed in the portal. The easiest way you can do this is to use the Vaadin Control Panel for Liferay add-on (also available from Vaadin Directory) to compile the portal widget set, as described in Section 13.9, "Vaadin Control Panel for Liferay".

13.10.2. Basic Communication

LiferayIPC is an invisible user interface component that can be used to send messages between two or more Vaadin portlets. You add it to an application layout as you would any regular user interface component.

```
LiferayIPC liferayipc = new LiferayIPC();
layout.addComponent(liferayipc);
```

You should be careful not to remove the invisible component from the portlet later if you modify the layout of the portlet.

The component can be used both for sending and receiving messages, as described next.

Sending Events

You can send an event (a message) with the `sendEvent()` method, which takes an event ID and the message data as parameters. The event is broadcast to all listening portlets. The event ID is a string that can be used to identify the recipient of an event or the event type.

```
liferayipc.sendEvent("hello", "This is Data");
```

If you need to send more complex data, you need to format or serialize it to a string representation as described in Section 13.10.5, "Serializing and Encoding Data".

Receiving Events

A portlet wishing to receive events (messages) from other portlets needs to register a listener in the component with `addListener()`.

The listener receives the messages in a **LiferayIPCEvent** object. Filtering events by the ID is built in into the listener handler, you give the listened event ID as the first parameter for the addListener(). The actual message data is held in the *data* property, which you can read with getData().

```
liferayipc.addListener("hello", new LiferayIPCEventListener() {
    public void eventReceived(LiferayIPCEvent event) {
        // Do something with the message data
        String data = event.getData();
        Notification.show("Received hello: " + data);
    }
});
```

A listener added to a **LiferayIPC** can be removed with removeListener().

13.10.3. Considerations

Both security and efficiency should be considered with inter-portlet communications when using the Vaadin IPC for Liferay.

Browser Security

As the message data is passed through the client-side (browser), any code running in the browser has access to the data. You should be careful not to expose any security-critical data in client-side messaging. Also, malicious code running in the browser could alter or fake messages. Sanitization can help with the latter problem and encryption to solve the both issues. You can also share the sensitive data through session attributes or a database and use the client-side IPC only to notify that the data is available.

Efficiency

Sending data through the browser requires loading and sending it in HTTP requests. The data is held in the memory space of the browser, and handling large data in the client-side JavaScript code can take time. Noticeably large message data can therefore reduce the responsiveness of the application and could, in extreme cases, go over browser limits for memory consumption or JavaScript execution time.

13.10.4. Communication Through Session Attributes

In many cases, such as when considering security or efficiency, it is better to pass the bulk data on the server-side and use the client-side IPC only for notifying the other portlet(s) that the data is available. Session attributes are a conveninent way of sharing data on the server-side. You can also share objects through them, not just strings.

The session variables have a *scope*, which should be `APPLICA-TION_SCOPE`. The "application" refers to the scope of the Java web application (WAR) that contains the portlets.

If the communicating portlets are in the same Java web application (WAR), no special configuration is needed. You can also communicate between portlets in different WARs, in which case you need to disable the `private-session-attributes` parameter in `liferay-portlet.xml` by setting it to `false`. Please see Liferay documentation for more information regarding the configuration.

You can also share Java objects between the portlets in the same WAR, not just strings. If the portlets are in different WARs, they normally have different class loaders, which could cause incompatibilities, so you can only communicate with strings and any object data needs to be serialized.

Session attributes are accessible through the **PortletSession** object, which you can access through the portlet context from the Vaadin **Application** class.

```
Person person = new Person(firstname, lastname, age);
...

PortletSession session =
        ((PortletApplicationContext2) getContext()).
            getPortletSession();

// Share the object
String key = "IPCDEMO_person";
session.setAttribute(key, person,
                     PortletSession.APPLICATION_SCOPE);

// Notify that it's available
liferayipc.sendEvent("ipc_demodata_available", key);
```

You can then receive the attribute in a **LiferayIPCEventListener** as follows:

```
public void eventReceived(LiferayIPCEvent event) {
    String key = event.getData();

    PortletSession session =
            ((PortletApplicationContext2)getContext()).
                getPortletSession();

    // Get the object reference
    Person person = (Person) session.getAttribute(key);

    // We can now use the object in our application
    BeanItem<Person> item = new BeanItem<Person>(person);
    form.setItemDataSource(item);
}
```

Notice that changes to a shared object bound to a user interface component are not updated automatically if it is changed in another portlet. The issue is the same as with double-binding in general.

13.10.5. Serializing and Encoding Data

The IPC events support transmitting only plain strings, so if you have object or other non-string data, you need to format or serialize it to a string representation. For example, the demo application formats the trivial data model as a semicolon-separated list as follows:

```
private void sendPersonViaClient(String firstName,
                        String lastName, int age) {
    liferayIPC_1.sendEvent("newPerson", firstName + ";" +
                        lastName + ";" + age);
}
```

You can use standard Java serialization for any classes that implement the `Serializable` interface. The transmitted data may not include any control characters, so you also need to encode the string, for example by using Base64 encoding.

```
// Some serializable object
MyBean mybean = new MyBean();
...

// Serialize
ByteArrayOutputStream baostr = new ByteArrayOutputStream();
ObjectOutputStream oostr;
try {
    oostr = new ObjectOutputStream(baostr);
    oostr.writeObject(mybean); // Serialize the object
    oostr.close();
} catch (IOException e) {
    Notification.show("IO PAN!"); // Complain
}
```

```
// Encode
BASE64Encoder encoder = new BASE64Encoder();
String encoded = encoder.encode(baostr.toByteArray());

// Send the IPC event to other portlet(s)
liferayipc.sendEvent("mybeanforyou", encoded);
```

You can then deserialize such a message at the receiving end as follows:

```
public void eventReceived(LiferayIPCEvent event) {
    String encoded = event.getData();

    // Decode and deserialize it
    BASE64Decoder decoder = new BASE64Decoder();
    try {
        byte[] data = decoder.decodeBuffer(encoded);
        ObjectInputStream ois =
                new ObjectInputStream(
                        new ByteArrayInputStream(data));

        // The deserialized bean
        MyBean deserialized = (MyBean) ois.readObject();
        ois.close();

        ... do something with the bean ...

    } catch (IOException e) {
        e.printStackTrace(); // Handle somehow
    } catch (ClassNotFoundException e) {
        e.printStackTrace(); // Handle somehow
    }
}
```

13.10.6. Communicating with Non-Vaadin Portlets

You can use the Vaadin IPC for Liferay to communicate also between a Vaadin application and other portlets, such as JSP portlets. The add-on passes the events as regular Liferay JavaScript events. The demo WAR includes two JSP portlets that demonstrate the communication.

When sending events from non-Vaadin portlet, fire the event using the JavaScript Liferay.fire() method with an event ID and message. For example, in JSP you could have:

```
<%@ taglib uri="http://java.sun.com/portlet_2_0"
            prefix="portlet" %>
<portlet:defineObjects />

<script>
function send_message() {
```

```
    Liferay.fire('hello', "Hello, I'm here!");
}
</script>

<input type="button" value="Send message"
       onclick="send_message()" />
```

You can receive events using a Liferay JavaScript event handler.
You define the handler with the `on()` method in the Liferay object.
It takes the event ID and a callback function as its parameters.
Again in JSP you could have:

```
<%@ taglib uri="http://java.sun.com/portlet_2_0"
           prefix="portlet" %>
<portlet:defineObjects />

<script>
Liferay.on('hello', function(event, data) {
    alert("Hello: " + data);
});
</script>
```

13.11. Remote Portlets with WSRP

Web Services for Remote Portlets (WSRP) is a way to deploy a portlet in one portal, a *producer*, and use it in another, a *consumer*. This is done using a special WSRP portlet that relays the user input from a consumer to an actual portlet running in a producer. The *Vaadin WSRP* add-on gives you the ability to run Vaadin portlets as remote WSRP portlets. The basic WSRP architecture is illustrated in Figure 13.8, "WSRP Architecture".

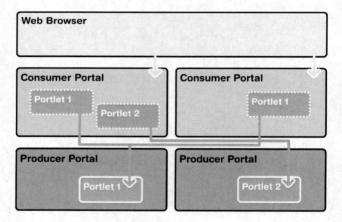

Figure 13.8. WSRP Architecture

In this documentation, we give the instructions for Liferay, but the Vaadin WSRP add-on should work in any other portal or non-portal server that supports WSRP. If you use other portal software, please refer to its documentation for the relevant parts of WSRP configuration.

The add-on is licensed under the same Apache License 2.0 as the Vaadin Framework itself.

13.11.1. Installing the Add-on

The Vaadin WSRP add-on is available as a JAR from the Vaadin Directory as well as from a Maven repository, as described in

Chapter 15, *Using Vaadin Add-ons*. Vaadin 6.6.0 or later is required.

You need to install the Vaadin WSRP JAR at least in the producer portals. A consumer only needs the widget set, but no JARs related to your Vaadin portlet, not even the Vaadin JAR.

You should put the Vaadin WSRP JAR in the `WEB-INF/lib` folder under the root context in the *producer* portal server. The location of the root context depends on the server, for example in Tomcat it is in `webapps/ROOT`.

Compiling the Widget Set

The Vaadin WSRP add-on contains a widget set, which you must compile into the Vaadin widget set installed in the portal. The widget set is needed in both the producer and consumer portals, but you do not need the WSRP JAR (or any other Vaadin JARs) in the consumer portal. You can avoid compiling the widget set by copying it (and the Vaadin themes) from the producer.

If you use Liferay, the easiest way to compile the widget set is to use the Vaadin Control Panel for Liferay add-on (also available from Vaadin Directory). Its use is described in detail in Section 13.9, "Vaadin Control Panel for Liferay". You can use the Control Panel to upgrade Vaadin, if you need, then select the **Vaadin WSRP** add-on, and compile the widget set. Once compiled in the producer, you can copy the `ROOT/html/VAADIN` folder to the corresponding folder in a consumer, or do the same compilation in the consumer separately.

For other portals than Liferay, a simple manual way to compile the widget set is to create a Vaadin project in Eclipse, add the WSRP JAR and any other required JARs to the `WebContent/WEB-INF/lib` folder, and click the **Compile Vaadin widgets** button. You need the Vaadin Plugin for Eclipse to do this.

13.11.2. Configuring a Remote Portlet

A portlet needs some configuration to be used as a remote portlet.

Portlet Configuration

You need to replace the regular Vaadin application portlet in your project to a WSRP portlet. Edit the `WEB-INF/portlet.xml` file and change the line:

```
<portlet-class>com.vaadin.terminal.gwt.server.ApplicationPort-
let2</portlet-class>
```

to the following:

```
<portlet-class>com.vaadin.addon.wsrp.WSRPApplicationPortlet</portlet-
class>
```

Other Portlet Configuration

WSRP support may need to be enabled in the portal-specific configuration. For example, to enable WSRP in Liferay, you need to enable the *remoteable* property in the `WEB-INF/liferay-port-let.xml` file for a portlet:

```
<remoteable>true</remoteable>
```

13.11.3. Producer Configuration

Once you have installed and Vaadin WSRP JAR in the producer portal, compiled the widget set, and deployed your portlet, you can configure it as a producer.

In Liferay, you can configure a WSRP portlet in the Control Panel as follows.

1. Open the Control Panel as an administrator and select **WSRP**.

2. Open the **Producers** tab and click **Add Producer** to create a new producer.

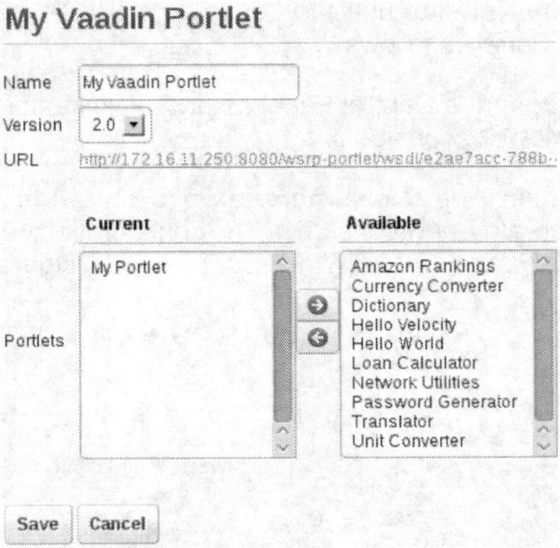

My Vaadin Portlet

Name	My Vaadin Portlet
Version	2.0
URL	http://172.16.11.250:8080/wsrp-portlet/wsdl/e2ae7acc-788b-...

Current   **Available**

My Portlet		Amazon Rankings
	→	Currency Converter
	←	Dictionary
Portlets		Hello Velocity
		Hello World
		Loan Calculator
		Network Utilities
		Password Generator
		Translator
		Unit Converter

Save   Cancel

Figure 13.9. WSRP Producer Configuration

3. Select your portlet from the **Available** portlets and click the left-arrow to select it as current.

4. Give the producer a **Name** and click **Save**.

The producer portlet is shown in the list. You need to copy the URL shown in the list when creating a consumer portlet in the consumer portal.

In other portals than Liferay, follow the instructions for the portal software to set up a portlet as a producer.

13.11.4. Consumer Configuration

Once you have configured a portlet as a producer in the producer portal, you can add it as a consumer portlet in a consumer portal. The consumer portlet is not a Vaadin portlet but a special WSRP portlet that relays the user input to the producer portlet in the other portal.

This requires that you have copied or compiled the widget set (and themes) in the consumer, as described earlier.

In Liferay, you first need to configure a WSRP consumer in the Control Panel as follows:

1. Open the Control Panel as an administrator and open the **WSRP** section.

2. Select the **Consumers** tab and click **Add Consumer** to create a new consumer. The configuration window is shown in Figure 13.10, "WSRP Consumer Configuration".

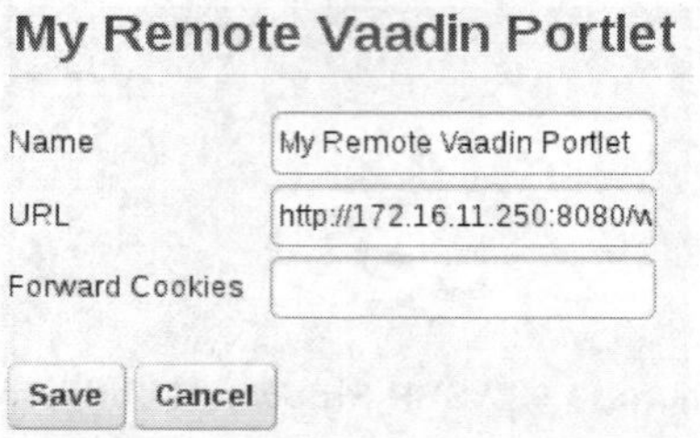

My Remote Vaadin Portlet

Name	My Remote Vaadin Portlet
URL	http://172.16.11.250:8080/w
Forward Cookies	

Save   Cancel

Figure 13.10. WSRP Consumer Configuration

3. Copy and paste the **URL** for the producer portlet from the producer portal configuration.

4. Give the consumer a **Name** and click **Save**.

5. In the consumer list, click **Actions → Manage Portlets** for the new consumer.

6. In the **Manage Portlets** view, click **New Portlet**.

7. Give the consumer portlet a **Name**, select the **Remote Portlet**, and click **Save**.

8. Go back to Liferay from the Control Panel by clicking **Back to Liferay**.

9. In the page where you want to add the portlet, click **Add → More... → WSRP**.

10. Your remote portlet should show up in the list. Click **Add** to add it to the page. You need to reload the page for the portlet to show up.

In other portals than Liferay, follow the instructions for the portal software to set up the portlet as a producer.

13.11.5. Advanced Configuration

Alternative Path for Vaadin Resources

The Vaadin WSRP implementation assumes that the widget set is located in `/html/VAADIN` URL. If you need to change this default to serve the `VAADIN` resource directory from some other URL, you have to extend the **WSRPApplicationPortlet** class and override the `getStaticFilesLocation()` method, which normally returns "/html". It should return the path under which the `VAADIN` directory is found.

If you extend the portlet class, you need to use your custom class in `portlet.xml`.

# Chapter 14

Rapid Development Using Vaadin and Roo

This chapter presents a tutorial for developing a basic application using rapid application development tools: Spring Roo and Vaadin Plugin for Eclipse. The application includes database binding with JPAContainer, internationalization, and testing with Vaadin TestBench.

14.1. Overview

In this tutorial, we develop a simple application while demonstrating also the basic tasks of making a typical business application:

- Creating a business data model using Roo
- Database binding using Java Persistence API (JPA) and the JPAContainer add-on
- Creating CRUD views using the Vaadin Plugin for Spring Roo
- Customizing views using Vaadin Plugin for Eclipse
- Using the Vaadin Calendar add-on
- User login with authentication and authorization
- Internationalization
- Using the Vaadin TestBench for regression testing
- Deploying the application to Cloud Foundry

Spring Roo is a rapid development tool for Java applications. It generates code that uses the Spring Framework, Java Persistence API, and Apache Maven. It also allows extending its functionality using add-ons, such as the Vaadin Plugin for Spring Roo. The Vaadin add-on can generate user interface views based on the data model definitions given to Roo. These views can then be customized and combined with views made with the visual editor of the Vaadin Plugin for Eclipse.

Vaadin JPAContainer is a **Container** that communicates with a JPA implementation of your choice, which in turn usually communicates with virtually any SQL database you choose. Then by binding the JPAContainer to a component such as a **Table** (in editable mode), you get a no-brainer CRUD component. As the edited table data is updated to the JPAContainer, which is linked to the JPA implementation, everything you do in the UI can immediately be reflected back to the database. JPAContainer is dual-licensed with the open source AGPL for free projects and CVAL for commercial applications.

Demo Application

For the purpose of this tutorial, we develop a simple business application. The work hour reporting application allows an employee to report work done for different projects.

For authentication, the application will have a login screen, where the user can also select the language. Business tasks are done in the main view, which will have a typical layout with a menu bar.

14.2. Setting Up the Environment

Let us begin with setting up the environment and creating the project. The tutorial requires installation of:

- Spring Roo (bundled with the SpringSource Tool Suite)
- Vaadin Plugin for Eclipse
- Vaadin Plugin for Spring Roo
- Vaadin Calendar Add-on
- Vaadin TestBench Add-on

The installation of Vaadin add-ons is covered later in Section 14.5, "Using Vaadin Add-ons in a Roo project" and Vaadin TestBench in Section 14.9, "Testing the Application".

14.2.1. Installing Spring Roo

The easiest way to get Spring Roo is to install the SpringSource Tool Suite (STS), which is a distribution of the Eclipse IDE packaged with Roo integration, among other things. You can also install Spring Roo as a command-line tool.

You can download the SpringSource Tool Suite from http://www.springsource.com/developer/sts. Please follow the installation instructions at the website. After installing, you can start STS by running the `STS` executable in the installation folder.

You need to install the Vaadin Plugin for Eclipse in STS. Please follow the instructions given in Section 2.2.1, "Vaadin Plugin for Eclipse".

14.2.2. Creating the Project

You can create a new Spring Roo project as follows:

1. Select **File → New → Spring Roo Project**.

2. Give the project a **Project name**. The name must be a proper identifier, that is, no spaces, etc.

3. Give the project a **Top-level package name**, such as `com.example.rapid`.

4. Make any other necessary project settings. None are required in this tutorial example. Finally, click **Next** and **Finish** to create the project. Creating a project can take a few seconds.

A Roo Shell is automatically opened for a new Roo project. If closed, you can open a new Roo Shell by selecting **Window → Show View → Roo Shell**.

14.2.3. Installing Vaadin Plugin for Spring Roo

Installing the Vaadin Plugin for Spring Roo is done in the Roo Shell. While the plugin installation is not project specific and it will work in all projects once installed, a Roo Shell can only be opened for an existing project.

1. If the Roo Shell is not already open, right-click the project folder in the **Package Explorer** and select **Spring Tools → Open Roo Shell**.

2. In the Roo Shell view enter:

```
roo> pgp trust --keyId 0xBF0451C0
roo> download accept terms of use
roo> addon install bundle --bundleSymbolicName
     com.vaadin.spring.roo.addon
```

14.2.4. Setting up the Roo Data Layer

Binding application data model to a database with Java Persistence API (JPA) is amazingly easy with Roo. You simply need to set up persistence as follows:

```
roo> persistence setup --provider ECLIPSELINK
                       --database HYPERSONIC_IN_MEMORY
```

The above example sets up persistence using the EclipseLink JPA layer and an in-memory HSQLDB database. Hitting **Ctrl+Space** completion shows the possible values for the `--provider` and `--database` parameters.

When using a real database, you need to configure the database connection in `src/main/resources/META-INF/spring/data-base.properties`.

14.3. Creating the Domain Model

Spring Roo automates the creation of a domain model. Using simple commands, it creates the entity classes and their property fields. As we enabled persistence for the project earlier, creating the entities also creates the JPA mappings between the domain objects and their underlying database representation.

14.3.1. Domain Model Design

The domain model of the work hour reporting system consists of three entities, illustrated in Figure 14.1, "Entity Diagram of the Domain Model". Employees working on projects, who are also the users of the system, are represented as **RapidUser** entities. Authorization is managed simply with an `admin` flag.

An employee uses the system to enter work entries, represented with the **WorkEntry** class. Each entry has starts and ends at a specific date and time and has a comment. A work entry is always associated with a project, represented in the **Project** class. A project has a name and ended projects can be disabled so that they can no longer be selected.

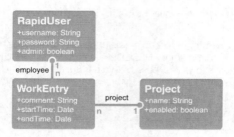

Figure 14.1. Entity Diagram of the Domain Model

14.3.2. Creating the Model in Roo

Roo Shell helps you in creating your model objects. The **entity** command creates a new entity class, specified with the `--class` parameter. Tilde (~) can be used to refer to the project package. The `--testAutomatically` option creates integration tests for the entity. As always with Roo Shell, hitting CTRL-SPACE can hint or autocomplete your commands.

```
roo> entity --class ~.domain.RapidUser --testAutomatically
```

The **field** command in Roo creates class properties. The first parameter for the command is the field type, such as `string`, `boolean`, or `date`. The name of the field is specified with the `--fieldName` parameter. The `--notNull` specifies that the field value may not be null. The `string` type as additional options, such as minimum (`--sizeMin`) and maximum (`--sizeMax`) length.

```
roo> field string --fieldName username --notNull --sizeMin 2
```

To create the domain model described earlier, the following commands need to be issued in all (including the ones explained above):

```
entity --class ~.domain.RapidUser --testAutomatically
field string --fieldName username --notNull --sizeMin 2
field string --fieldName password --notNull --sizeMin 4
field boolean --fieldName admin --primitive

entity --class ~.domain.Project --testAutomatically
field string --fieldName name --notNull --sizeMin 2 --sizeMax 255
field boolean --fieldName enabled --primitive

entity --class ~.domain.WorkEntry --testAutomatically
```

```
field string --fieldName comment --sizeMax 255
field reference --fieldName project --type ~.domain.Project --notNull
field reference --fieldName employee --type ~.domain.RapidUser --
notNull
field date --fieldName startTime --type java.util.Date --notNull
field date --fieldName endTime --type java.util.Date --notNull
```

The *reference* field type is used for references to other entities.
The entity type is given with the *--type* option.

As we gave the *--testAutomatically* parameter when we created
domain objects, Roo should have generated some tests automatically. To validate the domain model, type the following command
in the Roo Shell:

```
roo> perform tests
```

14.4. Creating Vaadin Application and CRUD Views

Spring Roo is essentially a code generator. As already seen in the
data model part of this tutorial, it will write a whole bunch of boiler
plate code for JPA entities. You get an even greater advantage of
Roo when you want a simple user interface around the domain
models.

By default, Spring Roo uses JSP pages (Spring MVC to be more
specific) to create basic CRUD (Create, Remove, Update, Delete)
views. This is covered in Roo's own tutorials. We choose a bit different route and use the Vaadin plugin for Roo to create an advanced Vaadin-based server-side RIA user interface for our
backend.

14.4.1. Creating the Application Skeleton

First, we use the **vaadin setup** command to create the basic application skeleton, on which we later build the user interface. Issue
the following command in the Roo shell:

```
vaadin setup --applicationPackage ~.web --baseName RapidWorkHours
--themeName rapid --useJpaContainer true
```

The command creates everything that you need or might need
later during development:

1. a "web" package where all your Vaadin related code will be added

2. an **Application** class

3. a `web.xml` file to configure Vaadin application for servlet containers

4. a theme

With `--useJpaContainer true`, we instruct the application to use JPAContainer later when we create the CRUD views. As JPAContainer is lazy-loading, this will save some memory in our application server in case the database grows a lot.

14.4.2. Generating CRUD Views

Next, we create the actual CRUD views. Issue the following command in the Roo Shell:

```
vaadin generate all --package ~.web.ui --visuallyComposable true
```

The command creates CRUD views for all the domain objects into web.ui package. The `--visuallyComposable` parameter instructs the Roo plugin to build views in such a way that we can later modify them with Vaadin Visual Designer. Without this parameter, the views are constructed in bit different manner, which may be bit more maintainable for advanced Vaadin users.

In case you add new domain objects later, you may issue this command again to create views for new domain objects.

14.4.3. Deploying to Development Server

At this point, we have a working Vaadin application ready, so we naturally want to see it in action. In the STS IDE, you can simply select the project and use **Run → Run as → Run on Server**. You can use the VMware vFabric server bundled with STS, but any other servlet container (such as the Jetty-based JEE Preview) should work fine as well.

In case you feel more comfortable in the Maven world, the project can also be deployed for testing with, for example, the `jetty:run` target. The Jetty plugin is automatically installed for the generated project.

14.5. Using Vaadin Add-ons in a Roo project

Complex Vaadin application often need to use some add-ons in addition to the core Vaadin. In our example project, we need the Vaadin Calendar and JPAContainer add-ons. The JPAContainer add-on is installed automatically by the Roo plugin, but the Calendar add-on needs to be installed manually.

We will next:

1. Install the Vaadin Calendar add-on

2. Compile the widget set

3. Configure the Deployment Assembly

The Vaadin Plugin for Roo supports installing add-ons from the Vaadin Directory and compiling the included widget sets.

14.5.1. Installing Add-ons

Open or select a Roo Shell and enter:

```
roo> vaadin addon install --artifactId vaadin-calendar
```

You can type the beginning of the command up to the `--artifact-Id`, followed by a space, and then hit **Ctrl+Space** for completion. It lists all the available add-ons in the Directory. If you enter the beginning of an add-on name, such as `vaadin-`, before the completion, it shows just those add-ons, as shown in Figure 14.2, "Getting List of Add-ons in Directory".

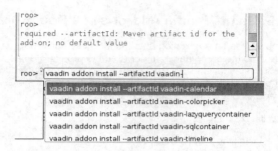

```
roo>
roo>
required --artifactId: Maven artifact id for the
add-on; no default value

roo> vaadin addon install --artifactId vaadin-

    vaadin addon install --artifactId vaadin-calendar
    vaadin addon install --artifactId vaadin-colorpicker
    vaadin addon install --artifactId vaadin-lazyquerycontainer
    vaadin addon install --artifactId vaadin-sqlcontainer
    vaadin addon install --artifactId vaadin-timeline
```

Figure 14.2. Getting List of Add-ons in Directory

14.5.2. Compiling the Widget Set

Add-ons that include custom widgets, in this case the Vaadin Calendar component, require compilation of a *widget set*, as described in detail in Chapter 15, *Using Vaadin Add-ons*. Roo makes the compilation simple, you only have to enter the following command in the Roo Shell:

```
roo> vaadin widgetset create
```

Executing the command can take considerable time, as it downloads all the necessary Maven dependencies on the first run. The actual widget set compilation takes usually between 20 to 60 seconds, depending on the hardware.

This creates a *combining widget set* that includes all the widget sets from different add-ons and also the default widget set of the Vaadin core library. The compiled widget set should appear in the target/rapid-0.1.0-SNAPSHOT/VAADIN/widgetsets/com.vaad-in.rapid.web.RapidWidgetset folder and be referenced in the web.xml deployment descriptor of the application.

Generally, only add-ons that introduce entirely new user interface components include a widget set that needs to be compiled. These are the majority of Vaadin add-ons. Add-ons providing a theme or container implementation do not include a widget set.

If you later add other add-ons, you need to issue the vaadin widgetset update command, which updates the combining widget set definition file. The vaadin widgetset compile command simply recompiles the widget set without updating the combining widget set definition file.

14.5.3. Configuring the Deployment Assembly

The widget set is compiled under the `target/rapid-0.1.0.BUILD-SNAPSHOT` folder, which is not included in the deployment path by default.

1. Open the project properties for the project

2. Select **Deployment Assembly**

3. Click **Add**

4. Select **Folder**

5. Select `target/rapid-0.1.0.BUILD-SNAPSHOT`

6. Click **Finish** and **OK** to save the settings

If you are using Maven to debug your application, you will face the same issue. As a workaround, use the `jetty-run` or `jetty:run-exploded` targets that use the target directory as the base directory for the web app. Another option is to modify the `gwt-maven-plugin` to compile the widget set to `src/main/webapp` with its `inplace` mode.

14.6. Customizing Views

For basic use, the entity views created by Roo work just fine. However in some cases, modifying the form or changing visible properties in the table component may be needed to satisfy critical end users. In this section, we discuss some methods how you can modify the application skeleton generated by Roo.

14.6.1. Modifying Roo generated entity form

As discussed in Section 14.4.1, "Creating the Application Skeleton", entity forms generated by Roo can be made compatible with the visual editor of the Eclipse plugin. If you gave the `--visually-Composable true` parameter for Roo when creating the views, you can open for example the `WorkEntryForm.java` file with the Visual Designer. For example, right-click on the the file in the **Project**

Explorer view. Then, choosing the **Design** view from the bottom of the screen opens the form generated by Roo in a graphical editor. Use the editor to organize the view according to your preferences. Also, add a **Label** component to the view and name it as `hoursLabel`.

When you switch back to the source view, you can immediately see the changes made by the visual mode. To fill proper value for the newly created `hoursLabel`, modify the `setItemDataSource()` method to call an `updateDuration()` method that you create to calculate the duration between start and the end times. The resulting value should be shown in the label. You might also call this method from a value change listener hooked to start and end time fields.

At any time you may switch between the source code editor and the visual editor without losing changes done on the other side. Just make sure not to modify parts of the code (methods and field declarations) that are marked with `@AutoGenerated` annotation.

14.6.2. Creating a Calendar View for Filling Work Entries

In this section, we build an alternative view for **WorkEntry** entities built around the Vaadin Calendar add-on. The Calendar displays filled entries for the end user in a nice graphical presentation. User can get a quick overview of what he has done during the week and it is also easy to spot if there is some missing entries. The user can also select and modify time ranges visually with the calendar, which speeds up the daily tasks.

Start by sketching the view with the Visual Designer.

1. Choose **File → New → Vaadin → Composite**

2. Fill in the proper package and class name (such as `~web.ui` and **CalendarView**). The Vaadin Plugin for Eclipse creates a class that extends **CustomComponent**.

3. Switch to the **Design** tab using the tab selector below the source code and the visual editor opens.

For our view we need three components: two **ComboBox**es to select the project and employee, and a **Calendar** from the add-on that we installed previously. Filtering may help you in finding them from the component list. Drag them to the the composite and sketch the view according to your preferences. Also use the **Properties** tab to give components more meaningful names and possibly fill in a suitable caption. When you return to the source code view, you can see the generated code.

Customizing Generated Code

The constructor has a comment to indicate the place where you should add your custom code. To make our view display some data, we need to connect the combo boxes to the data sources and provide events to the **Calendar** component via its **Calendar-EventProvider** interface. For the project and employee selectors, the easiest option is to use the **JPAContainer**.

When implementing the **CalendarEventProvider**, you need to extend the data model with a method that lists **WorkEntry** objects within a specific time ranges and also implement a light-weight wrapper for **WorkEntry** to make them compatible with the **Calendar** component.

Using Custom Views

Once you have some data sources connected, you most probably want to check out how your new view looks in the application. The Vaadin application skeleton generated by Roo uses the Navigator add-on and a generated `RapidEntityManagerView` (where Rapid is the application base name) class as the view controller. For complex applications, you might want to build your own navigation system, but for this application we can just modify the **RapidEntityManagerView** to include our custom views.

Let the composite implement the **org.vaadin.navigator.Navigator.View** interface and modify `addEntityViewsToList()` method in **RapidEntityManagerView** to include your custom view to the navigation. After that, deploy the application and verify the view is shown. You may add some test data in the **WorkEntry** views generated by Roo and check that it is shown in the **CalendarView**.

Adding New Entries

To allow users to add new entries via Calendar, implement a **RangeSelectHandler** and register it to the Calendar. In the handler, you can create an new instance of **WorkEntry**. Fill in the time range from the provided event object and default values for the project and employee fields that you can find through the combo boxes that we created earlier.

The new **WorkEntry** object now contains the most essential information, but it still has the default comment field. The user might also want to review the new entry. Here we can use the previously fine-tuned **WorkEntry** form that was originally automatically created by the Roo. Wrap the **WorkEntry** object in a **BeanItem** and pass it to a **WorkEntryForm** instance. As our Calendar component consumes quite a lot of space on the screen, it is best to show the editor form in a modal Window. Again, use your existing Java know-how and extract the recyclable parts to helper methods (such as `showEditorPopup(WorkEntry)`).

To fine-tune the usability of the view, you may add more hooks in the **Calendar**:

- **EventClickHandler** to open editor for existing event
- **EventMoveHandler** to adjust the time range
- **EventResizeHandler** to adjust the time range

14.6.3. Creating a Custom View for Reporting

Our example project also has a report view for easy listing of work entries. The query can be filtered by project, employee and the time range. Most of the process is similar to creating the calendar view, but in the **ReportView** one can survive with just standard Vaadin components. The table component at the bottom of the view lists entries matching the criteria defined by the controls above it.

When you have sketched the view connect selects to the data sources. Also hook a **JPAContainer** to the **Table**. Add **ChangeListener** to all fields and update filters in the **JPAContainer** instance hooked to the result table.

14.7. Authentication and Authorization

The goals of authentication and authorization are preventing unauthorized viewing and editing of data. In the case of our tutorial application, only administrators should be allowed to view and edit hours and projects entered by users other than themselves.

14.7.1. Implementing Authentication and Authorization

Since the requirements of the example project are very simple, all authentication is handled with a simple **Authenticator** class that checks if a certain user with a certain password exists in the database. The **Authenticator** could just as easily be implemented using Spring Security or some other security framework. The authenticator has two responsibilities:

1. Authenticate users based on a username / password pair

2. Keep track of views that require administrator privileges to access and answer the simple question: "Is this view accessible in the current session?"

This approach is too simplistic for a real project, but the basics should be fairly similar when integrating a framework such as Spring Security with Vaadin.

To authenticate users, the system needs to show a login view before letting users view any possibly sensitive data. For the example project, the Vaadin composite **LoginView** was created using Vaadin Visual Designer. By default the Visual Designer creates a **AbsoluteLayout** as the root layout. This was changed into a **VerticalLayout** and a **LoginForm** was placed inside of it. The login form was then aligned to the middle center, making it appear in the middle of the browser window when the login view is the only visible layout in the main window.

In order to display the login view before anything else, the main window, which is defined by the **RapidWindow** class has to be edited. Instead of setting the content of the window to a new **RapidEntityManagerView**, the content is set to the login view, unless a user is already logged in, and a **LoginListener** is registered to the login view. The login listener is called when the

"Login" button is clicked, and passed the values of the text fields in the login form. By default, a username and a password is passed in and these are passed off to the authenticator for authentication. If the authentication succeeds, the content of the **RapidWindow** is replaced with a new **RapidEntityManagerView**, just as before introducing the login view.

```
public class RapidWindow extends Window
        implements LoginListener {

    public RapidWindow() {
        if (RapidApplication.get().getUser() == null) {
            setContent(new LoginView(this));
        } else {
            showMainUI();
        }

        // select window theme
        setTheme("rapid");
    }

    public void showMainUI() {
        // entity manager
        setContent(new RapidEntityManagerView());
    }

    @Override
    public void onLogin(LoginEvent event) {
        String username = event.getLoginParameter("username");
        String password = event.getLoginParameter("password");
        if (Authenticator.login(username, password)) {
            showMainUI();
        }
    }

}
```

The check whether a user is already logged in is important, because of the multi-window support that is automatically enabled in all Vaadin projects created with Spring Roo. Without the check, a user could first log in as one user and then open a new window and log in as another user, causing both windows to be logged in as the latter user. This is because all windows open to the same application in the same browser share the same session, and only the last user to be logged in is stored in the session.

Authorization is handled in the `addEntityViewsToList()` method in **RapidEntityManagerView** class. Before the view is added to the list, the authenticator is asked whether the user is allowed access the view and only adds the view if the answer is `true`.

```
if (Authenticator.isViewAccessible(viewClass) &&
    Navigator.View.class.isAssignableFrom(viewClass) {
```

```
    navigator.addView(key, viewClass);
    ...
}
```

14.8. Internationalization

We want to have the user interface to be available in different languages. Details such as the formatting of dates has to change depending on the selected language.

The login view has a drop-down select that allows the user to choose the language. The application attempts to detect the preferred language reported by the browser, and defaults to English if the preferred language is not available. The preferred language is detected and the locale set in the application class, as follows:

```
public void init() {
    ...
    // Use the locale from the request as default.
    // Login uses this setting later.
    setLocale(((WebApplicationContext)getContext())
        .getBrowser().getLocale());
    ...
}
```

Now that we know the preferred language of the user, we can start internationalizing the application. Vaadin does not have a preferred way of doing internationalization, so you are free to choose whichever method you prefer. Quite often, the common Java practice of using **ResourceBundle**s and .properties files is sufficient, and this suits our application perfectly. Please refer to Java documentation for more details regarding internationalization in Java.

The *Externalize Strings* feature in the Eclipse IDE (and STS) will handle most of the boilerplate generation. In the **Package Explorer**, select the package that holds the UI classes (com.vaadin.rapid.web) and select **Source → Externalize Strings**. The dialog shows a list of files that contains strings that are yet to be translated - you need to open one at a time and externalize the strings. In the externalize dialog, first make sure the location of the messages.properties is suitable (and stays the same for all files you go trough), in our case we want it in the com.vaadin.rapid.web package. The IDE will generate the messages.properties and a **Messages** class the first time you run it. In the **String to extern-**

alize list, make sure that strings that do not need to be translated have an X mark and that strings that should be translated have a check mark. Also, change all keys for translated strings to something descriptive.

Figure 14.3. The Externalize Strings Dialog

Externalize Strings marks strings that should not be translated using a special comment in the code, so that the next time you run the function, it will only show the new strings or strings you have forgotten.

Note that if you externalize strings from a visually editable component, the Visual Editor can no longer open the component, because the generated code has been changed. This will probably be fixed in a future release of the Visual Editor, but for now you can go ahead and move the code rows that contain translations to the constructor.

Next, we will translate the names of the Views. We'll do this dynamically in the **RapidEntityManagerView** by prefixing the translation key with "View." and appending the view name (with spaces removed).

```
final String viewCaption = Messages.getString("View." + viewName);
```

In this application we do not want to translate the URI fragment that is shown in the browser, so we make some small changes to keep the viewName and the translated viewCaption separate throughout the code. Whether or not one wants to translate depends on the application - if you translate the fragment, it will be more descriptive in the users own language, but users with different language settings will not be able to share deep links.

To translate the column headers of the various tables, we add some code to the end of the refresh() in **AbstractEntityView**. This will allow us to translate the headers after the content has been set:

```
protected void refresh() {
    ...
    // Translate column headers
    Object[] columns = getTableColumns();
    String[] headers = new String[columns.length];
    for (int i = 0; i < headers.length; i++)
        headers[i] = Messages.getString(getClass().getSimpleName()
                + "." + columns[i].toString());
    table.setColumnHeaders(headers);
    ...
}
```

To translate boolean values and localize dates in the various tables, we modify the createTable() in **AbstractEntityView** so that it returns our own **RapidTable**, which overrides formatPropertyValue():

```
protected String formatPropertyValue(Object rowId, Object colId,
                                     Property property) {
    Object value = property.getValue();
    if (value instanceof Boolean) {
        // Translate boolean values
        return Messages.getString("Boolean."
            + ((Boolean) value).toString());
    } else if (value instanceof Date) {
        // Localize date/time
        return DateFormat.getDateTimeInstance(DateFormat.SHORT,
            DateFormat.SHORT, RapidApplication.get().getLocale())
            .format((Date) value);
    }
    return super.formatPropertyValue(rowId, colId, property);
}
```

There is one more translation task to do: **BeansValidation** (JSR 303) is used for validating values according to annotations on the entities. This process produces some messages that originate from the **BeansValidation**, and need to be translated separately. **BeansValidation** also uses property files, namely `ValidationMessages.properties`, that should be placed in the `src/main/resources` folder. To tell **BeansValidation** which locale to use we currently need some boilerplate - this will hopefully be fixed soon. In each **Form** class (**ProjectForm**, **RapidUserForm**, **WorkEntryForm**) we need to call a helper that goes trough our validators and sets the locale:

```
public void setItemDataSource(Item item) {
    ...
    for (Object propertyId : getBeanPropertyIds())
        ValidatorMessageUtil.updateValidators(
                getField(propertyId));
    ...
}
```

The helper method in **ValidatorMessageUtil** iterates trough the validators for the field, updating the locale.

14.9. Testing the Application

In the data model section, we already discussed briefly about automatic integration tests that Roo generates for the domain objects. They are a good start, but only ensure that simple CRUD methods work from domain model to the persistency layer. In serious application development, you should write tests for any additional business logic, as well for the UI layers.

14.9.1. Overview of Testing

Writing unit tests for the user interface layer of an application can be a time consuming task. Yet, they do not necessary ensure that the UI works properly. Deployment problems, timing issues, and the browser layer may still cause issues that break the UI. In this step of the tutorial, we will use the Vaadin TestBench to test the user interface layer. TestBench executes tests with real browsers, by simulating user actions in the browser. This way, we do not just test the UI layer, but the entire stack from JavaScripts running in the browser down to the database.

This currently describes the use of Vaadin TestBench version 2 - see Chapter 20, Vaadin TestBench for the documentation of Vaadin TestBench 3.

Vaadin TestBench tests are normally recorded with a browser plugin. Advanced users may fine tune the tests by hand and, for example, configure tests with parameters. Tests scripts are then converted into JUnit test cases, which can be integrated into an existing testing environment. Roo projects are based on the Maven build system, so we will configure the `pom.xml` of the project so that TestBench tests are run automatically. The TestBench setup and usage is discussed briefly. Please refer to Chapter 20, *Vaadin TestBench* in case you face problems.

To help the integration tests, we use the Maven Failsafe plugin. It is a testing plugin that automatically runs all tests named, for example, `*ITCase.java` in the test sources with the `verify` goal. The Failsafe plugin also provides necessary hooks where we can configure how our application server is started and stopped. If you want to test on a separate server, you can do just deploy and undeploy at these phases. The necessary Maven snippet can be found from the Failsafe project page.

14.9.2. Running the Test Server

The Jetty plugin should be already installed in your `pom.xml`, but we will configure Jetty to start automatically before the integration test phase and close cleanly when the tests have been run. Add the following XML snippet inside the definition of your Jetty plugin:

```xml
<executions>
    <!-- start and stop jetty (running our app) when running
         integration tests -->
    <execution>
        <id>start-jetty</id>
        <phase>pre-integration-test</phase>
        <goals>
            <goal>run-exploded</goal>
        </goals>
        <configuration>
            <scanIntervalSeconds>0</scanIntervalSeconds>
            <daemon>true</daemon>
            <stopKey>STOP</stopKey>
            <stopPort>8866</stopPort>
        </configuration>
    </execution>
    <execution>
        <id>stop-jetty</id>
```

```
        <phase>post-integration-test</phase>
        <goals>
            <goal>stop</goal>
        </goals>
        <configuration>
            <stopPort>8866</stopPort>
            <stopKey>STOP</stopKey>
        </configuration>
    </execution>
</executions>
```

To verify that the integration test system works, you can create a simple smoke test. Create a JUnit test case and name it as `SmokeTestITCase.java` and create a test method that connects to the test server. Verify that a proper kickstart page is returned. This verifies that the application is properly deployed for more advanced tests. Run your integration test with **mvn verify**. If this basic integration test passes fine, you are ready to continue setting up the TestBench.

14.9.3. Installing TestBench with Maven

TestBench is not available in any public Maven repository. Unless you have TestBench already installed, download it from vaadin.com/directory. Install the JAR to your local repository (or Maven proxy) by executing the following command in the install directory of TestBench:

```
mvn install::install-file -Dfile=vaadin-testbench-2.2.2.jar
-DgroupId=com.vaadin -DartifactId=testbench -Dversion=2.2.2
-Dpackaging=jar -DgeneratePom=true
```

You also need to specify the dependency `pom.xml` file of the project. Use the `test` scope as the JAR file is not needed in the actual application execution. We will need it when compiling test scripts from HTML to JUnit test cases, and also when executing the actual JUnit tests.

Notice that Vaadin TestBench is licensed with the Commercial Vaadin Add-on License. You can download the product for a 30-day free trial period with Maven, after which you need a license which you can buy from the Vaadin Directory.

14.9.4. Generating JUnit Tests

The test cases for Vaadin TestBench are recorded as HTML files and need to be compiled as JUnit tests . This needs to be automated.

Native scripts are kept in source repository as they are more maintainable than the compiled JUnit tests. The conversion is done by **com.vaadin.testbenc.DirectoryTestConverter** tool. You can use it most conveniently through the Maven Exec plugin. Configure it to be run at, for example, `generate-test-sources` and add generated java files to test sources. The Exec plugin has an option to do this, but you may need to use `build-helper-maven-plugin` instead.

14.9.5. Configuring System Properties

The test setup is now almost ready. As the last step, we need to provide some system properties to be defined for the JUnit tests generated by TestBench. Add the following configuration snippet to the configuration of the Failsafe plugin:

```
<configuration>
    <!-- Define some necessary system properties for -->
    <!-- TestBench JUnit tests.                       -->
    <systemPropertyVariables>
        <com.vaadin.testbench.tester.host>
            ${testbench.hubhost}
        </com.vaadin.testbench.tester.host>
        <com.vaadin.testbench.deployment.url>
            ${testbench.appurl}
        </com.vaadin.testbench.deployment.url>
        <com.vaadin.testbench.screenshot.directory>
            ${project.build.directory}/testbench-generated
        </com.vaadin.testbench.screenshot.directory>
    </systemPropertyVariables>
    <encoding>UTF-8</encoding>
</configuration>
```

Define the used parameters and you are ready to go. The `local-host` and `http://localhost:8080/${project.name}` will work fine for local testing. Save your scripts under `src/test/resources/` with the filenames ending with `ITCase.html`, and they will be automatically executed when you issue **mvn verify**. Your first test can simply login as the admin user and then assert some text to verify that the initial screen gets rendered.

14.9.6. Notes

Notice that we did not configure the TestBench hub (nor a remote control) to start and stop from Maven. Instead, we just defined the host where the hub is running. So, before actually executing the integration tests, make sure that the TestBench is up and running, as described in Chapter 20, *Vaadin TestBench*. Commonly, TestBench is used so that the hub and its slaves are running in a separate cluster, rather than on developer's workstations. If you have access to this kind of external hub, you can give its address as `com.vaadin.testbench.tester.host`. The `localhost` does not work as the deployment URL in this case, but you should use an URL which the test machines can access. If no separate test cluster is used, you might want to customize your Maven build to start and stop TestBench in a way similar to Jetty.

Your more advanced tests can then use the login test as a base and test various features. Record tests for at least basic CRUD actions for all entity types. To verify authorization code to work, you can also create a non-admin user in one test and verify with the new user that admin only features are not visible. Most actions can be recorded with the TestBench Recorder automatically, but there are some limitations. For example, selecting a time range in the Calendar view needs to be manually built using Selenium methods. (The TestBench version 2.2.0 also has a regression that adds an excess `selectWindow` command when logging in with LoginForm, so remove that command manually in case your test seems to fail in the very beginning.)

When building tests, notice that integration tests use the same database by default, so the data filled in the previous test will be visible during the next test. Tests are run in alphabetical order, so you may use a naming convention to control the test execution order.

14.10. Exception Handling

When something goes wrong in a Vaadin application, a small error indicator icon is shown on the control that was interacted with. When hovering over the icon, a tooltip containing the entire stack-trace of the exception is shown. No normal person (that is, other than a software developer) understands what this means and knows what to do.

In this section, we will remove the stack traces and replace them with error messages in terms that a normal user would understand.

14.10.1. Preventing Stacktraces in the UI

The autogenerated code lets the exceptions fall all the way through to the user interface. This can easily be changed by overriding the `terminalError()` method in the **Application** subclass.

```
@Override
public void terminalError(Terminal.ErrorEvent event) {
    Window errorWindow = findWindowForError(event);
    // Shows an error notification
    if (errorWindow != null) {
        errorWindow.showNotification(
            "An internal error has occurred, please " +
                "contact the administrator!",
            Notification.TYPE_ERROR_MESSAGE);
    }

    // print the error
    logger.log(Level.SEVERE,
        "An uncaught exception occurred: ",
        event.getThrowable());
}
```

14.10.2. Where to Catch Exceptions

The most likely places for errors to occur in the example application are when interacting with the database. Validation errors are already handled in the generated code, but errors due to constraint violations on the database level and communication failures need to be caught and handled correctly.

Almost all saving and deleting of entities is handled through the **AbstractEntityView**, which is the super type of all but one view. **CalendarView** is the custom view that does not extend **AbstractEntityView**, and thus needs to catch the exceptions separately. Almost all exceptions can be handled in a good way by handling them in **AbstractEntityView** and **CalendarView**. When an exception occurs, an error notification should be displayed to the user.

Handling Exceptions in AbstractEntityView

The Vaadin plug-in for Spring Roo generates the **AbstractEntityView** class for handling CRUD for all different entities in the application. This means that the methods that handle saving and deleting of entities can be changed to include customized exception handling. Roo generates an aspect, **AbstractEntityView_Roo_AbstractEntityView** containing the `doCommit()` and `doDelete()` methods. These methods can be changed by moving them to the **AbstractEntityView**, which will cause Roo to stop autogenerating the methods in the **AbstractEntityView_Roo_AbstractEntityView** aspect.

Move the methods to **AbstractEntityView** and surround the method contents with a `try...catch` block, catching all **Exception**s and showing a notification about which operation failed.

```
@Transactional
public void doDelete() {
    try {
        Object id = getIdForEntity(getEntityForItem(
                        getForm().getItemDataSource()));
        if (id != null) {
            getTable().removeItem(id);
        }
    } catch (Exception e) {
        logger.log(Level.SEVERE, "Could not delete entity", e);
        Notification.show("Deletion of the item failed.",
                        Notification.TYPE_ERROR_MESSAGE);
    }
}
```

Handling Exceptions in CalendarView

Since **CalendarView** is a custom view which doesn't extend **AbstractEntityView**, it also needs to handle exceptions. The calendar view does the same things as the other entity views, but with a different layout and logic.

Exception handling needs to be added to all code that persists or deletes data from the database. The **CalendarView** does this in several locations: When creating a new entry, when editing an entry, when moving an entry and when resizing an entry. E.g. the range select handler, which persists a work entry when it is first created should be changed to wrap the call to `workEntry.persist()` in a `try...catch` block.

```
@Override
public void rangeSelect(RangeSelectEvent event) {

    ...
    // Build a work entry
    ...

    try {
```

```
    workEntry.persist();
    showEditorPopup(workEntry, true);
} catch (Exception e) {
    logger.log(Level.SEVERE, "Could not store entity", e);
    Notification.show("Could not create a new " +
            "work entry due to an internal error.",
            Notification.TYPE_ERROR_MESSAGE);
}
}
```

In the rest of the code, all calls to `persist()`, `merge()` or `delete()`
are wrapped in `try...catch` blocks and a notification with a suitable message for each of the cases is displayed.

14.11. Deploying to Cloud Foundry

Cloud Foundry (`http://cloudfoundry.com/`) is a new platform-
as-a-service solution from SpringSource. Cloud Foundry makes it
extremely easy to deploy applications created with Spring Roo
and Vaadin to the cloud.

Before you can deploy to Cloud Foundry, you must register an
account at `http://cloudfoundry.com/`. The activation might take
some time, so you should do the registration several days before
you need the account.

14.11.1. Installing the Cloud Foundry Plug-in in STS

Installing the Cloud Foundry plug-in is easy. Open the STS Dashboard and select the **Extensions** tab in the lower-left corner of the
dashboard view. Scroll down to the **Server and Clouds** section
and choose the **Cloud Foundry integration plug-in** from there.
Click **Install** and follow the on-screen instructions.

14.11.2. Deploying the Application

Deploying the application is also very simple.

1. Open the **Servers** view, right-click somewhere in it, and
   create a **New → Server**.

2. In the **New Server** window, choose **VMWare → Cloud
   Foundry** and click **Next**.

3. Fill in the account information that you received by email
   from cloudfoundry.com and choose **VMware Cloud**

Foundry - http://api.cloudfoundry.com from the URL dropdown.

4. You can click 'Validate Account' to make sure that you filled in your password correctly.

5. Click 'Finish' to finish the installation of the Cloud Foundry server.

Once the new server is installed, you can add your project to it, just like you would add your project to any other server using the **Servers** view. Once added, right-click on the project and choose **Start**. This will ask for a name that identifies your project in the cloud as well as the URL to deploy to. After giving this information, the project will be uploaded and started in the cloud. After a few seconds, you should be able to visit the URL you provided and see your project in action.

14.11.3. Binding to the MySQL Service

The final part of our demonstration is to bind the application deployed in the Cloud Foundry to a real DBMS. In the following, we describe how you can bind the application to a MySQL database.

1. Bind a MySQL database to the application in Eclipse. In the **Cloud Foundry** view:

   a. Double-click the application deployed in Cloud Foundry

   b. Select **Services** and click **Add** in the upper-right corner

   c. Give the connection a name and choose a MySQL database

   d. Drag the created service from the **Services** panel to the **Services** table in the application

2. Remove the dependency to the HSQLDB that we used at first from `pom.xml`

3. Add the MySQL connector dependency as follows:

```
<dependency>
  <groupId>mysql</groupId>
  <artifactId>mysql-connector-java</artifactId>
```

```
        <version>5.1.15</version>
</dependency>
```

4. Add the Cloud Foundry runtime dependency as follows:

```
<dependency>
    <groupId>org.cloudfoundry</groupId>
    <artifactId>cloudfoundry-runtime</artifactId>
    <version>0.6.1</version>
</dependency>
```

5. Edit the `persistence.xml` file and change the **org.ec-lipse.persistence.platform.database.HSQLPlatform** class name to **org.eclipse.persistence.platform.data-base.MySQLPlatform**.

6. Edit the `applicationContext.xml` file and change the following line:

```
<beans xmlns="http://www.springframework.org/schema/beans"
xmlns:aop= ...
```

to the following:

```
<beans xmlns="http://www.springframework.org/schema/beans"
  xmlns:aop="http://www.springframework.org/schema/aop"
  xmlns:context="http://www.springframework.org/schema/con-
text"
  xmlns:jee="http://www.springframework.org/schema/jee"
  xmlns:tx="http://www.springframework.org/schema/tx"
  xmlns:xsi="http://www.w3.org/2001/XMLSchema-instance"
  xmlns:cloud="http://schema.cloudfoundry.org/spring"
  xsi:schemaLocation="http://www.springframe-
work.org/schema/aop http://www.springframe-
work.org/schema/aop/spring-aop-3.0.xsd http://www.springframe-
work.org/schema/beans http://www.springframe-
work.org/schema/beans/spring-beans-3.0.xsd http://www.spring-
framework.org/schema/context http://www.springframe-
work.org/schema/context/spring-context-3.0.xsd ht-
tp://www.springframework.org/schema/jee http://www.spring-
framework.org/schema/jee/spring-jee-3.0.xsd http://www.spring-
framework.org/schema/tx http://www.springframe-
work.org/schema/tx/spring-tx-3.0.xsd http://schema.cloud-
foundry.org/spring http://schema.cloudfoundry.org/spring/cloud-
foundry-spring.xsd">
```

7. Also in the `applicationContext.xml` replace the following:

```
<bean class="org.apache.commons.dbcp.BasicDataSource"
      destroy-method="close" id="dataSource">
  <property name="driverClassName"
            value="${database.driverClassName}"/>
```

```
    <property name="url" value="${database.url}"/>
    <property name="username" value="${database.username}"/>
    <property name="password" value="${database.password}"/>
</bean>
```

with the following:

```
<cloud:data-source id="dataSource" />
```

Part II

Vaadin Add-ons

Table of Contents

The Vaadin core library is just the beginning. Vaadin is designed to be highly extendable with third-party components, themes, data binding implementations, and tools. The add-ons are an important part of the Vaadin ecosystem, supporting also different business models for different needs.

Chapter 15

Using Vaadin
Add-ons

This chapter describes the installation of add-on components, themes, containers, and other tools from the Vaadin Directory and the use of commercial add-ons offered by Vaadin.

This edition is a draft. Many new features that will be included in Vaadin 7 are not yet covered in the draft and some of the content may in fact be outdated. For the most current version, please see the on-line edition available at `http://vaadin.com/book`.

15.1. Overview

In addition to the components, layouts, themes, and data sources built in into the core Vaadin library, many others are available as add-ons, either from the Vaadin Directory or from independent sources. Both commercial and free components exist under various licenses.

Installation of themes, data sources, and components built with server-side component composition is simple, just dropping a JAR package in a project and, usually, compiling the included widget set (the client-side implementation).

15.2. Downloading Add-ons from Vaadin Directory

Vaadin Directory at `http://vaadin.com/directory/` provides a rich collection of add-ons for Vaadin. You can download Directory add-on packages from the details page of an add-on.

1. Select the version; some add-ons have several versions available. The latest is shown by default, but you can choose another the version to download from the dropdown menu in the header of the details page.

2. Click **Download Now** and save the JAR or Zip file on your computer.

3. If the add-on is packaged in a Zip package, unzip the package and follow any instructions provided inside the package. Typically, you just need to copy a JAR file to your web project under the `WEB-INF/lib` directory.

4. Update and recompile your project. In Eclipse, select the project and press F5.

5. You need to compile the client-side implementations of the add-on components, that is, a *widget set*. This is the case for majority of add-ons, except for pure server-side, theme, or data binding add-ons. You must recompile the widget set if you install a new version of the add-on or the Vaadin library. See the subsequent sections for detailed instructions for compiling widget sets.

6. Update the project in web server and possibly restart the server.

After trying out an add-on, you can give some feedback to the author of the add-on by rating the add-on with one to five stars and optionally leaving a comment.

Please note the add-on license. While most commercial add-ons can be downloaded directly, you should note their license and other terms and conditions. Many are offered under a dual licensing agreement so that they can be used in open source projects for free, and many have a trial period for closed-source development.

15.3. Compiling Add-on Widget Sets

15.3.1. Compiling Widget Sets in Eclipse

To be able to compile widget sets in Eclipse, you need to have the Vaadin Plugin for Eclipse installed, as instructed in Section 2.2.1, "Vaadin Plugin for Eclipse".

An application can only have one widget set, so if you use multiple add-ons and possibly your own custom widgets, they need to be combined to a single widget set that inherits them. You can create the combining widget set manually and the Eclipse plugin simply update it when you add new add-ons. Otherwise, the Eclipse plugin automatically creates a project-specific widget set under the project root source folder.

The Eclipse plugin compiles widget sets automatically by default. They do not normally need to be recompiled after changes to server-side classes, so if the automatic recompilation get annoying, disable it from the project settings.

To compile the widget set(s) manually, click the **Compile Vaadin widgets** button in Eclipse toolbar or press **Ctrl+6**. You must re-compile the widget set(s) always when you install a new version of the add-on or of the Vaadin library.

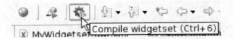

Figure 15.1. The Compile Vaadin widgets Button in Eclipse Toolbar

Further information on defining and compiling widget sets is given in Section 11.2.2, "Compiling the Widget Set", Section 11.11, "Defining a Client-Side Module Descriptor", and Section 11.12, "Compiling a Client-Side Module".

15.3.2. Compiling Widget Sets with an Ant Script

If you need to compile the widget set with an Ant script, you can find a script template at the URL https://vaadin.com/download/misc/build-widgetset-vaadin7.xml. You can copy the build script to your project and, once configured, use it by entering:

```
$ ant -f build-widgetset-vaadin7.xml
```

See Section 11.12, "Compiling a Client-Side Module" for details on configuring the build script and the available build targets, and Section 11.11, "Defining a Client-Side Module Descriptor" for information regarding the widget set definition file.

If you are using an IDE such as Eclipse, *always* remember to refresh the project to synchronize it with the filesystem after compiling the widget set outside Eclipse.

15.3.3. Troubleshooting

If you experience problems, do the following:

- Check the `.gwt.xml` widget set definition file under the widget set folder in the project root package. For example, if the project root package is `com.example.myproject`, the widget set definition file would be `com.example.myproject.widgetset.MyprojectWidgetset.gwt.xml`. See Section 11.11, "Defining a Client-Side Module Descriptor" for details on the contents of the widget set definition file.

- Check the `WEB-INF/web.xml` deployment descriptor and see that the servlet for your application has a widget set parameter, such as the following:

```
<init-param>
  <description>Application widgetset</description>
  <param-name>widgetset</param-name>
  <param-value>com.example.myproject.widgetset.MyprojectWidgetset</param-value>
</init-param>
```

- See the `VAADIN/widgetsets` directory and check that the widget set appears there. You can remove it and recompile to see that compilation works properly.

- Use the **Net** tab in Firebug to see that the widget set (and theme) is loaded properly.

- Use the `?debug` parameter for the application to see if there is any version conflict between the widget set and the Vaadin library, or the themes. See Section 12.3.1, "Debug Mode" for details.

- Refresh and recompile the project. In Eclipse, select the project and press **F5**, stop the server, clean the server temporary directories, and restart it.

- Check the Error Log view in Eclipse (or the IDE you use).

15.4. Removing Add-ons

Version mismatch problems with custom widget sets are a common source of grief for many beginners in Vaadin. If you need add-ons or your own custom components that include widget sets, you of course need to compile them, but otherwise it is unnecessary.

If you do not use any such add-ons or your own custom components, do the following:

1. If you are using the Eclipse plugin, disable automatic widget set compilation from project preferences, in the **Vaadin** category, by selecting **Suspend automatic widgetset builds**. This prevents accidental compilation of the unnecessary widget sets. You may want to do this anyhow as the automatic builds can be annoying. You can still always build the widget set with the button in the toolbar.

2. Remove all widget set folders from under the `VAADIN/widgetsets` folder.

3. Edit the `WEB-INF/web.xml` file and remove the *widgetset* init parameter from the servlet. It looks as follows:

```
<init-param>
  <description>Application widgetset</description>
  <param-name>widgetset</param-name>
  <param-value>com.vaadin.demo.colorpicker.widgetset.ColorPickerWidgetSet</param-value>
</init-param>
```

4. Refresh the project. In Eclipse, select the project and press F5, stop the server, clean the server temporary directories, and restart it.

At least in development environments, if you have extracted Vaadin themes to the VAADIN/themes folder, you should remove them and let them be loaded dynamically from the Vaadin JAR.

15.5. Using Add-ons in a Maven Project

To use add-ons in a project that uses Maven, you simply have to add them as dependencies in the POM. If the add-ons includes widget sets, as at least most component add-ons do, you also need to define and compile a project widget set.

Creating, compiling, and packaging a Vaadin project using Maven was described in Section 2.5, "Creating a Project with Maven".

15.5.1. Adding a Dependency

Vaadin Directory provides a Maven repository for all the add-ons in the Directory. You can view needed Maven dependency definitions by clicking the **Maven POM** button at the right side of the add-on view, as illustrated in Figure 15.2, "Maven POM Definitions in Vaadin Directory".

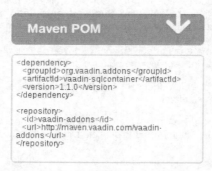

Figure 15.2. Maven POM Definitions in Vaadin Directory

You need to copy the dependency declaration to the pom.xml file in your project, under the /project/dependencies element.

```
...
<dependencies>
  <dependency>
    <groupId>com.vaadin</groupId>
    <artifactId>vaadin</artifactId>
    <version>${vaadin.version}</version>
  </dependency>
  <dependency>
    <groupId>org.vaadin.addons</groupId>
    <artifactId>vaadin-sqlcontainer</artifactId>
    <version>1.1.0</version>
  </dependency>
  ...
```

You can use the exact version number, as is done in the example above, or LATEST to always use the latest version of the add-on.

The POM excerpt given in Directory includes also a repository definition, but if you have used the vaadin-archetype-clean archetype when creating your project, it should already include the definition.

15.5.2. Enabling Widget Set Compilation

Most add-on components in Vaadin Directory include a *widget set* which must be compiled before using the add-on. Some add-ons, such as data binding add-ons or themes, do not include a widget set.

Configuring the POM

The configuration needed for compiling widget sets is included in the pom.xml created with the vaadin-archetype-clean archetype, but the elements are commented out. You just need to enable the configuration.

```
<!-- Compile custom GWT components or widget dependen-
cies with the GWT compiler -->
<!--
<plugin>
  <groupId>org.codehaus.mojo</groupId>
  ...
</plugin>
-->

...
```

```
<!--
<pluginRepositories>
</pluginRepositories>
-->

...

<dependencies>
...
  <!--
  <dependency>
    ...
  </dependency>
  -->
</dependencies>
```

Creating a Widget Set Definition File

Your project needs a widget set that combines the default widget set in the Vaadin core library with any widget sets from add-ons. This requires creating an empty *widget set definition file* (or *module file* in GWT terminology). The actual content of the file is generated automatically by searching the class path for widget sets (with the `vaadin:update-widgetset` as explained later), but you need to create an empty file.

Create a widget set directory in your project source directory.

```
$ mkdir project-name/src/main/java/your/company/gwt
```

Then create a `ProjectNameWidgetSet.gwt.xml` file in the directory with an empty `<module>` element as follows:

```
<module>
</module>
```

Enabling the Widget Set in the Application

The project widget set needs to be enabled in the `web.xml` deployment descriptor in the application. Edit the `src/main/webapp/WEB-INF/web.xml` file and add or modify the `widgetset` parameter for the servlet as follows.

```
<servlet>
  ...
```

```
  <init-param>
    <description>Widget Set to Use</description>
    <param-name>widgetset</param-name>
    <param-value>your.company.gwt.ProjectNameWidget-
Set</param-value>
  </init-param>
</servlet>
```

The parameter is the class name of the widget set, that is, without
the .gwt.xml extension and with the Java dot notation for class
names that include the package name.

This should complete the task of enabling a widget set compilation
and use in your project. Next, you need to update the project
widget set, as described in the next section.

15.5.3. Updating and Compiling the Project Widget Set

If you have enabled widget set compilation as described earlier
and created the project widget set, you need to update the widget
set to include the default widget set and any widget sets included
in add-ons. You can do this simply by running the vaadin:update-
widgetset goal in the project directory.

```
$ mvn vaadin:update-widgetset
...
[INFO] auto discovered modules [your.company.gwt.Pro-
jectNameWidgetSet]
[INFO] Updating widgetset your.company.gwt.Project-
NameWidgetSet
[ERROR] 27.10.2011 19:22:34 com.vaadin.terminal.gwt.wid-
getsetutils.ClassPathExplorer getAvailableWidgetSets
[ERROR] INFO: Widgetsets found from classpath:
[ERROR]          your.company.gwt.ProjectNameWidgetSet
in file:/home/magi/itmill/maventest/project-
name/src/main/java
[ERROR]          com.vaadin.terminal.gwt.DefaultWidgetSet
 in jar:file:/home/magi/.m2/repository/com/vaadin/vaad-
in/6.7.1/vaadin-6.7.1.jar!/
[ERROR]
[ERROR] 27.10.2011 19:22:34 com.vaadin.terminal.gwt.wid-
getsetutils.ClassPathExplorer getAvailableWidgetSets
```

```
[ERROR] INFO: Search took 8ms
...
```

Do not mind the "ERROR" labels, they are just an issue with the Vaadin Plugin for Maven.

If you later add other add-ons in the project, or remove some, you need to run the widget set update again.

The project widget set also needs to be compiled using the GWT Compiler. We enabled the Maven add-ons for GWT compilation in the previous section. You can compile the widget set with the gwt:compile goal as follows:

```
$ mvn gwt:compile
```

You need to recompile the widget set if you upgrade to a new version of Vaadin or any of the included widget sets. It is *not* done automatically by the package goal. If you have added or removed add-ons, you also need to run the vaadin:update-widgetset goal before the compilation.

This concludes the compilation of add-on widget sets. You still need to compile and package the actual application with the package goal, as described in Section 2.5, "Creating a Project with Maven".

Chapter 16

Vaadin Calendar

The Vaadin Calendar is a commercial add-on component for organizing and displaying calendar events. It can be used to view and manage events in monthly, weekly, and daily views.

16.1. Overview

The main features of the Vaadin Calendar include:

- Monthly, weekly, and daily views

- Two types of events: all-day events and events with a time range

- Add events directly, from a **Container**, or with an event provider

- Control the range of the visible dates

- Selecting and editing date or time range by dragging

- Drag and drop events to calendar

- Support for localization and timezones

The data source of the calendar can be practically anything, as its events are queried dynamically by the component. You can bind the calendar to a Vaadin container, or to any other data source by implementing an *event provider*.

Monthly and Weekly Views

The Vaadin Calendar has two types of views that are shown depending on the date range of the calendar. The *weekly view* displays a week by default. It can show anything between one to seven days a week, and is also used as a single-day view. The view mode is determined from the *date range* of the calendar, defined by a start and an end date. Calendar will be shown in a *monthly view* when the date range is over than one week (seven days) long. The date range is always calculated in an accuracy of one millisecond.

The monthly view, shown in Figure 16.1, "Monthly view with All-Day and Normal Events", can easily be used to control all types of events, but it is best suited for events that last for one or more days. You can drag the events to move them. In the figure, you can see two longer events that are highlighted with a blue and green background color. Other markings are shorter day events that last less than a 24 hours. These events can not be moved by dragging in the monthly view.

In Figure 16.2, "Weekly View", you can see four normal day events and also all-day events at the top of the time line grid.

Calendar Events

All occurrences in a calendar are represented as *events*. You have three ways to manage the calendar events: add them to the calendar and manage them by its API, from a Vaadin `Container`, or with an *event provider*.

Events are handled though the `CalendarEvent` interface. The concrete class of the event depends on the specific **CalendarEv-**

Figure 16.1. Monthly view with All-Day and Normal Events

entProvider used in the calendar. By default, **Calendar** uses a **BasicEventProvider** to provide events, which uses **BasicEvent** instances.

Vaadin Calendar does not depend on any particular data source implementation. Events are queried by the **Calendar** from the provider that just has to implement the `CalendarEventProvider` interface. It is up to the event provider that **Calendar** gets the correct events.

You can bind any Vaadin **Container** to a calendar, in which case a **ContainerEventProvider** is used transparently. The container must be ordered by start date and time of the events. See Section 9.5, "Collecting Items in Containers" for basic information about containers.

A calendar event requires a start time and an end time. These are the only mandatory properties. In addition, an event can also be set as an all-day event by setting the `all-day` property of the event.

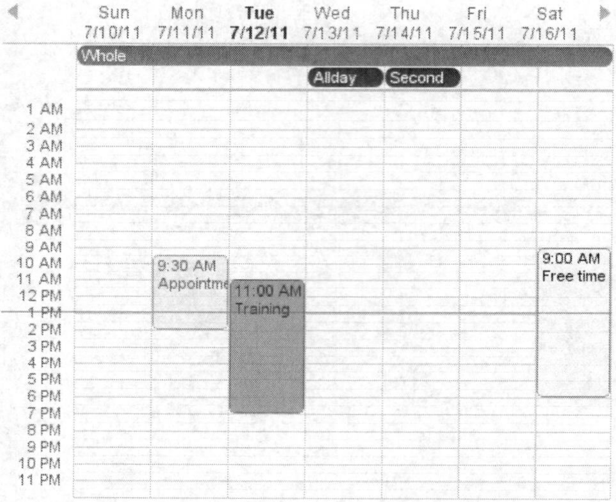

Figure 16.2. Weekly View

You can also set the `description` of an event, which is displayed as a tooltip in the user interface.

If the `all-day` field of the event is `true`, then the event is always rendered as an all-day event. In the monthly view, this means that no start time is displayed in the user interface and the event has an colored background. In the weekly view, all-day events are displayed in the upper part of the screen, and rendered similarly to the monthly view. In addition, when the time range of an event is 24 hours or longer, it is rendered as an all-day event in the monthly view.

When the time range of an event is equal or less than 24 hours, with the accuracy of one millisecond, the event is considered as a normal day event. Normal event has a start and end times that may be on different days.

Interaction

The date and week captions, as well as events, are clickable and the clicks can be listened for by the server. Also date/time range selections, event dragging, and event resizing can be listened by the server. Using the API, you have full control over the events caused by user interaction.

The weekly view has navigation buttons to navigate forward and backward in time. These actions are also listened by the server. Custom navigation can be implemented using event handlers, as described in Section 16.9, "Customizing the Calendar".

16.2. Installing Calendar

Vaadin Calendar is available for download from Vaadin Directory and from a Maven repository. Installing the add-on is the same as with Vaadin add-ons in general, so please refer to Chapter 15, *Using Vaadin Add-ons*. Vaadin Calendar includes a widget set, which you need to compile to your project widget set.

Licensing

When downloading the Vaadin Calendar add-on from Vaadin Directory, you need to choose the license.

Vaadin Calendar is a commercial product licensed under a dual-licensing scheme. The AGPL (GNU Affero General Public License) allows open-source development, while the CVAL (Commercial Vaadin Add-On License) needs to be purchased for closed-source use, including web deployments and internal use. With the CVAL license, you have a free 30-day trial period for evaluating the product.

Commercial licenses can be purchased from the Vaadin Directory, where you can also find the license details and download the Vaadin Calendar.

16.3. Basic Use

Use of Calendar requires two tasks after creating a **Calendar** instance: setting a time range for it and providing the calendar events. The time range controls its view mode; whether it is a daily, weekly, or monthly view.

16.3.1. Setting the Date Range

The view mode is controlled by the date range of the calendar. The weekly view is the default view mode. You can change the range by setting start and end dates for the calendar. The range must be between one and 60 days.

In the following, we set the calendar to show only one day, which is the current day.

```
cal.setStartDate(new Date());
cal.setEndDate(new Date());
```

Notice that although the range we set above is actually zero time long, the calendar still renders the time from 00:00 to 23:59. This is normal, as the Vaadin Calendar is guaranteed to render at least the date range provided, but may expand it. This behaviour is important to notice when we implement our own event providers.

16.3.2. Adding and Managing Events

The first thing the you will probably notice about the Calendar is that it is rather empty at first. The Calendar allows three different ways to add events:

- Add events directly to the **Calendar** object using the add-dEvent()

- Use a Container as a data source

- Use the *event provider* mechanism

The easiest way to add and manage events in a calendar is to use the basic event management API in the **Calendar**. You can add events with addEvent() and remove them with the removeEvent(). These methods will use the underlying event provider to write the modifications to the data source.

For example, the following adds a two-hour event starting from the current time. The standard Java **GregorianCalendar** provides various ways to manipulate date and time.

```
// Add a short event
GregorianCalendar start = new GregorianCalendar();
GregorianCalendar end   = new GregorianCalendar();
end.add(java.util.Calendar.HOUR, 2);
calendar.addEvent(new BasicEvent("Calendar study",
        "Learning how to use Vaadin Calendar",
        start.getTime(), end.getTime()));
```

Calendar uses by default a **BasicEventProvider**, which keeps the events in memory in an internal represenetation.

This adds a new event that lasts for 3 hours. As the BasicEventProvider and BasicEvent implement some optional event interfaces provided by the calendar package, there is no need to refresh the calendar. Just create events, set their properties and add them to the Event Provider.

16.3.3. Getting Events from a Container

You can use any Vaadin `Container` that implements the `Indexed` interface as the data source for calendar events. The **Calendar** will listen to change events from the container as well as write changes to the container. You can attach a container to a **Calendar** with `setContainerDataSource()`.

In the following example, we bind a **BeanItemContainer** that contains built-in **BasicEvent** events to a calendar.

```
// Create the calendar
Calendar calendar = new Calendar("Bound Calendar");

// Use a container of built-in BasicEvents
final BeanItemContainer<BasicEvent> container =
    new BeanItemContainer<BasicEvent>(BasicEvent.class);

// Create a meeting in the container
container.addBean(new BasicEvent("The Event", "Single Event",
            new GregorianCalendar(2012,1,14,12,00).getTime(),
            new GregorianCalendar(2012,1,14,14,00).getTime()));

// The container must be ordered by the start time. You
// have to sort the BIC every time after you have added
// or modified events.
container.sort(new Object[]{"start"}, new boolean[]{true});

calendar.setContainerDataSource(container, "caption",
    "description", "start", "end", "styleName");
```

The container must either use the default property IDs for event data, as defined in the `CalendarEvent` interface, or provide them as parameters for the `setContainerDataSource()` method, as we did in the example above.

Keeping the Container Ordered

The events in the container *must* be kept ordered by their start date/time. Failing to do so may and will result in the events not showing in the calendar properly.

Ordering depends on the container. With some containers, such as **BeanItemContainer**, you have to sort the container explicitly every time after you have added or modified events, usually with the `sort()` method, as we did in the example above. Some container, such as **JPAContainer**, keep the in container automatically order if you provide a sorting rule.

For example, you could order a **JPAContainer** by the following rule, assuming that the start date/time is held in the `startDate` property:

```
// The container must be ordered by start date. For JPAContainer
// we can just set up sorting once and it will stay ordered.
container.sort(new String[]{"startDate"}, new boolean[]{true});
```

Delegation of Event Management

Setting a container as the calendar data source with `setContainerDataSource()` automatically switches to **ContainerEventProvider**. You can manipulate the event data through the API in **Calendar** and the user can move and resize event through the user interface. The event provider delegates all such calendar operations to the container.

If you add events through the **Calendar** API, notice that you may be unable to create events of the type held in the container or adding them requires some container-specific operations. In such case, you may need to customize the `addEvent()` method.

For example, **JPAContainer** requires adding new items with `addEntity()`. You could first add the entity to the container or entity manager directly and then pass it to the `addEvent()`. That does not, however, work if the entity class does not implement `CalendarEvent`. This is actually the case always if the property names differ from the ones defined in the interface. You could handle creating the underlying entity objects in the `addEvent()` as follows:

```
// Create a JPAContainer
final JPAContainer<MyCalendarEvent> container =
    JPAContainerFactory.make(MyCalendarEvent.class,
                             "book-examples");

// Customize the event provider for adding events
// as entities
ContainerEventProvider cep =
        new ContainerEventProvider(container) {
    @Override
    public void addEvent(CalendarEvent event) {
        MyCalendarEvent entity = new MyCalendarEvent(
            event.getCaption(), event.getDescription(),
            event.getStart(), event.getEnd(),
            event.getStyleName());
        container.addEntity(entity);
    }
}

// Set the container as the data source
calendar.setEventProvider(cep);

// Now we can add events to the database through the calendar
BasicEvent event = new BasicEvent("The Event", "Single Event",
    new GregorianCalendar(2012,1,15,12,00).getTime(),
    new GregorianCalendar(2012,1,15,14,00).getTime());
calendar.addEvent(event);
```

16.4. Implementing an Event Provider

If the two simple ways of storing and managing events for a calendar are not enough, you may need to implement a custom event provider. It is the most flexible way of providing events. You need to attach the event provider to the **Calendar** using the setEvent-Provider() method.

Event queries are done by asking the event provider for all the events between two given dates. The range of these dates is guaranteed to be at least as long as the start and end dates set for the component. The component can, however, ask for a longer range to ensure correct rendering. In particular, all start dates are expanded to the start of the day, and all end dates are expanded to the end of the day.

16.4.1. Custom Events

An event provider could use the built-in **BasicEvent**, but it is usually more proper to define a custom event type that is bound directly to the data source. Custom events may be useful for some other purposes as well, such as when you need to add extra information to an event or customize how it is acquired.

Custom events must implement the `CalendarEvent` interface or extend an existing event class. The built-in **BasicEvent** class should serve as a good example of implementing simple events. It keeps the data in member variables.

```java
public class BasicEvent
        implements CalendarEventEditor, EventChangeNotifier {
    ...

    public String getCaption() {
        return caption;
    }

    public String getDescription() {
        return description;
    }

    public Date getEnd() {
        return end;
    }

    public Date getStart() {
        return start;
    }

    public String getStyleName() {
        return styleName;
    }

    public boolean isAllDay() {
        return isAllDay;
    }

    public void setCaption(String caption) {
        this.caption = caption;
        fireEventChange();
    }

    public void setDescription(String description) {
        this.description = description;
        fireEventChange();
    }

    public void setEnd(Date end) {
        this.end = end;
        fireEventChange();
    }

    public void setStart(Date start) {
        this.start = start;
        fireEventChange();
    }
```

```
public void setStyleName(String styleName) {
    this.styleName = styleName;
    fireEventChange();
}

public void setAllDay(boolean isAllDay) {
    this.isAllDay = isAllDay;
    fireEventChange();
}

public void addListener(EventChangeListener listener) {
    ...
}

public void removeListener(EventChangeListener listener) {
    ...
}

protected void fireEventChange() {...}
}
```

You may have noticed that there was some additional code in the **BasicEvent** that was not in the `CalendarEvent` interface. Namely **BasicEvent** also implements two additional interfaces:

`CalendarEditor`
> This interface defines setters for all the fields, and is required for some of the default handlers to work.

`EventChangeNotifier`
> This interface adds the possibility to listen for changes in the event, and enables the **Calendar** to render the changes immediately.

The start time and end time are mandatory, but caption, description, and style name are not. The style name is used as a part of the CSS class name for the HTML DOM element of the event.

In addition to the basic event interfaces, you can enhance the functionality of your event and event provider classes by using the **EventChange** and **EventSetChange** events. They let the **Calendar** component to know about changes in events and update itself accordingly. The **BasicEvent** and **BasicEventProvider** examples given earlier include a simple implementation of these interfaces.

16.4.2. Implementing the Event Provider

An event provider needs to implement the `CalendarEventProvider` interface. It has only one method to be implemented. Whenever the calendar is painted, getEvents(Date, Date) method is called and it must return a list of events between the given start and end time.

The following example implementation returns only one example event. The event starts from the current time and is five hours long.

```
public class MyEventProvider implements CalendarEventProvider{
    public List<Event> getEvents(Date startDate, Date endDate){
        List<Event> events = new ArrayList<Event>();
        GregorianCalendar cal = new GregorianCalendar();
        cal.setTime(new Date());

        Date start = cal.getTime();
        cal.add(GregorianCalendar.HOUR, 5);
        Date end = cal.getTime();
        BasicEvent event = new BasicEvent();
        event.setCaption("My Event");
        event.setDescription("My Event Description");
        event.setStart(start);
        event.setEnd(end);
        events.add(event);

        return events;
    }
}
```

It is important to notice that the **Calendar** may query for dates beyond the range defined by start date and end date. Particularly, it may expand the date range to make sure the user interface is rendered correctly.

16.5. Configuring the Appearance

Configuring the appearance of the Vaadin Calendar component is one of the basic tasks. At the least, you need to consider its sizing in your user interface. You also quite probably want to use some color or colors for events.

16.5.1. Sizing

The Vaadin Calendar supports the dynamic size system of Vaadin, with both defined and undefined sizes. When using defined sizes, the Calendar calculates the correct height for the cells so that it fits to the size given.

When using an undefined size for the calendar, all the sizes come from CSS. In addition, when the height is undefined, a scrollbar is displayed in the weekly view to better fit the cells to the user inter-

---

face. See the section called "Style for Undefined Size" for information about customizing the undefined sizes.

16.5.2. Styling

The Calendar has a default theme defined in the widget set. You may choose to overwrite the style names from the default theme file `calendar.css`. The file is located in a folder named `public` under the `src` folder in the JAR file. Vaadin will find the CSS from inside the JAR package.

Style for Undefined Size

Usually, you do not need to overwrite any of the default styles, but a Calendar with undefined size is a exception. Below is a list of style names that define the size of a Calendar with undefined size (these are the defaults from `calendar.css`):

```css
.v-calendar-month-sizedheight .v-calendar-month-day {
  height: 100px;
}

.v-calendar-month-sizedwidth .v-calendar-month-day {
  width: 100px;
}

.v-calendar-header-month-Hsized .v-calendar-header-day {
  width: 101px;
}

/* for IE */
.v-ie6 .v-calendar-header-month-Hsized .v-calendar-header-day {
  width: 104px;
}

/* for others */
.v-calendar-header-month-Hsized td:first-child {
  padding-left: 21px;
}

.v-calendar-header-day-Hsized {
  width: 200px;
}

.v-calendar-week-numbers-Vsized .v-calendar-week-number {
  height: 100px;
  line-height: 100px;
}

.v-calendar-week-wrapper-Vsized {
  height: 400px;
  overflow-x: hidden !important;
}
```

```
.v-calendar-times-Vsized .v-calendar-time {
  height: 38px;
}

.v-calendar-times-Hsized .v-calendar-time {
  width: 42px;
}

.v-calendar-day-times-Vsized .v-slot,.v-calendar-day-times-Vsized
.v-slot-even {
  height: 18px;
}

.v-calendar-day-times-Hsized, .v-calendar-day-times-Hsized .v-
slot,.v-calendar-day-times-Hsized .v-slot-even {
  width: 200px;
}
```

Event Style

Events can be styled with CSS by setting them a *style name suffix*.
The suffix is retrieved with the `getStyleName()` method in `Calen-
darEvent`. If you use **BasicEvent** events, you can set the suffix
with `setStyleName()`.

```
BasicEvent event = new BasicEvent("Wednesday Wonder", ...
);
event.setStyleName("mycolor");
calendar.addEvent(event);
```

Suffix `mycolor` would create `v-calendar-event-mycolor` class
for regular events and `v-calendar-event-mycolor-add-day` for
all-day events. You could style the events with the following rules:

```
.v-calendar .v-calendar-event-mycolor {}
.v-calendar .v-calendar-event-mycolor-all-day {}
.v-calendar .v-calendar-event-mycolor .v-calendar-event-caption {}
.v-calendar .v-calendar-event-mycolor .v-calendar-event-content {}
```

16.5.3. Visible Hours and Days

As we saw in Section 16.3.1, "Setting the Date Range", you can
set the range of dates that are shown by the Calendar. But what
if you wanted to show the entire month but hide the weekends? Or
show only hours from 8 to 16 in the weekly view? The `setVis-
ibleDays()` and `setVisibleHours()` methods allow you to do
that.

```
calendar.setVisibleDays(1,5);   // Monday to Friday
calendar.setVisibleHours(0,15); // Midnight until 4 pm
```

After the above settings, only weekdays from Monday to Friday would be shown. And when the calendar is in the weekly view, only the time range from 00:00 to 16:00 would be shown.

Note that the excluded times are never shown so you should take care when setting the date range. If the date range contains only dates / times that are excluded, nothing will be displayed. Also note that even if a date is not rendered because these settings, the event provider may still be queried for events for that date.

16.6. Drag and Drop

Vaadin Calendar can act as a drop target for drag and drop, described in Section 12.11, "Drag and Drop". With the functionality, the user could drag events, for example, from a table to a calendar.

To support dropping, a **Calendar** must have a drop handler. When the drop handler is set, the days in the monthly view and the time slots in the weekly view can receive drops. Other locations, such as day names in the weekly view, can not currently receive drops.

Calendar uses its own implementation of `TargetDetails`: **CalendarTargetdetails**. It holds information about the the drop location, which in the context of **Calendar** means the date and time. The drop target location can be retrieved via the `getDropTime()` method. If the drop is done in the monthly view, the returned date does not have exact time information. If the drop happened in the weekly view, the returned date also contains the start time of the slot.

Below is a short example of creating a drop handler and using the drop information to create a new event:

```
private Calendar createDDCalendar() {
  Calendar calendar = new Calendar();
  calendar.setDropHandler(new DropHandler() {
    public void drop(DragAndDropEvent event) {
      CalendarTargetDetails details =
              (CalendarTargetDetails) event.getTargetDetails();

      TableTransferable transferable =
              (TableTransferable) event.getTransferable();

      createEvent(details, transferable);
      removeTableRow(transferable);
    }
```

```
    public AcceptCriterion getAcceptCriterion() {
      return AcceptAll.get();
    }

  });

  return calendar;
}


protected void createEvent(CalendarTargetDetails details,
  TableTransferable transferable) {
  Date dropTime = details.getDropTime();
  java.util.Calendar timeCalendar = details.getTargetCalendar()
                        .getInternalCalendar();
  timeCalendar.setTime(dropTime);
  timeCalendar.add(java.util.Calendar.MINUTE, 120);
  Date endTime = timeCalendar.getTime();

  Item draggedItem = transferable.getSourceComponent().
                        getItem(transferable.getItemId());

  String eventType = (String)draggedItem.
                        getItemProperty("type").getValue();

  String eventDescription = "Attending: "
            + getParticipantString(
                (String[]) draggedItem.
                  getItemProperty("participants").getValue());

  BasicEvent newEvent = new BasicEvent();
  newEvent.setAllDay(!details.hasDropTime());
  newEvent.setCaption(eventType);
  newEvent.setDescription(eventDescription);
  newEvent.setStart(dropTime);
  newEvent.setEnd(endTime);

  BasicEventProvider ep = (BasicEventProvider) details
                    .getTargetCalendar().getEventProvider();
  ep.addEvent(newEvent);
}
```

16.7. Using the Context Menu

Vaadin Calendar allows the use of context menu (mouse right-click)
to manage events. As in other context menus in Vaadin, the menu
items are handled in Vaadin as *actions* by an *action handler*. To
enable a context menu, you have to implement a Vaadin Ac-
tion.Handler and add it to the calendar with addActionHand-
ler().

An action handler must implement two methods: getActions()
and handleAction(). The getActions() is called for each day
displayed in the calendar view. It should return a list of allowed

---

actions for that day, that is, the items of the context menu. The *target* parameter is the context of the click - a **CalendarDateRange** that spans over the day. The *sender* is the **Calendar** object.

The handleActions() receives the target context in the *target*. If the context menu was opened on an event, the target is the Event object, otherwise it is a **CalendarDateRange**.

16.8. Localization and Formatting

16.8.1. Setting the Locale and Time Zone

Month and weekday names are shown in the language of the locale setting of the **Calendar**. The translations are acquired from the standard Java locale data. By default, **Calendar** uses the system default locale for its internal calendar, but you can change it with setLocale(Locale locale). Setting the locale will update also other location specific date and time settings, such as the first day of the week, time zone, and time format. However, time zone and time format can be overridden by settings in the **Calendar**.

For example, the following would set the language to US English:

```
cal.setLocale(Locale.US);
```

The locale defines the default time zone. You can change it with the setTimeZone() method, which takes a **java.util.TimeZone** object as its parameter. Setting timezone to null will reset timezone to the locale default.

For example, the following would set the Finnish time zone, which is EET

```
cal.setTimeZone(TimeZone.getTimeZone("Europe/Hel-
sinki"));
```

16.8.2. Time and Date Caption Format

The time may be shown either in 24 or 12 hour format. The default format is defined by the locale, but you can change it with the setTimeFormat() method. Giving a null setting will reset the time format to the locale default.

```
cal.setTimeFormat(TimeFormat.Format12H);
```

You can change the format of the date captions in the week view with the `setWeeklyCaptionFormat(String dateFormatPattern)` method. The date format pattern should follow the format of the standard Java **java.text.SimpleDateFormat** class.

For example:

```
cal.setWeeklyCaptionFormat("dd-MM-yyyy");
```

16.9. Customizing the Calendar

In this section, we give a tutorial for how to make various basic customizations of the Vaadin Calendar. The event provider and styling was described earlier, so now we concentrate on other features of the Calendar API.

We use example code to demonstrate the customizations. You can find the source code of the example application on-line with the name `CustomizedCalendarDemo` at `http://dev.vaadin.com/svn/addons/Calendar`. Some of the less important code for this document has been left out to make the code more readable and shorter.

16.9.1. Overview of Handlers

Most of the handlers related to calendar events have sensible default handlers. These are found in the com.vaadin.ui.handler package. The default handlers and their functionalities are described below.

- **BasicBackwardHandler**. Handles clicking the back-button of the weekly view so that the viewed month is changed to the previous one.

- **BasicForwardHandler**. Handles clicking the forward-button of the weekly view so that the viewed month is changed to the next one.

- **BasicWeekClickHandler**. Handles clicking the week numbers int the monthly view so that the viewable date range is changed to the clicked week.

- **BasicDateClickHandler**. Handles clicking the dates on both the monthly view and the weekly view. Changes the viewable date range so that only the clicked day is visible.

- **BasicEventMoveHandler**. Handles moving the events in both monthly view and the weekly view. Events can be moved and their start and end dates are changed correctly, but only if the event implements **CalendarEventEditor** (implemented by **BasicEvent**).

- **BasicEventResizeHandler**. Handles resizing the events in the weekly view. Events can be resized and their start and end dates are changed correctly, but only if the event implements **CalendarEventEditor** (implemented by the **BasicEvent**).

All of these handlers are automatically set when creating a new **Calendar**. If you wish to disable some of the default functionality, you can simply set the corresponding handler to `null`. This will prevent the functionality from ever appearing on the user interface. For example, if you set the **EventMoveHandler** to `null`, the user will be unable to move events in the browser.

16.9.2. Creating a Calendar

Let us first create a new **Calendar** instance. Here we use our own event provider, the **MyEventProvider** described in Section 16.4.2, "Implementing the Event Provider".

```
Calendar cal = new Calendar(new MyEventProvider());
```

This initializes the Calendar. To customize the viewable date range, we must set a start and end date to it.

There is only one visible event in the timeline, starting from the current time. That is what our event provider passes to the client.

It would be nice to also be able to control the navigation forward and backward. The default navigation is provided by the default handlers, but perhaps we want to restrict the users so they can only navigate dates in the current year. Maybe we also want to pose some other restrictions to the clicking week numbers and dates.

These restrictions and other custom logic can be defined with custom handlers. You can find the handlers in the com.vaadin.ad-don.calendar.ui.handler package and they can be easily extended. Note that if you don not want to extend the default handlers, you are free to implement your own. The interfaces are described in `CalendarComponentEvents`.

16.9.3. Backward and Forward Navigation

Vaadin Calendar has only limited built-in navigation support. The weekly view has navigation buttons in the top left and top right corners.

You can handle backward and forward navigation with a `Backward-Listener` and `ForwardListener`.

```
cal.setHandler(new BasicBackwardHandler() {
  protected void setDates(BackwardEvent event,
                          Date start, Date end) {

    java.util.Calendar calendar = event.getComponent()
                                      .getInternalCalendar();
    if (isThisYear(calendar, end)
        && isThisYear(calendar, start)) {
      super.setDates(event, start, end);
    }
  }});
```

The forward navigation handler can be implemented in the same way. The example handler restricts the dates to the current year.

16.9.4. Date Click Handling

By default, clicking a date either in month or week view switches single-day view. The date click event is handled by a `DateClick-Handler`.

The following example handles click events so that when the user clicks the date header in the weekly view, it will switch to single-day view, and in the single-day view switch back to the weekly view.

```
cal.setHandler(new BasicDateClickHandler() {
  public void dateClick(DateClickEvent event) {
    Calendar cal = event.getComponent();
    long currentCalDateRange = cal.getEndDate().getTime()
                             - cal.getStartDate().getTime();

    if (currentCalDateRange < VCalendar.DAYINMILLIS) {
```

```
        // Change the date range to the current week
        cal.setStartDate(cal.getFirstDateForWeek(event.getDate()));
        cal.setEndDate(cal.getLastDateForWeek(event.getDate()));

    } else {
        // Default behaviour, change date range to one day
        super.dateClick(event);
    }
  }
});
```

16.9.5. Handling Week Clicks

The monthly view displays week numbers for each week row on
the left side of the date grid. The week number are clickable and
you can handle the click events by setting a WeekClickHandler
for the **Calendar** object. The default handler changes the date
range to be the clicked week.

In the following example, we add a week click handler that changes
the date range of the calendar to one week only if the start and
end dates of the week are in the current month.

```
cal.setHandler(new BasicWeekClickHandler() {
    protected void setDates(WeekClick event,
                           Date start, Date end) {
        java.util.Calendar calendar = event.getComponent()
                               .getInternalCalendar();
        if (isThisMonth(calendar, start)
            && isThisMonth(calendar, end)) {
            super.setDates(event, start, end);
        }
    }
});
```

16.9.6. Handling Event Clicks

The calendar events in all views are are clickable. There is no default handler. Just like the date and week click handlers, event
click handling is enabled by setting an EventClickHandler for
the **Calendar** object.

You can get hold of the clicked event by the getCalendarEvent()
method in the **EventClick** object passed to the handler, as shown
in the following example.

```
cal.addListener(new EventClickListener() {
    public void eventClick(EventClick event) {
        BasicEvent e = (BasicEvent) event.getCalendarEvent();

        // Do something with it
```

```
          new Notification("Event clicked: " + e.getCaption(),
              e.getDescription()).show(Page.getCurrent());
    }
});
```

16.9.7. Event Dragging

The user can drag an event to change its position in time. The default handler sets the start and end time of the event accordingly. You can do many things with a custom move handler, such as restrict moving events.

In the following example, we add a `EventMoveHandler` to a **Calendar**. The event handler updates the new position to the datasource, but only if the new dates are in the current month. This requires making some changes to the event provider class.

```
cal.setHandler(new BasicEventMoveHandler() {
  private java.util.Calendar javaCalendar;

  public void eventMove(MoveEvent event) {
    javaCalendar = event.getComponent().getInternalCalendar();
    super.eventMove(event);
  }

  protected void setDates(CalendarEventEditor event,
                          Date start, Date end) {
    if (isThisMonth(javaCalendar, start)
        && isThisMonth(javaCalendar, end)) {
      super.setDates(event, start, end);
    }
  }
});
```

For the above example to work, the example event provider presented earlier needs to be changed slightly so that it doesn't always create a new event when `getEvents()` is called.

```
public static class MyEventProvider
              implements CalendarEventProvider {
  private List<CalendarEvent> events =
      new ArrayList<CalendarEvent>();

  public MyEventProvider() {
    events = new ArrayList<CalendarEvent>();
    GregorianCalendar cal = new GregorianCalendar();
    cal.setTime(new Date());

    Date start = cal.getTime();
    cal.add(GregorianCalendar.HOUR, 5);
    Date end = cal.getTime();
    BasicEvent event = new BasicEvent();
    event.setCaption("My Event");
```

```
    event.setDescription("My Event Description");
    event.setStart(start);
    event.setEnd(end);
    events.add(event);
}

public void addEvent(CalendarEvent BasicEvent) {
    events.add(BasicEvent);
}

public List<CalendarEvent> getEvents(Date startDate,
                                     Date endDate) {
    return events;
}
}
```

After these changes, the user can move events around as earlier, but dropping an event, the start and end dates are checked by the server. Note that as the server-side must move the event in order for it to render to the place it was dropped. The server can also reject moves by not doing anything when the event is received.

16.9.8. Handling Drag Selection

Drag selection works both in the monthly and weekly views. To listen for drag selection, you can add a `RangeSelectListener` to the **Calendar**. There is no default handler for range select.

In the code example below, we create an new event when any date range is selected. Drag selection opens a window where the user is asked for a caption for the new event. After confirming, the new event is be passed to the event provider and calendar is updated. Note that as our example event provider and event classes do not implement the event change interface, we must refresh the **Calendar** manually after changing the events.

```
cal.setHandler(new RangeSelectHandler() {
  public void rangeSelect(RangeSelectEvent event) {
    BasicEvent calendarEvent = new BasicEvent();
    calendarEvent.setStart(event.getStart());
    calendarEvent.setEnd(event.getEnd());

    // Create popup window and add a form in it.
    VerticalLayout layout = new VerticalLayout();
    layout.setMargin(true);
    layout.setSpacing(true);

    final Window w = new Window(null, layout);
    ...

    // Wrap the calendar event to a BeanItem
    // and pass it to the form
```

```
        final BeanItem<CalendarEvent> item =
                        new BeanItem<CalendarEvent>(myEvent);

        final Form form = new Form();
        form.setItemDataSource(item);
        ...

        layout.addComponent(form);

        HorizontalLayout buttons = new HorizontalLayout();
        buttons.setSpacing(true);
        buttons.addComponent(new Button("OK", new ClickListener() {

            public void buttonClick(ClickEvent event) {
                form.commit();
                // Update event provider's data source
                provider.addEvent(item.getBean());
                // Calendar needs to be repainted
                cal.requestRepaint();
                getMainWindow().removeWindow(w);
            }
        }));

    ...
  }
});
```

16.9.9. Resizing Events

The user can resize an event by dragging from both ends to
change its start or end time. This offers a convenient way to change
event times without the need to type anything. The default resize
handler sets the start and end time of the event according to the
resize.

In the example below, we set a custom handler for resize events.
The handler prevents any event to be resized over 12 hours in
length. Note that this does not prevent the user from resizing an
event over 12 hours in the client. The resize will just be corrected
by the server.

```
cal.setHandler(new BasicEventResizeHandler() {
  private static final long twelveHoursInMs = 12*60*60*1000;

  protected void setDates(CalendarEventEditor event,
                    Date start, Date end) {
    long eventLength = end.getTime() - start.getTime();
    if (eventLength <= twelveHoursInMs) {
      super.setDates(event, start, end);
    }
  }
});
```

Chapter 17

Vaadin Timeline

17.1. Overview

Vaadin Timeline is an add-on component that gives the user an intuitive understanding of events and trends. A timeline consists of a time-axis depicting a desired time range and some events or values mapped to the time range.

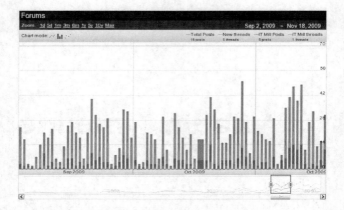

Figure 17.1. Vaadin Timeline Add-On Component

A timeline allows representing time-related data visually as graphs instead of numerical values. They are used commonly in almost all fields of business, science, and technology, such as in project management to map out milestones and goals, in geology to map out historical events, and perhaps most prominently in the stock market.

With Vaadin Timeline, you can represent almost any time-related statistical data that has a time-value mapping. Even several data sources can be used for comparison between data. This allows the user to better grasp of changes in the data and antipate forthcoming trends and problems.

Vaadin Timeline can be easily included in a Vaadin application and is highly customizable to suit almost any purpose. Timeline supports multiple graph types as well as events and markers. The user interaction with the Timeline is straight-forward and simple.

Book of Vaadin currently includes only an introduction to Vaadin Timeline. Please refer to the product documentation included in the installation package for further details.

Licensing

Vaadin Timeline is a commercial product licensed under a dual-licensing scheme. The AGPL (GNU Affero General Public License) allows open-source development. CVAL (Commercial Vaadin Add-On License) needs to be purchased for closed-source use, including web deployments as well as intranet use.

Commercial licenses can be purchased from the Vaadin Directory, where you can also find the license details and download the Vaadin Timeline.

Graph types

The Vaadin Timeline supports three graph types:

Line graphs
> Useful for representing continuous data, such as temperature changes or changes in stock price.

Bar graphs
> Useful for representing discrete or discontinuous data, such as market share or forum posts.

Scatter graphs
> Useful for representing discrete or discontinuous data.

If you have several graphs in the timeline, you can also stack them on top of each other instead of drawing them on top of each other by setting `setGraphStacking()` in **Timeline** to `true`.

Interaction Elements

The user can interact with the Vaadin Timeline in several ways.

On the bottom of the timeline there is a *scrollbar area* where you can move the time forward or backward in time by dragging the time range box or by clicking the left and right arrow buttons. You can change the time range by resizing the range box in the scrollbar area. You can also zoom with the mouse wheel when the pointer is inside the component.

Figure 17.2. Scrollbar Area

The middle area of the timeline is the *main area* where the selected time range is displayed. Time scale is shown below the main area. The time scale used depends on the zoom level and can be a time unit from hours to years. Value scale is displayed on the right side of the main area. The scale can be either a static value range or a range calculated from the displayed data set. The user can move in time by dragging the main area with the mouse left and right and zoom in and out by using the mouse wheel.

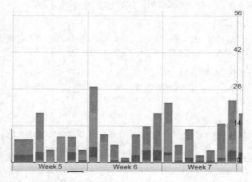

Figure 17.3. Main Area

You can select a *preset zoom level* with the buttons on the top the Timeline. This will change the displayed time range to match the zoom level. The zoom levels are fully customizable to suit the time range in the API.

Figure 17.4. Preset Zoom Buttons

The *current time range* is shown at the top-right corner of the component. Clicking the dates makes them editable, so that you can manually change them. *Graph legend* is shown below the time range. The legend explains what is represented by each bar on the graph and displays the current value when the user moves the mouse cursor over the graph.

Figure 17.5. Current Time Range and Graph Legend

Finally, the available *chart modes* are shown below the preset zoom levels options. The available graph modes can be set from the API.

Figure 17.6. Chart Mode

You can use or hide any of the features above can be shown or hidden depending on your needs. For example, if you only need to display a graph without any controls, you can hide all them from the API.

Event Markers

In addition to graphs, the timeline can have events. An event can be, for example, the time of a published advertisement in a graph that displays website hits. Combining the event data with the graphs enables the user to observe the relevance of the advertisement to the website hits visually.

Vaadin Timeline provides two types of event markers, as illustrated in Figure 17.7, "Timeline Event Markers".

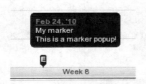 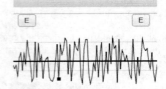

Figure 17.7. Timeline Event Markers

(On left) Marker with a customizable marker sign, for example, letter 'E'. The marker displays a caption which appears when the user hovers the pointer over the event.

(On right) Marker with button-like appearance with a marker sign and a caption.

Efficiency

Vaadin Timeline reduces the traffic between the server and the client by using two methods.

First of all, all the data that is presented in the component is dynamically fetched from the server as needed. This means that when the user scrolls the timeline view, the component continuously fetches data from the server. Also, only data that is visible to the user is transferred to the client. For example, if the timeline has data that has been measured once a second for an entire year, not all the data will be sent to the client. Only the data which can be rendered on the screen without overlapping is sent. This ensures that, even for large data sets, the loading time is small and only the necessary data is actually transferred over the network.

Second, Vaadin Timeline caches the data received from the server in the browser, so that the data is transferred over the network only once, if possible. This speeds up the time-range browsing when data can be fetched from the cache instead of reloading it over the network.

17.2. Using Timeline

17.2.1. Data Source Requirements

Vaadin Timeline uses Vaadin containers as data sources for both the graphs and the events. There are, however, some requirements for the containers to make them compatible with the Vaadin Timeline.

The containers have to implement `Container.Indexed` for the Vaadin Timeline to be able to use them. This is because the Vaadin Timeline dynamically fetches the data from the server when needed. This way large data sets can be used without having to load all data to the client-side at once and it brings a huge performance increase.

Another requirement is that the container has one property of type **java.util.Date** (or a class that can be cast to it), which contains the timestamp when a data point or event occurred. This property has to be set by using the `setGraphTimestampPropertyId()` in **Timeline**. The default property ID `timeline.Property-Id.TIMESTAMP` is used if no timestamp-property ID has been set.

A graph container also needs to have a *value* property that defines the value of the data point. This value can be any numerical value. The value property can be set with `setGraphValuePropertyId()` in **Timeline**. The default property ID `Timeline.PropertyId.VALUE` is used if no value property is given.

Below is an example of how a graph container could be constructed:

```
// Construct a container which implements Container.Indexed
IndexedContainer container = new IndexedContainer();

// Add the Timestamp property to the container
Object timestampProperty = "Our timestamp property";
container.addContainerProperty(timestampProperty,
                               java.util.Date.class, null);

// Add the value property
Object valueProperty = "Our value property";
container.addContainerProperty(valueProperty, Float.class, null);

// Our timeline
Timeline timeline = new Timeline();

// Add the container as a graph container
```

```
timeline.addGraphDataSource(container, timestampProperty,
                            valueProperty);
```

The event and marker containers are similar. They both need the *timestamp* property which should be of type **java.util.Date** and the *caption* property which should be a string. The marker container additionally needs a *value* property which is displayed in the marker popup.

Below is an example on how a marker or event container can be constructed:

```
// Create the container
IndexedContainer container = new IndexedContainer();

// Add the timestamp property
container.addContainerProperty(Timeline.PropertyId.TIMESTAMP,
                               Date.class, null);

// Add the caption property
container.addContainerProperty(Timeline.PropertyId.CAPTION,
                               String.class, "");

// Add the marker specific value property.
// Not needed for a event containers.
container.addContainerProperty(Timeline.PropertyId.VALUE,
                               String.class, "");

// Create the timeline with the container as both the marker
// and event data source
Timeline timeline = new Timeline();
timeline.setMarkerDataSource(container,
 Timeline.PropertyId.TIMESTAMP,
 Timeline.PropertyId.CAPTION,
 Timeline.PropertyId.VALUE);

timeline.setEventDataSource(container,
 Timeline.PropertyId.TIMESTAMP,
 Timeline.PropertyId.CAPTION);
```

The above example uses the default property IDs. You can change them to suit your needs.

The **Timeline** listens for changes in the containers and updates the graph accordingly. When it updates the graph and items are added or removed from the container, the currently selected date range will remain selected. The selection bar in the browser area moves to keep the current selection selected. If you want the selection to change when the contents of the container changes and keep the selection area stationary, you can disable the selection lock by setting setBrowserSelectionLock() to *false*.

17.2.2. Events and Listeners

Two types of events are available when using the Vaadin Timeline.

When the user modifies the selected date range by moving the date range selector, dragging the timeline, or by manually entering new dates, an event will be sent to the server with the information of what the current displayed date range is. To listen to these events you can attach a **DateRangeListener** which will receive the start and end dates of the current selection.

If you are using events in your graph then you can attach an **EventClickListener** to listen for clicks on the events. The listener will receive a list of itemIds from the event data source which are related to the click event. Since the events can be gathered into a single event icon if space is not sufficient for displaying them all, many item ids can be returned.

17.2.3. Configurability

The Vaadin Timeline is highly customizable and its outlook can be easily changed to suit your needs. The default view of the Timeline contains all the controls available but often all of them are not needed and can be hidden.

The following list contains the components that can be shown or hidden at your preference:

- Chart modes

- Textual date select

- Browser area (bottom part of the Timeline)

- Legend

- Zoom levels

- Caption

The outlook of the graphs themselves can also be changed for both the browser area and the main view. The following settings are available through the API:

- Graph outline color

- Graph outline width

- Graph caps (in line graphs only)

- Graph fill color

- Graph visibility

- Graph shadows

Other changes to the outlook of the component can easily be done by CSS.

Zoom levels are also fully customizable. Zoom levels are defined as milliseconds and can be added by calling the `addZoomLevel()` method. A zoom level always has a caption, which is the visible part in the zoom panel, and a millisecond amount.

By default the grid divides the graph into five equally spaced parts with a gray color. However, you can fully customize how the grid is drawn by using `setGridColor()` and `setVerticalGridLines()`.

17.2.4. Localization

By default the Vaadin Timeline uses English as its primary language for the captions and the default locale for the application to display the dates in the timeline.

You can change the different captions in the Timeline by using their corresponding setters:

- `setZoomLevelsCaption()` -- The caption appearing before the zoom levels

- `setChartModesCaption()` -- The caption appearing before the chart modes

Furthermore, you can also change the locale in which the Timeline shows the dates in the horizontal scale by specifying a valid locale using the `setLocale()` method of the timeline.

You can also configure in what format the dates appear in the horizontal scale or in the date select in the top-right corner by using the getDateFormats()-method which will return a **DateFormatInfo** object. By using its setters you can set specific formats for each date range in the scale. Please note that if you are using long date formats they might get clipped if the scale does not fit the whole formatted date.

17.3. Code example

17.3.1. Prerequisites

To get started using the Vaadin Timeline component you should first download the Vaadin eclipse plugin and install it. More information on getting it can be found at http://vaadin.com/eclipse.

Once you got the plugin installed create an example project by selecting **File → New → Other** and select **Vaadin Project**. Lets call it **MyTimelineDemo**.

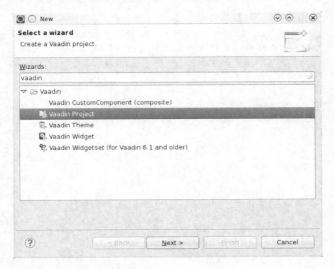

Figure 17.8. New Timeline Project

When the project is created you should add the Vaadin Timeline library to your project. This can be done by copying the timeline-

---

*.jar to the projects `WebContent/WEB-INF/lib` directory. When you copy the library into the folder you might get the message shown in Figure 17.9, "Widget set compilation".

Figure 17.9. Widget set compilation

You should answer Yes and let the widgetset get compiled. If you do not get the above message or you answer No then you have to compile the widgetset manually by selecting the icon. It might take a while until the widgetset gets compiled depending of how much resources your computer have.

Once the compilation is done the project file structure should look something as shown in Figure 17.10, "Timeline Example Project".

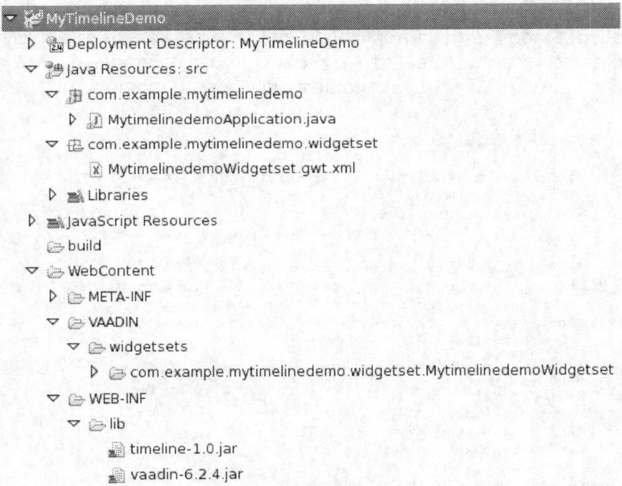

Figure 17.10. Timeline Example Project

Now you are ready to start developing with the Vaadin Timeline!

17.3.2. Create the data sources

To use the Vaadin Timeline you need to create some data sources for it. The Vaadin Timeline uses Container.Indexed containers as data sources for both the graphs and the markers and events. So lets start by creating a datasource which represents the graph we want to draw in the timeline.

For the Vaadin Timeline to understand how the data is constructed in the container we need to use specific property ids which describe what kind of data each property represents. For the Vaadin Timeline to work properly we will need to add two property ids, one for when the value was acquired and one for the value itself. The Vaadin Timeline has these both properties predefined as *Timeline.PropertyId.TIMESTAMP* and *Timeline.Property-Id.VALUE*. You can use the predefined ones or create your own if you wish.

So, lets create a container which meets the above stated specification. Open the main application class which was automatically created when we created the project (in our case `Mytimeline-demoApplication.java`) and add the following method.

```
/**
 * Creates a graph container with a month of random data
 */
public Container.Indexed createGraphDataSource(){

    // Create the container
    Container.Indexed container = new IndexedContainer();

    // Add the required property ids (use the default ones here)
    container.addContainerProperty(Timeline.PropertyId.TIMESTAMP,
        Date.class, null);
    container.addContainerProperty(Timeline.PropertyId.VALUE,
        Float.class, 0f);

    // Add some random data to the container
    Calendar cal = Calendar.getInstance();
    cal.add(Calendar.MONTH, -1);
    Date today = new Date();
    Random generator = new Random();

    while(cal.getTime().before(today)){
        // Create  a point in time
        Item item = container.addItem(cal.getTime());

        // Set the timestamp property
        item.getItemProperty(Timeline.PropertyId.TIMESTAMP)
            .setValue(cal.getTime());

        // Set the value property
        item.getItemProperty(Timeline.PropertyId.VALUE)
            .setValue(generator.nextFloat());

        cal.add(Calendar.DAY_OF_MONTH, 1);
    }

    return container;
}
```

This method will create an indexed container with some random points. As you can see we are using an **IndexedContainer** and define two properties to it which was discussed earlier. Then we just generate some random data in the container. Here we are using the default property ids for the timestamp and value but you could use your own if you wished. We'll see later how you would tell the Timeline which property ids to use if you used your own.

Next, lets add some markers to our graph. Markers are arrow like shapes in the bottom of the timeline with which you can mark some occurrence that happened at that time. To create markers you again have to create a data source for them. I'll first show you how the code to create them and then explain what it all means. Add the following method to the main Application class:

```
/**
 * Creates a marker container with a marker for each seven days
 *
 */
public Container.Indexed createMarkerDataSource(){

    // Create the container
    Container.Indexed container = new IndexedContainer();

    // Add the required property IDs (use the default ones here)
    container.addContainerProperty(Timeline.PropertyId.TIMESTAMP,
            Date.class, null);
    container.addContainerProperty(Timeline.PropertyId.CAPTION,
            String.class, "Our marker symbol");
    container.addContainerProperty(Timeline.PropertyId.VALUE,
            String.class, "Our description");

    // Add a marker for every seven days
    Calendar cal = Calendar.getInstance();
    cal.add(Calendar.MONTH, -1);
    Date today = new Date();
    SimpleDateFormat formatter =
            new SimpleDateFormat("EEE, MMM d, ''yy");
    while(cal.getTime().before(today)){
        // Create a point in time
        Item item = container.addItem(cal.getTime());

        // Set the timestamp property
        item.getItemProperty(Timeline.PropertyId.TIMESTAMP)
                .setValue(cal.getTime());

        // Set the caption property
        item.getItemProperty(Timeline.PropertyId.CAPTION)
                .setValue("M");

        // Set the value property
        item.getItemProperty(Timeline.PropertyId.VALUE).
            setValue("Today is "+formatter.format(cal.getTime()));

        cal.add(Calendar.DAY_OF_MONTH, 7);
    }

    return container;
}
```

Here we start the same as in the example with the graph container by creating an indexed container. Remember, all containers must be indexed containers when using the graph component.

We then add the timestamp property, caption property and value property.

The timestamp property is the same as in the graph container but the caption and value property differ. The caption property describes what kind of marker it is. The caption is displayed on top of the arrow shape in the Timeline so it should be a short symbol, preferably only one character long. The class of the caption property must be String.

The value property should also be a string and is displayed when the user hovers the mouse over the marker. This string can be arbitrarily long and normally should represent some kind of description of the marker.

The third kind of data sources are the event data sources. The events are displayed on top of the timeline and supports grouping and are clickable. They are represented as button like icons in the Timeline.

The event data sources are almost identical the to marker data sources except the value property is missing. Lets create an event data source and add events for each Sunday in out graph:

```
/**
 * Creates a event container with a marker for each sunday
 */
public Container.Indexed createEventDataSource(){

  // Create the container
  Container.Indexed container = new IndexedContainer();

  // Add the required property IDs (use the default ones here)
  container.addContainerProperty(Timeline.PropertyId.TIMESTAMP,
   Date.class, null);
  container.addContainerProperty(Timeline.PropertyId.CAPTION,
   String.class, "Our marker symbol");

  // Add a marker for every seven days
  Calendar cal = Calendar.getInstance();
  cal.add(Calendar.MONTH, -1);
  Date today = new Date();
  while(cal.getTime().before(today)){
   if(cal.get(Calendar.DAY_OF_WEEK) == Calendar.SUNDAY){
    // Create a point in time
    Item item = container.addItem(cal.getTime());

    // Set the timestamp property
    item.getItemProperty(Timeline.PropertyId.TIMESTAMP)
          .setValue(cal.getTime());
```

```
   // Set the caption property
   item.getItemProperty(Timeline.PropertyId.CAPTION)
    .setValue("Sunday");
 }
 cal.add(Calendar.DAY_OF_MONTH, 1);
}

return container;
}
```

As you can see the event container does not differ a whole lot from the marker containers. In use however they differ since they are groupable they can be closely put together and still be usable and you can add click listeners to them so you can catch user events. More on the click listeners later.

So now we have our three data sources ready to be displayed in our application. In the next chapter we will use them with our Timeline and see how they integrate with it.

17.3.3. Create the Vaadin Timeline

Okay, now that we have out data sources lets look at the init-method in our Vaadin Application. Lets start by creating our timeline, so add the following line to the end of the init-method in **MytimelinedemoApplication**:

```
Timeline timeline = new Timeline("Our timeline");
timeline.setWidth("100%");
```

This will create the timeline we want with a 100 percent width. Now lets add our data sources to the timeline:

```
timeline.addGraphDataSource(createGraphDataSource(),
                    Timeline.PropertyId.TIMESTAMP,
                    Timeline.PropertyId.VALUE);

timeline.setMarkerDataSource(createMarkerDataSource(),
                    Timeline.PropertyId.TIMESTAMP,
                    Timeline.PropertyId.CAPTION,
                    Timeline.PropertyId.VALUE);

timeline.setEventDataSource(createEventDataSource(),
                    Timeline.PropertyId.TIMESTAMP,

                    Timeline.PropertyId.CAPTION);
```

And finally add the timeline to the window. Here is the complete init-method:

```
@Override
public void init() {
    Window mainWindow = new Window("Mytimelinedemo Application");
    Label label = new Label("Hello Vaadin user");
    mainWindow.addComponent(label);
    setMainWindow(mainWindow);

    // Create the timeline
    Timeline timeline = new Timeline("Our timeline");

    // Create the data sources
    Container.Indexed graphDS  = createGraphDataSource();
    Container.Indexed markerDS = createMarkerDataSource();
    Container.Indexed eventDS  = createEventDataSource();

    // Add our data sources
    timeline.addGraphDataSource(graphDS,
                                Timeline.PropertyId.TIMESTAMP,
                                Timeline.PropertyId.VALUE);
    timeline.setMarkerDataSource(markerDS,
                                 Timeline.PropertyId.TIMESTAMP,
                                 Timeline.PropertyId.CAPTION,
                                 Timeline.PropertyId.VALUE);
    timeline.setEventDataSource(eventDS,
                                Timeline.PropertyId.TIMESTAMP,
                                Timeline.PropertyId.CAPTION);

    mainWindow.addComponent(timeline);
}
```

Now you should be able to start the application and browse the timeline. The result is shown in Figure 17.11, "Timeline Example Application".

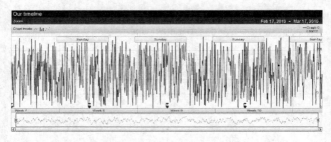

Figure 17.11. Timeline Example Application

17.3.4. Final Touches

Now that we have our timeline we would probably like to customize it a bit. There are many things you can do but lets start by giving our graph some style properties and a caption in the legend. This can be done as follows:

```
// Set the caption of the graph
timeline.setGraphLegend(graphDataSource, "Our cool graph");

// Set the color of the graph
timeline.setGraphOutlineColor(graphDataSource, Color.RED);

// Set the fill color of the graph
timeline.setGraphFillColor(graphDataSource, new Color(255,0,0,128));


// Set the width of the graph
timeline.setGraphOutlineThickness(2.0);
```

Lets do the same to the browser areas graph:

```
// Set the color of the browser graph
timeline.setBrowserOutlineColor(graphDataSource, Color.BLACK);

// Set the fill color of the graph
timeline.setBrowserFillColor(graphDataSource,
                             new Color(0,0,0,128));
```

And the result looks like this:

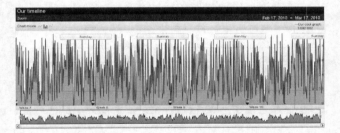

Figure 17.12. Styling Timeline

Okay, now that looks different. But there is still something missing. If you look in the upper left corner you will not see any zoom levels. No zoom levels are predefined so we will have to make our own. Since we are dealing with a month of data lets make a zoom level for a day, a week and a month. Zoom levels are given in milli-seconds so we will have to calculate how many milliseconds each of the zoom levels are. So lets add them by adding the following lines:

```
// Add some zoom levels
timeline.addZoomLevel("Day", 86400000L);
timeline.addZoomLevel("Week", 7 * 86400000L);
timeline.addZoomLevel("Month", 2629743830L);
```

Remember the events we added? You can now see them in the graph but their functionality is still a bit incomplete. We can add an event listener to the graph which will send an event each time the user clicks on one of the event buttons. To demonstrate this feature lets add an event listener which notifies the user what date the Sunday-button represents. Here is the code for that:

```
// Listen to click events from events
timeline.addListener(new Timeline.EventClickListener() {
    @Override
    public void eventClick(EventButtonClickEvent event) {
        Item item = eventDataSource.getItem(event.getItemIds()
                                .iterator().next());
        Date sunday = (Date) item.getItemProperty(
                    Timeline.PropertyId.TIMESTAMP).getValue();
        SimpleDateFormat formatter =
            new SimpleDateFormat("EEE, MMM d, ''yy");

        MyTimelineDemo.this.getMainWindow()
            .showNotification(formatter.format(sunday));
            }
    });
```

Now try clicking on the events and see what happens!

And here is the final demo application, yours will probably look a bit different since we are using random data.

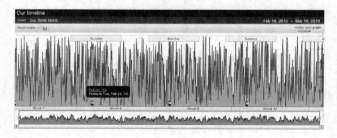

Figure 17.13. Final Example

Now we hope you have a basic understanding of how the Vaadin Timeline works and how it can be customized. There are still a few

---

features we left out of this tutorial like hiding unnecessary components from the timeline and adding multiple graphs to the timeline, but these are pretty self explanatory features and you probably can look them up in the JavaDoc.

We hope you enjoy the Vaadin Timeline and find it useful in your projects!

Vaadin JPAContainer

This chapter describes the use of the Vaadin JPAContainer add-on.

18.1. Overview

Vaadin JPAContainer add-on makes it possible to bind user interface components to a database easily using the Java Persistence API (JPA). It is an implementation of the `Container` interface described in Section 9.5, "Collecting Items in Containers". It supports a typical three-layer application architecture with an intermediate *domain model* between the user interface and the data access layer.

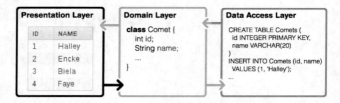

Figure 18.1. Three-Layer Architecture Using JPAContainer And JPA

The role of Java Persistence API is to handle persisting the domain model in the database. The database is typically a relational database. Vaadin JPAContainer binds the user interface components to the domain model and handles database access with JPA transparently.

JPA is really just an API definition and has many alternative implementations. Vaadin JPAContainer supports especially EclipseLink, which is the reference implementation of JPA, and Hibernate. Any other compliant implementation should work just as well. The architecture of an application using JPAContainer is shown in Figure 18.2, "JPAContainer Architecture".

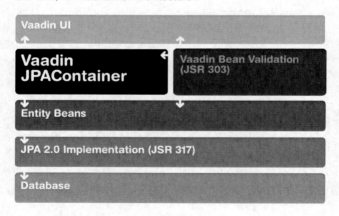

Figure 18.2. JPAContainer Architecture

Vaadin JPAContainer also plays together with the Vaadin Bean Validation add-on, which brings Java Bean Validation (JSR 303) to Vaadin applications.

Java Persistence API

Java Persistence API (JPA) is an API for object-relational mapping (ORM) of Java objects to a relational database. In JPA and entity-relationship modeling in general, a Java class is considered an *entity*. Class (or entity) instances correspond with a row in a database table and member variables of a class with columns. Entities can also have relationships with other entities.

The object-relational mapping is illustrated in Figure 18.3, "Object-Relational Mapping" with two entities with a one-to-many relationship.

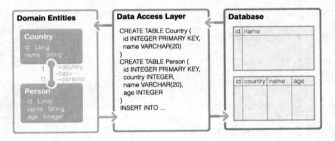

Figure 18.3. Object-Relational Mapping

The entity relationships are declared with metadata. With Vaadin JPAContainer, you provide the metadata with annotations in the entity classes. The JPA implementation uses reflection to read the annotations and defines a database model automatically from the class definitions. Definition of the domain model and the annotations are described in Section 18.3.1, "Persistence Metadata".

The main interface in JPA is the EntityManager, which allows making different kinds of queries either with the Java Persistence Query Language (JPQL), native SQL, or the Criteria API in JPA 2.0. You can always use the interface directly as well, using Vaadin JPAContainer only for binding the data to the user interface.

Vaadin JPAContainer supports JPA 2.0 (JSR 317).

JPAContainer Concepts

The **JPAContainer** is an implementation of the Vaadin `Container` interface that you can bind to user interface components such as **Table**, **Select**, etc.

The data access to the persistent entities is handled with a *entity provider*, as defined in the `EntityProvider` interface. JPAContainer provides a number of different entity providers for different use cases and optimizations. The built-in providers are described in Section 18.5, "Entity Providers".

Documentation and Support

In addition to this chapter in the book, the installation package includes the following documentation about JPAContainer:

- API Documentation

- JPAContainer Tutorial

- JPAContainer AddressBook Demo

- JPAContainer Demo

18.2. Installing

Vaadin JPAContainer can be installed either as an installation package, downloaded from the Vaadin Directory, or as a Maven dependency. You can also create a new JPAContainer-enabled Vaadin project using a Maven archetype.

18.2.1. Downloading the Package

Vaadin JPAContainer is available for download from the Vaadin Directory. Please see Section 15.2, "Downloading Add-ons from Vaadin Directory" for basic instructions for downloading from Directory. The download page also gives the dependency declaration needed for retrieving the library with Maven.

JPAContainer is a purely server-side component, so it does not include a widget set that you would need to compile.

Choosing the License

Vaadin JPAContainer is available under two licenses: Affero General Public License (AGPL) and Commercial Vaadin Add-on License (CVAL). If your project is compatible with the open-source AGPL, you can use the add-on for free. Otherwise you must acquire a sufficient number of CVAL licenses before the 30-day trial period ends. Vaadin JPAContainer is distributed as a separate installation package for each license.

Use of Vaadin JPAContainer with the CVAL license is included in the Vaadin PRO subscription.

18.2.2. Installation Package Content

Once extracted to a local folder, the contents of the installation directory are as follows:

README
: A readme file describing the package contents.

licensing.txt
: General information about licensing of JPAContainer.

license-xxxx-y.y.txt
: The full license text for the library.

vaadin-jpacontainer-xxxx-y.y-z.z.z.jar
: The actual Vaadin JPAContainer library. The xxxx is the license name and y.y its version number. The final z.z.z is the version number of the Vaadin JPAContainer.

vaadin-jpacontainer-xxxx-y.y-z.z.z-javadoc.jar
: JavaDoc documentation JAR for the library. You can use it for example in Eclipse by associating the JavaDoc JAR with the JPAContainer JAR in the build path settings of your project.

apidocs
: A folder containing the JavaDoc API documentation in plain HTML.

jpacontainer-tutorial.pdf
: The tutorial in PDF format.

```
jpacontainer-tutorial
```
> The tutorial in HTML format. The online version of the tutorial is always available at vaadin.com/download/jpacontainer-tutorial/.

```
jpacontainer-addressbook-demo
```
> The JPAContainer AddressBook Demo project covered in this tutorial. You can compile and package the application as a WAR with "**mvn** *package*" or launch it in the Jetty web browser with "**mvn** *jetty:run*". You can also import the demo project in Eclipse as described in the tutorial.

```
jpacontainer-demo-z.z.z.war
```
> The basic JPAContainer demo. It is somewhat more extensive than the AddressBook Demo.

18.2.3. Downloading with Maven

The download page in Vaadin Directory gives the dependency declaration needed for retrieving the Vaadin JPAContainer library with Maven. A separate dependency declaration is given for both available licenses for Vaadin JPAContainer.

For the CVAL License:

```
<dependency>
   <groupId>com.vaadin.addon</groupId>
   <artifactId>jpacontainer-addon-cval-2.0</artifactId>
   <version>2.0.0</version>
</dependency>
```

For the AGPL License:

```
<dependency>
   <groupId>com.vaadin.addon</groupId>
   <artifactId>jpacontainer-addon-agpl-3.0</artifactId>
   <version>2.0.0</version>
</dependency>
```

Use the LATEST version tag to automatically download the latest stable release or use a specific version number as done above.

See Section 15.5, "Using Add-ons in a Maven Project" for detailed instructions for using a Vaadin add-on with Maven.

Using the Maven Archetype

If you wish to create a new JPAContainer-enabled Vaadin project with Maven, you can use the `vaadin-archetype-jpacontainer` archetype. Please see Section 2.5, "Creating a Project with Maven" for details on creating a Vaadin project with a Maven archetype.

18.2.4. Including Libraries in Your Project

The Vaadin JPAContainer JAR must be included in the library folder of the web application. It is located in `WEB-INF/lib` path in a web application. In a normal Eclipse web projects the path is `WebContent/WEB-INF/lib`. In Maven projects the JARs are automatically included in the folder, as long as the dependencies are defined correctly.

You will need the following JARs:

- Vaadin Framework Library

- Vaadin JPAContainer

- Java Persistence API 2.0 (javax.persistence package)

- JPA implementation (EclipseLink, Hibernate, ...)

- Database driver or embedded engine (H2, HSQLDB, MySQL, PostgreSQL, ...)

If you use Eclipse, the Vaadin Framework library is automatically downloaded and updated by the Vaadin Plugin for Eclipse.

Optionally, you may need to also install the Vaadin BeanValidation add-on. If you do so, you also need an implementation of the Bean Validation, such as Hibernate Validator.

18.2.5. Persistence Configuration

Persistence configuration is done in a `persistence.xml` file. In a regular Eclipse project, it should be located in `WebContent/WEB-INF/classes/META-INF`. In a Maven project, it should be in `src/main/resources/META-INF`. The configuration includes the following:

- The persistence unit

- The persistence provider

- The database driver and connection

- Logging

The `persistence.xml` file is packaged as `WEB-INF/classes/META-INF/persistence.xml` in the WAR. This is done automatically in a Maven build at the package phase.

Persistence XML Schema

The beginning of a `persistence.xml` file defines the used schema and namespaces:

```
<?xml version="1.0" encoding="UTF-8"?>
<persistence
    xmlns="http://java.sun.com/xml/ns/persistence"
    xmlns:xsi="http://www.w3.org/2001/XMLSchema-instance"
    xsi:schemaLocation="
      http://java.sun.com/xml/ns/persistence
      http://java.sun.com/xml/ns/persistence/persist-
ence_2_0.xsd"
    version="2.0">
```

Defining the Persistence Unit

The root element of the persistence definition is persistence-unit. The name of the persistence unit is needed for creating **JPAContainer** instances from a **JPAContainerFactory**, as described in Section 18.4.1, "Creating **JPAContainer** with **JPAContainerFactory**" or when creating a JPA entity manager.

```
<persistence-unit name="addressbook">
```

Persistence provider is the JPA provider implementation used. For example, the JPAContainer AddressBook demo uses the EclipseLink JPA, which is defined as follows:

```
<provider>
    org.eclipse.persistence.jpa.PersistenceProvider
</provider>
```

The persistent classes need to be listed with a `<class>` element. Alternatively, you can allow including unlisted classes for persistence by overriding the `exclude-unlisted-classes` default as follows:

```
<exclude-unlisted-classes>false</exclude-unlisted-classes>
```

JPA provider specific parameters are given under the `properties` element.

```
<properties>
  ...
```

In the following section we give parameters for the EclipseLink JPA and H2 database used in the JPAContainer AddressBook Demo. Please refer to the documentation of the JPA provider you use for a complete reference of parameters.

Database Connection

EclipseLink allows using JDBC for database connection. For example, if we use the the H2 database, we define its driver here as follows:

```
<property name="eclipselink.jdbc.platform"
 value="org.eclipse.persistence.platform.database.H2Platform"/>
<property name="eclipselink.jdbc.driver"
         value="org.h2.Driver" />
```

Database connection is specified with a URL. For example, using an embedded H2 database stored in the home directory it would be as follows:

```
<property name="eclipselink.jdbc.url"
         value="jdbc:h2:~/my-app-h2db"/>
```

A hint: when using an embedded H2 database while developing a Vaadin application in Eclipse, you may want to add `;FILE_LOCK=NO` to the URL to avoid locking issues when redeploying.

We can just use the default user name and password for the H2 database:

```
<property name="eclipselink.jdbc.user" value="sa"/>
<property name="eclipselink.jdbc.password" value="sa"/>
```

Logging Configuration

JPA implementations as well as database engines like to produce logs and they should be configured in the persistence configuration. For example, if using EclipseLink JPA, you can get log that includes all SQL statements with the FINE logging level:

```
<property name="eclipselink.logging.level"
          value="FINE" />
```

Other Settings

The rest is some Data Definition Language settings for EclipseLink. During development, when we use generated example data, we want EclipseLink to drop tables before trying to create them. In production environments, you should use create-tables.

```
<property name="eclipselink.ddl-generation"
          value="drop-and-create-tables" />
```

And there is no need to generate SQL files, just execute them directly to the database.

```
<property name="eclipselink.ddl-generation.output-mode"
          value="database"/>
    </properties>
  </persistence-unit>
</persistence>
```

18.2.6. Troubleshooting

Below are some typical errors that you might get when using JPA. These are not specific to JPAContainer.

javax.persistence.PersistenceException: No Persistence provider for EntityManager
> The most typical cases for this error are that the persistence unit name is wrong in the source code or in the persist-ence.xml file, or that the persistence.xml is at a wrong place or has some other problem. Make sure that the persistence unit name matches and the persistence.xml is in WEB-INF/classes/META-INF folder in the deployment.

java.lang.IllegalArgumentException: The class is not an entity
> The class is missing from the set of persistent entities. If the persistence.xml does not have *exclude-unlisted-*

classes defined as `false`, the persistent entity classes should be listed with `<class>` elements.

18.3. Defining a Domain Model

Developing a persistent application begins with defining a domain model. A domain model consists of a number of entities (classes) and relationships between them.

Figure 18.4, "A Domain Model" illustrates a simple domain model as a UML class diagram. It has two entities: **Country** and **Person**. They have a "country has persons" relationship. This is a *one-to-many relationship* with one country having many persons, each of which belongs to just one country.

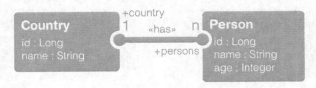

Figure 18.4. A Domain Model

Realized in Java, the classes are as follows:

```
public class Country {
    private Long    id;
    private String name;
    private Set<Person> persons;

    ... setters and getters ...
}

public class Person {
    private Long    id;
    private String  name;
    private Integer age;
    private Country country;

    ... setters and getters ...
}
```

You should make the classes proper beans by defining a default constructor and implementing the `Serializable` interface. A default constructor is required by the JPA entity manager for instantiating entities. Having the classes serializable is not required but often useful for other reasons.

After you have a basic domain model, you need to define the entity relationship metadata by annotating the classes.

18.3.1. Persistence Metadata

The entity relationships are defined with metadata. The metadata can be defined in an XML metadata file or with Java annotations defined in the javax.persistence package. With Vaadin JPAContainer, you need to provide the metadata as annotations.

For example, if we look at the Person class in the JPAContainer AddressBook Demo, we define various database-related metadata for the member variables of a class:

```
@Entity
public class Person {
    @Id
    @GeneratedValue(strategy = GenerationType.AUTO)
    private Long    id;

    private String  name;
    private Integer age;

    @ManyToOne
    private Country country;
```

The JPA implementation uses reflection to read the annotations and defines a database model automatically from the class definitions.

Let us look at some of the basic JPA metadata annotations. The annotations are defined in the javax.persistence package. Please refer to JPA reference documentation for the complete list of possible annotations.

Annotation: @Entity

Each class that is enabled as a persistent entity must have the @Entity annotation.

```
@Entity
public class Country {
```

Annotation: `@Id`

Entities must have an identifier that is used as the primary key for the table. It is used for various purposes in database queries, most commonly for joining tables.

```
@Id
@GeneratedValue(strategy = GenerationType.AUTO)
private Long id;
```

The identifier is generated automatically in the database. The strategy for generating the identifier is defined with the `@Generated-Value` annotation. Any generation type should work.

Annotation: `@OneToOne`

The `@OneToOne` annotation describes a one-to-one relationship where each entity of one type is associated with exactly one entity of another type. For example, the postal address of a person could be given as such.

```
@OneToOne
private Address address;
```

When using the JPAContainer **FieldFactory** to automatically create fields for a form, the `@OneToOne` relationship generates a nested **Form** to edit the data. See Section 18.8, "Automatic Form Generation" for more details.

Annotation: `@Embedded`

Just as with the `@OneToOne` annotation, `@Embedded` describes a one-to-one relationship, but says that the referenced entity should be stored as columns in the same table as the referencing entity.

```
@Embedded
private Address address;
```

The referenced entity class must have `@Embeddable` annotation.

The JPAContainer **FieldFactory** generates a nested **Form** for `@Embedded`, just as with `@OneToOne`.

Annotation: `@OneToMany`

The **Country** entity in the domain model has a *one-to-many* relationship with the **Person** entity ("country has persons"). This relationship is represented with the `@OneToMany` annotation. The *mappedBy* parameter names the corresponding back-reference in the **Person** entity.

```
@OneToMany(mappedBy = "country")
private Set<Person> persons;
```

When using the JPAContainer **FieldFactory** to automatically create fields for a form, the `@OneToMany` relationship generates a **Master-DetailEditor** for editing the items. See Section 18.8, "Automatic Form Generation" for more details.

Annotation: `@ElementCollection`

The `@ElementCollection` annotation can be used for one-to-many relationships to a collection of basic values such as **String** or **Integer**, or to entities annotated as `@Embeddable`. The referenced entities are stored in a separate table defined with a `@CollectionTable` annotation.

```
@ElementCollection
@CollectionTable(
    name="OLDPEOPLE",
    joinColumns=@JoinColumn(name="COUNTRY_ID"))
private Set<Person> persons;
```

JPAContainer **FieldFactory** generates a **MasterDetailEditor** for the `@ElementCollection` relationship, just as with `@OneToMany`.

Annotation: `@ManyToOne`

Many people can live in the same country. This would be represented with the `@ManyToOne` annotation in the **Person** class.

```
@ManyToOne
private Country country;
```

JPAContainer **FieldFactory** generates a **NativeSelect** for selecting an item from the collection. You can do so yourself as well in a custom field factory. Doing so you need to pay notice not to confuse the container between the referenced entity and its ID, which could even result in insertion of false entities in the database in some cases. You can translate between an entity and the entity ID using the **SingleSelectTranslator** as follows:

```
@Override
public Field createField(Item item, Object propertyId,
                         Component uiContext) {
    if (propertyId.equals("station")) {
        ComboBox box = new ComboBox("Station");

        // Translate between referenced entity and its ID
        box.setPropertyDataSource(
                new SingleSelectTranslator(box));

        box.setContainerDataSource(stationContainer);
        ...
```

The JPAContainer **FieldFactory** uses the translator internally, so using it also avoids the problem.

Annotation: `@Transient`

JPA assumes that all entity properties are persisted. Properties that should not be persisted should be marked as transient with the `@Transient` annotation.

```
@Transient
private Boolean superDepartment;
...
@Transient
public String getHierarchicalName() {
...
```

18.4. Basic Use of JPAContainer

Vaadin JPAContainer offers a highly flexible API that makes things easy in simple cases while allowing extensive flexibility in demanding cases. To begin with, it is a **Container**, as described in Section 9.5, "Collecting Items in Containers".

In this section, we look how to create and use **JPAContainer** instances. We assume that you have defined a domain model with JPA annotations, as described in the previous section.

18.4.1. Creating JPAContainer with JPAContainer-Factory

The **JPAContainerFactory** is the easy way to create **JPAContainers**. It provides a set of *make...()* factory methods for most cases that you will likely meet. Each factory method uses a different type of entity provider, which are described in Section 18.5, "Entity Providers".

The factory methods take the class type of the entity class as the first parameter. The second parameter is either a persistence unit name (persistence context) or an **EntityManager** instance.

```
// Create a persistent person container
JPAContainer<Person> persons =
    JPAContainerFactory.make(Person.class, "book-examples");

// You can add entities to the container as well
persons.addEntity(new Person("Marie-Louise Meilleur", 117));

// Set up sorting if the natural order is not appropriate
persons.sort(new String[]{"age", "name"},
            new boolean[]{false, false});

// Bind it to a component
Table personTable = new Table("The Persistent People", persons);
personTable.setVisibleColumns(new String[]{"id","name","age"});
layout.addComponent(personTable);
```

It's that easy. In fact, if you run the above code multiple times, you'll be annoyed by getting a new set of persons for each run - that's how persistent the container is. The basic `make()` uses a **CachedMutableLocalEntityProvider**, which allows modifying the container and its entities, as we do above by adding new entities.

When using just the persistence unit name, the factory creates an instance of **EntityManagerFactory** for the persistence unit and uses it to build entity managers. You can also create the entity managers yourself, as described later.

The entity providers associated with the different factory methods are as follows:

Table 18.1. JPAContainerFactory Methods

`make()`	**CachingMutableLocalEntityProvider**
`makeReadOnly()`	**CachingLocalEntityProvider**
`makeBatchable()`	**BatchableLocalEntityProvider**
`makeNonCached()`	**MutableLocalEntityProvider**
`makeNonCachedReadOnly()`	**LocalEntityProvider**

JPAContainerFactory holds a cache of entity manager factories for the different persistence units, making sure that any entity manager factory is created only once, as it is a heavy operation. You can access the cache to get a new entity manager with the `createEntityManagerForPersistenceUnit()` method.

```
// Get an entity manager
EntityManager em = JPAContainerFactory.
    createEntityManagerForPersistenceUnit("book-examples");

// Do a query
em.getTransaction().begin();
em.createQuery("DELETE FROM Person p").executeUpdate();
em.persist(new Person("Jeanne Calment", 122));
em.persist(new Person("Sarah Knauss", 119));
em.persist(new Person("Lucy Hannah", 117));
em.getTransaction().commit();

...
```

Notice that if you use update the persistent data with an entity manager outside a **JPAContainer** bound to the data, you need to refresh the container as described in Section 18.4.2, "Creating and Accessing Entities".

Creating JPAContainer Manually

While it is normally easiest to use a **JPAContainerFactory** to create **JPAContainer** instances, you may need to create them manually. It is necessary, for example, when you need to use a custom entity provider or extend **JPAContainer**.

First, we need to create an entity manager and then the entity provider, which we bind to a **JPAContainer**.

```
// We need a factory to create entity manager
EntityManagerFactory emf =
    Persistence.createEntityManagerFactory("book-examples");
```

```
// We need an entity manager to create entity provider
EntityManager em = emf.createEntityManager();

// We need an entity provider to create a container
CachingMutableLocalEntityProvider<Person> entityProvider =
    new CachingMutableLocalEntityProvider<Person>(Person.class,
                                                  em);

// And there we have it
JPAContainer<Person> persons =
        new JPAContainer<Person> (Person.class);
persons.setEntityProvider(entityProvider);
```

You could save the first step by asking the entity manager from the **JPAContainerFactory**.

18.4.2. Creating and Accessing Entities

JPAContainer integrates with the JPA entity manager, which you would normally use to create and access entities with JPA. You can use the entity manager for any purposes you may have, and then **JPAContainer** to bind entities to user interface components such as **Table**, **Tree**, any selection components, or a **Form**.

You can add new entities to a **JPAContainer** with the addEntity() method. It returns the item ID of the new entity.

```
Country france = new Country("France");
Object itemId = countries.addEntity(france);
```

The item ID used by **JPAContainer** is the value of the ID property (column) defined with the @Id annotation. In our **Country** entity, it would have **Long** type. It is generated by the entity manager when the entity is persisted and set with the setter for the ID proeprty.

Notice that the addEntity() method does *not* attach the entity instance given as the parameter. Instead, it creates a new instance. If you need to use the entity for some purpose, you need to get the actual managed entity from the container. You can get it with the item ID returned by addEntity().

```
// Create a new entity and add it to a container
Country france = new Country("France");
Object itemId = countries.addEntity(france);

// Get the managed entity
france = countries.getItem(itemId).getEntity();
```

```
// Use the managed entity in entity references
persons.addEntity(new Person("Jeanne Calment", 122,
france));
```

Entity Items

The `getItem()` method is defined in the normal Vaadin `Container` interface. It returns an **EntityItem**, which is a wrapper over the actual entity object. You can get the entity object with `getEntity()`.

An **EntityItem** can have a number of states: persistent, modified, dirty, and deleted. The dirty and deleted states are meaningful when using *container buffering*, while the modified state is meaningful when using *item buffering*. Both levels of buffering can be used together - user input is first written to the item buffer, then to the entity instance, and finally to the database.

The `isPersistent()` method tells if the item is actually persistent, that is, fetched from a persistent storage, or if it is just a transient entity created and buffered by the container.

The `isModified()` method checks whether the **EntityItem** has changes that are not yet committed to the entity instance. It is only relevant if the item buffering is enabled with `setWriteThrough(false)` for the item.

The `isDirty()` method checks whether the entity object has been modified after it was fetched from the entity provider. The dirty state is possible only when buffering is enabled for the container.

The `isDeleted()` method checks whether the item has been marked for deletion with `removeItem()` in a buffered container.

Refreshing JPAContainer

In cases where you change **JPAContainer** items outside the container, for example by through an `EntityManager`, or when they change in the database, you need to refresh the container.

The `EntityContainer` interface implemented by **JPAContainer** provides two methods to refresh a container. The `refresh()` discards all container caches and buffers and refreshes all loaded items in the container. All changes made to items provided by the container are discarded. The `refreshItem()` refreshes a single item.

18.4.3. Nested Properties

If you have a one-to-one or many-to-one relationship, you can define the properties of the referenced entity as *nested* in a **JPAContainer**. This way, you can access the properties directly through the container of the first entity type as if they were its properties. The interface is the same as with **BeanContainer** described in Section 9.5.1, "**BeanContainer**". You just need to add each nested property with `addNestedContainerProperty()` using dot-separated path to the property.

```
// Have a persistent container
JPAContainer<Person> persons =
    JPAContainerFactory.make(Person.class, "book-examples");

// Add a nested property to a many-to-one property
persons.addNestedContainerProperty("country.name");

// Show the persons in a table, except the "country" column,
// which is an object - show the nested property instead
Table personTable = new Table("The Persistent People", persons);
personTable.setVisibleColumns(new String[]{"name","age",
                                          "country.name"});

// Have a nicer caption for the country.name column
personTable.setColumnHeader("country.name", "Nationality");
```

The result is shown in Figure 18.5, "Nested Properties". Notice that the `country` property in the container remains after adding the nested property, so we had to make that column invisible. Alternatively, we could have redefined the `toString()` method in the country object to show the name instead of an object reference.

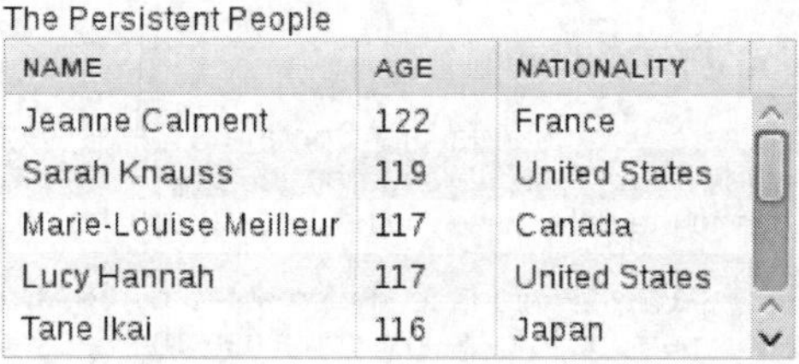

The Persistent People

NAME	AGE	NATIONALITY
Jeanne Calment	122	France
Sarah Knauss	119	United States
Marie-Louise Meilleur	117	Canada
Lucy Hannah	117	United States
Tane Ikai	116	Japan

Figure 18.5. Nested Properties

You can use the * wildcard to add all properties in a nested item, for example, "country.*".

18.4.4. Hierarchical Container

JPAContainer implements the `Container.Hierarchical` interface and can be bound to hierarchical components such as a **Tree** or **TreeTable**. The feature requires that the hierarchy is represented with a *parent* property that refers to the parent item. At database level, this would be a column with IDs.

The representation would be as follows:

```
@Entity
public class CelestialBody implements Serializable {
    @Id
    @GeneratedValue(strategy = GenerationType.IDENTITY)
    private Long    id;

    private String  name;

    @ManyToOne
    private CelestialBody parent;
    ...
} ...

// Create some entities
CelestialBody sun     = new CelestialBody("The Sun", null);
CelestialBody mercury = new CelestialBody("Mercury", sun);
CelestialBody venus   = new CelestialBody("Venus", sun);
CelestialBody earth   = new CelestialBody("Earth", sun);
CelestialBody moon    = new CelestialBody("The Moon", earth);
CelestialBody mars    = new CelestialBody("Mars", sun);
...
```

You set up a **JPAContainer** to have hierarchy by calling `setParentProperty()` with the name of the property that refers to the parent. Coincidentally, it is named "`parent`" in the example:

```
// Create the container
JPAContainer<CelestialBody> bodies =
    JPAContainerFactory.make(CelestialBody.class, "my-unit");

// Set it up for hierarchical representation
bodies.setParentProperty("parent");

// Bind it to a hierarchical component
Tree tree = new Tree("Celestial Bodies", bodies);
tree.setItemCaptionMode(Tree.ITEM_CAPTION_MODE_PROPERTY);
tree.setItemCaptionPropertyId("name");
```

You can use the `rootItemIds()` to acquire the item IDs of the root elements with no parent.

```
// Expand the tree
for (Object rootId: bodies.rootItemIds())
    tree.expandItemsRecursively(rootId);
```

Unsupported Hierarchical Features

Using `setParent()` in the container to define parenthood is not supported.

Also, the current implementation does not support *setChildrenAllowed()*, which controls whether the user can expand a node by clicking a toggle. The toggle is by default visible for all nodes, even if they have no children. The method is not supported because it would require storing the information outside the entities. You can override `areChildrenAllowed()` to implement the functionality using a custom logic.

```
// Customize JPAContainer to define the logic for
// displaying the node expansion indicator
JPAContainer<CelestialBody> bodies =
        new JPAContainer<CelestialBody>(CelestialBody.class) {
    @Override
    public boolean areChildrenAllowed(Object itemId) {
        // Some simple logic
        return getChildren(itemId).size() > 0;
    }
};
bodies.setEntityProvider(
    new CachingLocalEntityProvider<CelestialBody>(
        CelestialBody.class, em));
```

18.5. Entity Providers

Entity providers provide access to entities persisted in a data store. They are essentially wrappers over a JPA entity manager with optimizations and other features important when binding persistent data to a user interface.

The choise and use of entity providers is largely invisible if you create your **JPAContainer** instances with the **JPAContainerFactory**, which hides such details.

JPAContainer entity providers can be customized, which is necessary for some purposes. Entity providers can be Enterprise Java-

---

Beans (EJBs), which is useful when you use them in a Java EE application server.

18.5.1. Built-In Entity Providers

JPAContainer includes various kinds of built-in entity providers: caching and non-caching, read-write and read-only, and batchable.

Caching is useful for performance, but takes some memory for the cache and makes the provider stateful. *Batching*, that is, running updates in larger batches, can also enhance performance and be used together with caching. It is stateless, but doing updates is a bit more complex than otherwise.

Using a *read-only* container is preferable if read-write capability is not needed.

All built-in providers as *local* in the sense that they provide access to entities using a local JPA entity manager.

The **CachingMutableLocalEntityProvider** is usually recommended as the first choise for read-write access and **CachingLocalEntityProvider** for read-only access.

LocalEntityProvider

A read-only, lazy loading entity provider that does not perform caching and reads its data directly from an entity manager.

You can create the provider with `makeNonCachedReadOnly()` method in **JPAContainerFactory**.

MutableLocalEntityProvider

Extends **LocalEntityProvider** with write support. All changes are directly sent to the entity manager.

Transactions can be handled either internally by the provider, which is the default, or by the container. In the latter case, you can extend the class and annotate it, for example, as described in Section 18.5.1, "Built-In Entity Providers".

The provider can notify about updates to entities through the `EntityProviderChangeNotifier` interface.

BatchableLocalEntityProvider

A simple non-caching implementation of the `BatchableEntityProvider` interface. It extends **MutableLocalEntityProvider** and simply passes itself to the `batchUpdate()` callback method. This will work properly if the entities do not contain any references to other entities that are managed by the same container.

CachingLocalEntityProvider

A read-only, lazy loading entity provider that caches both entities and query results for different filter/sortBy combinations. When the cache gets full, the oldest entries in the cache are removed. The maximum number of entities and entity IDs to cache for each filter/sortBy combination can be configured in the provider. The cache can also be manually flushed. When the cache grows full, the oldest items are removed.

You can create the provider with `makeReadOnly()` method in **JPAContainerFactory**.

CachingMutableLocalEntityProvider

Just like **CachingLocalEntityProvider**, but with read-write access. For read access, caching works just like in the read-only provider. When an entity is added or updated, the cache is flushed in order to make sure the added or updated entity shows up correctly when using filters and/or sorting. When an entity is removed, only the filter/sortBy-caches that actually contain the item are flushed.

This is perhaps the most commonly entity provider that you should consider using for most tasks. You can create it with the `make()` method in **JPAContainerFactory**.

CachingBatchableLocalEntityProvider

This provider supports making updates in *batches*. You need to implement a `BatchUpdateCallback` that does all the updates and execute the batch by calling `batchUpdate()` on the provider.

The provider is an extension of the **CachingMutableLocalEntityProvider** that implements the `BatchableEntityProvider` interface. This will work properly if the entities do not contain any references to other entities that are managed by the same container.

You can create the provider with `makeBatchable()` method in **JPAContainerFactory**.

18.5.2. Using JNDI Entity Providers in JEE6 Environment

JPAContainer 2.0 introduced a new set of entity providers specifically for working in a JEE6 environment. In a JEE environment, you should use an entity manager provided by the application server and, usually, JTA transactions instead of transactions provided by JPA. Entity providers in com.vaadin.addon.jpacontainer.provider.jndijta package work mostly the same way as the normal providers discussed earlier, but use JNDI lookups to get reference to an EntityManager and to a JTA transaction.

The JNDI providers work with almost no special configuration at all. The **JPAContainerFactory** has factory methods for creating various JNDI provider types. The only thing that you commonly need to do is to expose the EntityManager to a JNDI address. By default, the JNDI providers look for the EntityManager from "java:comp/env/persistence/em". This can be done with the following snippet in web.xml or with similar configuration with annotations.

```
<persistence-context-ref>
  <persistence-context-ref-name>
    persistence/em
  </persistence-context-ref-name>
  <persistence-unit-name>MYPU</persistence-unit-name>
</persistence-context-ref>
```

The "MYPU" is the identifier of your persistence unit defined in your persistence.xml file.

If you choose to annotate your servlets (instead of using the web.xml file as described above), you can simply add the following annotation to your servlet.

```
@PersistenceContext(name="persistence/em",unitName="MYPU")
```

If you wish to use another address for the persistence context, you can define them with the setJndiAddresses() method. You can also define the location for the JTA **UserTransaction**, but that should be always accessible from "java:comp/UserTransaction" by the JEE6 specification.

18.5.3. Entity Providers as Enterprise Beans

Entity providers can be Enterprise JavaBeans (EJB). This may be useful if you use JPAContainer in a Java EE application server. In such case, you need to implement a custom entity provider that allows the server to inject the entity manager.

For example, if you need to use Java Transaction API (JTA) for JPA transactions, you can implement such entity provider as follows. Just extend a built-in entity provider of your choise and annotate the entity manager member as `@PersistenceContext`. Entity providers can be either stateless or stateful session beans. If you extend a caching entity provider, it has to be stateful.

```
@Stateless
@TransactionManagement
public class MyEntityProviderBean extends
    MutableLocalEntityProvider<MyEntity> {

    @PersistenceContext
    private EntityManager em;

    protected LocalEntityProviderBean() {
        super(MyEntity.class);
        setTransactionsHandledByProvider(false);
    }

    @Override
    @TransactionAttribute(TransactionAttributeType.REQUIRED)
    protected void runInTransaction(Runnable operation) {
        super.runInTransaction(operation);
    }

    @PostConstruct
    public void init() {
        setEntityManager(em);
        /*
         * The entity manager is transaction-scoped, which means
         * that the entities will be automatically detached when
         * the transaction is closed. Therefore, we do not need
         * to explicitly detach them.
         */
        setEntitiesDetached(false);
    }
}
```

If you have more than one EJB provider, you might want to create an abstract super class of the above and only define the entity type in implementations. You can implement an entity provider as a managed bean in Spring Framefork the same way.

18.6. Filtering JPAContainer

Normally, a **JPAContainer** contains all instances of a particular entity type in the persistence context. Hence, it is equivalent to a database table or query. Just like with database queries, you often want to narrow the results down. **JPAContainer** implements the `Filterable` interface in Vaadin containers, described in Section 9.5.4, "**Filterable** Containers". All filtering is done at the database level with queries, not in the container.

For example, let us filter all the people older than 117:

```
Filter filter = new Compare.Greater("age", 117);
persons.addContainerFilter(filter);
```

This would create a JPQL query somewhat as follows:

```
SELECT id FROM Person WHERE (AGE > 117)
```

The filtering implementation uses the JPA 2.0 Criteria API transparently. As the filtering is done at the database-level, custom filters that use the `Filterable` API do not work.

When using Hibernate, note that it does not support implicit joins. See Section 18.9.3, "Joins in Hibernate vs EclipseLink" for more details.

18.7. Querying with the Criteria API

When the `Filterable` API is not enough and you need to have more control, you can make queries directly with the JPA Criteria API. You may also need to customize sorting or joins, or otherwise modify the query in some way. To do so, you need to implement a `QueryModifierDelegate` that the JPAContainer entity provider calls when making a query. The easiest way to do this is to extend **DefaultQueryModifierDelegate**, which has empty implementations of all the methods so that you can only override the ones you need.

The entity provider calls specific `QueryModifierDelegate` methods at different stages while making a query. The stages are:

1. Start building a query

2. Add "ORDER BY" expression

3. Add "WHERE" expression (filter)

4. Finish building a query

Methods where you can modify the query are called before and after each stage as listed in the following table:

Table 18.2. QueryModifierDelegate Methods

queryWillBeBuilt()
orderByWillBeAdded()
orderByWasAdded()
filtersWillBeAdded()
filtersWereAdded()
queryHasBeenBuilt()

All the methods get two parameters. The CriteriaBuilder is a builder that you can use to build queries. The CriteriaQuery is the query being built.

You can use the getRoots().iterator().next() in CriteriaQuery to get the "root" that is queried, for example, the PERSON table, etc.

18.7.1. Filtering the Query

Let us consider a case where we modify the query for a **Person** container so that it includes only people over 116. This trivial example is identical to the one given earlier using the **Filterable** interface.

```
persons.getEntityProvider().setQueryModifierDelegate(
        new DefaultQueryModifierDelegate () {
    @Override
    public void filtersWillBeAdded(
            CriteriaBuilder criteriaBuilder,
            CriteriaQuery<?> query,
            List<Predicate> predicates) {
        Root<?> fromPerson = query.getRoots().iterator().next();

        // Add a "WHERE age > 116" expression
        Path<Integer> age = fromPerson.<Integer>get("age");
```

```
        predicates.add(criteriaBuilder.gt(age, 116));
    }
});
```

18.7.2. Compatibility

When building queries, you should consider the capabilities of the different JPA implementations. Regarding Hibernate, see Section 18.9.3, "Joins in Hibernate vs EclipseLink".

18.8. Automatic Form Generation

The JPAContainer **FieldFactory** is an implementation of the `FormFieldFactory` and `TableFieldFactory` interfaces that can generate fields based on JPA annotations in a POJO. It goes further than the **DefaultFieldFactory**, which only creates simple fields for the basic data types. This way, you can easily create forms to input entities or enable editing in tables.

The result is bit similar to what you can achieve with Spring Roo, as described in Section 14.4, "Creating Vaadin Application and CRUD Views". However, the form views are generated dynamically at run-time, whereas Roo generates static form views.

The generated defaults are as follows:

Annotation	Class Mapping
`@ManyToOne`	**NativeSelect**
`@OneToOne, @Embedded`	Nested **Form**
`@OneToMany, @ElementCollection`	**MasterDetailEditor** (see below)
`@ManyToMany`	Selectable **Table**

The field factory is recusive, so that you can edit a complex object tree with one form.

18.8.1. Configuring the Field Factory

The **FieldFactory** is highly configurable with various configuration settings and by extending. You need to make the configuration before

---

The setMultiSelectType() and setSingleSelectType() allow you to specify a selection component that is used instead of the default for a field with @ManyToMany and @ManyToOne annotation, respectively. The first parameter is the class type of the field, and the second parameter is the class type of a selection component. It must be a sub-class of **AbstractSelect**.

The setVisibleProperties() controls which properties (fields) are visible in generated forms, subforms, and tables. The first paramater is the class type for which the setting should be made, followed by the IDs of the visible properties.

The configuration should be done before binding the form to a data source as that is when the field generation is done.

Further configuration must be done by extending the many protected methods. Please see the API documentation for the complete list.

18.8.2. Using the Field Factory

The most basic use case for the JPAContainer **FieldFactory** is with a **Form** bound to a container item:

```
// Have a persistent container
final JPAContainer<Country> countries =
    JPAContainerFactory.make(Country.class, "book-examples");

// For selecting an item to edit
final Select countrySelect = new Select("Select a Country",
                                        countries);
countrySelect.setItemCaptionMode(Select.ITEM_CAPTION_MODE_PROPERTY);
countrySelect.setItemCaptionPropertyId("name");

// Country Editor
final Form  countryForm  = new Form();
countryForm.setCaption("Country Editor");
countryForm.addStyleName("bordered"); // Custom style
countryForm.setWidth("420px");
countryForm.setWriteThrough(false); // Enable buffering
countryForm.setEnabled(false);

// When an item is selected from the list...
countrySelect.addListener(new ValueChangeListener() {
    @Override
    public void valueChange(ValueChangeEvent event) {
        // Get the item to edit in the form
        Item countryItem =
            countries.getItem(event.getProperty().getValue());

        // Use a JPAContainer field factory
```

```
        // - no configuration is needed here
        final FieldFactory fieldFactory = new FieldFactory();
        countryForm.setFormFieldFactory(fieldFactory);

        // Edit the item in the form
        countryForm.setItemDataSource(countryItem);
        countryForm.setEnabled(true);

        // Handle saves on the form
        final Button save = new Button("Save");
        countryForm.getFooter().removeAllComponents();
        countryForm.getFooter().addComponent(save);
        save.addListener(new ClickListener() {
            @Override
            public void buttonClick(ClickEvent event) {
                try {
                    countryForm.commit();
                    countryForm.setEnabled(false);
                } catch (InvalidValueException e) {
                }
            }
        });
    }
});
countrySelect.setImmediate(true);
countrySelect.setNullSelectionAllowed(false);
```

This would create a form shown in Figure 18.6, "Using FieldFactory
with One-to-Many Relationship".

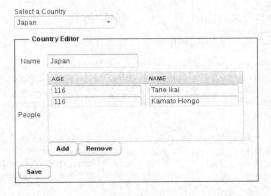

Figure 18.6. Using FieldFactory with One-to-Many Relationship

If you use Hibernate, you also need to pass an **EntityManager-PerRequestHelper**, either for the constructor or with `setEntity-ManagerPerRequestHelper()`, as described in Section 18.9.2, "The EntityManager-Per-Request pattern".

18.8.3. Master-Detail Editor

The **MasterDetailEditor** is a field component that allows editing an item property that has one-to-many relationship. The item can be a row in a table or bound to a form. It displays the referenced collection as an editable **Table** and allows adding and removing items in it.

You can use the **MasterDetailEditor** manually, or perhaps more commonly use a JPAContainer **FieldFactory** to create it automatically. As shown in the example in Figure 18.6, "Using FieldFactory with One-to-Many Relationship", the factory creates a **MasterDetailEditor** for all properties with a `@OneToMany` or an `@ElementCollection` annotation.

18.9. Using JPAContainer with Hibernate

Hibernate needs special handling in some cases.

18.9.1. Lazy loading

In order for lazy loading to work automatically, an entity must be attached to an entity manager. Unfortunately, Hibernate can not keep entity managers for long without problems. To work around the problem, you need to use a special lazy loading delegate for Hibernate.

JPAContainer entity providers handle lazy loading in delegates defined by the `LazyLoadingDelegate` interface. The default implementation for Hibernate is defined in **HibernateLazyLoadingDelegate**. You can instantiate one and use it in an entity provider with `setLazyLoadingDelegate()`.

The default implementation works so that whenever a lazy property is accessed through the Vaadin Property interface, the value is retrieved with a separate (JPA Criteria API) query using the currently active entity manager. The value is then manually attached

---

to the entity instance, which is detached from the entity manager. If this default implementation is not good enough, you may need to make your own implementation.

18.9.2. The EntityManager-Per-Request pattern

One issue with Hibernate is that it is designed for short-lived sessions. The lifetime of an entity manager is roughly that of a session. However, if an error occurs in a session or entity manager, the manager becomes unuseable. This causes big problems with long-lived sessions that would work fine with EclipseLink.

The recommended solution is to the *EntityManager-per-Request* pattern. It is highly recommended always when using Hibernate.

An entity manager can only be open during the request-response cycle of the Vaadin application servlet, so that one is created at the beginning of the request and closed at the end.

You can use the **EntityManagerPerRequestHelper** as follows:

1. Create a new instance in the constructor or `init()` method of your Vaadin application class.

2. Override `onRequestStart()` in the application class and call `requestStart()` in the helper instance.

3. Override `onRequestEnd()` in the application class and call `requestEnd()` in the helper.

4. Whenever a new **JPAContainer** instance is created in the application, register it in the helper by calling `addContainer()` with the container.

5. If you use the JPAContainer **FieldFactory**, as described in Section 18.8, "Automatic Form Generation", you need to set the helper for the factory either by passing it in the constructor (`new FieldFactory(myEMPRH)`) or with `setEntityManagerPerRequestHelper()`. The **FieldFactory** creates **JPAContainer**s internally and these instances need to be updated with the entity manager instances when they change between requests.

18.9.3. Joins in Hibernate vs EclipseLink

EclipseLink supports implicit joins, while Hibernate requires explicit joins. In SQL terms, an explicit join is a "`FROM a INNER JOIN b ON a.bid = b.id`" expression, while an implicit join is done in a WHERE clause, such as: "`FROM a,b WHERE a.bid = b.id`".

In a JPAContainer filter with EclipseLink, an implicit join would have form:

```
new Equal("skills.skill", s)
```

In Hibernate you would need to use **JoinFilter** for the explicit join:

```
new JoinFilter("skills", new Equal("skill", s))
```

Chapter 19

Mobile Applications with TouchKit

This chapter describes how to write mobile applications using the Vaadin TouchKit.

This chapter documents the use of TouchKit with Vaadin 6. The API of the add-on is not yet updated for Vaadin 7.

19.1. Overview

Web browsing is becoming ever increasingly mobile and web applications need to satisfy users with both desktop computers and mobile devices, such as phones and tablets. While the mobile browsers can show the pages just like in regular browsers, the screen size, finger accuracy, and mobile browser features need to be considered to make the experience more pleasant. Vaadin TouchKit gives the power of Vaadin for creating mobile user interfaces that complement the regular web user interfaces of your applications. Just like the purpose of the Vaadin Framework is to make desktop-like web applications, the purpose of TouchKit is to allow creation of web applications that give the look and feel akin to native mobile applications.

In this chapter, we first look into the special considerations of mobile browsing. Then, we look how to create a project that uses TouchKit. TouchKit offers a number of specialized mobile components, which are described in a dedicated section. We treat phone and tablet applications separately, and discuss testing briefly. Finally, we discuss the limitations of TouchKit briefly. In the chapter, we use a Mobile Mail application as an example for creating a web application that looks very much like a native mobile application.

Vaadin TouchKit is a commercial product licensed under a dual-licensing scheme. The AGPL license allows open-source development, while the CVAL license needs to be purchased for closed-source use, including web deployments and internal use. Commercial licenses can be purchased from the Vaadin Directory, where you can also find the license details and download Vaadin TouchKit.

19.2. Considerations Regarding Mobile Browsing

When developing applications that support mobile browsing, you need to consider various issues that are different from non-mobile use.

19.2.1. Mobile Human Interface

Mobile devices use very different human interfaces than regular computers. Perhaps the most evident feature is that the user can easily change the orientation of the display to switch between portrait and landscape views. This may change not just the dimensions of the display, but also the most useful layout.

There is often no physical but a virtual keyboard. You need to ensure that, when the virtual keyboard pops up, it does not hide the input field to which the user is trying to enter data. This should be handled by the browser, but you should in any case check that it does. This is largely a testing issue.

There is no "right-finger-button" and double-tap is not normally used in mobile user interfaces unlike the double-click with mouse. Instead, a "long tap" usually has the same meaning as the double click. Finger gestures also play a large role, such as using a vertical swipe gesture for scrolling instead of a scroll bar.

TouchKit helps with many of these special requirements for mobile applications.

19.2.2. Bandwidth

Mobile Internet connections are often significantly slower than with fixed lines. With a common 384 kbps connection, just loading the Vaadin client-side engine can take several seconds. This can be helped by compiling a widget set that includes only the used components.

Even with mobile broadband, the latency can be significant factor, especially with highly interactive rich applications. The latency is usually almost unnoticeable in fixed lines, typically less than 100 ms, while mobile Edge connections typically have latency around 500 ms, and sometimes much higher during hiccups. You may need to limit the use of the immediate mode, text change events, and polling.

19.2.3. Mobile Features

Phones and tablets have many integrated features that are often available in the browser interface as well. Location-awareness is one of the most recent features. And of course, you can also make phone calls.

19.2.4. Compatibility

The mobile browsing field is currently evolving at fast pace and the special conventions that are introduced by leading manufacturers may, in the next few years, stabilize as new web standards. The browser support in TouchKit concentrates on WebKit, which appears to be emerging as the leading mobile browser core. In addition to Apple's products, also the default browser in Android uses WebKit as the layout engine. Yet there are differences, as the Android's JavaScript engine, which is highly relevant for Vaadin, is the Google Chrome's V8 engine.

TouchKit aims to follow the quickly evolving APIs of these major platforms, with the assumption that other browsers will follow their lead in standardization. Other platforms will be supported if they rise in popularity.

Back Button

Some mobile devices, especially Android devices, have a dedicated back button, while iOS devices particularly do not. TouchKit does not provide any particular support for the button, but as it is a regular browser back button, you can handle it with URI fragments, as described in Section 12.9, "URI Fragment and History Management with **UriFragmentUtility**". For iOS, the browser back button is hidden if the user adds the application to the home screen, in which case you need to implement application-specific logic for the back-navigation.

19.3. Creating a Project Targeting Multiple Devices

19.3.1. Using TouchKit Add-on in a Project

You can install TouchKit as a Vaadin add-on or use it with Maven with the `vaadin-touchkit` dependency.

Deployment Descriptor

You need to use the special **TouchKitApplicationServlet** class instead of the regular **ApplicationServlet** in the `web.xml` deployment descriptor.

As TouchKit comes with a custom widget set, you need to define a combining widget set for your project. The combining widget set descriptor is automatically generated by the Vaadin Plugin for Eclipse and in Maven when you install or define the TouchKit add-on.

```
<servlet>
  <servlet-name>Vaadin Application Servlet</servlet-name>
  <servlet-class>com.vaadin.addon.touchkit.server.TouchKitApplica-
tionServlet</servlet-class>
  <init-param>
    <description>Vaadin application class to start</description>
    <param-name>application</param-name>
    <param-value>com.vaadin.demo.mobilemail.MobileMailApplica-
tion</param-value>
```

```
  </init-param>
  <init-param>
    <param-name>widgetset</param-name>
    <param-value>com.vaadin.demo.mobilemail.gwt.MobileMailWidget-
Set</param-value>
  </init-param>
</servlet>
```

19.3.2. Application

Mobile applications must extend the **TouchKitApplication** instead
of the regular **Application** class. Because much of the browser
information is not yet available when the init() method is called,
you should only set basic things like the main window and theme
there. The main window must be set and must be a **TouchKitWindow**, not a **Window** as in regular Vaadin applications.

```
public class MobileMailApplication extends TouchKitApplication {
    @Override
    public void init() {
        setMainWindow(new TouchKitWindow());

        // Using mobile mail theme
        setTheme("mobilemail");
    }
```

Most initialization has to be be done in onBrowserDetailsReady(),
including the decision to use a regular or a mobile browser interface. The decision is usually made using the user-agent information
available in the **WebBrowser** class and the width and height of
the main window.

```
public void onBrowserDetailsReady() {
    WebBrowser browser = getBrowser();
    float viewPortWidth = getMainWindow().getWidth();

    if (viewPortWidth < 600) {
        getMainWindow().setContent(new SmartphoneMainView());
    } else {
        getMainWindow().setContent(new TabletMainView());
    }
}
```

The demo application does not actually support regular browsers,
just notifies about the situation. The special mobile components in
TouchKit are not guaranteed to work at all in regular browsers. It
does give separate user interfaces for phones and tablets, as described in detail later.

19.4. Mobile User Interface Components

TouchKit introduces a number of components special to mobile
device user interfaces.

19.4.1. NavigationView

The **NavigationView** is a layout component that consists of a
navigation bar and a content area. The content area is scrollable,
so there is no need to use an inner panel component. In addition,
there can be an optional toolbar component at the bottom of the
view. **NavigationView** is often used inside a **NavigationManager**
to get view change animations.

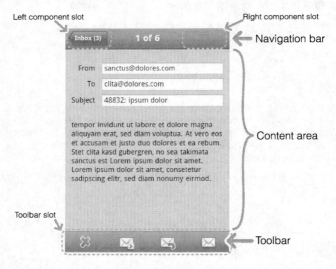

Figure 19.1. Layout of the NavigationView

NavigationView has a full size by default. The content area is
expanding, so that it takes all the space left over from the navigation
bar and toolbar.

Navigation Bar

The navigation bar at the top of **NavigationView** is a **Navigation-Bar** component. It has two component slots, with one on the left and one on the right. On the middle, there is a caption. You can use the **NavigationBar** elsewhere as well, such as for the toolbar.

The left slot is automatically filled with a **Back** button if you set the previous component with `setPreviousComponent()`. If you use the **NavigationView** inside a **NavigationManager**, the manager automaticaly sets the previous view when you navigate to it from another managed view.

You can get access to the navigation bar component with `getNavigationBar()` to use its manipulator methods directly, but **NavigationView** also offers some shorthand methods: `setLeftComponent()`, `setRightComponent()`, and a setter and a getter for the caption.

Toolbar

A slot for an optional toolbar is located at the bottom of the **NavigationView**. The toolbar can be any component, but a **Toolbar** component made for this purpose is included in TouchKit. It is described in Section 19.4.2, "**Toolbar**". You could also use a **HorizontalLayout** or **CssLayout**.

You usually fill the tool bar with **Button** components with an icon and no textual caption. You set the toolbar with `setToolbar()`.

Styling with CSS

```
.v-touchkit-navview { }
  .v-touchkit-navview-wrapper {}
  .v-touchkit-navview-toolbar {}
.v-touchkit-navview .v-touchkit-navview-notoolbar {}
```

The root element has the `v-touchkit-navview` class. The content area is wrapped inside a `v-touchkit-navview-wrapper` element. If the view has a toolbar, the toolbar slot has the `v-touchkit-navview-toolbar` style, but if not, the top-level element has the `v-touchkit-navview-notoolbar` style.

19.4.2. Toolbar

The **Toolbar** is a layout component that extends **CssLayout**, usually containing **Button** components. The toolbar has by default 100% horizontal width and a fixed height. The components are spread evenly in the horizontal direction. **Toolbar** is typically used in a **NavigationView**, as described in Section 19.4.1.

For a description of the inherited features, please refer to Section 6.3, "**VerticalLayout** and **HorizontalLayout**".

Styling with CSS

```
.v-touchkit-toolbar { }
```

The component has an overall `v-touchkit-toolbar` style in addition to the `v-csslayout` style of the superclass. Other style names are as for **CssLayout**.

19.4.3. NavigationManager

The **NavigationManager** is a visual effect component that gives sliding animation when switching between views. You can register three components: the currently displayed component, the previous one on the left, and the next component on the right. You can set these components with `setCurrentComponent()`, `setPreviousComponent()`, and `setNextComponent()`, respectively.

The **NavigationManager** component is illustrated in Figure 19.2, "**NavigationManager** with Three **NavigationView**s".

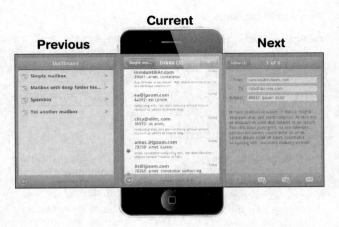

Figure 19.2. NavigationManager with Three NavigationViews

The navigation manager is important for responsiveness, because the previous and next components are cached and the slide animation started before server is contacted to load the new next or previous views.

Switching between the views is done programmatically according to user interaction; swipe gestures are not supported at the moment.

Handling View Changes

While you can put any components in the manager, some special features are enabled when using the **NavigationView**. When a view becomes visible, the `onBecomingVisible()` method in the view is called. You can override it, just remember to call the super-class method.

```
@Override
protected void onBecomingVisible() {
    super.onBecomingVisible();

    ...
}
```

Tracking Breadcrumbs

NavigationManager also handles *breadcrumb* tracking. The `navigateTo()` pushes the current view on the top of the bread-crumb stack and `navigateBack()` can be called to return to the previous breadcrumb level.

Notice that calling `navigateTo()` with the "previous" component is equivalent to calling `navigateBack()`.

19.4.4. NavigationButton

The **NavigationButton** is a special version of the regular **Button** designed for navigation inside a **NavigationManager**, as described in Section 19.4.3. Clicking the button will automatically navigate to the defined target view. The view change animation does not need to make a server request first, but starts immediately after clicking the button. If you leave the target view empty, an empty placeholder view is shown in the animation. The view is filled after it gets the content from the server.

You can give the target view either in the constructor or with `setTargetView()`.

```
NavigationView view = new NavigationView("A View");
...
NavigationButton button = new NavigationButton("Click");
button.setTargetView(view);
...
```

Notice that the automatic navigation will only work if the button is inside a **NavigationManager** (in a view inside it). If you just want to use the button as a visual element, you can use it like a regular **Button** and handle the click events with a **ClickListener**.

Styling with CSS

```
.v-touchkit-navbutton { }
  .v-touchkit-navbutton-desc { }
```

The component has an overall `v-touchkit-navbutton` style. If the component description is set with `setDescription()`, it is shown in a separate `<span>` element with the `v-touchkit-navbutton-desc` style.

19.4.5. Popover

Popover is much like a regular Vaadin sub-window, useful for quickly displaying some options or a small form related to an action. Unlike regular sub-windows, it does not support dragging or resizing by the user. It can have a caption, but usually does not. As sub-windows usually require a rather large screen size, the **Popover** is mainly applicable to tablet devices, but can be used also in phones with full size with `setSizeFull()`.

In the following, we extend **Popover** to use it. It is modal by default. Notice that the screen size is not available in the constructor, so we have to postpone using it to the `attach()` method.

```
public class ComposeView extends Popover {
    ...
    public ComposeView(boolean smartphone) {
        setClosable(false);

        ...

        // In phones use all space, in tablets just vertically
        if (smartphone) {
            setSizeFull();
        } else {
            setHeight("100%");
            center();
        }
    }

    @Override
    public void attach() {
        super.attach();

        // If tablet is wide, leave some space horizontally
        if (!smartphone) {
            if (getParent().getWidth() > 800) {
                setWidth("80%");
            } else {
                setWidth("100%");
            }
        }
    }
    ...
}
```

You add popover windows to an application-level **Window** object with `addWindow()`, just like sub-windows in a regular Vaadin application.

```
if (event.getButton() == emailButton) {
    ComposeView composeView = new ComposeView(smartphone);
    getWindow().addWindow(composeView);
```

```
        return;
}
```

The resulting user interface in a tablet device is shown in Figure 19.3, "**Popover** in a Tablet Device".

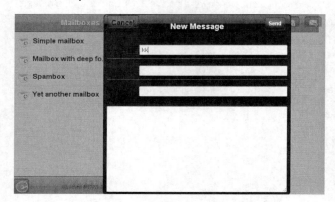

Figure 19.3. Popover in a Tablet Device

Alternatively, you can call the `showRelativeTo()`, which displays the sub-window relative to an existing component in the user interface.

```
Popover popover = new Popover();
popover.setContent(mailboxHierarchyView);
popover.setClosable(true);
popover.showRelativeTo(showMailboxHierarchyButton);
popover.setHeight(getParent().getHeight() - 100, UNITS_PIXELS);
```

In this case, you should not call `addWindow()` explicitly.

Styling with CSS

```
.v-touchkit-popover .v-touchkit-fullscreen { }
  .v-touchkit-popover .v-touchkit-relative { }
  .v-touchkit-popover .v-touchkit-plain { }
```

The component has an overall `v-touchkit-popover` style. If fullscreen, it also has the `v-touchkit-fullscreen` style, if positioned relatively it has `v-touchkit-relative`, and if not, the `v-touchkit-plain` style.

19.4.6. Switch

The **Switch** component is a **CheckBox** that looks like the switch button in Apple iOS.

```
Switch switch = new Switch();
switch.setCaption("Do I look like iOS?");
layout.addComponent(switch);
```

Styling with CSS

```
.v-touchkit-switch { }
  .v-touchkit-switch-slider { }
```

The component has an overall `v-touchkit-switch` style. The slider element has `v-touchkit-switch-slider` style.

19.4.7. ComponentGroup

The **ComponentGroup** is a layout component for grouping components. It uses margins, background color, and rounded corners to visualize the grouping. It extends **CssLayout** and behaves otherwise as such, except in having 100% default width. There is a vertical and a horizontal version of the component.

```
VerticalComponentGroup componentGroup = new VerticalCom-
ponentGroup();

// Name field
Component textField = new TextField("Name");
textField.setWidth("100%");
componentGroup.addComponent(textField);

// Email field
EmailField emailField = new EmailField("Email");
emailField.setWidth("100%");
componentGroup.addComponent(emailField);

// Number field
NumberField numberField = new NumberField("Age");
numberField.setWidth("100%");
componentGroup.addComponent(numberField);
```

Styling with CSS

```
.v-touchkit-componentgroup { }
.v-touchkit-componentgroup-h { }
```

The component has an overall `v-touchkit-componentgroup` style if vertical and `v-touchkit-componentgroup-h` if horizontal. If the component has a caption, the `v-touchkit-has-caption` style is added.

19.4.8. EmailField

The **EmailField** is just like the regular **TextField**, except that it has automatic capitalization and correction turned off. Mobile devices also recognize the field as an email field and can offer a virtual keyboard for the purpose, so that it includes the at (`@`) and period (`.`) characters, and possibly a shorthand for `.com`.

19.4.9. NumberField

The **NumberField** is just like the regular **TextField**, except that it is marked as a numeric input field for mobile devices, so that they will show a numeric virtual keyboard rather than the default alpha-numeric.

19.5. Mobile Features

19.5.1. Geolocation

The geolocation feature in TouchKit allows receiving the geographical location from the mobile device. The browser will ask the user to confirm that the web site is allowed to get the location information. Tapping **Share Location** gives the permission. The browser will give the position acquired by GPS, cellular positioning, or Wi-Fi positioning, as enabled in the device.

Geolocation is requested by calling `detectCurrentPosition()` in the **TouchKitWindow** main window of the application. You need to give a **PositionCallback** handler that receives the location in `onSuccess()` if acquired from the device successfully. The position is given in a **Position** object.

```
mainWindow.detectCurrentPosition(new PositionCallback() {
    public void onSuccess(Position position) {
        double latitude  = position.getLatitude();
```

```
        double longitude = position.getLongitude();
        double accuracy  = position.getAccuracy();

        ...
    }

    public void onFailure(int errorCode) {
        ...
    }
});
```

The position is given as degrees with fractions. The longitude is positive to East and negative to West of the Prime Meridian passing through Greenwich, following the convention for coordinate systems. The accuracy is given in meters.

The `onFailure()` is called if the positioning fails for some reason. The *errorCode* explains the reason. Error 1 is returned if the permission was denied, 2 if the position is unavailable, 3 on positioning timeout, and 0 on an unknown error.

Notice that geolocation can take significant time, depending on the location method used by the device. With Wi-Fi and cellular positioning, the time is usually less than 30 seconds. With GPS, it can reach minutes or longer, especially if the reception is bad.

19.6. Testing and Debugging on Mobile Devices

Testing places special challenges for mobile devices. The mobile browsers may not have much debugging features and you may not be able to install third-party debugging add-ons, such as Firebug.

19.6.1. Debugging

The debug mode, as described in Section 12.3, "Debug and Production Mode", works on mobile browsers as well, even if it is a bit harder to use.

The lack of FireBug and similar tools can be helped with simple client-side coding. For example, you can dump the HTML content of the page with the *innerHTML* property in the HTML DOM.

TouchKit supports especially WebKit-based browsers, which are used in iOS and Android devices. You can therefore reach a good compatibility by using a desktop browser based on WebKit. Features such as geolocation are also supported by desktop browsers. If you make your phone/tablet-detection and orientation detection using screen size, you can easily emulate the modes by resizing the browser.

Chapter 20

Vaadin TestBench

This chapter describes the installation and use of the Vaadin TestBench.

20.1. Overview

Quality assurance is one of the cornerstones of modern software development. Extending throughout the entire development process, quality assurance is the thread that binds the end product to the requirements. In iterative development processes, with ever shorter release cycles and continuous integration, the role of regression testing is central. The special nature of web applications creates many unique requirements for regression testing.

In a typical situation, you are developing a web application with Vaadin and want to ensure that only intended changes occur in its behaviour after modifying the code, without testing the application manually every time. There are two basic ways of detecting such regressions. Screenshots are the strictest way, but often just checking the displayed values in the HTML is better if you want to allow some flexibility for themeing, for example. You may also want to generate many different kinds of inputs to the application and check that they produce the desired outputs.

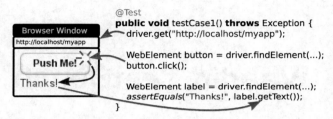

Figure 20.1. Controlling the Browser with WebDriver

Vaadin TestBench utilizes the Selenium WebDriver to control the browser from Java code, as illustrated in Figure 20.1, "Controlling the Browser with WebDriver". It can open a new browser window to start the application, interact with the components for example by clicking them, and then get the HTML element values.

You can develop such WebDriver unit tests along your application code, for example with JUnit, which is a widely used Java unit testing framework. You can also use a recorder that runs in the browser to create JUnit test case stubs, which you can then refine further with Java. You can run the tests as many times as you want in your workstation or in a distributed grid setup.

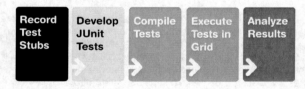

Figure 20.2. TestBench Workflow

The main features of Vaadin TestBench are:

- Record JUnit test case stubs in browser

- Develop tests in Java with the WebDriver

- Validate UI state by assertions and screen capture comparison

- Screen capture comparison with difference highlighting

- Distributed test grid for running tests

- Integration with unit testing

- Test with browsers on mobile devices

Execution of tests can be distributed over a grid of test nodes, which speeds up testing. The grid nodes can run different operating systems and have different browsers installed. In a minimal setup, such as for developing the tests, you can use Vaadin TestBench on just a single computer.

Based on Selenium

Vaadin TestBench is based on the Selenium web browser automation library. With the Selenium WebDriver API, you can control browsers straight from Java code. The TestBench Recorder is based on the Selenium IDE.

Selenium is augmented with Vaadin-specific extensions, such as:

- Proper handling of Ajax-based communications of Vaadin

- Exporting test case stubs from the Recorder

- Performance testing of Vaadin applications

- Screen capture comparison

- Finding HTML elements using a Vaadin selector

TestBench Components

The main components of Vaadin TestBench are:

- Vaadin TestBench Java Library

- Vaadin TestBench Recorder

The library includes WebDriver, which provides API to control a browser like a user would. This API can be used to build tests, for example, with JUnit. It also includes the grid hub and node servers, which you can use to run tests in a grid configuration.

The Vaadin TestBench Recorder is helpful for creating test case stubs. It is a Firefox extension that you install in your browser. It has a control panel to record test cases and play them back. You can play the test cases right in the recorder. You can then export the tests as JUnit tests, which you can edit further and then execute with the WebDriver.

Vaadin TestBench Library provides the central control logic for:

- Executing tests with the WebDriver

- Additional support for testing Vaadin-based applications

- Comparing screen captures with reference images

- Distributed testing with grid node and hub services

Requirements

Requirements for recording test cases with Vaadin TestBench Recorder:

- Mozilla Firefox

Requirements for running tests:

- Java JDK 1.6 or newer

- Browsers installed on test nodes as supported by Selenium WebDriver

  - Google Chrome

  - Internet Explorer

  - Mozilla Firefox

  - Opera

  - Mobile browsers: Android, iPhone

- Build system such as Ant or Maven to automate execution of tests during build process (recommended)

Continuous Integration Compatibility

Continuous integration means automatic compilation and testing of applications frequently, typically at least daily, but ideally every time when code changes are committed to the source repository. This practice allows catching integration problems early and finding the changes that first caused them to occur.

You can make unit tests with Vaadin TestBench just like you would do any other Java unit tests, so they work seamlessly with continuous integration systems. Vaadin TestBench is tested to work with at least TeamCity and Hudson/Jenkins build management and continuous integration servers, which all have special support for the JUnit unit testing framework.

Licensing and Trial Period

You can download Vaadin TestBench from Vaadin Directory and try it out for a free 30-day trial period, after which you are required to acquire the needed licenses. You can purchase licenses from the Directory. A license for Vaadin TestBench is also included in the Vaadin Pro Account subscription.

20.2. Installing Vaadin TestBench

Installation of Vaadin TestBench covers the following tasks:

- Download and unpack the Vaadin TestBench installation package

- Install Vaadin TestBench Recorder

- Install Vaadin TestBench Library

Which modules you need to install depends on whether you are developing tests or running existing tests. Two basic installation types are covered in these instructions:

- Test development installation on a workstation

- Distributed grid installation

20.2.1. Test Development Installation

In a typical test development setup, you install Vaadin TestBench on a workstation. You can use the TestBench Recorder to record test cases and export them as JUnit test case stubs. This is especially recommended if you are new to Vaadin TestBench and do not want to code from scratch. You can install the Recorder in Firefox as described in Section 20.2.6, "Installing the Recorder".

You may find it convenient to develop and execute tests under an IDE such as Eclipse. The special support for running JUnit test cases in Eclipse is described in Section 20.5.3, "Running JUnit Tests in Eclipse".

In such a test development setup, you do not need a grid hub or nodes. However, if you develop tests for a grid, you can run the tests, the grid hub, and one node all in your development workstation. A distributed setup is described in the following section.

20.2.2. A Distributed Testing Environment

Vaadin TestBench supports distributed execution of tests in a grid. A test grid consists of the following categories of hosts:

- One or more test servers executing the tests

- A grid hub

- Grid nodes

The components of a grid setup are illustrated in Figure 20.3, "Vaadin TestBench Grid Setup".

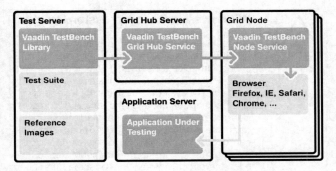

Figure 20.3. Vaadin TestBench Grid Setup

The grid hub is a service that handles communication between the JUnit test runner and the nodes. The nodes are services that perform the actual execution of test commands in the browser.

The hub requires very little resources, so you would typically run it either in the test server or on one of the nodes. You can run the tests, the hub, and one node all in one host, but in a fully distributed setup, you install the Vaadin TestBench components on separate hosts.

Controlling browsers over a distributed setup requires using a remote WebDriver. Grid development and use of the hub and nodes is described in Section 20.7, "Running Tests in an Distributed Environment".

20.2.3. Downloading and Unpacking the Installation Package

First, download the installation package `vaadin-testbench-3.0.0.zip` and extract the installation package where you can find it.

Windows

In Windows, use the default ZIP decompression feature to extract the package into your chosen directory, for example, `C:\dev`.

Windows Zip Decompression Problem

The default decompression program in Windows XP and Vista as well as some versions of WinRAR cannot unpack the installation package properly in certain cases. Decompression can result in an error such as: "The system cannot find the file specified." This can happen because the default decompression program is unable to handle long file paths where the total length exceeds 256 characters. This can occur, for example, if you try to unpack the package under Desktop. You should unpack the package directly into `c:\dev` or some other short path or use another decompression program.

Linux, MacOS X, and other UNIX

In Linux, Mac OS X, and other UNIX-like systems, you can use Info-ZIP or other ZIP software with the command:

```
$ unzip vaadin-testbench-3.0.0.zip
```

The contents of the installation package will be extracted under the current directory.

In Mac OS X, you can also double-click the package to extract it under the current folder in a folder with the same name as the package.

20.2.4. Installation Package Contents

The installation package contains the following:

documentation

    The documentation folder contains the TestBench library API documentation, a PDF excerpt of this chapter of Book of Vaadin, and the license.

example

    The example folder provides TestBench examples. An example Maven configuration POM is given, as well as the JUnit test Java source files. For a description of the contents, see Section 20.2.5, "Example Contents".

```
maven
```
The Maven folder contains version of the Vaadin TestBench libraries that you can install in your local Maven repository. Please follow the instructions in Section 20.5.5, "Executing Tests with Maven".

```
vaadin-testbench-recorder
```
This folder contains the Vaadin TestBench Recorder, which you can install in Firefox. Please follow the instructions in Section 20.2.6, "Installing the Recorder".

```
vaadin-testbench-standalone-3.0.0.jar
```
This is the Vaadin TestBench library. It is a standalone library that includes the Selenium WebDriver and many other required libraries.

```
vaadin-testbench-standalone-3.0.0-javadoc.jar
```
This is the JavaDoc API documentation for the TestBench library. If you use Eclipse, you can associate the JAR with the TestBench JAR in the project preferences, in the build path library settings.

20.2.5. Example Contents

The `example/maven` folder provides a number of examples for using Vaadin TestBench. The source code for the application to be tested, a desktop calculator application, is given in the `src/main/java` subfolder.

The tests examples given under the `src/test/java` subfolder, in the `com/vaadin/testbenchexample` package subfolder, are as follows:

```
SimpleCalculatorITCase.java
```
Demonstrates the basic use of WebDriver. Interacts with the buttons in the user interface by clicking them and checks the resulting value. Uses `By.id()` to access the elements.

```
LoopingCalculatorITCase.java
```
Otherwise as the simple example, but shows how to use looping to produce programmatic repetition to create a complex use case.

`ScreenshotITCase.java`
> Shows how to compare screenshots, as described in Section 20.6, "Taking and Comparing Screenshots". Some of the test cases include random input, so they require masked screenshot comparison to mask the random areas out.
>
> The included reference images were taken with Firefox on Mac OS X, so if you use another platform, they will fail. You will need to copy the error images to the reference screenshot folder and mask out the areas with the alpha channel as described in Section 20.6.3, "Taking Screenshots for Comparison".

`SelectorExamplesITCase.java`
> This example shows how to use different selectors:
>
> - `By.id()` - selecting by identifier
>
> - `By.xpath()` - selecting by an XPath expression

`VerifyExecutionTimeITCase.java`
> Shows how to time the execution of a test case and how to report it.

`AdvancedCommandsITCase.java`
> Demonstrates how to test tooltips (Section 20.5.10, "Testing Tooltips") and context menus. Uses debug IDs, XPath expressions, as well as CSS selectors to find the elements to check.

For information about running the examples with Maven, see Section 20.5.5, "Executing Tests with Maven".

20.2.6. Installing the Recorder

You can use the Vaadin TestBench Recorder in a test development environment to record test cases and to export them as JUnit test case stubs, which you can then develop further. This gives you a quick start when you are learning to use TestBench. Later you can use the Recorder to identify the HTML DOM paths of the user interface elements which you want to test.

After extracting the files from the installation package, do the following:

1. Change to the `vaadin-testbench-recorder` directory under the installation directory.

2. Open Mozilla Firefox

3. Either drag and drop the `vaadin-testbench-recorder-3.0.0.xpi` to an open Firefox window or open it from the menu with **File → Open File**.

4. Firefox will ask if you want to install the TestBench Recorder extension. Click **Install**.

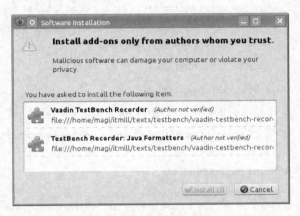

Figure 20.4. Installing Vaadin TestBench Recorder

5. After the installation of the add-on is finished, Firefox offers to restart. Click **Restart Now**.

Installation of a new version of Vaadin TestBench Recorder will overwrite an existing previous version.

After Firefox has restarted, navigate to a Vaadin application for which you want to record test cases, such as http://demo.vaadin.com/sampler.

20.2.7. Test Node Configuration

If you are running the tests in a grid environment, you need to make some configuration to the test nodes to get more stable results.

Operating system settings

Make any operating system settings that might interfere with the browser and how it is opened or closed. Typical problems include crash handler dialogs.

On Windows, disable error reporting in case a browser crashes as follows:

1. Open **control panel → System**

2. Select **Advanced** tab

3. Select **Error reporting**

4. Check that **Disable error reporting** is selected

5. Check that **But notify me when critical errors occur** is not selected

Settings for Screenshots

The screenshot comparison feature requires that the user interface of the browser stays constant. The exact features that interfere with testing depend on the browser and the operating system.

In general:

- Disable blinking cursor

- Use identical operating system themeing on every host

- Turn off any software that may suddenly pop up a new window

- Turn off screen saver

If using Windows and Internet Explorer, you should give also the following setting:

- Turn on **Allow active content to run in files on My Computer** under **Security settings**

20.3. Preparing an Application for Testing

Vaadin TestBench can usually test Vaadin applications as they are, especially if just taking screenshots. However, assertions on HTML elements require a DOM path to the element and this path is vulnerable to even small changes in the DOM structure. They might change because of your layout or UI logic, or if a new Vaadin version has some small changes. To make such problems less common, you can use *debug IDs* to refer to components.

```
public class ApplicationToBeTested extends Application {
    public void init() {
        final Window main = new Window("Test window");
        setMainWindow(main);

        // Create a button
        Button button = new Button("Push Me!");

        // Optional: give the button a unique debug ID
        button.setDebugId("main.button");

        // Do something when the button is clicked
        button.addListener(new ClickListener() {
            @Override
            public void buttonClick(ClickEvent event) {
                // This label will not have a set debug ID
                main.addComponent(new Label("Thanks!"));
            }
        });
        main.addComponent(button);
    }
}
```

The application is shown in Figure 20.5, "A Simple Application To Be Tested", with the button already clicked.

Thanks!

Figure 20.5. A Simple Application To Be Tested

The button would be rendered as a HTML element: `<div id="main.button" ...>...</div>`. The DOM element would then be accessible from the HTML page with: `driver.findEle-`

`ment(By.id="main.button")`. For the label, which doesn't have a debug ID, the path would be from the page root. A recorded test case stub for the above application is given in Section 20.5.1, "Starting From a Stub", which is further refined in this chapter.

20.4. Using Vaadin TestBench Recorder

The Vaadin TestBench Recorder is used for recording and exporting JUnit test stubs that you can then develop further.

The most important role for using the Recorder is to identify all user interface elements that you want to test - you can do all other test logic by coding. The elements are identified by a *selector*, which usually use an HTML document path that selects the element. By default, the Recorder records the paths using a Vaadin selector, where the root of the path is the application element. The path can also be an XPath expression or a CSS selector. It can use a debug ID that you can set in the application code.

You can play back recoded test cases and use the Recorder to make assertions and take screenshots for screen capture comparison. Then, you export the test stubs as JUnit Java source files which you can then develop further.

Figure 20.6. Recorder Workflow

The Recorder is available only for Mozilla Firefox. To run the recorded tests in other browsers, you need to export them as JUnit tests and launch the other browsers with the WebDriver, as described later.

20.4.1. Starting the Recorder

To start the Recorder:

1. Open Mozilla Firefox

2. Open the page with the application that you want to test

3. Select **Tools → Vaadin TestBench Recorder** in the Firefox menu

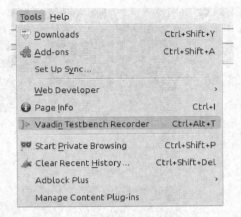

Figure 20.7. Starting Vaadin TestBench Recorder

The Vaadin TestBench Recorder window will open, as shown in Figure 20.8, "Vaadin TestBench Recorder Running".

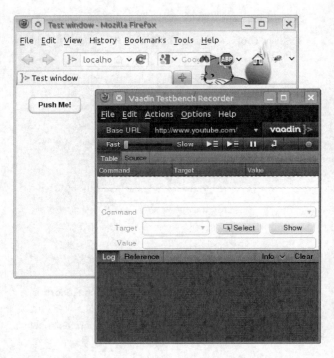

Figure 20.8. Vaadin TestBench Recorder Running

Recording is automatically enabled when the Recorder starts. This is indicated by the pressed ⦿ **Record** button.

20.4.2. Recording

While recording, you can interact with the application in (almost) any way you like. The Recorder records the interaction as commands in a test script, which is shown in tabular format in the Table tab and as HTML source code in the Source tab.

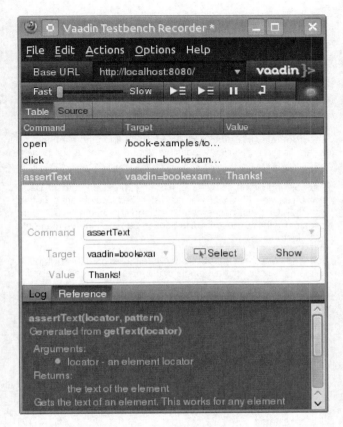

Figure 20.9. User Interaction Recorded as Commands

Please note the following:

- Changing browser tabs or opening a new browser window is not recommended, as any clicks and other actions will be recorded

- Passwords are considered to be normal text input and are stored in plain text

While recording, you can insert various commands such as assertions or take a screenshot by selecting the command from the Command list.

When you are finished, click the ⊚ **Record** button to stop recording.

20.4.3. Selectors

The Recorder supports various *selectors* that allow finding the HTML elements that are interacted upon and asserted. By default, Recorder uses the *Vaadin selector*, which finds the elements by an application identifier, a possible debug ID, and a component hierarchy path.

You can find elements by a plain XPath expression from the page root, an element ID, CSS style class, etc. The selectors are exported with the JUnit test cases as corresponding Vaadin or Selenium selector methods, described in Section 20.5.2, "Finding Elements by Selectors".

Some selectors are not applicable to all elements, for example if an element does not have an ID or it is outside the Vaadin application. In such case, another selector is used according to a preference order. You can change the order of the preferred selectors by selecting **Options → Options → Locator Builders** and dragging the selectors (or locators) to a preferred order. Normally, the Vaadin selector should be at top.

20.4.4. Playing Back Tests

After you have stopped recording, reset the application to the initial state and press ▶ **Play current test** to run the test again. You can use the ?restartApplication parameter for an application in the URL to restart it.

You can also play back tests saved in the HTML format by first opening a test in the Recorder with **File → Open**.

You can use the Fast Slow slider to control the playback speed, click **Pause** to interrupt the execution and **Resume** to continue. While paused, you can click **Step** to execute the script step-by-step.

Check that the test works as intended and no unintended or invalid commands are found; a test should run without errors.

20.4.5. Editing Tests

While the primary purpose of using the Recorder is to identify all user interface elements to be tested, you can also edit the tests at this point. You can insert various commands, such as assertions or taking a screenshot, in the test script during or after recording.

You insert a command by selecting an insertion point in the test script and right-clicking an element in the browser. A context menu opens and shows a selection of Recorder commands at the bottom. Selecting **Show All Available Commands** shows more commands. Commands inserted from the sub-menu are automatically added to the top-level context menu.

Figure 20.10, "Inserting commands in a test script" shows adding an assertion after clicking the button in the example application.

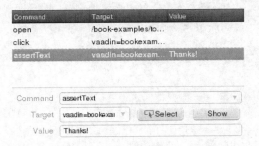

Figure 20.10. Inserting commands in a test script

Inserting a command from the context menu automatically selects the command in the **Command** field and fills in the target and value parameters.

You can also select the command manually from the **Command** list. The new command or comment will be added at the selected location, moving the selected location down. If the command requires a target element, click **Select** and then click an element in your application. A reference to the element is shown in the **Target** field and you can highlight the element by clicking **Show**. If the command expects some value, such as for comparing the element value, give it in the **Value** field.

Commands in a test script can be changed by selecting a command and changing the command, target, or value.

20.4.6. Exporting Tests

Once you have are satisfied with a test case, you need to export it as a JUnit test case stub.

You can save a test by selecting **File → Export → JUnit Test**.

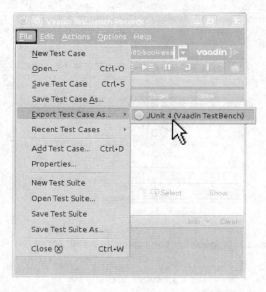

Figure 20.11. Exporting Test Case as JUnit Test

In the dialog that opens, enter a file name for the Java source file. The file contains a Java class with name **Testcase**, so you might want to name the file as Testcase.java. You can rename the class later.

20.4.7. Saving Tests

While exporting tests as JUnit tests is the normal case, the Recorder also allows saving test cases and test suites in a HTML format that can be loaded back in the Recorder. Vaadin TestBench does not support other use for these saved tests, but you may still find the feature useful if you like to develop test cases more with the Recorder.

20.5. Developing JUnit Tests

Tests are developed using the Selenium WebDriver, which is augmented with Vaadin TestBench API features useful for testing Vaadin applications.

Perhaps the easiest way to start developing tests is to use the Recorder to create a JUnit test stub, which is described in the next section. The main purpose of the recorder is to help identify the HTML DOM paths of the user interface elements that you want to interact with and use for assertions. Once you get the hang of coding tests, you should be able to do it without using the Recorder. Working with debug IDs and using a browser debugger, such as Firebug, is usually the easiest way to find out the DOM paths. You can also use the Recorder just to find the paths, and copy and paste them directly to your source code without going through the export hassle.

While this section describes the development of JUnit tests, Vaadin TestBench and the WebDriver are in no way specific to JUnit and you can use any test execution framework, or just regular Java applications, to develop TestBench tests.

20.5.1. Starting From a Stub

Let us assume that you recorded a simple application, as described earlier, and exported it as a JUnit stub. You can add it to a project in a suitable package. You may want to keep your test classes in a separate source tree in your application project, or in an altogether separate project, so that you do not have to include them in the web application WAR. Having them in the same project may be nicer for version control purposes.

You need to perform at least the following routine tasks:

- Rename the package

- Rename the class

- Check the base URL

- Clean up unnecessary code

A JUnit stub will look somewhat as follows:

```
package com.example.tests;

import java.util.regex.Pattern;
import java.util.concurrent.TimeUnit;
import org.junit.*;
import static org.junit.Assert.*;
import static org.hamcrest.CoreMatchers.*;
import org.openqa.selenium.*;
import org.openqa.selenium.firefox.FirefoxDriver;
import org.openqa.selenium.support.ui.Select;
import com.vaadin.testbench.By;
import com.vaadin.testbench.TestBench;
import com.vaadin.testbench.TestBenchTestCase;

public class Testcase1 extends TestBenchTestCase {
 private WebDriver driver;
 private String baseUrl;
 private StringBuffer verificationErrors = new StringBuffer();
```

The *verificationErrors* is used to collect some errors in some recorded commands, but can be removed if such commands are not used. You can also use it to collect non-fatal errors, for example screenshot comparison errors, and only fail on logic errors.

Test Setup

The set-up method, annotated with @Before, makes the basic configuration for the test. Most importantly, it creates the **Web-Driver** instance, which is for Firefox by default. Drivers for different browsers extend the **RemoteWebDriver** class - see the API type hierarchy for the complete list.

```
@Before
public void setUp() throws Exception {
    driver = TestBench.createDriver(new FirefoxDriver());
    baseUrl = "http://localhost:8080/myapp";
}
```

Check that the *baseUrl* is the correct URL for the application. It might not be.

Test Case Stub

The test case methods are marked with @Test annotation. They normally start by calling the get() method in the driver. This loads the URL in the browser.

Actual test commands usually call the findElement() method in the driver to get hold of an HTML element to work with. The button has the main.button ID, as we set that ID for the **Button** object with the setDebugId() method in the application. The HTML element is represented as a **WebElement** object.

```
@Test
public void testCase1() throws Exception {
    driver.get(concatUrl(baseUrl, "/myapp"));
    assertEquals("Push Me!", driver.findElement(By.vaadin(
        "bookexamplestobetested::PID_Smain.button")).getText());
    driver.findElement(By.vaadin(
        "bookexamplestobetested::PID_Smain.button")).click();
    assertEquals("Thanks!", driver.findElement(By.vaadin(
        "bookexamplestobetested::/VVerticalLayout[0]/"+
        "ChildComponentContainer[1]/VLabel[0]")).getText());
}
```

The get() call appends the application path to the base URL. If it is already included in the base URL, you can remove it.

After Testing

Finally after running all the test cases, the method annotated with @After is called. Calling quit() for the driver closes the browser window.

The stub includes code for collecting verification errors. If you do not collect those, as is often the case, you can remove the code.

```
@After
public void tearDown() throws Exception {
    driver.quit();

    String verificationErrorString =
        verificationErrors.toString();
    if (!"".equals(verificationErrorString)) {
        fail(verificationErrorString);
    }
}
```

20.5.2. Finding Elements by Selectors

The Selenium WebDriver API provides a number of different *selectors* for finding HTML DOM elements. The available selectors are defined as static methods in the **org.openqa.selenium.By** class. They create and return a **By** instance, which you can use for the `findElement()` method in **WebDriver**.

The ID, CSS class, and Vaadin selectors are described below. For others, we refer to the Selenium WebDriver API documentation.

Finding by ID

Selecting elements by their HTML element `id` attribute is usually the easiest way to select elements. It requires that you use debug IDs, as described in Section 20.3, "Preparing an Application for Testing". The debug ID is used as is for the `id` attribute of the top element of the component. Selecting is done by the `By.id()` selector.

For example, in the `SimpleCalculatorITCase.java` example we use the debug ID as follows to click on the calculator buttons:

```
@Test
public void testOnePlusTwo() throws Exception {
    openCalculator();

    // Click the buttons in the user interface
    getDriver().findElement(By.id("button_1")).click();
    getDriver().findElement(By.id("button_+")).click();
    getDriver().findElement(By.id("button_2")).click();
    getDriver().findElement(By.id("button_=")).click();

    // Get the result label value
    assertEquals("3.0", getDriver().findElement(
            By.id("display")).getText());
}
```

The ID selectors are used extensively in the TestBench examples.

Finding by Vaadin Selector

In addition to the Selenium selectors, Vaadin TestBench provides a *Vaadin selector*, which allows pointing to a Vaadin component by its layout path. The JUnit test cases saved from the Recorder use Vaadin selectors by default.

You can create a Vaadin selector with the `By.vaadin()` method. You need to use the Vaadin **By**, defined in the com.vaadin.test-bench package, which extends the Selenium **By**.

The other way is to use the `findElementByVaadinSelector()` method in the `TestBenchCommands` interface. It returns the **WebElement** object.

A Vaadin selector begins with an application identifier. It is the path to application without any slashes or other special characters. For example, `/book-examples/tobetested` would be `bookexamplestobetested`. After the identifier, comes two colons "`::`", followed by a slash-delimited component path to the component to be selected. The elements in the component path are client-side classes of the Vaadin user interfacer components. For example, the server-side **VerticalLayout** component has **VVertical-Layout** client-side counterpart. All path elements except the leaves are component containers, usually layouts. The exact contained component is identified by its index in brackets.

A reference to a debug ID is given with a `PID_S` suffix to the debug ID.

For example:

```
// Get the button's element.
// Use the debug ID given with setDebugId().
WebElement button = driver.findElement(By.vaadin(
    "bookexamplestobetested::PID_Smain.button"));

// Get the caption text
assertEquals("Push Me!", button.getText());

// And click it
button.click();

// Get the Label's element by full path
WebElement label = driver.findElement(By.vaadin(
    "bookexamplestobetested::/VVerticalLayout[0]/"+
    "ChildComponentContainer[1]/VLabel[0]"));

// Make the assertion
assertEquals("Thanks!", label.getText());
```

Finding by CSS Class

An element with a particular CSS style class name can be selected with the `By.className()` method. CSS selectors are useful for elements which have no ID, nor can be found easily from the component hierarchy, but do have a particular unique CSS style. Tooltips are one example, as they are floating `div` elements under the root element of the application. Their `v-tooltip` style makes it possible to select them as follows:

```
// Verify that the tooltip contains the expected text
String tooltipText = driver.findElement(
    By.className("v-tooltip")).getText();
```

For a complete example, see the `AdvancedCommandsITCase.java` file in the examples.

20.5.3. Running JUnit Tests in Eclipse

The Eclipse IDE integrates JUnit with nice control features. To run TestBench JUnit test cases in Eclipse, you need to do the following:

1. Add the TestBench JAR to a library folder in the project, such as `lib`. You should not put the library in `WEB-INF/lib` as it is not used by the Vaadin web application. Refresh the project by selecting it and pressing **F5**.

2. Right-click the project in Project Explorer and select **Properties**, and open the **Java Build Path** and the **Libraries** tab. Click **Add JARs**, navigate to the library folder, select the library, and click **OK**.

3. Switch to the **Order and Export** tab in the project properties. Make sure that the TestBench JAR is above the `gwt-dev.jar` (it may contain an old `httpclient` package), by selecting it and moving it with the **Up** and **Down** buttons.

4. Click **OK** to exit the project properties.

5. Right-click a test source file and select **Run As → JUnit Test**.

A JUnit view should appear, and it should open the Firefox browser, launch the application, run the test, and then close the browser window. If all goes well, you have a passed test case, which is reported in the JUnit view area in Eclipse, as illustrated in Figure 20.12, "Running JUnit Tests in Eclipse".

Figure 20.12. Running JUnit Tests in Eclipse

If you are using some other IDE, it might support JUnit tests as well. If not, you can run the tests using Ant or Maven.

20.5.4. Executing Tests with Ant

Apache Ant has built-in support for executing JUnit tests. To enable the support, you need to have the JUnit library `junit.jar` and its Ant integration library `ant-junit.jar` in the Ant classpath, as described in the Ant documentation.

Once enabled, you can use the `<junit>` task in an Ant script. The following example assumes that the source files are located under a `src` directory under the current directory and compiles them to the `classes` directory. The the class path is defined with the `classpath` reference ID and should include the TestBench JAR and all relevant dependencies.

```
<project default="run-tests">
    <path id="classpath">
        <fileset dir="lib"
                 includes="vaadin-testbench-standalone-*.jar" />
    </path>

    <!-- This target compiles the JUnit tests. -->
    <target name="compile-tests">
        <mkdir dir="classes" />
        <javac srcdir="src" destdir="classes"
               debug="on" encoding="utf-8">
            <classpath>
                <path refid="classpath" />
            </classpath>
```

```
            </javac>
    </target>

    <!-- This target calls JUnit -->
    <target name="run-tests" depends="compile-tests">
        <junit fork="yes">
            <classpath>
                <path refid="classpath" />
                <pathelement path="classes" />
            </classpath>

            <formatter type="brief" usefile="false" />

            <batchtest>
                <fileset dir="src">
                    <include name="**/**.java" />
                </fileset>
            </batchtest>
        </junit>
    </target>
</project>
```

You also need to deploy the application to test, and possibly launch a dedicated server for it.

20.5.5. Executing Tests with Maven

Executing JUnit tests with Vaadin TestBench under Maven requires installing the TestBench library in the local Maven repository and defining it as a dependency in any POM that needs to execute TestBench tests.

A complete example of a Maven test setup is given in the `ex-ample/maven` folder in the installation package. Please see the README file in the folder for further instructions.

Installing TestBench in Local Repository

You can install TestBench in the local Maven repository with the following commands:

```
$ cd maven
$ mvn install:install-file \
      -Dfile=vaadin-testbench-3.0.0-SNAPSHOT.jar \
      -Djavadoc=vaadin-testbench-3.0.0-SNAPSHOT-javadoc.jar \
      -DpomFile=pom.xml
```

The maven folder also includes an INSTALL file, which contains instructions for installing TestBench in Maven.

Defining TestBench as a Dependency

Once TestBench is installed in the local repository as instructed in the previous section, you can define it as a dependency in the Maven POM of your project as follows:

```
<dependency>
  <groupId>com.vaadin</groupId>
  <artifactId>vaadin-testbench</artifactId>
  <version>&version.testbench;-SNAPSHOT</version>
</dependency>
```

For instructions on how to create a new Vaadin project with Maven, please see Section 2.5, "Creating a Project with Maven".

Running the Tests

To compile and run the tests, simply execute the `test` lifecycle phase with Maven as follows:

```
$ mvn test
...
-------------------------------------------------------------
-
  T E S T S
-------------------------------------------------------------
-
Running TestBenchExample
Tests run: 6, Failures: 2, Errors: 0, Skipped: 1, Time
  elapsed: 36.736 sec <<< FAILURE!

Results :

Failed tests:
  testDemo(TestBenchExample): expected:<[5/17/]12> but
  was:<[17.6.20]12>
  testScreenshot(TestBenchExample): Screenshots differ

Tests run: 6, Failures: 2, Errors: 0, Skipped: 1
...
```

The example configuration starts Jetty to run the application that is tested. Error screenshots from screenshot comparison are written to the `target/testbench/errors` folder. To enable comparing them to "expected" screenshots, you need to copy the screenshots to the `src/test/resources/screenshots/reference/` folder.

See Section 20.6, "Taking and Comparing Screenshots" for more information regarding screenshots.

20.5.6. Test Setup

Test configuration is done in a method annotated with `@Before`. The method is executed before each test case. In a JUnit stub exported from Recorder, this is done in the `setUp()` method.

The basic configuration tasks are:

- Set TestBench parameters
- Create the web driver
- Do any other initialization

TestBench Parameters

TestBench parameters are defined with static methods in the **com.vaadin.testbench.Parameters** class. The parameters are mainly for screenshots and documented in Section 20.6, "Taking and Comparing Screenshots".

20.5.7. Creating and Closing a Web Driver

Vaadin TestBench uses Selenium WebDriver to execute tests in a browser. The **WebDriver** instance is created with the static `createDriver()` method in the **TestBench** class. It takes the driver as the parameter and returns it after registering it. The test cases must extend the **TestBenchTestCase** class, which manages the TestBench-specific features.

The basic way is to create the driver in a method annotated with the JUnit `@Before` annotation and close it in a method annotated with `@After`.

```
public class AdvancedTest extends TestBenchTestCase {
    private WebDriver driver;

    @Before
    public void setUp() throws Exception {
        ...
        driver = TestBench.createDriver(new FirefoxDriver());
    }
    ...
    @After
```

```
    public void tearDown() throws Exception {
        driver.quit();
    }
}
```

This creates the driver for each test you have in the test class, causing a new browser instance to be opened and closed. If you want to keep the browser open between the test, you can use `@BeforeClass` and `@AfterClass` methods to create and quit the driver. In that case, the methods as well as the driver instance have to be static.

```
public class AdvancedTest extends TestBenchTestCase {
    static private WebDriver driver;

    @BeforeClass
    static public void createDriver() throws Exception {
        driver = TestBench.createDriver(new Fire-
foxDriver());
    }
    ...
    @AfterClass
    static public void tearDown() throws Exception {
        driver.quit();
    }
}
```

20.5.8. Basic Test Case Structure

A typical test case does the following:

1. Open the URL

2. Navigate to desired state

   a. Find a HTML element (**WebElement**) for navigation

   b. Use `click()` and other commands to interact with the element

   c. Repeat with different elements until desired state is reached

3. Find a HTML element (**WebElement**) to check

4. Get and assert the value of the HTML element

5. Get a screenshot

The **WebDriver** allows finding HTML elements in a page in various ways, for example, with XPath expressions. The access methods are defined statically in the **By** class.

These tasks are realized in the following test code:

```
@Test
public void testCase1() throws Exception {
    driver.get(baseUrl + "/book-examples/tobetested");

    // Get the button's element.
    // (Actually the caption element inside the button.)
    // Use the debug ID given with setDebugId().
    WebElement button = driver.findElement(By.xpath(
        "//div[@id='main.button']/span/span"));

    // Get the caption text
    assertEquals("Push Me!", button.getText());

    // And click it. It's OK to click the caption element.
    button.click();

    // Get the Label's element.
    // Use the automatically generated ID.
    WebElement label = driver.findElement(By.xpath(
        "//div[@id='myapp-949693921']" +
        "/div/div[2]/div/div[2]/div/div"));

    // Make the assertion
    assertEquals("Thanks!", label.getText());
}
```

You can also use URI fragments in the URL to open the application at a specific state. For information about URI fragments, see Section 12.9, "URI Fragment and History Management with **UriFragmentUtility**".

You should use the JUnit assertion commands. They are static methods defined in the org.junit.Assert class, which you can import (for example) with:

```
import static org.junit.Assert.assertEquals;
```

Please see the Selenium API documentation for a complete reference of the element search methods in the **WebDriver** and **By** classes and for the interaction commands in the **WebElement** class.

TestBench has a collection of its own commands, defined in the TestBenchCommands interface. You can get a command object that you can use by calling testBench(driver) in a test case.

20.5.9. Waiting for Vaadin

Selenium is intended for regular web applications that load a page that is immediately rendered by the browser. Vaadin, on the other hand, is an Ajax framework where page is loaded just once and rendering is done in JavaScript. This takes more time so that the rendering might not be finished when the WebDriver continues executing the test. Vaadin TestBench allows waiting until the rendering is finished.

The waiting is automatically enabled. You can disable waiting by calling `disableWaitForVaadin()` in the `TestBenchCommands` interface. You can call it in a test case as follows:

```
testBench(driver).disableWaitForVaadin();
```

When disabled, you can wait for the rendering to finish by calling `waitForVaadin()` explicitly.

```
testBench(driver).waitForVaadin();
```

You can re-enable the waiting with `enableWaitForVaadin()` in the same interface.

20.5.10. Testing Tooltips

Component tooltips show when you hover the mouse over a component. Events caused by hovering are not recorded by Recorder, so this interaction requires special handling when testing.

Let us assume that you have set the tooltip as follows:

```
// Create a button with a debug ID
Button button = new Button("Push Me!");
button.setDebugId("main.button");

// Set the tooltip
button.setDescription("This is a tip");
```

The tooltip of a component is displayed with the `showTooltip()` method in the **TestBenchElementCommands** interface. You should wait a little to make sure it comes up. The floating tooltip element is not under the element of the component, but you can find it by `//div[@class='v-tooltip']` XPath expression.

```
@Test
public void testTooltip() throws Exception {
    driver.get(appUrl);

    // Get the button's element.
    // Use the debug ID given with setDebugId().
    WebElement button = driver.findElement(By.xpath(
        "//div[@id='main.button']/span/span"));

    // Show the tooltip
    testBenchElement(button).showTooltip();

    // Wait a little to make sure it's up
    Thread.sleep(1000);

    // Check that the tooltip text matches
    assertEquals("This is a tip", driver.findElement(
        By.xpath("//div[@class='v-tooltip']")).getText());

    // Compare a screenshot just to be sure
    assertTrue(testBench(driver).compareScreen("tooltip"));
}
```

20.5.11. Scrolling

Some Vaadin components, such as **Table** and **Panel** have a
scrollbar. To get hold of the scrollbar, you must first find the component element. Then, you need to get hold of the TestBenchElementCommands interface from the **WebElement** with testBenchEle-
ment(WebElement). The scroll() method in the interface scrolls
a vertical scrollbar down the number of pixels given as the parameter. The scrollLeft() scrolls a horizontal scrollbar by the given
number of pixels.

20.5.12. Testing Notifications

When testing notifications, you will need to close the notification
box. You need to get hold of the TestBenchElementCommands interface from the **WebElement** of the notification element with
testBenchElement(WebElement). The closeNotification()
method in the interface closes the notification.

20.5.13. Testing Context Menus

Opening context menus require special handling. You need to
create a Selenium **Actions** object to perform a context click on a
WebElement.

In the following example, we open a context menu in a **Table** component, find an item by its caption text, and click it.

```
// Select the table body element
WebElement e = getDriver().findElement(
        By.className("v-table-body"));

// Perform context click action to open the context menu
new Actions(getDriver()).moveToElement(e)
        .contextClick(e).perform();

// Select "Add Comment" from the opened menu
getDriver().findElement(
        By.xpath("//*[text() = 'Add Comment']")).click();
```

The complete example is given in the `AdvancedCommandsIT-Case.java` example source file.

20.5.14. Profiling Test Execution Time

It is not just that it works, but also how long it takes. Profiling test execution times consistently is not trivial, as a test environment can have different kinds of latency and interference. For example in a distributed setup, timings taken on the test server would include the latencies between the test server, the grid hub, a grid node running the browser, and the web server running the application. In such a setup, you could also expect interference between multiple test nodes, which all might make requests to a shared application server and possibly also share virtual machine resources.

Furthermore, in Vaadin applications, there are two sides which need to be profiled: the server-side, on which the application logic is executed, and the client-side, where it is rendered in the browser. Vaadin TestBench includes methods for measuring execution time both on the server-side and the client-side.

The `TestBenchCommands` interface offers the following methods for profiling test execution time:

`totalTimeSpentServicingRequests()`
> Returns the total time (in milliseconds) spent servicing requests in the application on the server-side. The timer starts when you first navigate to the application and hence start a new session. The time passes only when servicing requests for the particular session. The timer is shared in the servlet session, so if you have, for example, multiple portlets

in the same application (session), their execution times will be included in the same total.

Notice that if you are also interested in the client-side performance for the last request, you must call the `timeSpentRenderingLastRequest()` before calling this method. This is due to the fact that this method makes an extra server request, which will cause an empty response to be rendered.

`timeSpentServicingLastRequest()`
Returns the time (in milliseconds) spent servicing the last request in the application on the server-side. Notice that not all user interaction through the WebDriver cause server requests.

As with the total above, if you are also interested in the client-side performance for the last request, you must call the `timeSpentRenderingLastRequest()` before calling this method.

`totalTimeSpentRendering()`
Returns the total time (in milliseconds) spent rendering the user interface of the application on the client-side, that is, in the browser. This time only passes when the browser is rendering after interacting with it through the WebDriver. The timer is shared in the servlet session, so if you have, for example, multiple portlets in the same application (session), their execution times will be included in the same total.

`timeSpentRenderingLastRequest()`
Returns the time (in milliseconds) spent rendering user interface of the application after the last server request. Notice that not all user interaction through the WebDriver cause server requests.

If you also call the `timeSpentServicingLastRequest()` or `totalTimeSpentServicingRequests()`, you should do so before calling this method. The methods cause a server request, which will zero the rendering time measured by this method.

Generally, only interaction with fields in the *immediate* mode cause server requests. This includes button clicks. Some components, such as **Table**, also cause requests otherwise, such as when loading data while scrolling. Some interaction could cause multiple requests, such as when images are loaded from the server as the result of user interaction.

The following example is given in the `VerifyExecutionTimeIT-Case.java` file under the TestBench examples.

```
@Test
public void verifyServerExecutionTime() throws Exception {
    openCalculator();

    // Get start time on the server-side
    long currentSessionTime = testBench(getDriver())
            .totalTimeSpentServicingRequests();

    // Interact with the application
    calculateOnePlusTwo();

    // Calculate the passed processing time on the serve-side
    long timeSpentByServerForSimpleCalculation = testBench()
        .totalTimeSpentServicingRequests() - currentSessionTime;

    // Report the timing
    System.out.println("Calculating 1+2 took about "
            + timeSpentByServerForSimpleCalculation
            + "ms in servlets service method.");

    // Fail if the processing time was critically long
    if (timeSpentByServerForSimpleCalculation > 30) {
        fail("Simple calculation shouldn't take "
            + timeSpentByServerForSimpleCalculation + "ms!");
    }

    // Do the same with rendering time
    long totalTimeSpentRendering =
            testBench().totalTimeSpentRendering();
    System.out.println("Rendering UI took " +
            totalTimeSpentRendering + "ms");
    if (timeSpentByServerForSimpleCalculation > 400) {
        fail("Rendering UI shouldn't take "
            + timeSpentByServerForSimpleCalculation + "ms!");
    }

    // A regular assertion on the UI state
    assertEquals("3.0", getDriver().findElement(
                    By.id("display")).getText());
}
```

20.6. Taking and Comparing Screenshots

You can take and compare screenshots with reference screenshots taken earlier. If there are differences, you can fail the test case.

20.6.1. Screenshot Parameters

The screenshot configuration parameters are defined with static methods in the **com.vaadin.testbench.Parameters** class.

screenshotErrorDirectory (default: `null`)
> Defines the directory where screenshots for failed tests or comparisons are stored.

screenshotReferenceDirectory (default: `null`)
> Defines the directory where the reference images for screenshot comparison are stored.

captureScreenshotOnFailure (default: `true`)
> Defines whether screenshots are taken whenever an assertion fails.

screenshotComparisonTolerance (default: `0.01`)
> Screen comparison is usually not done with exact pixel values, because rendering in browser often has some tiny inconsistencies. Also image compression may cause small artifacts.

screenshotComparisonCursorDetection (default: `false`)
> Some field component get a blinking cursor when they have the focus. The cursor can cause unnecessary failures depending on whether the blink happens to make the cursor visible or invisible when taking a screenshot. This parameter enables cursor detection that tries to minimize these failures.

maxScreenshotRetries (default: 2)
> Sometimes a screenshot comparison may fail because the screen rendering has not yet finished, or there is a blinking cursor that is different from the reference screenshot. For these reasons, Vaadin TestBench retries the screenshot comparison for a number of times defined with this parameter.

screenshotRetryDelay (default: `500`)
> Delay in milliseconds for making a screenshot retry when a comparison fails.

For example:

```
@Before
public void setUp() throws Exception {
    Parameters.setScreenshotErrorDirectory(
        "screenshots/errors");
    Parameters.setScreenshotReferenceDirectory(
        "screenshots/reference");
    Parameters.setMaxScreenshotRetries(2);
    Parameters.setScreenshotComparisonTolerance(1.0);
    Parameters.setScreenshotRetryDelay(10);
    Parameters.setScreenshotComparisonCursorDetection(true);
    Parameters.setCaptureScreenshotOnFailure(true);
}
```

20.6.2. Taking Screenshots on Failure

Vaadin TestBench takes screenshots automatically when a test
fails, if the *captureScreenShotOnFailure* is enabled in TestBench
parameters. The screenshots are written to the error directory
defined with the *screenshotErrorDirectory* parameter.

You need to have the following in the setup method:

```
@Before
public void setUp() throws Exception {
    Parameters.setScreenshotErrorDirectory("screenshots/errors");
    Parameters.setCaptureScreenshotOnFailure(true);
    ...
}
```

20.6.3. Taking Screenshots for Comparison

Vaadin TestBench allows taking screenshots of the web browser
window with the `compareScreen()` command in the **TestBench-
Commands** interface. The method has a number of variants.

The `compareScreen(`**File**`)` takes a **File** object pointing to the reference image. In this case, a possible error image is written to the
error directory with the same file name. You can get a file object
to a reference image with the static `ImageFileUtil.getRefer-
enceScreenshotFile()` helper method.

```
assertTrue("Screenshots differ",
        testBench(driver).compareScreen(
            ImageFileUtil.getReferenceScreenshotFile(
                "myshot.png")));
```

The `compareScreen(`**String**`)` takes a base name of the screenshot.
It is appended with browser identifier and the file extension.

```
assertTrue(testBench(driver).compareScreen("tooltip"));
```

The compareScreen(**BufferedImage, String**) allows keeping the reference image in memory. An error image is written to a file with a name determined from the base name given as the second parameter.

Screenshots taken with the compareScreen() method are compared to a reference image stored in the reference image folder. If differences are found (or the reference image is missing), the comparison method returns false and stores the screenshot in the error folder. It also generates an HTML file that highlights the differing regions.

Screenshot Comparison Error Images

Screenshots with errors are written to the error folder, which is defined with the *screenshotErrorDirectory* parameter described in Section 20.6.1, "Screenshot Parameters".

For example, the error caused by a missing reference image could be written to screenshot/errors/tooltip_firefox_12.0.png. The image is shown in Figure 20.13, "A screenshot taken by a test run".

Figure 20.13. A screenshot taken by a test run

Screenshots cover the visible page area in the browser. The size of the browser is therefore relevant for screenshot comparison. The browser is normally sized with a predefined default size. You can set the size of the browser window with, for example,

```
driver.manage().window().setSize(new   Dimension(1024,
768));
```
in the `@Before` method. The size includes any browser chrome, so the actual screenshot size will be smaller.

Reference Images

Reference images are expected to be found in the reference image folder, as defined with the `screenshotReferenceDirectory` parameter described in Section 20.6.1, "Screenshot Parameters". To create a reference image, just copy a screenshot from the `errors/` directory to the `reference/` directory.

For example:

```
$ cp screenshot/errors/tooltip_firefox_12.0.png screenshot/ref-
erence/
```

Now, when the proper reference image exists, rerunning the test outputs success:

```
$ java ...
JUnit version 4.5
.
Time: 18.222

OK (1 test)
```

You can also supply multiple versions of the reference images by appending an underscore and an index to the filenames. For example:

```
tooltip_firefox_12.0.png
tooltip_firefox_12.0_1.png
tooltip_firefox_12.0_2.png
```

This can be useful in certain situations when there actually are more than one "correct" reference.

Masking Screenshots

You can make masked screenshot comparison with reference images that have non-opaque regions. Non-opaque pixels in the reference image, that is, ones with less than 1.0 value, are ignored in the screenshot comparison.

Visualization of Differences in Screenshots with Highlighting

Vaadin TestBench supports advanced difference visualization between a captured screenshot and the reference image. A difference report is written to a HTML file that has the same name as the failed screenshot, but with `.html` suffix. The reports are written to the same `errors/` folder as the screenshots from the failed tests.

The differences in the images are highlighted with blue rectangles. Moving the mouse pointer over a square shows the difference area as it appears in the reference image. Clicking the image switches the entire view to the reference image and back. Text "**Image for this run**" is displayed in the top-left corner to identify the currently displayed screenshot.

Figure 20.14, "The reference image and a highlighted error image" shows a difference report with three differences. Date fields are a typical cause of differences in screenshots.

Figure 20.14. The reference image and a highlighted error image

20.6.4. Practices for Handling Screenshots

Access to the screenshot reference image directory should be arranged so that a developer who can view the results can copy the valid images to the reference directory. One possibility is to store the reference images in a version control system and check-out them to the `reference/` directory.

A build system or a continuous integration system can be configured to automatically collect and store the screenshots as build
artifacts.

20.6.5. Known Compatibility Problems

Screenshots when running Internet Explorer 9 in Compatibility
Mode

Internet Explorer prior to version 9 adds a two-pixel border
around the content area. Version 9 no longer does this and
as a result screenshots taken using Internet Explorer 9 running in compatibility mode (IE7/IE8) will include the two pixel
border, contrary to what the older versions of Internet Explorer do.

20.7. Running Tests in an Distributed Envir-onment

A distributed test environment consists of a grid hub and a number
of test nodes. The hub listens to calls from test runners and delegates them to the grid nodes. Different nodes can run on different
operating system platforms and have different browsers installed.

A basic distributed installation was covered in Section 20.2.2, "A
Distributed Testing Environment".

20.7.1. Running Tests Remotely

Remote tests are just like locally executed JUnit tests, except instead of using a browser driver, you use a **RemoteWebDriver**
that can connect to the hub. The hub delegates the connection to
a grid node with the desired capabilities, that is, which browsers
are installed in a suitable node. The capabilities are described with
a **DesiredCapabilities** object.

For example, in the example tests given in the `example` folder, we
create and use a remote driver as follows:

```
@Test
public void testRemoteWebDriver() throws MalformedURLException {
    // Require Firefox in the test node
    DesiredCapabilities capability =
        DesiredCapabilities.firefox();

    // Create a remote web driver that connects to a hub
```

```
// running in the local host
WebDriver driver = TestBench.createDriver(
    new RemoteWebDriver(new URL(
        "http://localhost:4444/wd/hub"), capability));

// Then use it to run a test as you would use any web driver
try {
    driver.navigate().to(
        "http://demo.vaadin.com/sampler#TreeActions");
    WebElement e = driver.findElement(By.xpath(
        "//div[@class='v-tree-node-caption']"+
        "/div[span='Desktops']"));
    new Actions(driver).moveToElement(e).contextClick(e)
        .perform();
} finally {
    driver.quit();
}
}
```

Running the example requires that the hub service and the nodes are running. Starting them is described in the subsequent sections. Please refer to Selenium documentation for more detailed information.

20.7.2. Starting the Hub

The TestBench grid hub listens to calls from test runners and delegates them to the grid nodes. The grid hub service is included in the Vaadin TestBench JAR and you can start it with the following command:

```
$ java -jar \
    vaadin-testbench-standalone-3.0.0.jar \
    -role hub
```

You can open the control interface of the hub also with a web browser. Using the default port, just open URL http://localhost:4444/. Once you have started one or more grid nodes, as instructed in the next section, the "console" page displays a list of the grid nodes with their browser capabilities.

20.7.3. Starting a Grid Node

A TestBench grid node listens to calls from the hub and is capable of opening a browser. The grid node service is included in the Vaadin TestBench JAR and you can start it with the following command:

```
$ java -jar \
      vaadin-testbench-standalone-3.0.0.jar \
      -role node \
      -hub http://localhost:4444/grid/register
```

The node registers itself in the grid hub and you need to give the address of the hub with the *-hub* parameter.

You can run one grid node in the same host as the hub, as is done in the example above with the localhost address. In such case notice that, at least in OS X, you may need to duplicate the JAR to a separate copy to use it to run a grid node service.

20.7.4. Mobile Testing

Vaadin TestBench includes an iPhone and an Android driver, with which you can test on mobile devices. The tests can be run either in a device or in an emulator/simulator.

The actual testing is just like with any WebDriver, using either the **IPhoneDriver** or the **AndroidDriver**. The Android driver assumes that the hub (android-server) is installed in the emulator and forwarded to port 8080 in localhost, while the iPhone driver assumes port 3001. You can also use the **RemoteWebDriver** with either the iphone() or the android() capability, and specify the hub URI explicitly.

The mobile testing setup is covered in detail in the Selenium documentation for both the IPhoneDriver and the AndroidDriver.

Appendix A

Migrating from Vaadin 6

A.1. Overview

The Vaadin 7 API is more clearly for the web. Earlier many web concepts were more abstracted from the developer, while now they are more easily accessible. For example, the `init()` method receives as a parameter HTTP request data, which was earlier more difficult to obtain. Also the new central concept of **Root** is for web use where Vaadin applications are often embedded in web pages.

A.2. The Role of Root

The "main window" concept in Vaadin 6 is replaced with *root*. A root is in most cases what "main window" used to be in Vaadin 6, and in most code you can simply change **Window** to **Root**.

Even more visibly, a Vaadin application does not any longer extend **Application**, but **Root**.

Consider a Vaadin 6 application:

```
public class MyApplication extends Application {
    @Override
    public void init() {
        mainWindow = new Window("Myportlet Application");
```

```
        setMainWindow(mainWindow);

        mainWindow.addComponent(new Label("Hello, world!"));

        ...
    }
}
```

In Vaadin 7, the equivalent is:

```
public class MyRoot extends Root {
    @Override
    protected void init(WrappedRequest request) {
        addComponent(new Label("Hello, world!"));
        ...
    }
}
```

The new **WrappedRequest** contains request data received in the initial request, which was previously only available by implementing HttpServletRequestListener in the application class.

Appendix B

Songs of Vaadin

Vaadin is a mythological creature in Finnish folklore, the goddess and divine ancestor of the mountain reindeer. It appears frequently in the poetic mythos, often as the trustworthy steed of either *Seppo Ilmarinen* or *Väinämöinen*, the two divine hero figures. In many of the stories, it is referred to as *Steed of Seppo* or *Seponratsu* in Finnish. An artifact itself, according to most accounts, Vaadin helped Seppo Ilmarinen in his quests to find the knowledge necessary to forge magical artefacts, such as *Sampo*.

Some of the Vaadin poems were collected by *Elias Lönnrot*, but he left them out of *Kalevala*, the Finnish epic poem, as they were somewhat detached from the main theme and would have created inconsistencies with the poems included in the epos. Lönnrot edited Kalevala heavily and it represents a selection from a much larger and more diverse body of collected poems. Many of the accounts regarding Vaadin were sung by shamans, and still are. A shamanistic tradition, centered on the tales of Seppo and Vaadin, still lives in South-Western Finland, around the city of Turku. Some research in the folklore suggests that the origin of Vaadin is as a shamanistic animal spirit used during trance for voyaging to *Tuonela*, the Land of Dead, with its mechanical construction reflecting the shamanistic tools used for guiding the trance. While the shamanistic interpretation of the origins is disputed by a majority of the research community in a maximalist sense, it is considered a potentially important component in the collection of traditions that preserve the folklore.

Origin or birth poems, *synnyt* in Finnish, provide the most distinct accounts of mythological artefacts in the Finnish folklore, as origin poems or songs were central in the traditional magical practices. Vaadin is no exception and its origin poems are numerous. In many of the versions, Vaadin was created in a mill, for which Seppo had built the millstone. After many a year, grinding the sacred acorns of the *Great Oak* (a version of the *World Tree* in Finnish mythology), the millstone had become saturated with the magical juices of the acorns. Seppo found that the stone could be used to make tools. He cut it in many pieces and built a toolkit suitable for fashioning spider web into any imaginable shape. When Seppo started making Sampo, he needed a steed that would help him find the precious components and the knowledge he required. The magical tools became the skeleton of Vaadin.

> *"Lost, his mind was,*
> *gone, was his understanding,*
> *ran away, were his memories,*
> *in the vast land of hills of stone.*
> *Make a steed he had to,*
> *forge bone out of stone,*
> *flesh out of moss,*
> *and skin of bark of the birch.*
> *The length of his hammer,*
> *he put as the spine and the hip,*
> *bellows as the lungs,*
> *tongs as the legs, paired.*
> *So woke Vaadin from the first slumber,*
> *lichen did Seppo give her for eating,*
> *mead did he give her for drinking,*
> *then mounted her for the journey."*

Other versions associate the creation with Väinämöinen instead of Seppo Ilmarinen, and give different accounts for the materials. This ambiguity can be largely explained through the frequent co-operation between Väinämöinen and Seppo in the mythos.

The Kalevala associates a perverted Vaadin-like creature with the evil antagonist *Hiisi*. The creature, *Elk of Hiisi*, is chased by *Lemminkäinen*, the third hero in Kalevala. While this is antithetical to the other accounts of Vaadin, it is noteworthy in how it blurs the distinction between the mountain reindeer and elk, and how it makes clear that the steed is an artificial construct.

But the boast was heard by Hiisi,
And by Juutas comprehended;
And an elk was formed by Hiisi,
And a reindeer formed by Juutas,
With a head of rotten timber,
Horns composed of willow-branches,
Feet of ropes the swamps which border,
Shins of sticks from out the marshes;
And his back was formed of fence-stakes,
Sinews formed of dryest grass-stalks,
Eyes of water-lily flowers,
Ears of leaves of water-lily,
And his hide was formed of pine-bark,
And his flesh of rotten timber.
(Translation by W. F. Kirby, 1907)

Nevertheless, proper names are rarely used, so the identity of the steed or steeds remains largely implicit in the myths and, because of the differences in the origin myths, can not be unambiguously associated with a unique identity.

The theme of animal ancestor gods is common in the Finnish myth, as we can see in the widespread worship of *Tapio*, the lord of the bear and the forest. With respect to Vaadin, the identification of the animal is not completely clear. The Finnish word *vaadin* refers specifically to an adult female of the semi-domesticated mountain reindeer, which lives in the Northern Finland in Lapland as well as in the Northern Sweden and Norway. On the other hand, the Finnish folklore represented in Kalevala and other collections has been collected from Southern Finland, where the mountain reindeer does not exist. Nevertheless, Southern Finnish folklore and Kalevala do include many other elements as well that are distinctively from Lapland, such as the hunting of the Elk of Hiisi, so we may assume that the folklore reflects a record of cultural interaction. The distinction between the northern mountain reindeer and the deer species of Southern Finland, the forest reindeer and the elk, is clear in the modern language, but may have been less clear in old Finnish dialects, as is reflected in the Kalevala account. *Peura*, reindeer, may have been a generic word for a wild animal, as can be seen in *jalopeura*, the old Finnish word for lion. Kalevala uses the *poropeura* in the Lemminkäinen story to distinguish the specific sub-type of reindeer. The identification is further complicated by the fact that other lines of poems included in Kalevala often refer to a horse in association with Seppo and Väinämöinen. To some extent, this could be due to the use of the word for horse as a generic name for a steed. While a mountain reindeer is not suitable for riding, animal gods are typically portrayed as uncommonly large in mythology, even to the extremes, so the identification fits quite well in the variety of magical mounts.

The mythology related to Vaadin, especially as represented in Kalevala, locates some important characters and people in *Pohjola*, a mythical land in the north from where all evil originates, according to most accounts. For example, *Louhi* or Pohjolan emäntä, Queen of Pohjola, is the primary antagonist in the Kalevala mythos. Both Seppo Ilmarinen and Väinämöinen make services to Louhi to earn the hand of her daughters for marriage. Vaadin is often mentioned in connection with these services, such as the making of Sampo. On the other hand, as Sampo can be identified with the mill mentioned in creation stories of Vaadin, its identification in the stories becomes unclear.

While beginning its life as an artifact, Vaadin is later represented as an antropomorphic divine being. This is in contrast with the *Bride of Gold*, another creation of Seppo, which failed to become a fully living and thinking being. Finding magical ways around fundamental problems in life are central in Kalevala. In some areas, magical solutions are morally acceptable, while in others they are not and the successes and failures in the mythos reflect this ethic. Research in the folklore regarding the Bride of Gold myth has provided support for a theory that creating a wife would go against very fundamental social rules of courting and mating, paralleling the disapproval of "playing god" in acts involving life and death (though "cheating death" is usually considered a positive act). The main motivation of the protagonists in Kalevala is courting young daughters, which always ends in failure, usually for similar reasons. Animals, such as Vaadin, are outside the social context and considered to belong in the same category with tools and machines. The Vaadin myths present a noteworthy example of this categorization of animals and tools in the same category at an archetypal level.

The Vaadin myths parallel the *Sleipnir* myths in the Scandinavian mythology. This connection is especially visible for the connection of Väinämöinen with *Odin*, who used Sleipnir in his journeys. The use of tongs for the legs of Vaadin actually suggests eight legs,

---

which is the distinguishing attribute of Sleipnir. While Sleipnir is almost universally depicted as a horse, the exact identification of the steed may have changed during the transmission between the cultures.

The *Bridle of Vaadin* is a special artifact itself. There is no headstall, but only the rein, detached from the creature, kept in the hand of the rider. The rein is a chain or set of "gadgets" used for controlling the creature. The rein was built of web with special tools, with Seppo wearing magnifying goggles to work out the small details.

The significance and cultural influence of Vaadin can be seen in its identification with a constellation in the traditional Finnish constellation system. The famous French astronomer *Pierre Charles Le Monnier* (1715-99), who visited Lapland, introduced the constellation to international star charts with the name *Tarandus vel Rangifer*. The constellation was present in many star charts of the time, perhaps most notably in the *Uranographia* published in 1801 by *Johann Elert Bode*, as shown in Figure B.1, "Constellation of Tarandus vel Rangifer in Bode's Uranographia (1801)". It was later removed in the unification of the constellation system towards the Greek mythology.

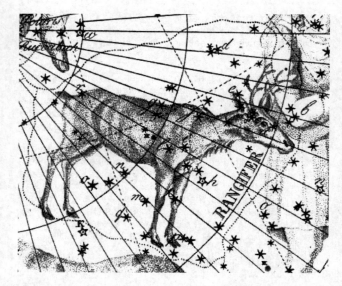

Figure B.1. Constellation of Tarandus vel Rangifer in Bode's Uranographia (1801)

Index

Symbols

@Connect, 342

A

AbstractComponent, 91, 95
AbstractComponentContainer, 91
AbstractField, 91
add-ons
    creating, **369**
addContainerFilter(), 321
addNestedContainerProperty(), 317
AJAX, 10, 48, **49**
Alignment, 250-252
And (filter), 323

C

caption property, 99
Client-Side Engine, 47, **51**
compatibility, 286
Component, 91
Component interface, 93, 95
    caption, 99
    description, 100
    enabled, 102
    icon, 103
    locale, 104
    read-only, 107
    style name, 109
    visible, 109
ComponentState, 342
connector, 342
Container, 315-324
    Filterable, 170, 321-324
CSS, 48, 49, 277-294

compatibility, 286
introduction, 279-286
CustomComponent, 261-276

D

Data Model, 48
description property, 100
DOM, 49
Drag and Drop, 411-423
    Accept Criteria, 416-420

E

Eclipse
    widget development, 343-347
enabled property, 102
Equal (filter), 322
events, 48
executeJavaScript(), 400

F

Field, 95-98
Filter (in Container), 321-324

G

getLocale(), 105
Google Web Toolkit, 5, 10, 47, 48, **50**, 51, 204
    GWT Module Descriptor, 520
    themeing, 281
    widgets, **341-371**
Greater (filter), 322
GreaterOrEqual (filter), 322

H

HorizontalSplitPanel, 232-235
HTML templates, 48
HTTP, 47

vaadin }>

Commercial Offering

vaadin }> thinking of U and I

Building stunning web user
interfaces is easy with the
Vaadin Framework. It is a
solid, maintainable base
for secure applications that
work with all major web
browsers.

The Vaadin Framework is optimized for development speed – your
team can build the final product in the time it takes to create a
prototype. This allows you to focus on creating better applications.
Having control over web technology is easier when you let Vaadin
take care of browsers, communications and other details.

Better
Results
Faster

Vaadin offers services, tools and components to complement the free open source framework and a very active open source community. The commercial offering helps you to create an amazing user experience and gets your product on the market faster.
Save time and money, see how >>

Apache-licensed Vaadin Framework

Access to free add-on components

Public discussion forum

1:1 developer support

Knowledgebase

Bug fix priority and custom builds

Feature voting

Licenses to commercial Vaadin add-ons:

- TouchKit for supporting mobile touch devices
- JPA Container for Java Persistence API support
- TestBench for user interface test automation
- Flexible calendar and data visualization components

JRebel for speeding up development cycle

Vaadin expert participation to customer projects

Outsourced product development

Account manager, signed agreement, invoicing

Price

Free	Pro Account	Key Account
✔	✔	✔
✔	✔	✔
✔	✔	✔
	Available for $230 / h	25h included
	✔	✔
	✔	✔
	✔	✔
	subscription	perpetual
	✔	✔
		available
		available
		✔
0	$90 per month per developer	$9900 per year for up to 6 developers

Boosting Productivity With:
Pro Account:

Pro Account is an online service that supports professional developers in building software on top of the Vaadin Framework.

Tools and components

The service includes licenses to all the commercial developer tools and add-on components created by the Vaadin team. Get the benefits of touch-optimized components, proper support for JPA and other add-ons that help you build better applications. Build solid user interface level regression tests and eliminate wait times from the development process with the tools included.

Warranty and support

The support channel helps you resolve problems and gets you in touch with the team that built Vaadin whenever you need guidance or a new feature. If you encounter any problems, we'll fix them and give you a custom build before the next product release to keep your development team on track.

Subscribe online at vaadin.com/pro-account

Building Success Together:
Key Account:

Key Account is a customized service solution for your development team. Our experts are actively involved in your project, making sure it will be a success.

Directly from the authors
As the authors of Vaadin Framework who have participated in software projects using it for over a decade, our team can bring valuable insight to your project. Our mission is to enable the creation of amazing web-based solutions – it is up to you to choose how we can serve your project best.

Professional tools and expertise
Our service is tailored to your needs. The tools, components and guarantees included are the foundation we build on. They are complemented by expert participation in your project when requested and outsourced development services when your team is too busy to do everything by themselves.

Contact us for a Key Account offer tailored to your needs at vaadin.com/contact

Vaadin
Training

The best way to get started with Vaadin is to take part in one of our training courses. You will learn all the necessary skills in the most efficient way. You can also ask for an offer on a customized workshop tailored to your needs.

Read more, see the training calendar and sign up at vaadin.com/training